THE HERESIES OF JAN PATOČKA

Northwestern University
Studies in Phenomenology
and
Existential Philosophy

General Editor Anthony J. Steinbock

THE HERESIES OF JAN PATOČKA

Phenomenology, History, and Politics

James Dodd

Northwestern University Press
Evanston, Illinois

Northwestern University Press
www.nupress.northwestern.edu

Copyright © 2023 by Northwestern University. Published 2023 by Northwestern University Press. All rights reserved.

Printed in the United States of America

10 9 8 7 6 5 4 3 2 1

ISBN 978-0-8101-4586-3 (paper)
ISBN 978-0-8101-4587-0 (cloth)
ISBN 978-0-8101-4588-7 (ebook)

Cataloging-in-Publication Data are available from the Library of Congress.

In memoriam, Krzysztof Michalski (1948–2013)
and Erazim Kohák (1933–2020)

Contents

	Preface	ix
	Acknowledgments	xi
	Introduction: Philosophy in Troubled Times	3
1	On an Asubjective Phenomenology	21
2	On the Body	61
3	On the Three Movements of Human Existence	83
4	On the Care for the Soul	127
5	On Sacrifice	171
6	On Hope	203
7	On Dissidence	229
	Conclusion: Legacies	255
	Epilogue	263
	Notes	267
	Index	295

Preface

Academic life has a reputation, not at all unfounded, for a certain inwardness, for being comfortable only when at least an arm's remove from the outside world, where like lotus eaters its practitioners seek immunity from practical exigencies in favor of what its apologists would describe as the "life of the mind." At its best, this inwardness promises the cultivation of an understanding that, thanks to a peculiarly ironic freedom, privileges insight over mere persuasion, judgment over conformity, responsibility over thoughtlessness.

This inwardness of the life of the mind relies on the successful maintenance of a certain comforting relief from history, from the conflicts, divisions, and urgent questions that mark a given era. Naturally this is delusional. History never gives the finite mind a chance to catch its breath. Yet it is a useful delusion, and its protective veil has served to cultivate successive generations of teachers and students, offering those who have experienced it a sense of unbroken continuity of interest and care, despite all the obstacles. For in the end, any real continuity of academic life is at best an ideal. At bottom there is only our tenuous grasp of a shared goal of understanding, whether within or against a tradition, or both, the pursuit of which is continually fractured and rendered problematic by the inevitable contingencies and misunderstandings that define our times, and not least ourselves.

This book is an attempt to honor this ideal in the memory of my teachers, Krzysztof Michalski and Erazim Kohák, two central European philosophers who many years ago introduced me to the idea of philosophy as a living tradition. They are two philosophical spirits who have nourished me over the years, and with whom I continue to have a deep bond both intellectual and personal, even if now only in memory.

At the same time, as I dedicate my modest offerings in this book to their legacy, I have to confess that there are aspects of their intellectual and spiritual personae that will forever remain closed to me, perhaps for reasons of the history that we otherwise managed happily to ignore during my years as their student. I have not shared their experiences, I am the product of a very different time, and a very different place than the postwar central Europe from which these two quintessential Europeans developed their perspectives on the tasks of understanding. Most importantly, I do not share their easy affinity with the legacies of Europe and European identity, nor would I want to, at least not in the same way.

Yet I can say that each, in his own ultimately idiosyncratic fashion, awoke within me and many others in similar stages of their intellectual development the beginnings of that interest and care basic to philosophy at its best, whether European or not, and in a way wholly commensurate with the pedagogical legacy of the epistolary mentor of the one and the fellow countryman of the other: Jan Patočka.

Acknowledgments

This book has benefited from many discussions over the years with a wide variety of scholars of the work of Jan Patočka in multiple venues in various countries, but above all in conjunction with my regular visits to the Institute for Human Sciences in Vienna, which I have had the fortune to enjoy since the early 1990s. I wish to thank in particular the former director of the Jan Patočka Archive, Klaus Nellen, and its current director, Ludger Hagedorn, whose collective generosity and friendship have been invaluable. I am also grateful to Nicolas de Warren, whose philosophical acumen and intellectual generosity, not to mention friendship, have been influential on my thinking on all matters philosophical and beyond since we were students together at Boston University in the 1980s.

The inspiration for this book crystallized in a small reading group on Patočka's *Heretical Essays* and *Plato and Europe* at the New School for Social Research in 2015. An early outline structured the seminar "'Europe Is Dead': Philosophy, History, and Politics in the Thought of Jan Patočka" that I offered at the Transregional Center for Democratic Studies in Wrocław, Poland, in the summer of 2018. I wish to thank Elzbieta Matynia for the kind invitation to take part in such a wonderful program, and the participants of both the reading group and the seminar for a wealth of thoughtful and lively discussions.

Shorter and less developed versions of parts of several chapters have appeared elsewhere: "O co usilovala asubjektivní fenomenologie," trans. Jan Frei, in *Filosofický časopis* 6, no. 65 (2017): 855–71 and "Sobre la promesa de una fenomenología asubjetiva," trans. Jorge Enrique Publido Blanco, in *Aporía: Revista Internacional de Investigaciones Filosóficas* 3 (2019): 77–95 (parts of chapters 1 and 2); "Patočka and the Metaphysics of Sacrifice," in *Studies in East European Thought* 72, no. 3 (2020) (the core of chapter 5); and "*Polemos* in Jan Patočka's Political Thought," in *Thinking after Europe: Jan Patočka and Politics*, ed. Francesco Tava (London: Rowman and Littlefield, 2016), 77–94 (parts of chapter 7).

THE HERESIES OF JAN PATOČKA

Introduction

Philosophy in Troubled Times

Spring

In 1968, as the result of the reform policies of the Alexander Dubček regime introduced early that year and the resulting climate of what was to become known as the "Prague Spring," the Czech philosopher Jan Patočka was allowed, after a hiatus of almost two decades, to return to lecturing at Charles University in Prague.[1] In the brief interlude between the end of the German occupation at the close of the Second World War and the Communist takeover in 1949, Patočka had similarly returned to university teaching from a long absence, given that Czech universities had been closed during the war. Then, his refusal to join the Communist Party had soon led to his expulsion from the university; in 1968, Patočka's return would also be short-lived, and for comparable reasons.

As was the case in the late 1940s, the late 1960s were troubled times. When Patočka began his lectures in the fall of 1968, which were transcribed by his students and eventually published as samizdat in the 1980s under the title *Body, Community, Language, World* (*Tělo, společenství, jazyk, svět*),[2] the Warsaw Pact armies had invaded just weeks before, and the long process of enforced conformity instituted in the normalization policies of the regime was already underway, ultimately forcing Patočka, once again, out of the university by 1972. Spring was over.

The itinerary of Patočka's brief career of public teaching is worth noting. From 1945 to 1950, apart from several offerings in phenomenology, the focus had largely been on the history of philosophy, including lectures on Socrates, Plato, and Aristotle. In the 1968–69 semester the focus would be phenomenology, and the attempt to articulate, critically, the philosophical legacies of Edmund Husserl and Martin Heidegger. The 1968–69 lectures, coupled with a series of articles published in *Filosofický časopis* in 1965–66 specifically devoted to an exposition of Husserl's philosophy,[3] are a remarkable body of work, combining a tour de force of the history of the problem of the subjective body from ancient to modern philosophy with a powerful demonstration of the living potential of phenomenology as a philosophy of the present. Patočka's teaching spoke to a widespread yearning at the time, one arguably still in force today, for a thinking that committed itself to an understanding of the human condition in its concreteness and historicity.

The 1968–69 lectures will play a central role in this book, since they articulate in a singular fashion Patočka's philosophical project in the 1960s and 1970s. They also point to something else, something that belongs to the dynamic of the times in which they were presented, and which bears directly on Patočka's own personal history. It is not a mere supplementary detail to note that these lectures were given in the wake of the Russian invasion in August 1968 and the inauguration of normalization that would grip Czechoslovakia's social and political life right up to the Velvet Revolution in 1989. The lectures Patočka addressed to his audience in the lecture hall were not wholly indifferent to the turmoil outside, as if intellectual reflection could affect a distant insouciance regarding the collapse of hopes and aspirations that characterized the events of 1968. Patočka's thinking cannot be fully understood unless one recognizes in it an example of a nuanced meditation on the very possibility of a philosophical life in precisely the times in which he lived—the troubled times of repeatedly disappointed springs in which the aspirations of the intellectual were frustrated by the constraints of public and political life imposed by successive regimes of domination and ideological control on the one hand, and the catastrophes of war and revolution on the other.

This observation is not only germane to the world after 1968. There is little in Patočka's intellectual history that was not, in some form or another, shaped by the extreme events of the past century, the myriad catastrophes that were consistently coupled with experiences of tantalizing springs promising hope and renewal. Born in 1907 in Turnov, Bohemia, Patočka came of age during the interwar period, in a region of Europe devastated by the First World War, and then reborn in the formation of the group of nations that emerged in the wake of the dissolution of the defeated Austro-Hungarian Empire. Here spring had taken the form of Tomáš Garrigue Masaryk's democratic Czechoslovakia, which arguably embodied the hope of a new Europe, one putatively founded on a religiously infused humanism that not only stood against the old, sclerotic forms of authoritarianism and the norms of privilege, but also promised a spiritual bulwark against what was most pernicious and socially destabilizing in a modern order of increasing atomism and alienation. Yet this spring, too, would be short-lived. In the wake of Munich, the eclipse of the democratic project embodied in the new Czechoslovak state marked the beginning of a period of even more destruction and political upheaval.

The failure, both politically and intellectually, of Masaryk's Czechoslovakia had a profound influence on the young Patočka, who never ceased to reflect on the fate of Masaryk's national project and the broader historical trends in which it was enmeshed. It was arguably against the backdrop of his understanding of the legacy of this project that Patočka interpreted the situation in 1968, seeing the latter at least in part as a call to articulate the hope for a more humane existence that had been embodied in prewar Czechoslovakia on more solid philosophical and political grounds. And again, it was against the background of this history that Patočka understood the need to preserve this hope in the wake of yet another disappointed spring, as a struggle against those who would work to suppress that hope until 1989, a subsequent spring that Patočka would not live to see.

The repeated disappointments of the failed springs of these years understandably led, if not to despair, then at least to an experienced caution. Accordingly, Patočka's reflections on Masaryk were consistently critical, from beginning to end; they contain little patience for Masaryk's optimism, even if at the same time they express an obvious admiration for the elder philosopher.[4] Patočka's critique is perhaps the most incisive on precisely the question of the understanding of modernity, with regard to both the rise of modernity generally and, keeping in mind the closing months of 1968, the specific situation of a world increasingly characterized by technology and the mass mobilization of power. This situation was epitomized for Patočka by the terrifying experience of world war, something that he went so far as to identify as the essence of the twentieth century in the dark closing essay of the *Heretical Essays*.[5]

Patočka's world, like that of Masaryk, was thus one of crisis. The sense of crisis comes out with particular poignance at the beginning of *Plato and Europe*, a transcription of a series of private seminars that Patočka held after 1972.[6] Whatever the importance of the public university lectures, it is in these private seminars that Patočka's real legacy as a teacher is established, for they form the unique milieu of an effort to live a philosophical existence in a world increasingly hostile to the life of the mind.[7]

At the beginning of *Plato and Europe*, Patočka invites his listeners to reflect on their situation, on what it could mean to pursue something like philosophy at all in the world today, one so marked by the twilight of such a hopeful spring. Patočka broadens the circle of concern, finding echoes as it were of a life unsettled well beyond the borders of eastern Europe. One such concern was the looming ecological crisis that had been described in a recent report released by the Club of Rome, with its warning of an imminent ecological catastrophe as the result of the overconsumption of natural resources.[8] Another was a speech given by the avant-garde Romanian playwright Eugène Ionesco in Salzburg, which gave powerful expression to a general sense of the helplessness experienced by individuals who have become ever more subject to their lives being defined and manipulated by forces that seem to be wholly outside of their control.[9] The theme was a familiar one: already in the last years of the nineteenth century, Masaryk too had emphasized similar experiences of alienation, which he identified as the cause behind a marked increase in suicides. And finally, Patočka cites Max Scheler, who had written in the 1920s about the "disequilibrium" that had marked the opening of the century, expressing a sense of a time out of joint, of the order of things somehow fundamentally unsettled and spinning inexorably into chaos.[10]

As varied as these echoes may be, some quite specific to recent history and the current local context, some shared by all human beings on the planet, some responding to a very real and defined threat, and some to a more general sense of unease and instability, they all belong, Patočka suggests, to the unitary phenomenon of a common situation. And it is precisely as a reflection on the problem of this common situation—in its most universal sense, the human condition—that philosophy provides a potential resource for living in troubled times. When spring is over, philosophy remains.

Europe Is Dead

One could of course add Husserl to the list of the thinkers of crisis as well. Husserl above all comes to mind when Patočka, in *Plato and Europe*, observes that, for Scheler and many other thinkers of crisis, the problem had always been articulated in terms in which Europe was assumed to be the center of gravity when reflecting on the condition of modern humanity.[11] The assumption had always been that it was Europe, whether in the guise of the rise of scientific culture since the Renaissance or in Enlightenment culture generally, that had inaugurated the modern age, and thus it would be Europe which would develop the conditions necessary for equilibrium, for shaping the contemporary world in such a way that would respond adequately to the spiritual contradictions of modern existence.

This was certainly the guiding assumption of Husserl, as can be seen in a series of reflections on the question of Europe and contemporary history dating from the closing years of the First World War, and which culminates in part 1 of *The Crisis of European Sciences*.[12] Patočka had a personal connection to this phase of Husserl's thinking, having studied with the master in Freiburg in the 1930s. In 1935, in conjunction with the Prague Cercle philosophique, of which he was the secretary,

Patočka helped orchestrate Husserl's invitation to lecture in Prague.[13] These lectures would form the basis of part 1 of the *Crisis*, but it was Husserl's lectures in Vienna several months earlier, "The Crisis of European Humanity and Philosophy," that contained several themes that would remain essential to Patočka's own thinking about Europe throughout his career, and thus merit closer consideration.[14]

The central thesis of Husserl's Vienna lecture is that philosophy, both as idea and tradition, can tell us something essential about Europe, and with that serve as the point of departure for understanding and responding to its contemporary crisis. The thesis is not so much that philosophy is somehow exclusively European, or that it represents an available spiritual resource with which Europe can come to terms with its current state of decline. The point is far stronger: philosophy as such is constitutive of the very idea of Europe: the ideal of a rational culture just *is* the guiding telos of European existence. Other cultures may cultivate philosophies, but it is only Europe that has made philosophy its guiding idea. Thus if "the European nations are sick," and "Europe itself, it is said, is in crisis,"[15] it is for Husserl a function of this ideal falling into a state of decline.

Europe is in this sense for Husserl essentially an *idea*; it is not merely a geographical concept, or a cultural formation with a particular history, past or present, though these may be involved as well, if only in a non-essential way. The condition and fate of Europe are thus that of an idea, the idea of rational, philosophical life, a scientific vocation both committed to truth and responsible for itself, and it is as this idea that Husserl appeals to Europe in the situation in the 1930s.

This claim that Europe is primarily a teleological idea, one that may or may not be reflected in any given historical phenomenon, at least on the concrete level, borders on the unfalsifiable, and has rarely been embraced by the more empirically minded.[16] It is difficult to counter such skepticism. At best, "Europe" is a relatively coherent concept when it is used to designate the diverse nexus of histories that make up the western tip of the Eurasian continent in the wake of the gradual disappearance of the Western Roman Empire. Anything more than this—historical claims regarding how and when, or even whether, there emerges a common, transnational European identity, or of a cultural unity that speaks to a fundamental way of life, and just what characterizes this identity and this way of life—becomes far more problematic. What is worse, the entire discussion is often overburdened by endless ideological debates that are more in tune with the political struggles of the moment, than with the development of a cogent historical understanding of the contingent portion of humanity included arbitrarily under the title of "Europe."

And in fact, Husserl's reflections on Europe are probably better understood in the context of precisely the political struggles of the moment—and in the 1930s these struggles were, for the cosmopolitan and scientifically oriented like Husserl, an aging university professor with a Bohemian Jewish background, unambiguously existential. This was the real source of much of the force of Husserl's thinking on Europe in works such as the *Crisis*, and in the end the question was for him the question of the survival of a worldview, fashioned largely in the nineteenth century, that saw things in terms of the progress of scientific culture.

Yet at the same time there is more to Husserl's thesis than these echoes of the ideological struggles of 1930s Europe. Above all, history is not understood here to be a mere contingent expression of the ideal of reason that Husserl identifies as definitive of Europe; instead, the idea of reason itself, Husserl argues, is intrinsically historical. There is thus something deeper at work in Husserl's reflections. He is striving to articulate a conception of humanity as not only historically determined in an external sense of being subject to specific conditions, but one in which the very consciousness of existence takes the form of a historical self-understanding. And more, Husserl's is a conception of humanity in which historical self-understanding is inseparable from *universality*—historical humanity, conscious of its actions in the horizon of historical becoming, becomes in Husserl's thinking essentially equivalent to a *universal humanity*.

This means that the idea of reason can itself only be illuminated through historical reflection, and in two interrelated senses. The first relies on the figure of the self-projection of the idea into the future, which for Husserl takes the form of an embrace of the task to realize a self-sustaining rational world. The telos in play here is one that is embedded in human action, and in a fashion that requires the progressive understanding of its meaning. Reason thus becomes the guiding ideal of history, a consciously posited practical imperative to realize not only a certain form of life, but of the world as well. The idea of Europe in Husserl's account is not a given basis for identity, for identifying who one is as a member of a given cultural community. It is a challenge, an imperative to be, to exist in a certain way. If universality can also be said to emerge as a particular cultural reality, it is one only to the extent that such a reality can embody the task of transformation into something that transcends its particularity. If Husserl's thinking is Eurocentric, it is only because he believes that Europe remains contested ground for the universal, and with that a peculiar magnet for anyone called to the task.

More specifically, the concrete historical emergence of this idea is described by Husserl as the appearance of individuals and communities dedicated to reason as the task of realizing a rational world, the forms of which conform to rational self-justification. If decisive, the emergence of such individuals and communities represents for Husserl the breakthrough to an "epoch of mankind which now seeks to live, and only can live, in the free shaping of its existence, its historical life, through ideas of reason, through infinite tasks."[17] This is precisely the idea of philosophy for Husserl, "which makes itself known, from the standpoint of universal mankind as such, as the breakthrough and the developmental beginning of a new human epoch."[18]

That the tasks of such a life are infinite implies the impossibility of their being completed in a finite sense, thus yielding an end-state or complete form of being. This means that "Europe," taken in a finite historical sense, is not and can never be "universal humanity" in anything but a purely aspirational form. Universal humanity is an open horizon, visible at all only as a passage beyond the finite; if its meaning is historically conditioned by a beginning, as in Husserl's (frankly mythical) description of the beginning of Europe in Greek philosophy, it is only as a rupture of whatever belongs to the settled finitude of that beginning.

This means that what Husserl calls the "inborn teleology" of Europe, the orientation of the infinite task of universality, stands in necessary contrast and dissonance with the empirical, finite, concrete life of Europeans—however defined. Any philosophy, any Europe for that matter, is as a given empirical formation of the spirit only an anticipation of the ideal, a progression towards its realization, or it is a retreat from it and is its negation and obfuscation:

> But now this is the danger point: "philosophy"; here we must certainly distinguish between philosophy as a historical fact at a given time and philosophy as an idea, as the idea of an infinite task. Any philosophy that exists at a given historical time is a more or less successful attempt to realize the guiding idea of the infinity and at the same time even the totality of truths.[19]

If so, then any specific form of historical existence should never be considered an unambiguously secure gain or loss. It is for this reason that Husserl in the Vienna lecture contrasts the "spiritual teleology" of the idea of philosophy, of Europe, with the idea of a natural teleology of development that would proceed as a sequence of closed and repeatable forms, as if it were possible to posit a schema of historical transformation in which cultures would develop beyond their particularity into "European" forms progressively more rational and universal. Instead, Husserl argues, there is a chronically incomplete and open character of meaning that is implicitly true of any properly "spiritual" unity:

> There is, for essential reasons, no zoology of peoples. They are spiritual unities; they do not have, and in particular the supernational unity of Europe does not have, a mature shape that has ever been reached or could be reached as a shape that is regularly repeated. Psychic humanity [*seelisches Menschentum*] has never been complete and never will be, and can never repeat itself. The spiritual *telos* of European humanity, in which the particular telos of particular nations and of individual men is contained, lies in the infinite, is an infinite idea toward which, in concealment, the whole spiritual becoming aims, so to speak.[20]

This dimension of Husserl's argument, not often sufficiently emphasized, is important to bear in mind. It suggests that it would be a mistake to identify the perspective of universal reason with any given cultural form. It would also be a mistake to assume that it is a static, superhistorical perspective that would provide a domain of comparison for the relative development of the same. It is operative only in the historical movement of spiritual life, in the projection of life towards an ideal yet to be fully understood and which can become a theme at all only in a reflection motivated by a sense of historical becoming, one that in important ways always operates at the expense of one's own particularity.

The second sense of historical reflection that would illuminate this "spiritual history" is oriented not to the future projected by the task of the ideal, but to the origin, to the beginning or irruption of the projection towards the telos of the idea. This is again part of how Husserl understands the human consciousness of historicity, specifically its role as condition for the tasks of reason: it is an awareness not only of the task represented by the future, but of the sense of the emergence of this task represented by the past. That the two come together into a kind of circuit of sense justifies talk of a "tradition." To pursue the task of reason is thus a distinctively historical affair, one contingent upon success in not only projecting a coherent goal based on what one has inherited, but in turn making sense of that very inheritance, thus setting into motion the question of the origin.

In both the Vienna and Prague lectures, Husserl tells the familiar story of the emergence of the idea of philosophy as a specifically Greek event, thus tied to a time and a place:

> Spiritual Europe has a birthplace. By this I mean not a geographical birthplace, in one land, though this is also true, but rather a spiritual birthplace in a nation or in individual men and human groups of this nation. It is the ancient Greek nation in the seventh and sixth centuries B.C.[21]

Yet philosophy, or this "new attitude" that emerges in ancient Greece, is even for Husserl not unproblematically "Greek." This is not simply a question of the validity of designating a specific cultural-historical site as having the honor of being the "first"—that it was the ancient Greeks who should claim this title can and has been contested, and rightly so—but again points to the idea that philosophy as such, as a striving after infinite tasks, stands in necessary tension with any such finite origin. As a tradition, philosophy must have an origin; but the terminus of the tradition, the ideal of a rational humanity, is not circumscribed by the mere affirmation of the specific identity of what preceded it, but instead stands in an intrinsically critical-reflective relation to the same. Philosophy is thus a very peculiar kind of tradition, one which carries with it a sense of an origin that is not genuinely bound to the site of its emergence: "Unlike all other cultural works, philosophy is not a movement of interest which is bound to the soil of the national tradition."[22] Husserl's claim that Greece was the beginning of philosophy should thus be taken more as a kind of parable of history than a fact of history, an idealized story of the birth of the universal from particularity.

This means that, however essential philosophy is to Europe as an idea, it is not bound, at least not ultimately, to the soil of Europe. This, however, just intensifies the problem of the meaning of the origin, and by extension just what is meant by talking of the "tradition" of philosophy, if that is to mean more than its simple embodiment in specific literary practices. For the way Husserl sets up his reflection, it is almost as if he intends to argue that the tradition of philosophy is in the end really a kind of anti-tradition, a disruption of the continuity and settled meaning that would seem to characterize the idea of a tradition. Husserl seems to argue as if the very closure and settled character of traditions makes transcendence towards the task of universality possible. Traditions exist to be broken.

One might even speculate that the beginning of something like philosophy, if is it to be understood as a critique of tradition, is always possible, and perhaps even common. Dissatisfaction with how things have been done, a desire for renewal or just to escape the boredom of the familiar, is perhaps all that is needed to posit the most basic conditions for philosophy. The difficulty in Husserl's conception is to understand how the origin of philosophy does not just lie in the desire to break free from the hold of tradition, but how in turn the taking root of this desire itself marks the emergence of a tradition, and with that of a peculiar historical continuity that renews itself over time, generating that span between the moment of its emergence and the projection of the ideal as a task, or an end.

Here Denis Guénoun's theses on Europe serve to add an important nuance to Husserl's position, without necessarily rejecting it in its essentials.[23] Guénoun contends that "Europe" designates not the original movement of universality, of the irruption of the philosophical attitude—this is the position ascribed by Husserl to Greek consciousness, or better the position in which Greek consciousness as origin is disrupted, at best living with the new universal attitude in a state of tension. "Europe" rather designates the project of *returning* this universality back into something particular, something that would hold the universal in place as that which can properly be called one's "own." As such, the pretense of Europe is to attempt to infuse its particularity with the movement, and force, of the universal, but in a way circumscribed, and if not properly domesticated, then at least subjected to the strictures of power, thereby leveraging the universal into a form of self-affirmation as European, as bound to the soil of Europe or European continentality.

Husserl himself does not of course problematize Europe in this way; for him, the difference between a Europe that serves as a vehicle for the realization of universal humanity and the Europe that sees itself as the traditional heir of philosophy and scientific rationalism is of negligible importance. The danger he refers to in the Vienna lecture—and remember, this is 1935—is not of a Europe that would claim universal rationality as its own, thus usurping the ideal of reason for the purposes of self-affirmation, but of a Europe that would seek to break free from the constraints of rational culture altogether, in favor of an embrace of the irrational and the unlimited self-affirmation of relatively closed forms of life.

Nevertheless, Guénoun's deeper point remains relevant: there is an inherent strangeness to the universality of Europe; however essential it may be to its traditions, universality is also disruptive, something essentially "other" that problematizes the very particularity of Europe.[24] In his own way, Husserl also emphasizes this strangeness: if Europe never ceases to be conditioned by its traditional forms, its national and folk identities, then philosophy is only a part of Europe if it also takes the form of a kind of stranger within, leading inevitably to conflict:

> Clearly this [spread of philosophy] leads not simply to a homogenous transformation of the generally satisfactory life of the national state but probably to great internal schisms in which this life and the whole national culture suffer an upheaval. Those conservatives who were satisfied with the tradition and the philosophical men will fight each other, and the struggle will surely occur in the sphere of political power. The

persecution begins at the very beginnings of philosophy. Men who live for these ideas become objects of contempt.[25]

The conflict in question is not merely one of ideas. It has to do with the very way humans are in tune with their surrounding world, or how they comport themselves in relation to the exigencies of existence. Husserl tries to capture this dimension by describing a contrast of attitudes (*Einstellungen*). One is pre-scientific and "natural," in the sense of an orientation to the horizon of the given and the obvious, naively functioning as a bedrock of human life: "natural life can be characterized as a life naively, straightforwardly directed at the world, the world being always in a certain sense consciously present as a universal horizon, without, however, being thematic at such."[26] The other attitude is "theoretical," critical in posture, striving to take nothing for granted, to openly question everything that falls within the scope of pre-theoretical life. These attitudes clearly contradict one another, but at the same time they can also interpenetrate one another. For the questions that drive the theoretical can only find traction in tension with the natural attitude; if theoretical life represents a new orientation, it is only as a reorientation to what had been given before: "Thus the theoretical attitude, in its newness, refers back to a previous attitude, one which was earlier the norm; [with reference to this] it is characterized as a reorientation [*Umstellung*]."[27]

Husserl thus describes the irruption of the theoretical attitude, of *theōria*, as a reattunement of existence. It is not the outright dissolution of the natural attitude, but a vocational unity taking place within its horizon, one that takes the form of a periodic disruption alternating with a recalibration of the whole of natural existence. This in effect specifies the meaning of the "infinite task" of rational life as an inner reorientation and recalibration of concrete, "natural" existence, the interests of which remain operative throughout:

> The individual men who reorient themselves, as men within their universal life-community (their nation), continue to have their natural interests, each his individual interests; through no reorientation can they simply lose them; this would mean that each would cease to be what he has become from birth onward. In any circumstances, then, the reorientation can only be a periodical one; it can have habitually enduring validity for one's whole remaining life only in the form of an unconditional resolve of the will to take up, at periodic but internally unified points of time, the same attitude and, through this continuity that intentionally bridges the gaps, to sustain its new sort of interests as

valid and as ongoing projects and to realize them through corresponding cultural structures.[28]

This dynamic however is, in the long term, moving towards an increasing embeddedness of *theōria* in the particular forms of life, an ongoing revolution of its most basic orientation: "Scientific culture under the guidance of ideas of infinity means, then, a revolutionization [*Revolutionierung*] of the whole culture, a revolutionization of the whole manner in which mankind creates culture. It also means a revolutionization of [its] historicity, which is now the history of the cutting-off of finite mankind's development [*Geschichte des Entwerdens des endlichen Menschentums*] as it becomes mankind with infinite tasks."[29]

For Husserl, "Europe" is nothing less than the name for the historical vanguard of this *Entwerdens*, this curtailment of the preponderance of a finite, closed humanity; it is the name for the wave of critique, or the praxis of "the universal critique of all life and all life-goals, all cultural products and systems that have already arisen out of the life of man; and thus it also becomes a critique of mankind itself and of the values which guide it explicitly or implicitly."[30] Or again, "Europe" names neither a place nor a group of cultures, but the finite vehicle of an infinite "praxis whose aim is to elevate mankind through universal scientific reason, according to norms of truth of all forms, to transform it from the bottom up into a new humanity made capable of an absolute self-responsibility on the basis of absolute theoretical insights."[31]

Though "Europe" for Husserl in an important sense represents the inevitable curtailment of its own finite identity in favor of the ideal of a universal rational humanity, he nevertheless assumes that it can still be the title for the vanguard of reason, that it is still the inevitable point of reference for the ideal of a philosophical life in truth. With this, as Patočka points out, Husserl shares with Scheler and others the assumption that the question of modern humanity is precisely the question of Europe. Yet, Patočka asks his listeners some forty years after the composition of Husserl's *Crisis*, is such an assumption still meaningful? Is Europe still the inevitable point of departure for the self-determination of a universal humanity, as it has time and again been taken to be? Or has the center instead shifted, so that in fact the question is and can no longer be Europe, even as the imperfect and incomplete expression of an ideal, but must instead be more directly about humans in a planetary sense, a humanity as such in relation to a now global society?

Patočka's answer is unequivocal. It can only be planetary, whatever that means or can mean, for *Europe is dead*:

I think this question really must be answered in the affirmative: it regards man in his relationship to the planet. It is clear today, when Europe has come to an end. Europe, that two-thousand-year-old construction, which managed to lift up mankind to an altogether new degree of self-reflection and consciousness, and strength and power as well, when this historical reality, which for a long time supposed that it encompassed all of mankind, that it is mankind and that all else is worthy of neglect, is definitively at an end.[32]

If Europe is nevertheless still a question, a problem, it is now one of how, in the situation of the existence of planetary humanity, the legacy of Europe still has some meaning, still speaks to humans in a way that quickens reflection and provides an orientation for posing the burning questions of the times.

The problem of legacy in fact forms one of the fundamental leitmotifs of Patočka's philosophical reflections on Europe, and the legacy in question is usually understood as emerging directly from catastrophes. This is characteristic of the historical reflections one finds in *Plato and Europe* as well as the *Heretical Essays*, in which Patočka describes the spiritual legacy of Europe emerging from a series of failures, the itinerary of which spans very different, if also interrelated, cultural and political formations: the emergence of Platonic philosophy in the wake of the failure of the polis, irrevocable after the Peloponnesian War; the rise of the Roman Empire as a "universal city" in the wake of the collapse of republican political and moral cohesion; the rise of Christendom and the medieval world in the wake of the political and social collapse of the Roman Empire; the rise of modern mathematical science in the wake of the collapse of a philosophy, a wisdom, grounded in the coupling of faith and ancient metaphysics; and the final catastrophe, the death of Europe itself as an ideal in the total war of the twentieth century. Each catastrophe points to the specific conditions, the given situation in which the ideal and task of philosophy is rediscovered, or a legacy is confirmed precisely in the recognition of its failure or disappearance. Catastrophes and responses to catastrophes constitute for Patočka the real fabric of the philosophical tradition: "through catastrophe[s], despite their destructive consequences, this heritage is spread through the world."[33]

The result of this perspective is that the historical narrative for Patočka is considerably more complex than it was for Husserl. It is also arguable that the details of the actual history are more important for Patočka than they had been for Husserl, and for philosophical reasons. No parables here. To be sure, much of Patočka's account follows faithfully the broad outlines of contemporary archaeology and historiography, for which he obviously had a voracious appetite. On a deeper level, however, Patočka's repeated emphases on the breaks, ruptures, discontinuities, and disasters of this familiar history take each station along the way as an opportunity to glimpse an underlying problematicity of human existence that he takes to be in play throughout. The legacies at work here, in other words, are not complete and fixed paradigms and archetypes, preserved by tradition in ways that make them both transparent and practically efficacious. There is no inborn teleology that drives the whole, whether in the sense of an unbroken development of spirit, or even in the more nuanced teleology of the ideal that one finds in Husserl. There is instead a manifold of contingent legacies that almost from the very beginning are transmitted through distortions, forgetting, failures, and forms of life that ultimately prove to be dead ends, but through which, if properly understood, one can catch a glimpse of the fundamental existential structures of human life. Europe, in other words, is most interesting for Patočka when it is either not yet Europe, but the problem of a future Europe guiding a reflection on Mesopotamia or ancient Greece, or a past form of Europe in the grip of one or another state of collapse.

In the end, Patočka's is a project not so much keen to preserve a given idea of Europe, as to rediscover the potential force of a philosophical ideal of life in the wake of its twilight. His reconstruction of the legacies of Europe, above all those of philosophy, in the end serves to frame an ontological inquiry into human existence, just as it frames a reflection on the current situation at the beginning of *Plato and Europe*. The three are inextricably intertwined; and it is here that one can see how phenomenology—and the importance of the project of the 1968–69 lectures—fit into Patočka's overall philosophical itinerary.

Phenomenology and the Hopes of Philosophy

Patočka's emphasis in the beginning of *Plato and Europe* on the human situation in which he and his listeners find themselves already introduces the ontological problematic, in a subtle and compelling way. For what is a "situation"? On the one hand, it is something eminently concrete: a situation is what roots humans, fixes them in terms of very specific conditions. One is defined by the situation, it designates those facts that have come together to constitute that profile of existence which at any given point is called a life, as well as the specific set of material and spiritual conditions that provide the ground for understanding, and confirming, what and who one in fact is. A reflection on the situation is aimed at the clarification of life in its very concreteness, in the hope of arriving at a self-understanding capable of surveying the terrain of existence, compensating for the otherwise opaque self-understanding of the given moment.

Something else goes with this. However opaque, there is also always something open in a situation, something undecided that forms an essential thread that runs through any context of life. Situations are not hermetically sealed; they are not given as a perfectly closed positivity, but always remain open with respect to their meaning. A situation is thus more than a state of affairs; it is that as well, but it distorts things if one fails to recognize how the moment is also bent towards its future. This encompasses what, if anything, remains to be decided—what action to take, what response to make with regard to the situation illuminated in reflection, what meaning to affirm, what to deny or defend oneself against. It also encompasses a sensitivity to the contingency of things, an awareness that what is the case is only contingently so, that it is not unproblematic and settled that concrete life has taken precisely the shape that it has. In some situations, the more hopeless ones in which life reveals itself to be a burden, this experience of openness takes the form of a sense of decline, of the awareness that the world has somehow taken a wrong turn, that it has in some important way departed from its own intrinsic meaning—again that feeling that time is out of joint, that there is a fundamental disequilibrium that has come to mark indelibly the collective life of humanity. Such sentiments speak not simply about facts and conditions, but also how it is that the world is encountered in the light of its possibilities.

In both senses the situation represents a figure of *manifestation*—it is not just the state of the world, but the way the world presents itself, the way that things appear and make themselves known. Manifestation is in turn not a simple relation between two things, but a relation between something that shows itself and someone to whom something—a given entity or complex of entities, or even a situation in its opacity and openness—appears. This is the most basic structure of a phenomenological ontology: the relation of the human being as openness to the manifestation of things, to the "how" things appear in their relation to subjects, those beings who "see" things and inhabit the space not of their mere existence, but the dynamics of their appearance.

Another basic thesis of phenomenology, prominent in both Husserl and Heidegger, is that this space of manifestation is specifically that of an understanding, and the manner of manifestation of things in understanding is precisely the ground of truth. But it is equally the ground of untruth, of falsity and distortion. Humans live among not only things that manifest themselves in their truth, but also things which manifest themselves as what they are not. A being capable of cultivating a relation to truth is equally a being capable of cultivating the myriad forms of untruth, from the obliviousness of forgetting to the distorting machinations of the lie. This theme, already central to ancient philosophy, in turn becomes central to phenomenology, above all in the thought of Heidegger.[34]

It is this ontology of the human being as a being who inhabits the horizon of manifestation, of truth and untruth, that forms the bedrock of Patočka's reflections on Europe. For the core legacy of Europe—which for Patočka as for Husserl is precisely the legacy of philosophy—is according to Patočka's argument the *care for the soul*. The soul is that being for whom truth is a possibility, for whom it has become possible to inhabit the space of manifestation, of appearance, in such a way that prejudices all perspectives in favor of the truth. The care for the soul is the care for a life in truth, understood as an ontological possibility of human existence.

In this way phenomenology, understood as a philosophy of manifestation, of the relation of phenomenality that makes possible a care for both the true and the self, reveals for Patočka the promise of a more fundamental ontological understanding of the meaning of human existence implicit in the care for the soul. If the legacy of Europe reveals something essential about the situation of contemporary humanity, and philosophy reveals something essential about Europe, then phenomenology will reveal something essential about philosophy. This *in nuce* had also been the position of Husserl, and in fact much of Patočka's philosophical development, from his early work on the problem of the "natural" world to his philosophy of history, can be inscribed within the horizon of reflection opened by Husserl's *Crisis of European Sciences*.

Yet this really represents only a point of departure. Phenomenology, and possibly philosophy as well, will become something very different for Patočka than it had been for Husserl, as will all the legacies and hopes that Patočka will continue to subsume under the title of "Europe."

Outline

In general terms, Patočka's thinking can be characterized as a philosophy of history rooted in a phenomenological ontology that provides its most essential philosophical impetus. Patočka offers a reflection on the human condition, defined as an intimate relation to what it means to be, what it means to be manifest, and with that present in the world. Patočka is thus a philosopher who devotes himself to the perennial questions of human existence, seeking an understanding, or at least a glimpse, of the eternal. Yet at the same time, Patočka's is a thinking that situates itself in the historical moment, that not only acknowledges its times, but seeks to provide an essential expression of the metaphysics of the age—the truth, the way of being, as well as the exigencies and challenges of what it means to be a human being in the twentieth century. It is an age when, after the death of Europe and the apparent eclipse of the care for the soul, the philosopher emerges as a unique kind of wanderer, heir to the legacies of catastrophe, but for all that committed once again to the life of Socratic questioning.

Patočka is also much more than this. He is not only a philosopher of history and the human condition, but a historian of philosophy of the first rank, making notable contributions to the field of Renaissance studies (above all on Comenius) and Aristotle scholarship, much of which has been recognized in the literature over the years and some of which still awaits a full reception.[35] Moreover, Patočka is not only a philosopher who reflected on the contemporary situation of Europe, but took action within it, serving as one of the spokespersons, along with Václav Havel, of the Charter 77 dissident movement, an act that ultimately cost him his life. If that were not already enough, Patočka is also a towering figure in modern Czech intellectual history, equal to Masaryk, with a unique understanding of the history and culture of central Europe, expressed in writings on Czech history and critical forays into literature and the philosophy of art.[36]

Any single study of Patočka's thought, facing the usual demands of scholarly economy, risks reducing the richness of his writings to a cluster of themes that, however otherwise essential they may be, ultimately belie the complexity of the corpus in which they are embedded. This study is no different. It is not and cannot be exhaustive. The attempt in what follows is to show how the development of Patočka's idea of phenomenology acts as a constant source of inspiration for his thinking on the meaning of history, the problem of Europe, and the tasks of political existence. The guiding thesis is uncontroversial: the problems of phenomenological philosophy, history, and political life form an inseparable unity in Patočka's thought. And the goal is modest: the aim is to orchestrate a broad reflection on the meaning of the legacy of Patočka's philosophy, some half century after his death.

The form of what follows will thus be more of an essay on Patočka's thought than an exhaustive scholarly monograph, which in any case would be a task better left to others who are far more capable than this author.[37] It seeks to enter into the flow of Patočka's reflections, essaying different points of entry and exploring the different registers of a complex body of work, instead of submitting it to a master interpretation whose arc would terminate in a definite concluding thesis that would belie its prevailing open, even experimental character. If this yields something of a discursive, wandering quality to what follows, it is intentional. The aim is to capture something of the experience of reading Patočka's writings, in which a unity of thinking is progressively deepened through a series of projects begun and abandoned, only to be rediscovered in different forms and lines of reflection that often emerge out of trenchant self-critique. The argument is not that Patočka's work is fragmentary, which would simply be false; but only that he was too responsible a thinker to be lured by the sirens of systematic philosophy and easily formulated conclusions. The hope is that an essay that serves as a guide and companion to the reading of the complex philosophical gestures one encounters in the writings of the Czech philosopher offers perhaps the most appropriate means to explore their enduring power.

1

On an Asubjective Phenomenology

World as a Philosophical Problem

The guiding theme of Jan Patočka's philosophy is undoubtedly that of the world. "The problem of philosophy," as Patočka puts it in 1936, formulating a conviction that will remain in force throughout his philosophical career, "is the world as a whole."[1] The world is the whole of what exists, what can be said to be; its problematic turns on the question of in just what sense the "whole" itself can be said to be, and with that, in what sense the world as a whole can be established as a coherent theme for philosophical reflection. The world is also that thanks to which humans are what they are; it is that from out of which they emerge, individually and collectively, and into which they project their possibilities. Its problematic thus covers equally the problem of the essence of human existence itself.

In a sense, the world is both the most concrete and the most abstract of problems. It is concrete when it takes the form of an insistence on the importance of remaining true to the world as we experience it, to those concrete relations that make up the whole of human existence in the common horizon of life. It is abstract when it dissolves into generalities that, perhaps of necessity, lack definition, substance, or a way forward for thinking, even if it remains incontrovertible that even in its most abstract of forms philosophy is in the end about "the world." Patočka's thinking accepts the challenge of navigating between these extremes, in that for him the theme of the world, or at least its philosophical form, is not something given, but must be established—the world as a theme of reflection, in other words, is a terrain, a ground that must be secured.

The success in bringing the problem of the world into play at all is central to Patočka's account of philosophy, both in its history and its essential aims. Philosophy for Patočka begins with an act of transcendence, one thanks to which the world, ever present in the functioning of life but not in the form of a problem taken up for itself, becomes an explicit concern. The friction that marks this act of transcendence, the tug of resistance it must overcome, comes from life itself, from the ordinary movement of humans in a given world in which the immediate understanding (or mystery) of things dominates the moment. In everyday life, the world remains on the edges of concern, present at best in the guise of the vague generality of "everything." This means that the world as a whole can come into view only when the natural prerogative of the interests and concerns of the moment is broken, and thinking, in the form of reflection, moves beyond the fixed circuit of a pre-given familiarity with how things are.

Patočka often illustrates this transcending of the ordinary with a description of the emergence of mathematical thinking, or more specifically a particular experience that such thinking can offer: namely the astonishment, first won by insight, at the frustration of a certain anticipation of order, and in its wake an encounter with something wholly unexpected.[2] A striking example of this is the discovery of the incommensurability of the diagonal and side of a square, an insight that disrupted an entire attitude towards the nature of the real that had been characteristic of the ancient Pythagoreans (and, as goes the legend, may have cost at least one of them, a fellow named Hippasus, his life). It is not so much the astonishment—in the sense of *thaumazein*, here citing both Plato and Aristotle[3]—that there exists a deeper, more fundamental reality, populated by new, strange objects (such as irrational numbers), as it is the experience of a shift of relation with regard to the ordinary, the experience of which occasions a dizzying perplexity. The familiar world itself, obvious in its everyday indifference, finds itself circumscribed by a new way of relating to what is that does not limit itself to the closed rhythms of familiarity and their indefinite extension, but is capable of suspending them in favor of a different mode of inquiry that follows different expectations. Out of the perplexity of such aporias there arises a peculiar kind of freedom, opened by the movement of aporetic thinking itself, which Patočka characterizes as the formation of a fundamental mode of access—for mathematical objects are "something accessible to us not from *external givenness* but from *internal freedom*."[4]

Something similar is the case with the shift, which for Patočka is coincidental with the very origin of philosophy, that leads to a reorientation to the world as a whole, and not simply to a new domain of paradoxical things. Yet in this case the shift is more complicated, for it is a shift, one might say, from the world in one sense, to the same world but in a vastly different sense. This different sense of the world also becomes accessible thanks to an internal freedom, but at the same time it brings with it an experience of a necessity of something of which one had been previously unaware. It is not so much the necessity of insight characteristic of mathematical objects, as it is a revealed necessity discovered at the heart of ordinary relations with things, one that belongs essentially to the functioning of experience itself, as its unspoken condition and possibility. Accordingly, if the whole comes into view only through a free transcendence, then at the same time what comes into view is precisely the whole *in its necessity*:

> It [the world as a whole] is pre-present, as obvious, in the "functioning" experiential sequences, in the reference of their "and so on" which leads us from one given to the next, from one present to another present. It must, however, be first *explicitly torn out* of this everyday obvious functioning before we can note that this process of approximation, perennially incomplete, presupposes the being, the existence of the *whole* which requires an act of transcendence, at once free and necessary—free insofar as it can be done only once we *break free* of what is momentarily given and so forced on us, and necessary, because to deny it would mean to deny experience itself in its functioning.[5]

The world, affirmed in its necessity, emerges in harmony with an act of freedom. The result is that the world is no longer a hidden, implicitly functioning necessity forced on humans in the form of a pre-given familiarity, an opaque relatedness of all things to the open-ended process of their becoming. It now unfolds within a free relation to what is worldly. Yet at the same time, this new affirmation remains in tension with the everyday; the dominance of the latter, which takes the form of the preponderance of the multiplicity of things over the whole of what is, remains in effect. The necessity represented by the world as a whole is in this way a peculiar kind of disappearing, self-obfuscating necessity, one always already absorbed into the determinations of things, like a light that cedes its space to the things it allows to appear in clarity:

> The world [*svět*], the circle of light [*světlo*] in which I see every activity and thing facing me, all I determine to do, vanishes totally in the clarity of that determination.... We do not originally see and live the *world as world* but rather as the things and projects within it.[6]

If things are what they are only thanks to their relation to this whole, this "circle of light" with its newfound necessity, then the nature of this relation has to itself be determined. Moreover, this determination is not an immediate result of any given exercise of the free transcendence towards the whole of what is. At most this yields a question, the possibility of which is perhaps established, but never in a form that immediately yields a coherent self-understanding of its significance. For Patočka, the history of philosophy is to a great extent determined by various ways of addressing the hidden potential of this reorientation of humans towards the whole of what is. It is experienced as a reorientation because philosophy always emerges in contrast with the nonphilosophical. However essential it may be to humanity, philosophy is not its first, most original expression.

In this respect, the significance of philosophy is not that it was the first to pose the question of the whole, or even to describe, much less codify the peculiar experience of *thaumazein*. Such a claim is not only unprovable but, arguably, an insignificant prize, since the bare transcendence that differentiates the familiar world from the horizon opened by the sense of wonder need be neither unique nor uncommon. What counts is what emerges in its wake, how the question of the whole, glimpsed in wonder, finds its articulation as an explicit problem. In the Greek manner of such thinking, which Patočka never fails to take as paradigmatic, the particular articulation of the sense of the whole is captured in the figure of *phusis*, of the drama of manifestation as the emergence from nothing and the return to nothing, of coming to be and passing away. Greek thinking from its earliest beginnings, culminating in the philosophy of Aristotle, submits *phusis* to discourse, in the attempt to articulate the movement of this drama of manifestation in a set of fixed, stable meanings that together constitute a unified understanding of the world. Here the necessity of the whole finds its expression in concepts, as does the relation of the whole to things. The whole is that ground thanks to which things are what they are, and emerge and perish the way they do, thereby fitting into a global coherence that is comprehended and comprehensible in a fixed manner, or in accordance with what is eternal, unchanging.[7]

The essence of Greek thinking, in other words, lies in its particular articulation of the question of the whole in terms of a *science*, an *epistēmē*, where philosophy, that reorientation of human existence towards the possibilities of transcendence, takes a decidedly conceptual form:

> Thus, gradually, on the basis of the discovery of the world as a process of manifestation and in the effort to comprehend, embrace, and surround this manifestation there emerges philosophy as a science and science as a part of philosophy, that is, of global comprehension.[8]

Philosophy, or at least Greek philosophy, thus begins for Patočka with a reorientation, a self-transcendence of everyday understanding; it matures as an articulation of the whole from out of this reorientation. Yet this articulation is at once a fulfillment of a promise—that the things encountered in wonder can be *thought*, grasped in insight, and spoken of meaningfully with concepts—but also its ultimate obfuscation. In the form it comes to take in Greek thinking and those traditions that find their beginnings in its basic insights, philosophy tends to an ossification that obscures its originary potential. For the radical emphasis on the meaning of the eternal in its understanding of the whole as something fixed and unchanging ultimately leads to a metaphysical framework that consistently lends itself to a lifeless, univocal articulation of things, one that belies the open diversity of forms that make up the very body of factical life, forms that govern the world both natural and human. The particularity of Greek thinking, its progressive emphasis on an understanding committed to the fixed and the unchanging, introduces a seductiveness of closed, fixed conceptual forms that risk deadening the sense of both the dynamic drama of *phusis* and the startled transcendence of *thaumazein*. Greek philosophy begins in the rush of wonder, but lists inexorably towards boredom.

This is perhaps most poignantly exemplified in the case of human relations. The more rigid, the more univocally applied the determinations of metaphysics become, the more relations among humans, political but not limited to the political, become inscrutable and misunderstood:

> The projects we undertake are focused on our personal, exclusive goals but they are meaningful only in reciprocity, in the mutuality of mirroring and mutual penetration with others. As long as the turn from things to the world is not carried through to this dimension, as long as there is no realization of the originality of the living relation in which others cease to be mere things (even if governed together with me by the same cosmic norms of harmony and justice), the discovery of the world cannot take place except along the lines of the impersonal and so of the "lifeless"; hence also the appeal for the Greek philosopher of what is comprehensive and transcendent, global and permanent, though lifeless and internally empty, of ideas, of mathematical entities, of logical relations. In a world so understood there cannot ultimately dwell the meaning of manifestation, such a world is stripped of it and vacuous—it has to be transcended if we are to overcome the fossilization brought about by the discovery and uncovering, but impersonal and so ineffective philosophizing in the matrix of transtemporal presence in its unity with rigorous science.[9]

Philosophy for Patočka, one might conclude, really begins only once its beginning has itself become a problem; namely, the problem of retracing that original movement from familiar things to the problematic world that had once opened the possibility of something like a philosophy at all. It is not a return to wonder, so much as a re-dedication to the promise, the hope, that the experience of wonder once seemed to have given. Now the friction to be overcome that would make such a repetition possible is no longer merely the preeminence of the everyday, the forced givenness of the moment, but the tendency of habits of thinking to fossilize reflection into the rigid conceptual schemas of Greek-like metaphysics, and with that the dominance of the impersonal.

Yet Patočka's point is not simply that the person, or personal being, should be at the center of philosophical reflection. In fact, even in his own account of the history of Western metaphysics, it always had been just that, though in progressively degenerate forms. The Platonic articulation of the eternal as the unchanging reality of Idea had been accompanied by an ethic of personal discipline and responsibility that spoke directly to the spiritual needs of the self. The care for the soul (*epimeleia tēs psuchēs*) accordingly shares a common genesis with the metaphysics of the *idea*. Likewise, the question of personal existence stands at the center of another set of metaphysical theses, those that form the core of modern philosophy: the Baconian idea of the *regnum hominis*, the Cartesian figure of humans as the *maîtres et possesseurs de la nature*, in short, the determination of the subject as will and as power that belongs to the foundations of the metaphysics of modern philosophy and science. Throughout, the legacy or legacies of Western thinking do not amount to a mere jettisoning of the problem of the person, as a progressively de-personalized and alienated articulation of the same.

Patočka often cites Kant as giving the problem of subjectivity the decisive form that it will take within modern philosophy—namely, the form of a task of uncovering the constitutive logic of objectivity, which in turn is understood as governing the relation between the person and the whole of what is. In Kant this takes the form of the question of what it is that can be known; but also what can be hoped, in the wake of what ought to be done, thus yielding three fundamental questions of philosophy that can be summed up in the question "What is a human being?"[10] This Kantian impulse is further developed in the post-Kantian philosophies of German Idealism, in which the project of reestablishing the relation of human beings to the whole is a fundamental goal, one that again takes the form of the establishment of a newfound orientation to subjectivity, to life in its concreteness, meant to replace the all-too-static ontology of Greek metaphysics, but still inscribed within its traditional forms.

In this way, the problem of the world in its modern form is indissociable from the problem of the subject, of subjective being and its transcendental function as the origin of the logic of experience, of life. It takes shape, in Patočka's language, as the problem of the "natural" world—the world natural to human existence, both in terms of the conditions of possibility for the encounterability of things, as well as a reflection on what is commensurable with those interests, concerns, and projects of human existence. The problem of the world, in other words, is the problem of life; and the problem of life is the problem of subjectivity, the being of which illuminates a fundamental continuity between human beings and their world.

It is this modern focus on subjectivity, unfolding essentially as the task of articulating a logic of experience, that Patočka considers to be fundamental to phenomenology. Yet what stands out with regard to phenomenology, beginning with Husserl, is a decidedly non-metaphysical impulse, one that strives to articulate the meaning of the whole of the world without forcing it into the fetters of fixed, univocal concepts. Thus, unlike other heirs to the Greek metaphysical tradition, phenomenology promises to explore the continuity of humans and their world as something that is perhaps not closed, but open:

> Another conception of the question that led to the rise of Greek philosophy is emerging, of the question for the drama of the world, for being which bestows meaning on all that is and sets each particular a priori into a meaningful framework. It is a conception which also sees the meaning of philosophy in setting humans free for a prevenient continuity of the world and of being, but so analyzes the continuity that as a consequence of these analyses we might doubt whether that continuity can itself ever be surveyed as a whole, mastered, and exhausted.[11]

Heidegger is certainly being alluded to here, but what Patočka describes is no less the case with Husserl. The promise that originally attracted Patočka to Husserl's thinking was one of a renewed understanding of the meaning of the whole, of the world as it is uncovered in an original act of philosophical transcendence; it is the promise of reimagining the intrinsic essence of subjective existence as being-in-the-world, where the comprehension of the world as a horizon of meaning in turn allows for a reflection on the meaning of human life, personal human existence, as fundamentally bound up with and in the same movement. It is also the promise of a renewed critical stance, offering a penetrating interpretation of philosophy, whose history offers as many obstacles to self-comprehension as points of departure for inspiration and understanding. Husserl's phenomenology stands, in short, for the promise of a renewal of philosophy as a whole, of its vocation, purpose, and hope, and thus nothing less than the retracing of a path of freedom from the naive rhythms of given natural existence to a life of insight and understanding. Phenomenology promises, in other words, nothing less than the world.

CHAPTER 1

World of Life

Something like a history of the concept of the world thus belongs to Patočka's intellectual itinerary, and from the very beginning, starting with the historical sections of his 1936 habilitation thesis already cited above, *The Natural World as Philosophical Problem*. This historical interest in the problem of the natural world, however, finds its motivation, and ultimate bearings, in a specific phase of this history, one in which Husserl's thinking played an integral part, and which determined the horizon of the problem as it was understood by the end of the nineteenth century, above all in the rise and fall of positivism as one of the dominant intellectual trends of the times.

Husserl himself would often credit positivism as an influence on his own thinking; and specifically with regard to the problem of the natural world, it was above all the work of Richard Avenarius, the German-Swiss philosopher and founder of empirio-criticism, that would prove decisive. Avenarius, in works such as *Kritik der reinen Erfahrung* and *Der menschliche Weltbegriff*, argued for a concept of the world that had its origin in the natural experience of humans that arises purely from being in the world, among things and others, as the horizon of what is "found in advance" (*Vorgefundene*). Avenarius sought to contrast this fund of pre-found, natural understanding with the representation of the world established by the methods of natural science, revealing the metaphysical exaggerations of the latter by way of a contest with the illuminating, and ultimately legitimating force of "pure experience."[12]

Husserl's conception of the natural attitude and its world, central to the project of *Ideas I* (1913), and later the concept of the lifeworld (*Lebenswelt*), central to the project of the *Crisis*, were deeply influenced by Avenarius, and in two interrelated senses.[13] The first was Avenarius's idea of a naive, natural experience of the world that is not only juxtaposed with the natural scientific understanding of the world, but constantly affirmed in its inner integrity within natural life. Life itself, independently of the schemas of science, formulates an understanding immanent to the unfolding of concrete experience with the things of its surroundings, an understanding that is never completely abandoned. Second, and perhaps even more importantly, is the idea of a descriptive approach to this natural concept of the world, where description takes the form of a direct, unmediated relation to things as they are experienced, thus representing a mode of access that affirms a relative autonomy of the natural concept of the world in contrast to natural scientific explanation.

Husserl, who was critical of the ultimate naturalistic aims of Avenarius's project,[14] radicalizes both of these gestures in his idea of a descriptive eidetics on the one hand, and a significantly expanded conception of the natural world on the other.[15] This latter gesture, in part inspired by Wilhelm Dilthey's *The Formation of the Historical World in the Human Sciences*,[16] extends the sense of the natural world from the domain of physical nature to that of persons, communities, and history. Like Dilthey, Husserl argues that these "personalistic" dimensions of the world of human life operate on an evidentiary and phenomenal basis distinct from that of the natural sciences, and thus must be approached with a different methodological and conceptual repertoire.

From the beginning, though reaching an unprecedented level of sophistication in the *Crisis*, Husserl's analysis of the natural world unfolds as a descriptive elaboration of the structures of meaning implicit in what belongs to the world of everyday life. The constant emphasis that runs throughout is the world in its *obviousness* (*Selbstverständlichkeit*), its immediate comprehensibility. This is the obviousness of one's being in a world in which one is both a person in pursuit of ends and one who stands in turn as means for the ends of others, the obviousness that individuals are both "subjects" and "objects" in this sense; the obviousness that one exists in a world populated not only by individuals but by communities, some proximate and some distant, composed of others who comport themselves in the same horizon of the same scope of obviousness. That such things are obvious is not a mere contingent fact but belongs to the overall style of natural life; it points, in other words, to something essential. For Husserl, the obvious is something that provides an index to the species of validity that accords to natural being, and thus is a proper theme for philosophy, as it was for Avenarius, even if at the same time it is a validity that, in everyday life, there is no reason to even bring up:

> Naturally, all these things are the most obvious of the obvious. Must one speak about them, and with so much ado? In life certainly not. But not as a philosopher either? Is this not the opening-up of a realm, indeed an infinite realm, of always ready and available but never questioned ontic validities? Are they not *constant presuppositions* of scientific and, at the highest level, philosophical thinking?[17]

There is a tension here, however. The obviousness of the lifeworld, its taken-for-granted validity, in effect obscures those accomplishments thanks to which these presuppositions are valid, precisely in their obviousness. What is obvious need not be questioned, at least not in the natural course of life. Moreover, the obviousness of the lifeworld, for Husserl—and this will be a target of critique for Patočka—represents a guiding clue to the anonymous accomplishments of the subjectivity that establishes the validities of natural life as a whole. All the validities of the lifeworld are for Husserl first and foremost the spiritual acquisition of a formation of sense (*Sinngebilde*). At its most fundamental level, the world is ultimately manifest in the unity of a sense-formation constituted by the accomplishments of an "ultimately functioning subjectivity":

> We shall come to understand that the world which constantly exists for us through the flowing alteration of manners of givenness is a universal spiritual acquisition [*geistiger Erwerb*], having developed as such and at the same time continuing to develop as the unity of a spiritual form [*geistigen Gestalt*], as a meaning-formation [*Sinngebilde*]—as the formation [*Gebilde*] of a universal, ultimately functioning subjectivity [*letztfungierenden Subjektivität*].[18]

The overall aim of part 3 of the *Crisis*, from which these quotes are taken, is to develop the problematic of the lifeworld as a "way" to transcendental philosophy, understood as the analysis of this "universale letztfungierende Subjektivität." It begins where part 2 left off, namely with a critique of Kant, whose "incomprehensibly mythical" constructions,[19] rooted in classical Lockean psychology, ultimately obfuscate the cogency of the transcendental problematic. Instead Husserl proposes the thematic of the lifeworld, that domain of validities which for Kant had remained invisible as "an unquestioned ground of presuppositions,"[20] and which would serve as the methodological ground for the progressive clarification of the problem of subjectivity.

Clarification is needed in order to compensate for a certain blindness characteristic of the natural attitude, but this includes the need to understand the need for such clarity in the first place. To illustrate the task of the clarification of transcendental subjectivity, Husserl evokes the thought-experiment credited to Wilhelm von Helmholtz, in which one imagines beings who live confined to a two-dimensional plane, oblivious to its depth. Phenomenological reflection can accordingly be likened to breaking through an initial obliviousness of life confined to the surface of the everyday (the *Flächenleben* of Helmholtz) to the depth dimensions that exist just beneath the surface (*Tiefenleben*), and which come into view only thanks to a fundamental change of perspective.[21]

The image is suggestive, and helps make an essential point about a peculiar closure of obviousness characteristic of the natural world. Obviousness does not mean transparency; if it is a mode of understanding, it is one that lacks a motivation to make the origins of this understanding something explicit, openly articulated, and so in this sense it remains stubbornly opaque in its unquestionableness. Natural life naturally pulls itself again and again towards its own surface, like a kind of undertow in reverse.

The analysis of the lifeworld, or the comprehension of its "peculiar being-sense [*Seinssinn*]," is thus from the beginning beset with "difficulties,"[22] and on several levels. The most immediate is the obviousness that shrouds its deeper dimensions. In addition to this, there also stands in the way the effects of a whole range of attitudes, habits, and ways of thinking germane to the scientific attitude itself. For the thematization of the lifeworld is nothing short of taking up something that is systematically repressed in the scientific mindset, namely everything that is "subject-relative." There is thus something of a collusion between a natural resistance and a learned, culturally conditioned refusal, which together result in something like a fault line within natural life, one that runs along the tension between the scientific attitude premised on the deep suspicion of the validity of anything subject-relative, and a "prescientific life" for which, on the contrary, "what is actually first is the 'merely subjective-relative.'"[23] The obstinacy of scientific life keeps pre-scientific life at arm's length, while the obviousness of the latter is obliviously indifferent to the rejections of the former, the pair together forming a kind of not wanting to see what does not care to be seen anyway.

Yet this fault line is inscribed in the unity of the world itself. It only seems that we live in two worlds, for in the end there is only one world, however elusive its overall structure. Science may be an overcoming of the subject-relative, Husserl argues, but only in a fashion that remains within the horizon of the overall validity of the lifeworld. Objectivity, as the orienting terminus of the scientific attitude, is itself ultimately something relative to the subject, and precisely in a way that relies on the original evidentiary basis of the lifeworld. For science, Husserl never fails to emphasize, is a concrete human praxis, and as such is irrevocably embedded in the lifeworld; its perspective, however predicated on the contrast between evidence in the theoretical-logical sense and the "originary" evidence of the lifeworld itself, nevertheless is ultimately grounded on the latter as its fundamental and incontrovertible premise.[24] However "ideal" the truth of the sciences, however true in itself the objective world may be, its sense is ultimately something that can only be understood relative to subjective accomplishments of meaning. Which leads to something of a paradoxical situation: "Thus [the idea of a] true world in any sense, and within it our own being, becomes an enigma in respect to the sense of this being."[25]

For Husserl, the resolution of this paradox lies in the analysis of the lifeworld itself, in all its obviousness, an analysis that reveals the essential structures that govern the modes of evidence and validity for life as a whole. Whatever the scientific prejudices against the subjective may be, the lifeworld is not a mere flux of random relativities, but bears within itself a universal structure, whose a priori is itself not relative, and which forms the basis for the clarification of the accomplishments of all subjective-relative evidence or truth:

> What is needed, then, would be a systematic division of the universal structures—universal life-world *a priori* and universal "objective" *a priori*—and then also a division among the universal inquiries according to the way in which the "objective" *a priori* is grounded in the "subjective-relative" *a priori* of the life-world or how, for example, mathematical self-evidence has its source of meaning and source of legitimacy in the self-evidence of the life-world.[26]

Methodologically, this requires the *epochē*—the suspension not, as in *Ideas I*, of a general thesis putatively operative in the natural attitude, but instead a "turning of interest" (*Interessenwendung*) that turns away from, or refrains from being carried away by, the natural "straightforwardly living into the world" (*Dahinleben*) characteristic of natural life.[27] The *epochē* is a turning away from the naive acceptance of the pre-given towards an active reflection on what lies in the depth of this pre-givenness, or from the world as terminus of natural interest to the world as "ground validity [*Bodengeltung*] of natural life."[28] This is not, as Husserl stresses, a shift from one interpretation of the world to another, or a shift from one articulation of the world in terms of one interest to that of another, finite and therefore limited, or relative understanding of things. It is instead an interest in the ground of all interests as a whole, the basis for the full scope or range with regard to how the world "is" for subjects at all.

It is in this sense that the *epochē* yields not a *concept* of the world, as was the case in Avenarius, but rather the world as *phenomenon*, or the syntheses of manifestation that condition the emergence of any world-understanding, any mode of apprehension of the whole:

> This is not a "view," an "interpretation" bestowed upon the world. Every view about . . . , every opinion about "the" world, has its ground in the pregiven world. It is from this very ground that I have freed myself through the *epochē*; I stand *above* the world, which has now become for me, in a quite peculiar sense, a *phenomenon*.[29]

Here Husserl's departure not only from Avenarius and Kant is in play, but also from his own, more Cartesian approach found in texts such as *Ideas I* and the *Cartesian Meditations*.[30] Now the *epochē* is meant to yield neither an element nor a principle of experience that would stand as isolated in abstraction and justified with regressive arguments, and so it breaks with at least some aspects of the Kantian analytic. Yet at the same time, what the *epochē* opens is not merely a region of being characterized by its own distinctive modes of cognition, as is the case in Husserl's more Cartesian-inspired reflections. The *epochē* instead opens onto an experience of its own, consistent with natural life but recalibrated along the lines of the promise of a latent intuitivity of its own transcendental ground, in this way representing an experience turned from its surface to its depth, to again evoke Helmholtz's plane beings. The *epochē* inaugurates nothing less, in other words, than a "transcendental experience":

> And the gaze made free by the *epochē* must likewise be, in its own way, an experiencing gaze. [But] the accomplishment of the total transformation of attitude must consist in the fact that the infinity of actual and possible world-experience transforms itself into the infinity of actual and possible "transcendental experience," in which, as a first step, the world and the natural experience of it are experienced as "phenomenon."[31]

It is worth emphasizing this peculiarity of Husserl's transcendentalism, because it provides a useful axis around which to understand both the young Patočka's embrace of Husserl's philosophy and the motivations for his subsequent critique. For there are, one might argue, two potentially divergent paths that are opened in Husserl's thinking, which can be expressed in terms of the contrast between two directions indicated in part 3 of the *Crisis*. The first is the path to transcendental subjectivity itself, through what Husserl here and elsewhere describes as the analysis of an a priori system of correlations between world, things, and manners of givenness founded on the accomplishments of transcendental subjectivity:

> No matter where we turn, every entity that is valid for me and every conceivable subject as existing in actuality is thus correlatively—and with essential necessity—an index of its systematic multiplicities. Each one indicates an ideal general set of actual and possible experiential manners of givenness, each of which is an appearance of this one entity...[32]

The lifeworld thus serves as a horizon of clues for the transcendental problematic of elaborating the a priori correlation of manifest world and subjective-transcendental accomplishments. This system of correlations, thanks to which manifestation is keyed universally to the synthetic accomplishments of subjective life in such a way that determines the very horizon of the determinability of all being, justifies in Husserl's eyes the concept of transcendental *constitution*, the "original formation of meaning"[33] that governs the manifestation of beings. In this way, the becoming-manifest of things in the horizon of subjective life is understood as the securing, by way of transcendental constitution, of a manifold of abiding validities, of truths for which and thanks to which something like a world is understood at all.

There is more to this, however. Subjectivity is an inherent plurality; accordingly, "subjective life" must be understood here in an explicitly intersubjective sense, thus establishing a transcendental horizon of the idea of the world as a spiritual accomplishment, a formation of meaning or sense that is comprehensible only within the nexus of a decisively *interpersonal* comprehension. An even more fundamental structure constitutive of all sense-formation is that of *time*. That subjective life is horizonal, whether individual or communal; that its understanding is rooted in synthetic accomplishments; that it always unfolds intentionally as a movement towards . . . , an interest in things that unfolds in expectations rooted in retentions—all this points to a more originary description of *Sinnbildung* as something that is essentially *temporal* in character:

> This represents the beginnings of new dimensions of temporalization, or of time and its time content—quite apart from the fact (which is not to be elucidated here) that the constitution of every level and sort of entity is a temporalization which gives to each distinctive meaning of an entity in the constitutive system its own temporal form, whereas only through the all-inclusive, universal synthesis which constitutes the world do all these times come together synthetically into the unity of one time.[34]

Yet Husserl also recognizes a second path, or direction of analysis that sustains itself based purely on the evidence of the lifeworld alone, and which is quite independent of the *epochē* and the problems of transcendental constitution. The problematic of the lifeworld, the realization of the fault line that runs between the abiding and conditioning validities of the lifeworld and a scientific perspective that strives for a theoretical autonomy from all that is subject-relative, is not something securable only by the transcendental *epochē*, but can also be pursued within the natural attitude—with modifications—in what Husserl describes as an "ontology of the lifeworld."[35] Here Husserl's argument is similar to his defense of the idea in other works of a pure phenomenological psychology, another example of an a priori science purified of objectivistic prejudices, all of whose theses can be transmuted onto a properly transcendental register, but which can also be articulated within the more circumscribed orbit of non-transcendental but still eidetic clarification.[36] Here too the lifeworld can be elaborated descriptively, including the fundamental dimensions of intersubjectivity and temporality, just short of a full deployment of the transcendental *epoché* proper that would present the synthesis of the world-whole in terms of a correlation of manifestation and a priori subjective accomplishment.

There is thus a certain wedge in Husserl's presentation of phenomenology that can be explored between the problem of the natural world—the task of the clarification of the horizon of sense thanks to which we encounter things and ourselves, its conditions and structural characteristics—and the project of an ultimate clarification of the same grounded in transcendental subjectivity. The integrity of the former need not be completely contingent upon that of the latter; moreover, one can ask whether the "way" through the lifeworld may lead somewhere other than to the analysis of a "letztfungierende Subjektivität," either to a transcendentalism of a different kind, or to an ontology in a new, not only non-metaphysical but perhaps also non-subjectivistic key.

It is also a wedge that can, mutatis mutandis, be used to frame Patočka's own philosophical development, indicating how in moving away from Husserl's transcendental idealism Patočka in fact develops a latent potential of the broader Husserlian project. In moving away from one Husserl, one might say that Patočka in fact moves closer to another. This is perhaps best illustrated with a look at Patočka's *The Natural World as a Philosophical Problem* which, as already suggested above, determines Patočka's intellectual trajectory in decisive ways.

Unfulfillable Intentionality

It is not surprising that Patočka would take both the publication in 1970 of the second edition (the first was in 1936) of *The Natural World as a Philosophical Problem* and its translation into French in 1976 as opportunities not only to revisit a youthful work, but to use it as a measure of his mature understanding of phenomenological philosophy. The original work itself, as Patočka emphasizes in his afterword to the French translation, was not an original work, but rather was meant to endorse and give expression to Husserl's transcendental philosophy, specifically in the form that one finds developed in the *Crisis*.[37] It therefore stands as a good point of departure for exploring what Patočka had originally found compelling in Husserl's philosophy, as well as how far, after over thirty years of reflection, he had moved away from it.

As already adduced in the introduction, much of what was originally compelling about Husserl's philosophy for Patočka had to do with a sense of the urgent need for philosophy in contemporary Europe. Patočka takes pains in *The Natural World* to link his reflections to the "nihilistic mood" of the times, as Husserl had done in his lecture given in Prague the year before. Patočka in 1936 paints a picture of a fractured world, split between the natural spiritual context of everyday human life and the world as depicted by objective natural science, with the rationality of the latter seemingly out of step with the spiritual interests and needs of the former. "In our vital need," as Husserl himself put it in the *Crisis*, "this science has nothing to say to us."[38] This dissonance, Patočka argues, impacts the "life-feeling" of contemporary humanity, whose experience of the world shaped by scientific self-understanding finds its sense of freedom rendered valueless, a "mere *effectus non efficax*."[39] Humans take themselves to be more and more like things: overwhelmed by a sense of alienation, "man lives in the fundamental apperception of his unfreedom," Patočka declares, "he feels himself the agent of objective forces, perceives himself not as a person but rather as a thing."[40] Unsettled, humans succumb more and more to the despair of a hopeless inability to shake free from alienating social roles determined by increasingly dehumanizing forms of reification, and instead they list between the Charybdis of existential anxiety and the Scylla of "the thousand distractions so abundantly offered by modern life."[41]

The crisis is one of subjective self-understanding, and its resolution can only occur in the form of a renewed understanding of the subjectivity of life. Thus the urgent need for philosophical reflection. For a more fundamental, originary understanding of subjectivity poses, the youthful Patočka argues, the potential for introducing a new factor, a third term that would unite a fractured world:

> This third term can be nothing but the subjective activity that shapes both worlds, in different yet, in both cases, lawful, ordered ways. The unity underlying the crisis cannot be the unity of the things composing the world; rather, it must be the dynamic unity of the acts performed by the mind or spirit.[42]

Transcendental philosophy—specifically in the form of transcendental phenomenology—is conceived here as the premise of a renewed experience of freedom: to be free is to be something other than an object, a mere thing; it is to be something that is not imposed from the outside, but which flows out from one's "innermost core," thereby opening the way for "upsurges of new creativity."[43] To affirm in the most radical way the validity of this sense of free being is to embrace subjectivity as something unconditionally prior, something that is nothing less than the core sense of the world as a whole. To the extent that Husserl's transcendental reflection promises a methodological route to the illumination of pure subjectivity, it in turn offers a route to an embrace of a freedom of this kind; to the extent that such an embrace of freedom is at all possible, then something like the affirmation of the human world is possible as well. Patočka in 1936 explicitly endorses this promise of Husserl's philosophy, right down to the claim that subjectivity, reflectively articulated in the phenomenological reduction, represents the fundamental core of the world as a whole, an absolute illuminated by the method of an absolute reflection: "We claim that such a methodical procedure is possible and that on its basis it becomes clear that the transcendental, i.e., preexistent subjectivity *is* the world."[44]

For all the continuity of Patočka's thinking, his subsequent rejection of these claims of Husserlian phenomenological reflection to have uncovered the absolute ground of the world is an exception that stands out in its decisiveness. It is perhaps most definitively stated in a passage from the long commentary appended to the 1970 edition of *The Natural World*:

> We can no longer identify with the conception of phenomenological reflection that we held to in the original version of our *Natural World*. We can no longer accept the interpretation of the "phenomenological reduction" as the gateway to the absolute. We do not accept absolute reflection.[45]

Patočka's departure from Husserl is conclusive, but it also remains in many ways an immanent critique, one that retains a basic commitment, though modified, to many of the essentials of Husserlian phenomenology. On the one hand, Patočka endeavors to free the phenomenological theme of the world from its reduction to transcendental subjectivity, which he believed had been mistakenly identified by Husserl as the unique, univocal origin of the sense-formations of the world.[46] Husserl had argued consistently for a very strong sense of this identification: transcendental subjectivity is the origin of not only the articulations of the world accomplished within the sense-formations (*Sinnbildungen*) of culture and spiritual activity generally, but the sense of the world as a horizon as well: the very movement of life as living, as unfolding in the horizon of what is, has its essential origins in the structure of conscious life as a self-temporalizing, absolute stream of being. Patočka argues strongly against this conception of a transcendental origin but, on the other hand, without losing hold of a central insight that is nevertheless embodied therein: namely, that there is an essential role reserved for subjectivity in any description of the specifically horizonal character of the world. Even if the horizonal character of the world is not reducible to the absolute of a transcendentally functioning subjectivity, nevertheless this functioning—or, to evoke an image that will prove essential to Patočka's reformulation of the phenomenological project, its *movement*—remains as an essential dimension of life, in any sense.

How Patočka understands a non-absolute, post-idealist conception of subjectivity can be illustrated with a look at his 1967 essay "The 'Natural' World and Phenomenology."[47] Here Patočka describes two poles constitutive of the natural world as a concrete, lived reality of an existence in horizons. The first pole takes the form of a periphery, an outer horizon that circumscribes the reach of the plenum of things encountered in the surrounding world. This includes, or rather envelops, the spatiality in which things are coordinated in accordance with structures of proximity and distance. As in Heidegger, the sense in which human existence is "in" the world is in part determined by the manner in which humans as spatial beings project themselves as the negating of distances, whose conditioning terminus is the whole of life as a kind of being-in-remove.[48]

The second pole takes the form of a subjective inwardness, standing in tension with the periphery, and stamping the spatiality of the world with the form of an individual and individuated perspective.[49] Natural life is thus described by Patočka as both a projection into things, a being-outside of itself, and a reticence of inwardness at the heart of transcendence. Existence here is not a mere dispersal into an outside, but an encounter marked by the individuating factor of an indelible ownness of personal life. Thanks to the tension coordinated by these two poles, the world unfolds in terms of the forward progression of personal life as a movement outwards, the subjectivity of which is as fundamental as the distance of otherness marked by the periphery. It is a life that moves from the near and the familiar outwards to the foreign and the alien: "there always is the polarity of that to which I belong and which is *essentially* near (as distinct from what is only *actually* near), and of that which is essentially far, foreign, so that in its very being the world is dichotomized between the familiar and the alien."[50]

Descriptions of this polarity of which subjective inwardness is an essential component are only viable, however, if one resists understanding the inwardness of the subject along the lines of a Cartesian conception of immanence, where it would assume the character of a privileged region of existence, one that is essentially closed. For Patočka, Husserl's subjectivism comes down to the assertion that the relation between subject and world can be understood wholly in terms of what is contained and secured in subjective immanence, understood as just such a privileged region of access. The result is that, all too often, in Patočka's view, the transcendental absolute appears in Husserl as an ocean of immanence in which objects, reduced to being the mere foci of intentional acts, appear as islands, with the complex dialectics of immanence and transcendence being thereby obfuscated.[51]

Nevertheless, this criticism of Husserl's Cartesianism by Patočka should not be understood as an attempt to reestablish a naive realism, for which the putative privilege of subjectivity would yield to the claim that there is no difference in being that would distinguish subjective from non-subjective existence. Instead, the aim is to understand the difference between subjectivity and objectivity on its own "natural" terms, as a tension constitutive of a dynamic of immanence and transcendence, a tension between the inwardness of subject-relative situatedness and the movement of outward projection. Any description of this tension between inwardness and periphery, selfhood and horizon, must therefore evade the obfuscations of Cartesian immanence, but it must also avoid any reprise of an equally obfuscating realism that would insist on a conception of the subject as a thing among things.

Patočka's critique is thus not so much centered on the concept of subjectivity, or even on its transcendental status, as on its absolutization, as if subjectivity harbored within itself an immunity to any sense of being dependent on what is outside, and is thus *nulla "re" indiget ad existendum,* as Husserl himself puts it in *Ideas I,* appropriating the Cartesian definition of substance.[52] Nor is his critique premised on the demand for thinking to proceed independently of the position of the subject. The subject-relative character of the lifeworld, such a central thesis of the *Crisis,* will instead be deepened by Patočka in fundamental ways. His critique is directed at the Cartesian conflation of the necessity of subjective being with a secured point of departure for reflection, one that not only establishes a universal vantage point on all experience of things, but which does so in a fashion that is impervious to the problematicity of transcendence.

For Patočka, the problem of the whole, of how the whole can become a theme within worldly existence and in that sense become "philosophical," is to be conceived such that this perspective is never non-problematic, never absolute, at least in the Cartesian sense. In this way meaning, and with it intentionality as the life of meaning, is described by Patočka not only as something embedded in the horizon of existence, but as *horizonal in its basic essence,* and in this sense meaning can be said to be something "worldly."[53] Moreover, this horizonal character of meaning still represents for Patočka a kind of a priori. Or rather, the horizonal character of meaning belongs to the a priori that the world itself represents and which, as he articulates it in an unpublished text from the early 1970s, contrasts sharply with the Husserlian conception of a priori as an essence, an *eidos* grasped through an ideation rooted in the experience of particular things. According to Patočka:

> The concept of the world is not a general essence, for there is only the one world, a setting-into-idea [*In-Idee-Setzen*] here has no meaning. The one world as in principle One is nevertheless not an empirical, but an *a priori* datum, for it cannot be traced back to either individual experience or operations with the same. The world is no universality, but a whole and for *this* reason *a priori*.[54]

The world for Patočka is not a priori in the sense of a fixed, ideally repeatable unity of sense that can be grasped through a multiplicity of its instantiations, the repetition of which is firmly grounded in the subjectively accomplished double act of repetition and grasping of an identical essence across a spectrum of particularities. The world is a universality, but not one that is fixed by an intentional act that would *constitute* it as an identity, or the identical pole of an intentional accomplishment. The world, in short, is not a *general something* brought to intuition by an ideating consciousness, but the pure encompassing priority that characterizes the pre-given whole.[55]

The horizon of the world thus represents a unique sense of the a priori, and with that of a necessity, one which cannot, however, be understood in terms of tracking intentional forms as so many routes to fulfillment. That the world is horizonal, or that being in the world unfolds in intentional existence which not only brings to manifestation things in the world, but the world as a whole, represents for Patočka a horizon of intentionality that *cannot be fulfilled*:

> Horizonal consciousness can never be translated into nonhorizonal consciousness, even though every act is an act within a horizon. *A horizon is not an intention that could be fulfilled.* A horizon is *always equally integral*; only its relation to what stands before the horizon as before its background changes. The horizon is the background of a particular foreground: everything actual can and must separate out of the inactuality and return into it.[56]

If the idea of a transcendental horizon is of a subjective perspective in which all fulfillment, all manner of phenomenality is prescribed—and hence the idea of an a priori correlation between objective form and subjective accomplishment that is the goal of Husserl's reduction—then the very horizonality of the world, understood in this sense, disrupts the completeness of such an a priori. The world is not something that can be captured in the constitutive forms that govern any perspective, transcendental or not; it is instead the a priori that fixes the inner meaning of perspective as something relative, something that, again along the lines of the polarity of existence, emerges out of that which is prior to all possible perspectives:

> All [these descriptions of horizon, background and foreground] are metaphors which state, essentially, that an actual perspective does not constitute being; there is being prior to it and independent of it, there is being even without a perspective, but there is no perspective without being. The global horizon of the world means that a pre-given whole is always and in every respect (temporally, spatially, with respect to content) beyond the limits of all actual[ity]. The world is always more than a perspective can grasp of it.[57]

This is not all that far from Husserl's own understanding of the a priori of the world *as world*, which had always at best fitted uncomfortably within the project of an a priori correlation of objective form and subjective accomplishment. For in Husserl, as well, the world as a horizon was never something that could be included as a thing among things, even that special kind of logical construction that is an ensemble:

> Things, objects (always understood purely in the sense of the life-world), are "given" as being valid for us in each case (in some mode or other of ontic certainty) but in principle only in such a way that we are conscious of them as things or objects *within the world-horizon*. Each one is something, "something of" the world of which we are constantly conscious as a horizon. . . . The world, on the other hand, does not exist as *an* entity, as an object, but exists with such uniqueness that the plural makes no sense when applied to it. Every plural, and every singular drawn from it, presupposes the world-horizon.[58]

Yet for Husserl, the horizonal character of the world did not mean that the intentionality of object experience is irrelevant to its analysis. Husserl's argument is, in effect, that the meaning of the world, the meaning of the whole, is always understood as something that is manifest first and foremost by way of the experience of an order of things, one made possible by the life of an understanding that is primarily ("naturally") oriented to the appearance of individual objects or their ensembles and objective relations.[59] The world itself is not a general thing for Husserl, just as little as it is for Patočka, but for all that it is comprehensible only *in terms of things*, or better, the possibilities that are germane to objectification, or to reason as a comprehension of an order. "We are conscious of this horizon only as a horizon for existing objects; without particular objects of consciousness it cannot be actual [*aktuell*]."[60] This is the reason why Husserl's conception of phenomenology as an eidetics of lived experience was aimed ultimately at an analysis of the universal structures that make up the constitution of the world as a unity of a *nature*, or of a unity that takes the form of a totality of rationally ordered objectivities, the manifestation of which is grounded in the eidetically governed accomplishments of subjectivity.

It would be a mistake to view this orientation to object experience as a naive prejudice on the part of Husserl, as it is sometimes portrayed.[61] The idea that the whole of the world first comes to be genuinely meaningful only as an order and ordering of things represents an important and influential philosophical conviction, one that finds powerful expression in Husserl's thought. It in turn leads Husserl to a whole host of insights regarding the nature of scientific rationality, as well as the tradition, culture, and the history of reason in the broadest of senses. In the end, Patočka more than appreciates this aspect of Husserl's thinking,[62] seeking not so much to reject it *tout court* as to find ways to supplement it, by showing that the phenomenological theme of the world is more than the constitution of nature as an order of things, that it represents a universality that is not reducible to reason, but is instead inwardly constitutive of the very movement of our lives as horizonal beings.

The result is that the "transcendental subject" in Patočka is not so much excised from phenomenological reflection, as problematized. Patočka's critique is aimed at a reformulation of phenomenology along the lines of a non-subjectivist, non-Cartesian reflection capable of capturing the ontological structure of a being that lives from out of and towards that which is always more than an order of things. Accordingly, "the method of reflection we hold to at present," Patočka claims in his 1970 commentary on his early work, "cannot be that of the uncovering of hidden intentionalities by means of objective clues."[63] The result of any such project can only be that the being of intentional life, or the being on which is founded the unity of the world of life, remains doggedly in question.

To bring this question into focus, and the horizon of understanding it indicates, amounts to nothing less than bringing into focus the a priori of the world, that unfulfillable intentional terminus on which everything depends. This requires an essential innovation in phenomenological method, which Patočka programmatically articulates in the 1970s under the rubric of an "asubjective phenomenology."

The Problem of Meaning

One might think fruitfully of Patočka's project of an asubjective phenomenology as the attempt at a kind of philosophical anthropology, as Patočka himself suggests at the end of an important essay from the period, "*Epochē* and Reduction."[64] Such a project would recognize the relative autonomy of subjective life, yet in a manner that would emphasize its finitude in lieu of any attempt to root it in an absolute. It would accordingly maintain the distinction in essence between thingly and human being, but without reducing either the former to a mere index of subjective accomplishments of meaning, or the latter to pure spirit. Moreover, it would maintain the open-ended character of Husserl's investigations, refusing to be determined inwardly by either the vestiges of Cartesianism or a global critique of metaphysics, as in Heidegger.

Patočka's approach turns precisely on assessing Husserl's breakthrough of a radicalized reflection on phenomenality in the spirit of a deep suspicion of a philosophy of consciousness or, better, of immanence as the proper context of its pursuit. Accordingly, Patočka argues in a critical examination of Husserl's subjectivism from 1971, the main hindrance is "Husserl's adherence to Brentano's dogma of an original access to the psychical in a kind of advertence to oneself as an object." Even if, as the "Appendix to the Sixth Logical Investigation" shows,[65] Husserl understands this access differently, he nevertheless

> never doubts the existence of acts as lived-experiences that are themselves originally accessible in reflection. He even makes them the basis of appearing. All understanding is acquired on this basis and all explanation of the world and of worldly beings can be traced back to it. We might even venture the thesis that it was the systematic execution of this task that led Husserl to pose the basic transcendental question in his own way, and that the Cartesianism often claimed to be what fatefully led Husserl to the theory of the absolute being of pure consciousness is nothing other than a piece of unresolved Brentanoism.[66]

Patočka's resistance to Husserl's transcendentalism is not meant to be the rejection, as already emphasized above, of a subjective component forming a structural feature of phenomenality. What appears, appears for someone; the manner in which the orientation of the subject, its thetic posture and the ways in which it conditions appearance, are not being challenged here. "What we are arguing against," Patočka explains, "is the claim that one can make this basis of appearing in yet another object for a possible 'inner perception' that grasps it 'originally,' or that one can grasp it in an alleged 'reflection on pure lived-experience.'"[67]

The ground of appearing is not something that itself appears; the understanding in which something is grasped as identical through shifting perspectives is not something that avails itself of an originary, objectifying intuition: "that it must be possible to grasp the understanding once more in the original, i.e., in reflection, is an arbitrary assumption."[68] The problem, therefore, is that Husserl confuses the essential role of understanding, those subjective accomplishments interwoven with all manifestation, with a being that is distinct from what is manifest in experience itself, but which can nevertheless be brought to an intuitive, objectifying clarification:

> But does it follow that these accomplishments themselves would be originally accessible in an objectifying act of reflection? Or can all of this only be gathered in precisely the same way from phenomena? Are they not as much appearances in a field of appearing as are things, which they let appear? In the field of appearing, things let what belongs to the I [*das Ichliche*] come to the fore [*zum Vorschein*] just as much as what belongs to the I, for its part, lets things appear. But what belongs to the I cannot be grasped in itself and in an "absolute way."[69]

Thus the opportunity—opened by Husserl but obfuscated by an undigested "Brentanoism"—is for a conception of a phenomenal field, limited to the appearing as such, without reduction to either what appears in it or the being of the subject to whom the appearance appears. A phenomenal field, or a concept of the phenomenon, in other words, that is not indexed to something that "is" in such a way that it could play the role of the preexistent ground of manifestation, but is wholly the being of that which allows the manifestation of that which is other:

> There is a phenomenal field, a being [*ein Sein*] of the phenomenon as such, which cannot be traced back to anything existent which appears in it. This field can never be explained on the basis of anything existent, be it objective in the manner of a natural thing or subjective in the manner of the I. The phenomenal field is in principle not autonomous. It is impossible for it to be an absolutely self-contained being [*Seiendes*],

because its whole essence consists in manifesting, disclosing and presenting other beings.[70]

This conception of the phenomenal field draws on two ideas, from Heidegger and Husserl respectively, though again with modifications of each. The first is Heidegger's theme of *Seinsverständnis*, the understanding of being that is inwardly constitutive of *Dasein*'s self-projection as being-in-the-world, "from which both appearing things and we ourselves take on those determinations that are characteristic of things and of us as beings."[71] *Dasein* is, to the extent to which it not only has itself as a concern, but more fundamentally out of an understanding of the horizon of the meaning of being as a whole. Yet Patočka wants to resist at least one side of Heidegger, where the ecstatic structure of this understanding is interpreted as the free projection of the world, which might suggest again a subjective autonomy that has no place for Patočka in understanding the human relation to the world:

> It is not we, our *Dasein*, that in projecting the world [*im Weltentwurf*] gives us to know the meaning of world-content, i.e., to which being we can relate and how. It is the understanding of Being, the phenomenon as such, that grants this; and it is neither possible nor necessary to look for more. The transcendence of *Dasein* is not a stepping out of oneself or projecting oneself somewhere outside oneself. In this sense, it is not a "project," but an essential being-outside-oneself and finding-oneself [*Sich-empfangen*].[72]

This same thesis—of a subjectivity that is an essential play between being-outside oneself and finding oneself, and thus an encounter with oneself as outside, given in the world—also conditions Patočka's appropriation of the second idea, this time from Husserl: that of a transcendental experience. This can be illustrated by turning again to "*Epochē* and Reduction," in which Patočka briefly sketches a critique of the *Fundamentalbetrachtung* of Husserl's *Ideas I*. The *Fundamentalbetrachtung* is of course the central methodological section of the *Ideas*: here the concepts of *epochē* and reduction are introduced, and the phenomenological program outlined. It is also the most metaphysical part of the text, introducing what amounts to a double ontology: the being of the world characterized as "objective or mediated being," the meaning of which is relative to manifestation, and the being of this manifestation itself taken as "subjective or immediately accessible being."[73] This ontological divide is meant to clarify the meaning of the reduction, but as Patočka emphasizes, "as one can easily observe, this ontology is not grounded in transcendental experience, but in reflection on the mode of access to that which is accessible within it."[74]

Curiously, Husserl in the *Ideas* situates his initial argument for the absolute being of consciousness effectively outside of the phenomenological *epochē* proper: the affirmation of the absolute being of transcendental life by way of an eidetics of consciousness (or an "eidetic reduction") is meant to pave the way for understanding the possibility of the phenomenological *epochē* and reduction. Thus, even for Husserl the ontological distinction of world and consciousness is not necessarily taken to be the direct result of a description of transcendental life.[75] Yet it was certainly not meant to be incompatible with it, and in the course of transcendental investigation the aim is arguably to confirm its validity—and this is precisely where Patočka lodges his critique: "By his desire for a twofold ontology . . . Husserl finds himself forced into an inconsistency with transcendental experience itself, which thus demands that he make further distinctions that are, however, not more helpful."[76] And in fact the descriptive characteristics of transcendence and immanence, once the *epochē* has been embraced and phenomenological investigation is underway, more often than not bleed into each other: the putative "nonadumbrative" character of pure consciousness, entailing a pure, adequate givenness, which had meant to be its distinctive signature, is progressively undermined by Husserl's own analyses of inner time-consciousness, in which the entire model of apprehension/content of apprehension is suspended, sending the conceit of a consciousness unambiguously present to itself into increasingly troubled waters. The nature of the real phenomenological absolute, gestured at but not fully explicated by Husserl in §81 of *Ideas I*, remains elusive.

Consciousness, subjective life, intentionality, all of this is inextricable from transcendence; immanence is itself a posture of transcendence: to insist on its radical autonomy from the world as a premise of the transcendental problematic is incompatible with the experience that frames it. Likewise, the methodological procedure of reduction, understood as underwritten by the putative autonomy of the being of immanence, skews the whole presentation of the transcendental field in the direction of an unjustified subjectivism. Patočka's methodological solution in "*Epochē* und Reduction," which in turn represents a core gesture of his asubjective phenomenology, is to replace the *epochē*-reduction axis of reflection formulated by Husserl with an *unrestricted epochē* in which the being of subjective immanence is suspended on an equal par with that of objective transcendence:

We may now pose the question of what would happen were the *epochē* not brought to a halt in the face of the thesis of my own self [*des eigenen Selbst*], but made in a wholly universal way? In an *epochē* thus performed, I certainly do not doubt what is indubitable, i.e., the self-positing *cogito*. Yet I do not employ this, as it were, "automatic" thesis, I make no use of it. . . . In this setting, the *epochē* is not an access to some being or pre-being [*Seienden oder Vor-Seienden*], whether it is worldly or non-worldly, but perhaps it is then immediately an access to appearing as such, instead of to what appears.[77]

The subject thus remains, even as a transcendental phenomenological theme, but now with an a priori explicated from out of its own decidedly worldly-transcendent phenomenality:

> What belongs to the I [*das Ichliche*] is arguably never perceived in itself and by itself, nor is it ever immediately experienced. Rather, I is only experienced as the organisational centre of a universal structure of appearance that cannot be reduced to a being as such, appearing in its particularity [*Einzelsein*]. We call this structure "world" and are justified in calling it this, since it is that which is encountered in the *epochē* and thereby neither denied nor contested, but brought to light only out of its original anonymity. The self is only what it is in its being exposed [*Auseinandersetzung*] to the world.[78]

If Patočka characterizes this approach as an *asubjective* phenomenology, this is not meant in the sense of a *non-subjective* phenomenology, precisely because the I remains as the "organisational centre of a universal structure of appearance" which is nothing less than the "world." Again the problem is one of the a priori of the world, of that field of phenomenality that enables all being, subjective and objective, to become manifest—to the subject. "Does the world thereby become something subjective?" Patočka asks towards the end of "*Epochē* and Reduction." No, if by "subjective" is meant a constituent part of subjectivity, where the world would then be identical in substance to the subject. But if "subjective" means "that to which the subject relates [*verhält*] as the horizon of its understanding," then "the world is subjective . . . and it is the *epochē* that opens access to this aspect of the subjective."[79]

An important feature of this approach is how Patočka's critical revision of Husserl's concept of subjectivity conditions the concept of *intentionality* as a philosophical theme. More precisely, Patočka's approach challenges the extent to which Husserl's mature theory of intentionality can be said to define the problem of *meaning* in a complete manner. Like for Heidegger, the problem of meaning will always remain central to Patočka's thinking; for both philosophers, the ontological question is always one of the *meaning* of being. The critique of subjectivism is accordingly not a departure from the problem of meaning: the basic question remains how human existence encounters itself as a task, a project of existence, and the world as the horizon of this understanding. The guiding thread of the analysis remains the manifold ways that humans grasp themselves as a question of understanding, or a problem of individual meaning embedded in the meaning of the whole.

It is in regard to the philosophical theme of meaning, more so than the problem of the metaphysical status of the ego, that Patočka's conception of an asubjective phenomenology holds the most promise. Yet it is on this level also the most problematic, since it brings into play a basic reorientation with regard to meaning or sense, thus requiring a different conception of what one can expect from meaning. For asubjective phenomenology implies that the accomplishments of understanding, or the way meaning provides orientation, are no longer identified solely with intentional acts that have as their chief content an articulated presence, or a posited unity of sense, if by that we imply something *complete* and *accomplished*. In Patočka's hands, the problem of meaning is instead transformed into a reflection on an unfolding movement that manifests itself in a wide variety of forms, of which unified acts of thinking and their complete accomplishments represent only a partial, if also important, subset of examples. The result is that the field of meaning, and the kind of "whole" that it represents, emerges in Patočka's descriptions as something determined by the dynamics of an understanding that is at bottom more of a riddle for itself than an order of accomplished belief. The meaning of the world, which in Husserl tends to take the guise of a tissue of beliefs in constant states of modalization and reformation, in Patočka tends to assume the look of a tissue of questions, provisionally answered at best but always open to an indwelling mystery or problematicity. If the being of human existence remains for Patočka the being of an understanding, then it is of a decisively *problematic* understanding.

This approach to the field of meaning as a concrete manifestation of problematic understanding lies behind Patočka's lifelong interest in phenomena such as myths, works of literature, and language itself as subjects for philosophical interrogation. As illustrative we can point to the beginning of the 1969 essay "What Is Existence?"[80] which opens with a description of a selection of literary characters from the novels of William Faulkner, Thomas Mann, and Fyodor Dostoevsky. Patočka introduces these fictions as points of departure for a reflection on the concept of existence, taking each as expressions of an understanding of what it means to be. One finds no "intentional analysis" here, at least not in the form in which the intentional unity of a body of habits and abiding beliefs is analyzed as given accomplishments that would lend themselves to explication and comprehension. That would require the assumption of unequivocal achievements of sense at decisive junctures, thereby forming the joints organizing the whole, to evoke a metaphor of Plato's. Instead, sense lives here more in the realm of metaphor, unities of meaning that certainly are established, but in a way that falls short of a representation of an order of things.

The far more equivocal world of literary expressions thus predominates, such as Mann's portrait of Adrian Leverkühn in *Doctor Faustus*, and these expressions are taken to be problematic representations that illuminate human existence in ways that we perhaps comprehend, but which hardly avail themselves of fixed interpretations. The portrait of Leverkühn is of a riddle, shot through with both the familiar and the alien, the comprehensible and the irrational, the human and the monstrous. Like that of Goethe's Faust, Mann's portrait provides reflection with a thick metaphorical field of play, one intimately related to the phenomenality of a decidedly problematic life. If phenomenology still operates here on the level of description, it is not one that operates by remaining true to what is available in immediate intuition elicited by an image or imagination, but to a far more anarchic and opaque evocation of the fundamental play of often indeterminate forces that make up the core of human life.[81]

In such exercises, philosophical reflection still entails an attempt to make "meaning" into an object, or at least a theme; it is just that what counts are not only those cases in which meaning is something closed and determinate, an accomplishment that can be grasped in terms of given or even anticipated univocity. Meaning—or perhaps the kind of meaning that counts from a philosophical point of view—is instead understood to be something that can only be shifting and indeterminate, opaque and ambiguous. Meaning is accordingly something more like a continuously enriched question than a position, or a belief that would submit itself to an analysis into partial accomplishments and justifications. The portrait of Adrian Leverkühn is thus attractive precisely because here meaning, the meaning that not only comes to expression but governs a life, represents a contested unity, a problematicity of sense that indicates, precisely in its opacity, more clearly the philosophical problem of existence itself.

Selfhood, Reflection, and Clarity

Descriptions of the life of problematic meaning, in which Patočka strives to illuminate the patterns that make up the lived concreteness or existential density of lived experience, are also at the core of Patočka's approach to the problem of *selfhood*. This involves in turn taking up the problem of the "I," or the ego of classical phenomenology, but now from an asubjective perspective.

Far from neglecting the theme of the I, an asubjective approach to phenomenology is committed to an exploration of multiple senses of self, I, and personhood that belong to the projection of human existence in the world.[82] And here, too, the theme of horizon proves to be central. The I, for Patočka, is "a horizon by its very nature," one that is implicated in intricate ways with the horizon of the world, as well as the fundamental structures of subjective inwardness.[83]

Husserl too had explored much of this terrain, and in a similar spirit. Refusing to reduce the I to an intellectual spontaneity or a logical subject, he pursued a broad set of analyses of the concrete, personal ego, its relation to the body, to habitualities, to affective drives, and the various forms of communal selfhood and identity.[84] Patočka's approach is broadly compatible with many of these analyses in their specifics, even if it conflicts with the broader agenda of constitutional analysis, and in fact one might point to his reflections on selfhood as some of the richest, and most promising, contributions of the whole of Patočka's phenomenology.

To illustrate this, Patočka's complex and wide-ranging engagement with the problem of selfhood can be approached by way of a consideration of a key Husserlian theme, that of reflection, which had already played such a prominent role in Patočka's critique of Husserl:

> A philosophical consideration meant to grasp what, in all experience, is the primal ground of all meaning, cannot do without reflection. Reflection, self-apprehension, is its element. The scope, the nature, the meaning, and the possibility of reflection remain, however, problematic.[85]

Here again the critique of Husserl's subjectivism is decisive.[86] Patočka identifies three presuppositions of Husserl's operative understanding of properly philosophical reflection: (a) such reflection is not motivated by mundane but by pure theoretical interest, and is thus "free"; (b) reflection proper is the pure apperception of the stream of experience as an "object," specifically the object that the subject is for itself, not in its mere appearance, but in its being in itself; and (c) the cogito of such reflection guarantees the absolute evidence of the object of reflection, the stream of experience.[87]

Patočka's critique turns on the second presupposition: namely, that it is in and as a view on something, an object observed, that the self grasps itself. Is this not a distortion of what, in its essence, is the being of practical comportment? Does a practical being encounter itself originally as a determinate structure of lived experience or as an object of inner observation of the same? Or more pointedly: "In reducing the essence of the ego to the question of its lived-experiences are we not eschewing its true nature?"[88]

Despite this critique, there remains a deeper connection with Husserl's approach that is worth considering. Take, for example, Patočka's suggestion in his 1968–69 lectures that reflection should be understood as belonging to the domain of appresentation, and thus as something that unfolds in the context of the relation with others: "The primordial act of reflection is probably something that belongs to the realm of appresentation. I appresent myself as I am in the other life."[89] The idea is that primitive reflection is not a form of direct seeing, but a decidedly *appresented* seeing, one grounded in the dynamic awareness of being seen by others. Patočka goes on to argue that the seeing of oneself thanks to being seen by others accordingly forms the context of a first encounter with oneself as a "self." Self-reflection is thus something originary: the self does not begin fully formed, and only then becomes reflected back to itself from others; rather, the very being of the self unfolds primarily in the reflective arc intrinsic to the logic of encounter with others, thanks to which the self is introduced into life in a primary sense.

One important implication of Patočka's description is that, even though the "self" is given by others, it is not so in a univocal sense. The giving of the self is inwardly determined by a dialectical process, one in which the originary movement of one's existence forms the essential catalyst, the irreplaceable ground necessary for setting the reflective encounter in motion. The other gives oneself to oneself, but only in a movement that one *is*, and thanks to which one is in a position to receive this gift of selfhood at all. This means that, in the arc of reflection, the being that one is, the understanding that one is, both begins from oneself and is effectively *modified from within*: in going out from oneself towards others, towards the world, one simultaneously meets a return, a modification of one's seeing encounter with the other into a seeing encounter with oneself.

Patočka's conception of this structure of reflection can be read as a critical rearticulation of a key thesis of Husserl's. In *Ideas I* and elsewhere, Husserl argues that reflection involves a basic modification of consciousness.[90] For Husserl—and this is perhaps where he frees himself the most from the Brentanean notion of inner perception—reflection represents a countermovement to the "natural" immersion of the self in things, that fascination with what is other than consciousness, which in turn obscures the presence of intentional life to itself in favor of the manifestation of things in the world. Reflection is a modification of natural consciousness that results in a kind of limited reversal of its natural polarity, one thanks to which the relation of consciousness to things becomes articulated on its own terms, instead of remaining in lockstep with the prejudice of allowing things to guide all unfolding of manifestation. Reflection in this way represents a modification of one mode of seeing into another, allowing for the revelation of patterns of phenomenality that would otherwise only operate anonymously in natural life.

Conceiving of reflection as just such a countermovement, and more, that its essential relation to selfhood just is this countermovement, is precisely Patočka's thesis:

> We believe, on the contrary, that reflection, however radical, even that which performs the *epochē* with respect to all preconceptions, is a countermove against the automatic tendency of life not to see itself as it is, to look away from itself, from its essential uncertainty concerning itself and its possibilities—against our tendency to turn elsewhere or take refuge in illusions and false tranquility, blinding ourselves to our own sight which would expose us and paralyze our myopic security regarding the pitfalls of human existence. Reflection is a countermove against the *interestedness* of naïve life.[91]

Patočka's approach deepens the account of the modification at the origin of reflection, precisely by providing an alternative conception of the "natural" existence of consciousness presupposed in Husserl's account. For Husserl, the modification relevant to reflection has its origin in a native capacity of natural consciousness: "original," unmodified consciousness harbors the ability to modulate its form, shifting from a non-reflective, original mode of manifestation to a reflective one, thereby capturing its being in the self-evidence of the cogito. Patočka's suggestion that reflection be situated in the sphere of appresentation, by contrast, inaugurates a much more complex and dynamic account of the modification at the origin of reflection. Here, the "seeing" that emerges in reflection, the turning to oneself along a track transformed by being seen by the other but without being replaced by the other, is not rooted in the bare potential of human existence to effectively present or objectify itself in a variety of different modes. Reflection is here indeed a modification, even a transformation, but it is not rooted in the immediate freedom of consciousness to direct the course of its manner of manifestation. It is instead rooted in an original condition of human life as standing in relation to what is not immediately given, or open for what is non-present, but appresented, to saturate the ground of its existence, thereby giving rise to a unique form of self-manifestation inwardly determined by otherness. For the "appresented" self that one *is*, that self who enters life through the inner conduit of a return from the equally appresented other, carries with it the otherness of the other, that same otherness which in turn constitutes an original parameter of that going out from oneself at all.

In other words, reflection interpreted through the dynamics of appresentation posits a mode of seeing that has its origin not in a free capacity of consciousness, but in the otherness, quasi-presence, and horizonality of a life originally lived outwards from itself. Life is being described here by Patočka as something that is *always already modification*, one without any hint of the presence of an unmodified self as its ground or origin. The specter of solipsism that had always haunted classical phenomenology, of an ipseity that would render the tendency to inwardness into an autonomous sphere of being, is thereby vanquished.

The very fact that we are practical beings lends considerable weight to this thesis. We are never, Patočka argues, living in relation to mere things, but are always already in the flow of an ongoing praxis, extended in time and "stages of possible realization," which belies the idea that it makes sense for our own being to be "*given* in the mode of immanent givenness in the sense of a self-presence of an absolute being."[92] To make such a claim for the modifications of reflection would be to embrace the idea that life in reflection is something radically different from prereflective life, from the life lived in and among things.

Yet this yields, Patočka claims, a dilemma with regard to what reflection actually achieves with regard to grasping its ground, the selfhood of subjective being:

> Either we understand the concept of reflection as such an absolute givenness (but then reflection will really and truly be a leap into a mode of being radically different from the being of prereflective life), or we have to *divest* the concept of reflection of its character of accessing a being of absolute immanence, a being that does not "give itself in adumbrations" (i.e., in perspectives).[93]

If Patočka's approach to the problem of reflection is, at least to some extent, in continuity with the basic thesis of Husserl's regarding the role of modification, then it is equally the case that he breaks with Husserl's belief that consciousness can capture what is essential regarding its being as access to the world through an *objectifying* reflection.[94] Patočka thus embraces the second horn of the dilemma, but at the same time, recognizing that it considerably disrupts traditional conceptions of self-knowledge, he couples it with the pursuit of a new conception of *clarity* and of the reflection that cultivates it: "If we can show a clarity that is in principle nonobjectival, and if all objectival, objectifying clarity, all modalities of this objectification, are rooted in it, then we have gone beyond Husserl with the help of a Husserlian motif."[95]

Though Patočka does not put it in these terms, this promises to build in interesting ways on the Husserlian gesture, characteristic of his thought since at least the *Logical Investigations*, to expand what counts in philosophy as an "object." Husserl had sought to orchestrate a countermovement to the progressive limitations on the concept of object or thing that form an important thread of the complex legacy of empiricism, above all the insistence that only individual, particular entities could count as paradigmatic objective referents, thus excluding generalities. We could perhaps reformulate Patočka's proposal as the attempt to show that the essential limits of what can count as an object, once they have been articulated in the broadest possible sense, cannot in turn furnish us with a clear determination of the limits of clarity. The point would then be that *clarity is more than objectivity*, more than the positionality of belief or the thetic accomplishments of thought in general.

A contrast with the sketch of a theory of reflection that Husserl presents in *Ideas I* can help determine more precisely where the two thinkers part ways. Phenomenological reflection in *Ideas I* is described as a living self-engagement, a modality in which the flow of consciousness becomes manifest to and for itself; yet at the same time, the originary manifestation of this flow, which Husserl elsewhere goes so far as to describe as a "Heraclitean flux,"[96] at first falls outside of the scope of clarity, even as it is being affirmed in its originary givenness.[97] Reflection alone is not clarification; we must learn to see what is present in reflection, or what reflection at most promises to make visible, but has not yet actually achieved. Husserl's way forward is to argue that, for consciousness to be brought to clarity, it must be brought to *evidence*, which in turn must take the form of some manner of objectification; otherwise, consciousness may be given, but it remains locked in obscurity.

Patočka, by contrast, forgoes what he takes to be the prejudice that access to being only comes to fruition, to completion, when it settles into a form of objectivity, whether empirical or eidetic. Instead, Patočka's conviction is that human existence always already has access to itself, that in its very being it moves within a kind of nonobjective but nevertheless original clarity. We learn how to explore this clarity of existence not through evidence, but in terms of the lived possibilities it gives us, since our existence *just is* an openness to what is, to what manifests itself: "Being that relates to its own being is at the same time unlocked for itself in some sense. The possibility of reflection is rooted in this openness."[98]

Something else goes with this, and again involves the task of confronting the residual Cartesianism in classical phenomenology, in particular the thesis that the self-certainty of the *ego-cogito* brings with it a kind of *self-transparency*. Patočka pushes back hard against what he takes to be a bias towards affirming this thesis in Husserl's philosophy:

> What is experience, consciousness? A clarity interpenetrated by obscurity. Is it really something I can grasp in full clarity in inner vision, making it totally transparent to itself? Or is human experience by its very nature something essentially different from what can be given in object experience? That is a question which Husserl never raised.[99]

And again, Heidegger is central to Patočka's own attempt to raise just this question: "Heidegger asks what our approach to our own being is. Is it a view of being? is it a self-consciousness? a look turned to myself?"[100]

Patočka's answer to this question is decidedly "yes and no," an ambivalence signaled further on in the same text just quoted: "An inward look is naturally also a part of what we are, but our own being has a more direct access to itself."[101] This statement is made in the context of Patočka's discussion of what he takes to be the practical orientation of Heidegger's philosophy, at least as it had been articulated in the first division of *Being and Time*. As projected action, *Dasein*'s understanding of itself is in a basic sense "non-objectifying," in that the scope of its self-understanding is not limited to the domain of objective self-representation. This recognition of the importance of practical, non-objectifying dimensions of human life, along with the theme of the tendency for self-obfuscation or fallenness, represents for Patočka "the great advantages of Heidegger's over Husserl's phenomenology."[102]

Yet in Patočka's thinking the emphasis is, in the end, not so much on the primacy of the *practical* per se, as on the *personal* character that characterizes human action as a manner of being. Or better, the emphasis is not on the fact that human beings act, that their lives are occupied with practical affairs, but that they act out of a *non-indifference* to self, and with that out of an awareness of what is at stake in one's existence. Analyzed by Heidegger under the heading of *Sorge* (care), this concern with self, which determines the horizon of the existential task, is as much an accomplishment of meaning as it is the successful performance of some practice or other.[103] This means that, as it was also in Heidegger, the point is not so much to favor the practical sphere over the theoretical, as to argue that there is a common, existential root for both in the care-structure of *Dasein*.

The result is that the theme of ownness (*Eigenheit*) is arguably more important for Patočka than any kind of pragmatism that one might be tempted to adduce from *Being and Time*. An analysis of ownness forms the basis for Patočka's critique of conceptions of egoity or I-hood that would overlook this basic existential characteristic in favor of a concept of the I as foundation or first construct, whereby what is at play in ownness ossifies into a kind of structural principle of composition.

As illustrative of this critique, consider the following passage from the 1968–69 lectures:

> Heidegger's assertion concerning the ownness of existence is not designed to deny the I, it is enough if it turns out that the I—if we understand it as the last or the first we have to posit, as the foundation of all other theses—is in this respect already something derivative, something we see from the viewpoint of a being that can be analyzed into parts so that here is the foundation, here is a construct upon it, then further and further constructs upon that.[104]

The result of any such "foundational" conception is that the I effectively becomes interpreted in terms of a basic indifference to self: the being of care, the living of life as a task of being, is replaced by an anonymous principle of organization. Against this, and following Heidegger, Patočka argues that "we need to grasp the I in the context of that being which relates to its own being, to which its being is not indifferent, I as a task, being as a task, being which accepts and achieves itself."[105]

One consequence of this is that phenomenological reflection does not operate above the world, as if it were possible to establish a nonparticipatory view on truth, but remains always enmeshed in its accomplishments, in a clarity that is at the same time the enactment of unclarity.[106] Thus the I in Patočka, once its problematic is correctly understood, remains at the center of the program of an asubjective phenomenology, for it remains a key element in that manner of being thanks to which the self as task unfolds. Yet the I here no longer plays the role of a *fundamentum*, a structural-architectonic guarantor of order and evidence, but is instead a *spatium*, defined by ownness, or the concrete play of the ways humans are open to themselves and the world.

The Principle of All Principles

Taken together, these basic elements of an asubjective phenomenology—the analysis of the world as unfulfillable presence, the unrestricted *epochē* and the sense of autonomous phenomenality it sets into motion, the recalibration of the analysis of meaning towards problematicity, the situating of a theory of reflection in appresentation, the critique of a structural conception of the I in favor of elevating the theme of ownness as the *spatium* of the self—can be taken as driving towards a fundamental revision of Husserl's famous "principle of all principles" from §24 of *Ideas I*:

> No conceivable theory can make us stray from the *principle of all principles*: that each intuition affording [something] in an originary way [originär gebende Anschauung] *is a legitimate source of knowledge*, that *whatever presents itself to us in "Intuition" in an originary way* (so to speak, in its actuality in person [*in seiner leibhaften Wirklichkeit*]) *is to be taken simply as what it affords itself as*, but *only within the limitations in which it affords itself there*.[107]

The general tendency of Patočka's appropriation of classical phenomenology is to disrupt a reading of this principle that would privilege givenness in the sense of *self*-givenness (*Selbstgegebenheit*), or the accomplished givenness of something "as" it itself, thanks to the constitutive dynamics of intentional life that feed on the potentialities of bringing things into the clarity of *objective being*.[108] Here again it is reflection, or at least a reflection that would settle in an objectification, a self-presence in givenness, that comes under critical pressure in Patočka's engagement with Husserl, especially when the given under consideration is *oneself*. Namely, the question is whether the trajectory in reflection from what we might call original to clarified self-presence yields a genuine grasp of the self in its most originary sense:

> The self-presence of something in the original does not yet guarantee that it is given in its *originary* mode. Husserl's criterion of philosophical truth, the requirement of responsibility based on reflection, is not enough. True, in reflection I am in some sense given to myself, but is that I in the most original sense? Is reflection in the sense of self-objectification the gateway to myself? Need we not go further, extending the concept of reflection to include also that philosophical procedure which grasps not only what is given, but also the inward implication of the meaning of the given, pointing beyond?[109]

Here nothing less than the movement towards the self-givenness of human existence itself becomes suspect, in that it is possibly implicated in a collusion to obscure a dynamic of existence of which the I present in reflection, given there as "I myself," is perhaps at best only a derivative, even illusory self-presentation. The skeptical import of this question is generalized to include a critique of Husserl's conception of properly philosophical reflection, as grounded on his principle of all principles: for it implies that the methodological principle of shaping reflection in such a way that is designed to cleave close to the hold that the accomplishments of self-givenness have on subjective experience threatens to obscure a more primordial truth of that experience itself. To fashion oneself into an impartial observer of intentional life, to leave unchallenged the face of accomplished self-givenness that life has achieved for the ends of its manifestation in reflection, risks, however free of any theoretical prejudice it may be, succumbing to a basic naivete regarding the nature of the givenness of subjective existence.[110]

Moreover, this willful naivete of the mere reflective observer risks obscuring the question of the existential meaning of reflection itself. For reflection, Patočka argues, is grounded in the openness of that original access of humans to their own being, the sense in which existence itself is unlocked to itself, precisely in the mode of non-indifference. And here Patočka means precisely the non-indifference of a being that must *seek itself out*, that is non-indifferent first and foremost because it is originally a *problem* for itself:

> Therein—that this relation is concerned with itself, that it cares about itself—lies the possibility of reflection. Reflection derives from the fact that we are not initially given to ourselves but rather must seek ourselves. It does not mean self-perception, self-observation.[111]

For Patočka, this is precisely the advantage of Heidegger's analytic of *Dasein*:

> The existential analysis [of Heidegger] does not exclude a reflective grasping, conceived of, however, not as a mere internal intuition, but as an *understanding* of *Dasein*'s own being which exhausts itself in its accomplishment, so that its features are not "moments" or qualities of an object but rather modes of its being, modes of its comportment, modes of its relating to its own being.[112]

Thus the challenge to Husserl: Patočka proposes an idea of reflection as nothing but the forward movement of problematic life itself, one that shapes and produces an "I," a self, as a project, in contrast to the Husserlian conception of reflection that seeks to be "disinterested," in the sense in which it seeks to shape or modify *essentially nothing*, striving to establish itself as a perfectly transparent medium in which life becomes unequivocally manifest to itself.

One should exercise some caution here, and not exaggerate the point animating this challenge. Nor should one take Husserl to be a naive proponent of consciousness as some "mirror of nature," for whom pure *theōria* stands perennially as a univocal axis of orientation. Life for Husserl is saturated with interests and motivations that belong to its very essence; the point was never to cut reflection off from the interests of life, but to shape reflection in such a way as to provide a neutral space that would allow the very complexities of interested life to be manifest, to appear in whatever forms it has accomplished for itself in its being. There is an interest in disinterestedness.

If, however, we follow Husserl further and characterize this mode of transparent reflection as something "absolute," rooted in the originary givenness of an equally absolute experience that ultimately provides form and direction to all manifestation, then the meaning of Patočka's alternative becomes clear. Reflection, for Patočka, in contrast to observation, however artfully established, is "a part of human life in the world, the moment of authentic human life"[113]—*which means that it cannot ultimately be neutral*, it cannot abstain from the task of grappling with the tendencies of self-discovery, self-loss, and self-obfuscation that belong to the very movement of human existence. Philosophically, neutrality is a false harbor, a ruse of scientific formalism that ultimately evades the existential task of reflection itself.[114]

Another way to express Patočka's point is that what is problematic about the Husserlian absolute is an apparent attempt to suspend the *partiality* of life as a presupposition for the articulation of the phenomenality of the phenomenon, as if impartiality would guarantee a perspective (even a "scientific" perspective) on the drama of manifestation. Or as if phenomenality, the secret of appearing, were something intrinsically neutral, and at all approachable only in a subjective posture that would secure its own commensurate neutrality. Patočka's doubt arises from a sense that there is a basic limit to any exercise of neutrality in philosophical matters, and more: that the inner bond between human existence and manifestation is not in any way something "neutral." This doubt is aimed squarely at Husserl's conviction—argued by him, it should be said, with a pathos and insight equal to Patočka's—that just such neutrality is essential for the very possibility of philosophical autonomy, thanks to which the field of phenomena, and with it life itself, can be authentically articulated for thinking.

In what sense is philosophy, then, to take the form of reflection? If Patočka affirms the centrality of reflection, what ultimately guides it? The promise of reflection put forward by Husserl was of a certain distance, one that allowed a disengagement with existence, a minimal suspension, that would prepare the basis for a neutral phenomenality to appear, thus securing an objectivity at the heart of subjective self-understanding. The philosopher takes the manners in which things are given and, through the modification of reflection, turns toward the subjective accomplishments, the implicit intentionalities that constitute givenness, in a mode of objectifying distance that is free from interest. If Patočka rejects this conception, it is only because for him any reflection must be rooted in the movements of life more broadly construed, guided by an understanding of its temporality and modes of becoming: "It [reflection] stems from an understanding of the three fundamental *ecstases* of temporality and of the movements of existence anchored in them."[115]

One must thus turn to the problem of movement, of existence as movement—which is nothing less than an understanding of existence as essentially corporeal, bodily in character. This is the subject of the next chapter.

2

On the Body

Movement as a Philosophical Theme

The problems of reflection broached in the last chapter are central to the question of the very possibility of philosophy. Reflection is the indispensable medium of philosophical inquiry, just as it is of any inquiry at all. Arguably, both the potential for philosophy to be frustrated by the resistance of natural life, as well as for its breakthrough in relation to the same, lie in the conditions cleared by the exercises of reflection. The source of both its power and vulnerability, it would not be misleading to assert that the history of philosophy is at bottom the history of reflection.

As argued in the previous chapter, there is a thesis of Husserl's regarding reflection that Patočka implicitly retains, and which will prove decisive in what follows: namely the conception of reflection as *modification*. Reflection is not so much one discrete act among others, as it is a total modification of the overall phenomenality of consciousness. The distance exercised in reflection is thus not some local appendage of conscious life, but something established at the very core of its functioning.

Underscoring its originality, Husserl in *Ideas I* compares the modification of reflection to that of the self-temporalization of the stream of consciousness.[1] Consciousness, as an intrinsically temporal being, is in a process of constant self-modification, continuously passing from the impressional now into the immediately retained past, which is in turn mirrored by the modification of its protentional projection into the future. Temporalization, too, is a form of self-distancing, and one that is even more fundamental than reflection, and in fact for Husserl the latter is founded upon the former: the modification of reflecting consciousness is that of a self-grasping, an arc of vision that takes place within its own flowing retentional-protentional horizons. If the modification of reflection is a kind of self-distancing of consciousness, it is one that follows the circuit of the more originary self-distancing of inner time-consciousness itself. Reflection can thus be described in Husserl as a form of higher-order self-distancing that unfolds in the space opened by the originary self-distancing modifications of time.

There are many other examples in Husserl's writings of forms of self-distancing that are essential to the being of consciousness, all of which are, as in the case of reflection, founded on the original self-distancing of temporalization: memory, as the presencing or presentification (*Vergegenwärtigung*) of past experiences of the I in its present circuit of perception; the imagination (*Phantasie*), in which the I splits off from perceptual life into the quasi-world of the imagined, all the while retaining its place in the actuality of the non-imagined; and empathy (*Einfühlung*), in which the I apperceptively perceives in a non-original way a life that is not its own.[2]

One can understand Patočka's approach as the interpretation of all such instances of self-distancing together as expressions of an underlying ontological structure: human existence as essentially a being-in-distance or, more precisely, the being of *movement*. Patočka's overriding thesis is that all the species of distance operative in the diverse phenomena founded on temporalization are concomitant with and conditioned by the very movement that human existence is, precisely as a temporal being. The most basic parameters and characteristic comportments of the existential movement of human existence thus provide the only possible basis for understanding their essence.

The appeal to movement as an ontological category, one that captures something fundamental about what it means to be, is of course not new. Already Aristotle in the *Physics* offers a conception of movement that articulates the sense in which the possible, something that is not actual, can be said to "be" at all. For movement (change of place, but also qualitative transformations)[3] is the appearance of a possibility on the way, so to speak, towards the fulfillment of its end, its *terminus ad quem*, its actualization. Movement is the being of possibility once the process of its actualization has begun, but before it has come to rest in its culmination or completion. Movement, in other words, is the manner in which something is still at a distance from its target, which is nothing other than itself. In Aristotle, movement in this way provides insight into what it means to be in the realm of *phusis*, where everything is in that in-between of coming to be and passing away—including human life.[4]

It is important to stress that Aristotle is arguing that a movement as a *whole* comes to appearance as a unity of continuous phases, not as an assemblage of discontinuous parts.[5] Movement is perceived as something whole in an originary sense, not as a result of a synthesis of elements that would take place only at the end of a gathering together of the different parts of the whole. This of course does not mean that one has, in advance, the entirety of a movement already in view: the "whole" here is instead something that appears in a phenomenality in which each of its elements looks past a discrete moment of actualization towards its integration into an organized multiplicity, one that lies not in the actuality of the present but in the twin non-being of the past and the future.

One of Patočka's examples (inspired by Bergson) is a melody: when listening to a melodic phrase, the individual tones or notes are present in the mode of ceding to a whole of the melody, which is always what it is only in the form of a process, a coming into view that may aim at something established and settled, but which itself is neither, or is at best only partially established in the peculiar actuality of its being as emergence.[6] Aristotle's own example in the *Physics* is the building of a house, or how the "house" as an end, a *telos* of the activity of building, emerges in the progressive assembly of its material components.[7] The possible being of the house, contained in the materials used, those appropriate for house making, is actualized in the movement of building the house. The "whole" of the house being built is present in the course of its building, not as a completed house somehow floating ephemerally above the activity of building, but precisely in its status as still-possible being that is on the way to being realized in the activity of building. Movement, in this sense of the actual presence of the possible as potentiality, is accordingly characterized by Aristotle as the "actualization of what is potentially, insofar as it is such."[8]

What is attractive for Patočka about this Aristotelian conception of movement is, as it was for Heidegger,[9] the idea that the figure of the possible is not something relegated to the status of a non-being thanks to its association with the non-being of the future, or to an abstract projection of the intellect, or to an imagination that posits the possible in at best something like a quasi-being. Possibility instead has *being*, in the sense that it possesses a characteristic phenomenality all its own, and with that it stands in concrete relation to a given context or situation, even if at the same time it is something intrinsically incomplete, and thus also a form of *non-being*. As potentiality (*dunamis*), possibility in this way belongs inherently to the world, as an essential mode of being in which things become manifest or are revealed.

This in turn suggests a way to understand human transcendence, the posture humans assume in the openness of the world, as a comportment towards possibilities: human being is a movement in which the possibilities it projects itself towards do not lie outside or beyond given, actual being; but find their actuality precisely *as* possibilities in the concrete character of human comportment itself, understood as a movement in the Aristotelian sense of the "actuality of potentiality as such." If possibility is in this way a coherent mode of being, then to characterize human existence or *Dasein* as a being-in-possibilities—or for that matter a being-in-distance—is not ipso facto its relegation to the status of non-being in the sense of sheer nothing, but to recognize human reality as one for which the being of the possible is higher than the actual.

There is, however, an important caveat to Patočka's appropriation of these Aristotelian motifs. For Aristotle, movement or change requires some basis, some prior, finished or completed actuality thanks to which the being of potentiality has some stabilizing framework.[10] Thus the being of potentiality, of *dunamis*, is always something inaugurated, carried, and contained by what is properly actual. Movement is always on the surface, so to speak (and sometimes literally, as in a change of color), of something that does not move. This, Patočka argues, cannot be the case with human comportment, understood as a being-in-possibilities; there is no "prior" actuality that could be identified as the bearer of human possibility. This includes the traditional metaphysical candidate of "soul" or "subject" that would remain present throughout as a substratum, a *hupokeimenon* or substance that would indifferently bear human comportment without itself being a comportment. Nothing—and this is a guiding thesis of Patočka's thinking—in human existence is indifferent to existence, indifferent to the dynamics of the emergence of life; there is nothing that would function like a mute screen onto which would be played the drama of one's story:

> To understand the movement of human existence, for that we need to radicalize Aristotle's conception of movement. The possibilities that ground movement have no preexisting bearer, no necessary referent standing statically at their foundation, but rather all synthesis, all inner interconnection of movement takes place within it alone.[11]

There will be some notable exceptions to this, as will become clear below, but in principle this thesis will be operative in Patočka's thinking.

The challenge of this radicalization of Aristotle's conception of movement is to rearticulate what it means for a movement to be nevertheless *situated*, to have a beginning somewhere, thanks to which the horizon of emergence becomes realized as something decidedly concrete, but at the same time to be expressive of the fundamental sense of freedom that belongs to human transcendence. This is arguably the decisive part of the itinerary in Patočka's elaboration of what he takes to be the movement characteristic of human existence as a being-in-possibilities.

The first and perhaps most basic step in this direction is to relate movement to the philosophical problem of the *body*. Patočka's thesis will be that all human situatedness is founded on the corporeity of human existence, and subject to its dynamic. This is so much the case that it would not be an exaggeration to claim that the philosophy of movement in Patočka amounts in the end to a philosophy of the body, understood as the central organizing structure of human comportment in the world.

The Body and Movement

Though the Aristotelian impulse is central to Patočka's project of a philosophy of movement, Heidegger's influence is no less important, above all the analyses of spatiality and the comportments of *Dasein* included in the elaboration of the structure of care in *Being and Time*. Heidegger's existential interpretation of the fundamental structure of care, *Dasein*'s being ahead of itself as already in the world among things, as the unity of temporal *extases*, provides in rough outline the formal structure of Patočka's conception of movement. Likewise, the guiding insight of Heidegger's, that human existence as a being in possibilities, as the open clarity of praxis, precisely is the being of time, remains equally germane throughout Patočka's reflections.[12]

Yet Patočka's philosophy of movement is also predicated on a critique of Heidegger, who for Patočka failed to fully appreciate the phenomenon of the body, the result being a certain excessively formal articulation of the existentiality of *Dasein*:

> It does seem that Heidegger's analytics makes his ontology of existence excessively formal; though praxis is the original form of clarity, he never takes into consideration the fact that the original praxis is necessarily and in principle the activity of a *bodily* subject, that embodiment must therefore have an ontological status which cannot be identical with the body's being come across as present here and now.[13]

Patočka's basic claim is that the body is the site of an original assumption of existence. To be a body—to be one's own body—is the *conditio sine qua non* of one's own becoming as a freely acting subject. The structures of bodily comportment are for this reason not simply given "in" the world, they belong in essential ways to the very manifestation of the world itself: the world is as implicit in the manifestation of the body, as the body is in the manifestation of the world.

Heidegger's neglect of the body as a properly ontological theme creates in this way the appearance of a cleft between the existential task that *Dasein* is for itself, its practical being articulated in the structure of care, and the lived concreteness of its existence, or that dynamic dimension of facticity that belongs precisely to the body, as the ontological basis upon which it is possible to assume any life at all, any possibilities as my own. What is missing, in other words, is an account of how the task of life becomes concrete:

> What makes the link between the "for the sake of" [the task *Dasein* is for itself] and what follows from it as our concrete task is left unsolved in Heidegger's schema. I believe the link resides in life's embodiment—what I can do is given by what makes it possible for me to do anything at all, and that is my corporeality, which I *must take over* prior to all free possibilities.[14]

Though Heidegger's analyses of care remain a vital presupposition in his reflections, in the end it is Husserl's analyses of the body in texts such as *Ideas II* and elsewhere that will provide Patočka with the guiding clues for the elaboration of the body as an ontological theme. Perhaps the most important example of this is Patočka's appropriation of Husserl's distinction between the body as organ of subjective volition and action, the lived or subject-body (*Leib*), and the body as a thing among things of nature (*Körper*). In *Ideas II* this distinction is orchestrated along the lines of a contrast between two attitudes: one naturalistic, folding an account of the body into a general account of what it is to be a thing in the system of objectively determinate nature; and the other personalistic, articulating the body in accordance with a range of subjective interests and motivations that structure an interpersonal environment populated by persons and things of meaning, value, and use.[15] The body belongs to both "worlds," and represents an axis of differentiation between them; it is also the site in which they come together and are coordinated into a whole. For the body not only forms the basis for the distinction between human being as a physical reality, a natural existence, and human being as the site of praxis, of motivated action and meaning, but is also the possibility of a certain inter-translatability between the two. All that is physical in the human being is the potential bearer of personalistic patterns of action and meaning, and likewise, all that is personalistic is rooted primordially in a physical existence that provides the context for its incipient presence. However different, they form a circuit of mutual interpretation, each providing the basis for a profile of the meaningfulness of the other.

Like any translation (the analogy is neither Patočka's nor Husserl's), there remains a certain opacity on both sides, an incommunicability that resists complete transparency. On the one hand, the body is experienced as the organ of free subjective movement; it is that basis on which the willing, sensing I engages directly with the world, and is in this way the immediate expression of life in the first person, of what it means concretely to say "I." On the other hand, the body is also the terminus of reification, in which the self disappears into a thinghood indistinguishable from any other thing of nature, shifting in this way ineluctably from the first to the third person, from "I" to "it." Shadowed by its own transition into the third person, a tendency that lies at the very heart of the constitutive unity of its sense, the "I" is never purely either "I" or "it," but a continuous transition—or translation—from one to the other and back again.

Here Patočka cites the example from Husserl—one which Merleau-Ponty developed as well, though perhaps with a less ontological bent—of one hand touching the other hand of the same body. In one hand touching the other, the body is manifest as both the sensing organ of perception and the object sensed; it is the organ in which sensing and willing are localized, but only in such a way that it itself appears as something determinate at the other side of sensing, as a thing. Being-touched by itself, the self-manifestation of the body as thing is unstable, taking its own turn in kind as the sensing organ for which the other hand, at first sensing but now the sensed, becomes manifest as a given thing. Each hand is in this way inscribed in a kind of circle of continuously disrupted and reconstituted mutual objectification, each of the pair taking its turn as subject and object without ever completely becoming either.[16]

In this way the body is indeed an object, present in the experience of touch, yet insofar as it also passes over into the modes of sensing it is at most a kind of quasi-object, subject to a circuit of constituting/constituted, the stability of which is undermined from within by the contradiction between being in the first person and being in the third that runs through its core.[17] Moreover, the body is only this, in Husserl's expression, "strangely incompletely constituted thing"[18] on a tactile level: in the other senses such as seeing and hearing, one finds no comparable circuit of disruption and reconstitution. The distances here are of a different order, and contrast with what Patočka, as did Husserl before him (and in fact Aristotle as well), takes to be the more originary phenomenon of touch.

As such, tactile presence is the primary phenomenality of subjective corporeity, the mode of first encounter of the subject with itself as concrete life. Accordingly, the relation of the tactile body to other fields of sense and modes of activity is marked by the function of being the center of orientation, that coordinating point of reference within which everything in perceptual life is balanced. The center of proprioception is something felt, thanks to which the body carries itself through its fields of sensuous perception, including the visible and the auditory. Orientation is of course germane not only to sense perception, but to all the forms of bodily movement in general, and with that to all the relevant comportments of the volitional subject that hold sway in the body. The subjective body is, to use Husserl's expression, defined by an original form of volition in the form of the "I can"—I can move, I can stand, raise my head, walk towards, grasp, reposition my view, everything contained in the ambulatory perceptions of the proprioceptive or kinesthetic subject. These simple movements of the body represent, on one level, the free flow of subjective volition in the comportment of its body towards this or that task, this or that end.[19]

The body as a thing does not of course simply melt away in the expression of the "I can," as if replaced by a free action that is only accidentally associated with it. Yet it does represent a sense in which the body as third person cedes ground, so to speak, for potentialities that can only be properly pursued in the first person. To the extent that the body as thing cedes ground in this way, the freedom of the "I can" can be integrated into physical existence in the form of an organized, oriented field of play within the complexes of sensibility and meaning. This field of corporeal action in the end represents a series of conditions on which freedom remains uniquely dependent:

> The bodily "I can" is the consciousness of freedom. Only an incarnate being integrated into the rest of reality in a bodily aesthesiological, meaning-bestowing, meaningful field can be free. It is, however, a *freedom in dependence*. In order to bring anything whatever about, we depend on this bodily field and on all that opens before us within it.[20]

Though he never truly breaks from this essentially Husserlian schema of the subject-body/body-thing (*Leibkörper*), Patočka's analysis nevertheless goes beyond Husserl in some decisive respects.[21] Perhaps the most important of these is the broadening of the thematic of bodily comportment along the lines of the philosophy of movement sketched above. The body for Patočka, as center of orientation and dependent freedom, takes on the significance of the primordial ontological structure of human movement. The body not only moves, or is moved by the willing subject, but is instead *essentially movement*, the very embodiment of subjective existence itself, thus forming the foundational, or *first possibility* of human existence:

> No doubt, everything I accomplish is enacted for the sake of my being, but at the same time there is a *fundamental* possibility that must be open to me, a possibility without which all the others merely float in the air, baseless, senseless, and unrealizable. This, the primordial, is thus no contingent thing, nothing ontic; rather, *as first possibility*, its ontological status

is the basis for all existence. , . . This ontological basis is corporeality *as the possibility of movement.*[22]

This first possibility, or first movement, is described by Patočka as oriented by three parameters that in turn define its role in the manifestation of the horizon of the world. Two of these parameters are developments of the account of the twin poles of subjective inwardness and periphery already met earlier in the discussion of the problem of the world, and the role of these structures allows for a reintroduction of the problem of the world from the perspective of Patočka's philosophy of movement. However, it is only with a third parameter, itself related to the problem of concrete reflection also sketched above, that Patočka's presentation of the movement of human existence is complete as a function of worldly orientation: namely, the relation to other subjects, present also as embodied, as a conditioning of worldly orientation taken as a whole.

Taking each of the parameters in turn, the first, already described above, fixes the pole of subjective inwardness as something *rooted*, an inward pull or reticence of transcendence at the core of any perspective a subject may have within the open span of its environment. The body provides a better sense of what this entails: the subject-body as movement is rooted in its function as a center of orientation, of the freedom of the "I can." This is not a mere arbitrary marker set by the free subject; it is instead grounded in the facticity of its physical being. The I exists only to the extent to which it assumes, takes on, engages a corporeal base that it does not originally create, but is given as the initial ground of its possibility as a self. Subjective inwardness is thus rooted in the reticence of a corporeity that the subject never completely assimilates or dissolves, and which it can only *assume* as the given basis of its individuation. However much the body is one's own project as an acting, willing subject, however plastic its response to will and decision, it always retains this inward reticence in the face of human transcendence, rendering provisional any sense in which one *is* one's body. For the I is its body, or the body of the I is itself, only in a conditioned sense, only to the extent that or so long as one's body yields to one's will or allows itself to be assumed as the basis of freedom. Accordingly, one is always limited from within by a reserve at the core of one's being that is not oneself, but which one remains dependent upon, and which can always disrupt projects as an obstacle, just as much as it can facilitate their success.

The fact that the I is embodied means that there is an ineluctable otherness at the core of its being. Its movement is not a purely fluid emanation of freedom, but is subject to the potential immobility of an unfreedom that it can never completely elude. The body in this sense is not something one *is*, but something one *has*, which at first designates a distance that always separates the self from the body: "In this sense, then, we are not our body. With respect to the body-object we are always at a distance."[23] The I *has* a body precisely because, as an I, it can never be a pure object, a mere thing, and thus the I stands at a distance from the body-thing, for "only that which cannot be a pure object can be at a distance."[24] This is not a distance that can be crossed in the sense of erased: to cease to be at a distance from the body would be precisely to eradicate freedom, it would be simply to be the thing that the I is as body at the expense of the movement of transcendence that the I exists as a being who acts and wills from having a body.

This differentiation between the body one is and the body one has lies at the core of the sense of the body as movement: the body the I has is the function of the dependent, limited transcendence of the body the I is. The body as movement is the emergence of a potential freedom, a being that can never be a mere thing, from the thing in which it in turn disappears. The "I can" is accordingly not the body-thing, but the subject that, across a distance, "holds sway," maintaining itself in a state of tension with an unfree ground on which it nevertheless relies in order to be at all, and into which it inevitably retreats in inactive passivity, such as sleep or death, conditions in which the body as thing no longer cedes ground to free comportment.

This tension of transcendence that differentiates the body one is from the body one has is understood by Patočka in explicitly temporal terms, again relating a figure of distance to the modifications of temporal life: "for the I is not possible except as a transcendence or, more precisely, as a dominance in time, as something that is neither at the mercy of the passivity of the inner stream nor scattered through the objective moments of time."[25]

It is important to stress that to have a body does not mean that it becomes a mere possession, a mere instrument at an arm's remove from the freedom of subjective volition, as if transcendence and the assumption of the body as first possibility represented a kind of closed arc of reification. If the I has a body across a distance that marks its difference with object-being as a whole, it is also a distance that witnesses a constant transition of freedom precisely into being an object, though never with a complete abdication of its status as free: "I-freedom, I-dominance, is a constant transition into an object, that it is constantly escaping from freedom to the other shore of objectivity without thereby losing its inner identity and so responsibility for what it does as active and creative."[26] The I is dominant only over that which ultimately marks the finite, limited character of that very sway of freedom.

This can be understood as a deepening of Husserl's analysis of the circuit of disrupted and reconstituted objectivity characteristic of the lived body discussed earlier, though now with closer attention paid to the ontological implications of the temporality or temporal distance constitutive of subjective being. This becomes even more clear with Patočka's emphasis on the importance of *habit*. Husserl is again the inspiration: the subject-body is not only a center of orientation, thanks to which the "I can" assumes the profile of an empirical reality; it is also the body of habits, those concrete patterns of bodily comportment that take shape in time as an abiding acquisition of given capacities to act. The horizon of the holding-sway of the "I can" is not one of a pure transcendence, but is pre-populated by habitual responses, projections, and patterns of action whose being is decisively rooted in the past. The subject is thus embodied not only in having a body as a physical basis for action, but also as the substrate of habitualities, of that which presages the paths of action that it is able to assume. All human life depends on habit in this sense to act at all, for there to be a sense for what can or cannot be done.[27]

The body is thus not only sheer opaque objectivity, but also the concrete legacy of the past, the nexus of a myriad of habits that condition and open the possibilities of the "I can." Habits belong essentially to the body which one has, and stand at that same remove of distance as the physical body. The I is not its habits, or rather, to borrow an expression from Sartre, the I is its habits in the mode of not being its habits: they constitute the situation the I is, in tension with which the I exists as their transcendence. Habits amount to the objectified and embodied remnants of past experiences, past actions that discovered the possibilities of bodily comportments first in rough, and then in progressively more determinate forms. Habits are in this way the legacies of the past self returning to the present from the far shore of objectivity as conditioning factors, forming part of the essential terrain of the transcendence of the I, which can only "be" from the basis of the given past:

> Its [subjective being's] subjectivity is freedom and freedom is always acting; acting, however, is possible only when I have the power, when I can, and I can only when I have a body at my disposal, a body that obeys me; when, that is, my I is the subject of corporeal habitualities. That in turn means that I cannot be only an absolute presence but must also be a substrate of what I have accumulated already; and since I can accumulate only on the basis of an already present definite ability to use a body, we can say that even innate dispositions are *already here* and in that sense past—I can be a free being only on the basis of a past, on the ground of a relation to it.[28]

The implication is that the body-thing does not yield immediately to the dominance of the I, to freedom; it yields only on terms conditioned by the accumulated history of freedom that the I has already been, those ways in which the body has already yielded, ceded space for the possibility of free action. If subjective inwardness is something rooted in the body, it is not in the body as sheer objecthood, but rather in the mediated being of habits, of unique corporeal conditions that are established for every individual in terms of their own past. The dialectic of distance between the I as a dominance in time and the body it "has" as its condition for action is in this way organized by habit, the result being that the free I is not a thing, but nor is it entirely not a thing, but is rather "corporeal in its entire substance."[29]

The role of habit, along with the fundamental condition of the body as need, suggests that the concreteness of one's freedom is something that needs to be settled, taken care of, for it to be able to be at all. Needs call for satisfaction, for a care for self that secures what sustains the physical body. Habits as well need to be cared for, to the extent that they must be cultivated over time, both learned and practiced. One is free only on the basis of the past embodied in habit; and the body is that from which the I can act, only to the extent that it takes the form of a foundation of past action made substantial in corporeal habitualities. The I is thus rooted in the unfree ground of past freedom, in the legacies of past success that give definite shape to free being as a properly spiritual formation.

The Body and World

The ontological rootedness of the body also expresses something essential about the *worldly* character of the body. Patočka describes the movement of the body as standing in relation to the world as a whole, in the sense that human comportment always unfolds relative to the world as an immobile referent that circumscribes the horizon of its freedom. In the 1967 essay already cited earlier, "The 'Natural' World and Phenomenology," Patočka rather poetically describes this immobile referent of bodily comportment as the "earth."[30] The language here evokes Heidegger, but the metaphor is not all that alien to Husserl: for the earth, as Husserl also argues, in a primordial sense does not move, it is that originary *archē* of immobility implicit in all movement, and from which movement projects itself.[31]

The rootedness of the body in the earth takes the form not only of an inner referent, but also of a *force*, one that inwardly sustains life, forming the essential parameters of the bedrock dependency of finite bodily existence as a state of need. The earth is what humans ultimately draw upon in their response to the exigencies of need, it is that without which the body would not be physically possible—the air one breathes, the food one consumes, the firm ground upon which one stands. The body is accordingly described by Patočka as rooted in a state of existential dependency, inwardly conditioned by a need not only for a point of departure, for some solid "ground under one's feet," but also for an enduring force that sustains the very possibility of its projection. The body one has in the sense of what stands in need of care, what must be addressed for one to be at all, is part of that unfree ground of need, and as such represents the most basic set of tasks for the cultivation of free existence:

> The body is not only the act center which initiates action but is also that at which its dynamics aim: it is hungry or thirsty, it desires air, light, movement. . . . It is thus the starting point of an action which returns to it in satisfaction, and the polarity of dissatisfaction-satisfaction lies at the root of *need*. The body is in need *in principle*, not accidentally; it wants to be constantly cared for, and in this caring-for it is always *dependent* on its field.[32]

Along with the first parameter of subjective inwardness and rootedness, the second parameter is equally constitutive of the body as movement: the peripheral distance Patočka interprets, again in Heideggerian language, with the metaphor of the "sky," which he describes as the open distance that bonds the world as horizon to itself.[33] As in Heidegger, the sky is associated with the movement of an understanding that projects possibilities, opens the future, and pulls subjective existence outwards from itself. However rooted transcendence may be, however consumed its dynamism is by need, it is ultimately a countermovement in tension with everything that holds it in closure, pulling away from what holds it back. The periphery stands as the outermost beyond of this pulling-free, the constant referent of a being that can never be fully reduced to the necessity of returning to itself in satisfaction and sustenance, securing what a body cannot do without.

There are thus two poles of the movement of human, corporeal life: the inward pole of rootedness, of the oriented corporeal field fundamentally rooted in the earth, and the outer, peripheral pole of the sky. Here one can see that Patočka's break with Aristotle's insistence that the being of movement requires the presence of a prior actuality must be subjected to a caveat. If Aristotle's argument comes down to the thesis that all movement requires a referential ground that does not move, then here too the earth and the sky do not move, and with that they define, of necessity, the horizon of movement. To be sure, the earth and the sky are no "things," no objects or substances that would stand as complete and upon which movement would be somehow grafted, which is what Aristotle seems to have had in mind. Nevertheless, the movement of human existence that Patočka describes is pulled in various directions beyond itself, even in directions that ultimately refer to a dependency on what does not move, thus repeating the Aristotelian figure of the need for a "prior actuality," at least in an extended ontological sense.

In this way the earth and the sky represent constant poles of the movement of human life in horizons, together composing an inner solidity that runs through the openness of the possible. They are not actualities in Aristotle's sense, since they are neither complete nor settled, but they are given, even immobile parameters constitutive of the horizon of the world. The horizon of the world as both earth and sky thus denotes an openness, and ultimately that of possibility itself, but it is not a wholly fluid dynamic; it binds, conditions, and even contains. This means that the movement of human existence is not free of friction, density, ballast, effort, condition, and even the self-enclosure and finality epitomized by thinghood.

The movement of the body that unfolds between the earth and sky—or between the rooted inwardness of oriented comportment animated by existential need and the peripheral horizon of projected freedom—is described by Patočka as triangulated by a third parameter, a primordial *center*. This center represents an existential structure whose most important component, Patočka argues, is a relation to the being of others, other corporeal beings who also exist in the region between earth and sky. And the emphasis is precisely on others as embodied: the dialectic of freedom and body-thing is not something in spite of which the I encounters another I, but the very ground of the presence of the other. Bodily existence is the condition for the possibility of the transcendental constitution of the other, and that precisely as a terrain uniquely prepared by the dialectic of the first-person I and the third-person thing of the body:

> Here then is the deepest, "transcendental" significance of objective corporeity—it is the locus on which the realization of thou-ness can build. The first and third person are the inner presuppositions of the realization of the second person.[34]

With the elaboration of these three parameters Patočka fixes a basic, general structure for an analysis of the movements of human existence as constitutive of the natural world: "Contact with others is the primordial, most important component of the *center* of the natural world whose *ground* is the earth and whose *periphery* is the sky."[35]

This place of others in the center of things is in turn important for understanding spatiality, which is essential to any account of the a priori of the world. Here again the oriented structure of the bodily field is key, and with the theme of the other it receives an important supplement. Along with the functioning of the tactile body in proprioception, bodily comportment is also marked by a spatiality that relates directly to the way that human existence stands in relation to itself through the other, not in an accidental, but an essential sense. In this way, Patočka's analyses of the body supplement and deepen the reflection on selfhood and the other discussed in the last chapter. For the spatiality of the body is not only that through which the other as "you" is transcendentally possible, approachable in the horizon of a bodily field in which the other as body is manifest; it is equally the possibility of relating to oneself as a self, as an "I." The bodily I carries itself, handles its comportments in accordance with patterns of self-relation that find their originary genesis in relations with others structured precisely as movements of bodily comportment.

This means that the drama of subjective transcendence at the core of Patočka's descriptions of the body does not only take place between the I and its body; the entire complex is mediated by the bodily presence of others. Husserl and Heidegger had emphasized this as well: however precisely formulated its mathematical definition may be, space unrelated to others, untouched by subjectivity, is in the end an abstraction from an experienced basis that is irreducibly intersubjective.[36] Similarly, however illuminating phenomenological descriptions of bodily self-comportment in the first person may be, the full picture is missing without the eventual emphasis on this intersubjective dimension.

The inner bond of spatiality and the other is a key theme in Patočka's account of the movement of human existence, and lies at the root of fundamental existential phenomena such as vulnerability, the need to be accepted, and the possibilities for cooperative satisfaction of the basic conditions of life.[37] Vulnerability and need in particular are primordial expressions of the basic truth that human existence, its meaning and manner of being in the world, always takes place in relation to a dialectic with the other. Again, the reason for this is the intrinsic finitude of subjective life: the sustaining conditions for the free I as a dominance in time, as a being that assumes the body as its first possibility, generating a sustaining past in the form of the cultivation of habit and the practices of satisfaction—all of this assumes the presence of others on whom I depend for protection, sustenance, community, life. Relations with others determine our very sense of self, for they determine the most basic conditions for encountering the possibility that one is for oneself at all.

Not only do relations with others establish who we are, but they also *localize* personal, bodily existence in the world:

> Our body is a life which is spatial in itself and of itself, producing its location in space and making itself spatial. Personal being is not a being like a thing but rather a self-relation which, to actualize this relation, must go round about through another being. We relate to ourselves by relating to the other, to more and more things and ultimately to the universe as such, so locating ourselves in the world.[38]

It is important to emphasize that these relations with others and things thanks to which humans find (or better, produce) their place in the world are not determined in a static way, they are not even altogether given. They have an intrinsic horizonal character, which means that they involve modalities of obscurity, absence, and incompleteness. Others are as much an open transcendence as the I, as much a question for themselves in the process of articulating itself between the satisfaction of earthly needs and the open horizon of the world's possibilities. If others are central and not incidental to one's self-relation, orientation, and localization in the world, and thus are vital to the dynamics of self-understanding on all levels, it is not because they provide the self-understanding of the I ready-made, but because they ultimately share a common horizon of life in which such understanding remains indelibly problematic, incurably open.

Yet at the same time the relations of self and other are not wholly fluid; they also have a characteristic density, which is the result of how the body lives in its horizons. Living in horizons, Patočka argues, the momentum of human life transfers a certain actuality to what is not yet, what is absent or indeterminate; possibilities themselves thicken in the course of a life, extending reality beyond the narrow confines of what is unequivocally established and given: "With the help of the transference of actuality, far more is present to me as real than what is actually given: whatever stands in some relation to the self-given is also actual."[39] This includes the possibilities found in things, but also the trajectories of other lives with which one lives in dependency and cooperation, to the extent that all of human existence is the movement of being pulled into an *outside*, or being subject to a centrifugal flow of things and other selves, all of which force the I to turn away from itself and towards the horizon of the world. Humans are again in this way beings of distance, or better, beings who live in the peculiar actuality of distances:

> Things beyond our senses are present to us. Even what can never be given in the original, like the experience of others, becomes actual. We live by relating constantly to the experience of others in the world as to something actually given. Living in horizons, the transference of actuality, points to a powerful centrifugal stream that governs our life—out of ourselves, to the world. We live turned away from ourselves, we have always already transcended ourselves in the direction of the world, of its ever more remote regions.[40]

Yet this outward movement is as much toward oneself as toward that which is not oneself. The movement of human life is equally bound to the constant demand of being pulled into itself, as it were, in the sense that life is pulled outside of itself towards the horizon of its *own* non-givenness which is, in many ways, more real than whatever can count unequivocally as its given actuality. The old thesis that possibility is higher than actuality thereby finds affirmation in Patočka's thinking, but at the same time it is also coupled with the thesis that being in possibilities projects before itself a natural prejudice for the positivity of the actual, thanks to which the horizon of the world is experienced as something ineluctably *real*. The world is something eminently real, as a world for oneself and for others, who together project into its horizon an actuality that seeks to belie its incompleteness and openness, making it something definite and fixed. Living in possibilities continues to imply the open "not yet" of the future, but it is also rooted in the virtual realities of anticipated realization, realities that capture the self in their web as much as what is genuinely present, and which on that basis draws human life outwards from itself.

The Origin of Openness

Patočka's philosophy of movement—which is at bottom a philosophy of the body—also includes numerous reflections on the important phenomena of affectivity and instinct. Here too there is a basis appropriated from Husserl's phenomenology, but as in the case with the a priori of the world and the modification of reflection, the themes of affectivity and instinct undergo a certain recalibration in Patočka's approach, one that again extends the scope and detail of the ontological problematic.

In Husserl, the theme of affectivity tends to be limited, for the most part, to its role in the fashioning of understanding in the domain of perceptual judgment. In Heidegger there is a similar limitation, with affectivity only coming under consideration thanks to the role played by mood or attunement (*Stimmung*) in the way *Dasein* is brought before itself as an existence, a project.[41] In general, affectivity and instinct are, arguably, never fully treated on their own terms by either philosopher; their analysis is always subordinate to another purpose, namely the phenomenological interpretation of human understanding.

The result, Patočka observes, is that modes of being other than the human remain ontologically obscure, even those that are evidently contained in the human as aspects or dimensions of its existence:

> It remains an unresolved problem how we could trace out, how we could ontologically delimit affectivity and emotionality in something that is *merely* living, that lacks existence. We need to deal with it, though, because our human existence in a (working, pragmatic) world presupposes the existence of the childish and the animal-like within us.[42]

Patočka's suggestion that we pursue the themes of affectivity and instinct beyond the limitations of a reflection on their role in understanding—whether it be Husserl's theory of judgment or Heidegger's analytic of *Dasein* as a *Seinsverständnis*—has the potential to open a phenomenological perspective on the philosophical problem of human animality. The idea is that affectivity and instinct belong to a form of life, of movement, that is more basic, more primordial than a life shaped by understanding, and which represents a form of bodily comportment more directly integrated within the immanence of the world.

Husserl and Heidegger could be said to already anticipate the general direction in which the description of human animality might unfold. For both, the understanding, whether respectively characterized as an accomplishment of sense-bestowal or thrown projection, takes the form of a departure, and with that, once again, a kind of distance from what belongs to the realm of affectivity. This is part of the significance of the contrast, at play in both Husserl and Heidegger, of the passivity of the past with the future-oriented directedness of active transcendence. For both thinkers, the distance thanks to which the understanding achieves its fundamental trajectory is constituted in terms of a basic temporal structure governed by the contrast between the past and the future, which can be said to take the general form of a contrast between something *closed* and something *open*. The already-been, the pastness of the past, is something unrepeatable, inaccessible to the free projection of possibility, and is in this sense closed; the not-yet or the to-be of the future is, by contrast, the very ground of accessibility, of an open comportment to possible being. Yet the distance between the closure of the one and the openness of the other is not a static given, an enduring form of the present moment, but is bound up with the sense of the passage of time, or of a dynamic tension between what is, what has been, and what will be. The past is not simply closed, but ever-closing; likewise, the future is not an open terrain of the possible, but the movement of its opening-access. Understanding—or the kind of *grasping* it represents—operates in the oscillation between a past continuously being absorbed in its closure and a future opening constantly out of the closure of the past, but without the one ever being severed from the other.

Pure affectivity is thus not something one posits before oneself; its happening is always, as it were, already over by the time awareness and understanding manage to respond. In this sense affectivity is something that is always closing behind us, becoming progressively enveloped in the depth of what the understanding subject had already been before it came to exercise itself as an understanding projecting itself out to the future. Patočka identifies this figure as belonging to the core of the subject-body, experienced as an elusive depth of the body with which the subject is never coextensive, thus again emphasizing that distance between the primordial freedom of the I as existence and its corporeal basis:

> The primordial I, the primordial freedom is something I *am* in the purest sense of the word, never something I *have*. A free being, however, not only is but also *has* a body *at its disposal*, is in charge of its body, that is, of a corporeal subject and presubject with which *not only* is it never fully coextensive but which in some respects ever elude it, containing presuppositions, instinctual matrices, situational moments which are never fully *before* us, finally even a purely objectively material substrate which as a dark, naturally causal bearer of its *own* vitality is also in some sense coextensive with me.[43]

Temporalization is again central to understanding how this is structured. If we bracket for the moment further reflection on the understanding, we can see that the very passage of time suggests, implicit in one aspect of its dynamic, a potential relation to the world that is *not yet* marked by the full distance of understanding, where the oscillation between the closure of the past and the openness of the future has not yet unwound itself. In this way, our experience of time itself suggests the possibility of a being that is not yet a movement which realizes the full meaning of the passage of time, that leaves unrealized time as the potential ground for the establishment of a life in distances, and instead remains a lingering in *proximity*:

> Does not this distantiating mode of life [so *Dasein* as understanding-projection], by being a duality of the given and the not given, of the present and the absent, of being and not being, itself presuppose a level of life where that remove with respect to things does not yet obtain—where there is a different, distinctive mode of life, where what is in our case only one dimension is a whole distinctive mode of living, an entire relation to the world?[44]

Such a relation to the world, Patočka suggests, endures within us as a pre-subjective level of our own life. As a dimension of our existence that is not yet existence, this "animality," to give it another name, is presented in Patočka's descriptions of the movement of human existence as a disrupted, repressed dimension.[45] Yet at the same time it has a positive role, in that it provides life, precisely as bodily, with a palpable sense of *depth*—the past we carry within ourselves as bodily existences outstrips the acquisitions of habit and everything else that belongs to freedom, to consciousness. This depth of living speaks instead to a passive, indifferent continuity with all that is. Here a sense of cosmic wholeness intrinsic to the raw meaning of the world finds its root, a profound indifference of the whole that can never be unambiguously incorporated into an understanding that has always already left it behind in favor of meaning.

Animality is, however, not for all that a condition of pure meaninglessness. Affectivity, however passive, is not pure indifference, nor is instinct empty, mechanical behavior. Animal life too is movement, the being of possibility; likewise, all the bodily phenomena described earlier regarding the oriented space of bodily comportment, the satisfaction of corporeal needs, the spatiality of the other, all of this remains in play. Yet life that lists towards pure animality establishes itself within the immanence of a closed, indifferent world, a dark background that has not yet been opened for anyone, thus affirming an essential anonymity of the inwardness of animal life.

This potential for an analysis of human animality is one of the more heretical promises of Patočka's asubjective phenomenology, once it has evolved into a full philosophy of body and movement. It is heretical in that it departs from a long-standing prohibition in classical phenomenology against any incursion of philosophical anthropology. Husserl's firewall against such incursions could be said to lie in the idea of an anonymously functioning transcendental subjectivity that, in and of itself, must be sharply distinguished from anything "human," at least in the sense of what would be included in the range of empirical human phenomena, including the evolution of the human animal form.[46] Likewise, Heidegger takes some pains early in *Being and Time* to distance his project of fundamental ontology from philosophical anthropology, and could perhaps consider the matter settled once his focus turns more and more to the problem of Being as such, leaving behind even the analysis of *Dasein* in its everydayness in favor of the history of Being and the questioning germane to its construction.[47]

In Patočka, one might argue, existential analysis neither affirms the thesis of an anonymously functioning subjectivity, as a kind of absolute being of irrevocable distance (and with that of accomplished time) that would form the definitive horizon of all experience, nor does it wholly map onto Heidegger's turn that would seemingly decenter the self-understanding of *Dasein* in favor of an equally anonymous trajectory of distancing in the form of the destiny of Being. Inspired here by Eugen Fink, Patočka instead seeks to revive the possibility of a more ancient sense of the world as the event of manifestation, as a great *mysterium* irreducible to subjectivity and its dynamics of experience and understanding, if also lying implicit throughout:

> It is a condition for the appearance of an existent that it be somewhere, at some time, always within some understanding of time and space. Is there not then within us some understanding—unclear, anticipatory, unobjectifiable—of this antecedent whole? Might we not thus receive into an ontological context that which creates the light for appearing—the whole of all that is, the world in the strong sense of the word? Would we not in that way rehabilitate the ancient idea of *phusis* as *archē*?[48]

The central problem that finds expression in this figure of what we might call the "creation of appearing" out of the antecedent whole of radical indifference—and thus the establishment of the openness of human comportment in that which is radically other than freedom—is that of individuation. The body is the individuation of temporal being; its movement cannot be understood solely in terms of the phenomenal dynamics that unfold in the light of the world, but must include the condition of an irreducible and ultimately hidden origin from which things emerge and into which they disappear.

The theme of animality as a life in radical proximity to the unfree depth of the world as that out of which all being emerges as *phusis* represents a considerable deepening of the problem of the body, and with that perhaps the most radical departure from the Husserlian, and perhaps even Heideggerian origins of the problem. The body, grasped as an existential movement, is described by Patočka as situated on a primordial boundary line between a whole that is eternally indifferent to itself, and the movement of an existence that is essentially non-indifferent, an issue for and pursuit of itself. The closer individuated life cleaves to this boundary, the more animal the existence; the further it stretches beyond it, the more human the animal.

The phenomenality of the body could then be described as marked by the dynamic between an insurmountable cosmic refusal to appear and a constant striving to see, to let appearing be; likewise, between an eternally unfree ground of openness, and the free embrace of the same. This tension is what stands in the end for Patočka as the formative origin of the productive movement of manifestation. And it is also the body which thus ensures that any experience of the self, any search for oneself, involves both of these seemingly irreconcilable dimensions as aspects of being in the world, for their intermingling is nothing less than the very bond of individuation and worldhood:

> It is as corporeal that we are individual. In their corporeity, humans stand at the boundary between being, indifferent to itself and to all else, and existence in the sense of a pure relation to the totality of all there is. On the basis of their corporeity humans are not only the beings of distance but also the beings of proximity, rooted beings, not only innerworldly beings but also beings in the world.[49]

This yields a contrast between the idea of human existence as openness, an opening onto the world, and that thanks to which beings appear, or are brought out of themselves and into manifestation. Thus again we hear the echo of the ancient idea of *phusis*, of the primordial world itself as the basis for manifestation, for individuation—the non-individuated night as ground of manifestation: "Things would then be what they are by virtue not of the secondarily human opening but already of the primordial, 'physical' opening of what is by being."[50] Human openness thus would be one of clarity, of an individuating non-indifferent encounter with what is, in contrast to the indifference of the night of being on the one hand, and the first stirrings of life emerging out of the primordial night on the other. Human movement, then, in its most primordial sense, is for Patočka precisely the transition from the revealing of *phusis* to the clarity of non-indifference, or "the middle term between the two fundamental ways in which being uncovers existents and thereby shows itself to be their origin and ruling principle, *archē*."[51]

3

On the Three Movements of Human Existence

Openness and History

The elements of the philosophy of movement outlined in the last chapter, which had in turn emerged from the project of an asubjective phenomenology as a critique of the classical phenomenologies of Husserl and Heidegger, only develop into a full-scale philosophical anthropology with Patočka's elaboration of what he characterizes as the three basic, primordial movements of human existence. The elaboration of these three movements provides in turn a unique philosophical perspective for Patočka's reflections on Europe, the contemporary situation, and the possibility of philosophy as such, and arguably stand at the very center of his mature philosophy.

The three movements of existence can also be seen as an extension, and deepening, of the theme of openness introduced at the end of the last chapter. This can be illustrated with a look at the opening discussion in Patočka's *Heretical Essays* on the theme of *prehistory* ("Reflections on Prehistory"). Patočka here advances the guiding thesis that human existence is primordially an openness to what manifests itself, not incidentally, but in a way constitutive of the very possibility of being human. Thanks to this primordial openness, things both human and other than human are provided a foundation for becoming manifest, for "coming to their own being, that is, of becoming phenomenon, of manifesting themselves."[1]

Openness is not something univocal, but takes on various forms and complex structures, not least of which is the fact that human openness is something *cultivated*. That openness is cultivated in turn entails that openness is intrinsically historical, and the "world" it gives rise to, "if by 'the world' we understand the structure of the way that what there is can appear to humans,"[2] is tied to at least a particular time and more often than not also to a particular place. A historical epoch is by implication not something that simply happens, but is defined by an accomplishment of a manner of articulating the sense of things, and with that the cultivation of openness. As such, the accomplishments of human openness are also something that can be transmitted or handed down, becoming an organic part of other times and places, even those that exhibit often very different modes of manifestation.

Language, Patočka emphasizes, is perhaps the most primordial example of both the cultivation of openness and its transmission. Language represents a kind of secondary phenomenality, an accomplishment of articulation that serves openness as a constant resource for passing on "what has been seen," whereby language becomes "the foundation of a comportment which represents a widening of openness and which serves it."[3] Language is perhaps the most striking example of the cultivation of openness, given precisely its universal human scope, but it is also part of a broader canvas of practices and comportments, such as "religion, myth, art, and sacrifice."[4] Each of these should be taken in a very broad sense, and the list should be left open, since clearly any communal or cultural activity that generates forms of tradition both limited and enduring with an eye to their permanence are relevant here, from drinking and eating rituals to local mannerisms of speech, dress, and gesture.

Openness is in this way something dynamic, life in movement; humans are not mere witnesses to manifestation, but live lives that unfold within it, take root in it, and thereby shape its movements in ways that yield specific forms of consciousness and experience. Openness thus yields not only a world, but worlds; and worlds not only for individuals, but thanks to the transmissability of traditions, potentially for everyone:

> The opening of the world . . . is ever historical in all its forms, contingent on the self-manifestations of phenomena and on the doings of humans who preserve and transmit. Openness is ever an event in the life of individuals, yet through tradition it concerns and relates to all.[5]

Openness is of course an important theme in Heidegger, and much of Patočka's discourse here can be read as the appropriation of a key Heideggerian motif. Of special relevance is the thesis in Heidegger that openness belongs to the basic structure of *Dasein* as standing in truth, in the clearing that it is.[6] In Heidegger this is tied, as in Patočka, explicitly to human freedom—not freedom as a capacity to choose, or as a matter of inclination or constraint, but freedom precisely as the movement of openness. According to Heidegger:

> Freedom is not merely what common sense is content to let pass under this name: the caprice, turning up occasionally in our choosing, of inclining in this or that direction. Freedom is not mere absence of constraint with respect to what we can or cannot do. Nor is it on the other hand

mere readiness for what is required and necessary (and so somehow a being). Prior to all this ("negative" and "positive" freedom), freedom is engagement in the disclosure of beings as such. Disclosedness itself is conserved in ek-sistent engagement, through which the openness of the open region, i.e., the "there" ["*Da*"], is what it is.[7]

However, Patočka argues, in Heidegger, freedom as engagement in openness is by and large pursued through a reflection on those manners of human comportment that are directly oriented towards openness, to truth, so for example in art, philosophy, and science. Such an approach does not, for Patočka, capture the full range of human comportment, which is not in all its forms aimed at the *explicit* cultivation of openness, even if at the same time all such forms belong to its horizon and with that count among its fundamental conditions:

> Open comportment . . . ever dependent on phenomena, is of a temporal-historical nature; it is always in movement, coming out of the darkness and flowing into the darkness of concealment, and with respect to meaning breaks up into various partial movements. Only one of these is oriented to the theme of openness, manifestation, unconcealment, and its transmission. Others focus on the rooting of humans in the open realm of the common world of humans and on the protection and preservation of that world.[8]

All human life is lived in the open, but not all of it is directed towards its explicit cultivation. All of freedom presupposes disclosedness, but the concrete unfolding of life in disclosedness is not a matter of pure freedom. And if the cultivation of openness is in turn something intrinsically historical, then even if all human life is historical, it is not always lived in the explicit mode of a historically oriented consciousness or self-understanding. By extension, this means that it is possible for there to be more or less historically determined epochs, or forms of communal life in which history unfolds in ways that do not make it explicitly a theme, favoring instead other tendencies of equal human primordiality.

In this way the problem of something like a "prehistory" or even a "non-history" presents itself. If we are to attempt to understand history, the meaning of history—the chief aim of the *Heretical Essays*—then a reflection on forms of the "natural world" that are mute with regard to history becomes a clear desideratum. It is equally clear that such an attempt requires more than an orientation to what is explicitly aimed at in the cultivation of openness. A broader view is needed, one that is attuned to the full range of the dimensions of existence.

CHAPTER 3

In this connection, Patočka cites as a resource for such a project Hannah Arendt's *The Human Condition*, with its elucidation of the roles of labor, work, and action in the constitution of the human world, a line of reflection that recalls Aristotle's distinctions of *poiēsis, praxis,* and *theōria*.[9] Just as Arendt's categories of analysis do not completely map onto Aristotle's, so Patočka's do not completely map onto Arendt's. Nevertheless, the two projects are fruitfully read in conjunction, their differences perhaps deepening an understanding of the implications of each.

Central to the reflections of Patočka and to some extent Arendt as well is the thesis that the question of the origin of a properly historical existence entails the emergence of a specific political-communal form of life. For Patočka, this is in turn coextensive with the question of the possibility of philosophy itself, for philosophy begins, he is convinced, only where history and politics have already taken hold. Accordingly, a reflection on prehistory aims to describe the context of possibility in which something like both politics and philosophy can emerge as the twin progenies of history.

This double (or perhaps triple) beginning in Patočka's account is intrinsically problematic in character, not only given the obvious problems of historical reconstruction, but in its essence. Prehistory does not simply designate a preparatory empirical development in which the conditions for the possibility of politics and philosophy, and thus history proper, are neatly put into place. It designates instead a condition against which both must struggle, since prehistory represents as much an original impediment to the beginning of philosophical existence, as it does its condition of possibility:

> Philosophy does not begin *ex abrupto*; it does not come into the spiritual world where it merely fills in some kind of empty space. Rather, it comes into the spiritual world where there exists something that both helps and hinders its origin and development. It hinders before it helps.[10]

The emergence of the form of historicity that opens the shared horizon of politics and philosophy is a struggle, one in which not only is the possibility of historical existence at stake, but equally something that must in the end be sacrificed in order for history to emerge as a form of self-consciousness. The gain of history comes only at the loss of prehistory. The beginning of history is for Patočka, as it was for Arendt, a decentering of a pre-historical order, a fundamental recalibration of the human landscape in order to open onto something that had always been excluded. In Arendt, this is understood in terms of the rise of the distinction in the ancient Greek world between *oikos* and *polis*, between the sphere of private life and public action, and the gradual precedence of the latter over the former. In Patočka, it will be a decentering of what he describes as the mythical world, in which empire and universe cease to move within the immanence of a shared household with the gods, and life instead surges upward in an adventure of uniquely exposed, transcendent humanity. At bottom, in both thinkers it is a shift from a given world of closed meaning, locked in cyclical patterns that are closer to nature than to human initiative, to an open horizon of a fundamentally shaken, problematic world. Something remarkable is thereby gained, but something is also irretrievably lost:

> To uncover what is hidden in manifestation entails questioning, it means discovering the problematic character not of this or that but of the whole as such, as well as the life that is rigorously integrated into it. Once, however, that question had been posed, humans set out on a long journey they had not traveled hitherto, a journey from which they might gain something but also decidedly lose a great deal. It is the journey of history.[11]

If prehistory is a preparation for history, providing its fundamental possibility, it is one that, paradoxically, also stands in opposition to the same. An interesting example of this is how writing emerges in the context of ancient civilizations characterized by prehistory. Patočka argues that writing in this context is coextensive with the will to tradition and preservation; one might also note that writing is ranged under what Arendt describes as the domain of work, of the efficacy of *homo faber*, and thus among activities such as architecture, literature, and art. Writing and these other activities originally serve the overall aim to create a life form that endures, that can stand against the inevitable loss represented by the endless, repetitive rhythms of consumption and biological life.[12] In this way the emergence of writing represents "a new, extremely effective medium for the petrification of life forms," affording humanity a "petrified memory" that in itself "does not arise in the context of human acts aimed at endowing life with a new meaning."[13]

In writing, the past becomes manifest in a new way, and is present in a fashion that exceeds the capacities of traditions of oral transmission and the symbols of ritual practice. Writing makes effectively available for reflection a past that had, before writing, been more or less immemorial. This thought leads Patočka to distinguish levels of prehistory, thus recognizing the unique kind of pastness that belongs to what remains anonymous because of the absence of its petrification in the human artifice (to adopt an expression of Arendt's), and the "level of prehistory in which a collective memory is preserved in the form of a written tradition."[14] One might cite as evidence here, as does Patočka, the Linear B tablets from Knossos, which appear to be limited to the recording of the economic transactions of the ancient palace, thus representing a minimal form of temporary preservation meant only to buttress the material functioning of the community. Another, very different permutation of this will to preserve are the texts that record the Babylonian origin myth Enuma Elish and the Gilgamesh epic from the library of Ashurbanipal at Nineveh; here too belong the first written versions of Greek oral epic in Homer and Hesiod. Writing in all these cases arguably follows, at least initially, the dominant ethos of the practices it is used to supplement, whether they be material or economic transactions, or the telling of stories related to gods and humans and the distant origins of all things.

This assessment of archaic writing as rooted in a will to preservation and permanence allows us to sharpen the thesis that prehistory both frustrates and provides the impetus for history. As petrified memory, writing potentially frustrates this impetus by further ossifying forms of traditionality against the loosening of its fetters in forgetting, thereby not only easing the burden of sustainability, but also offering stubborn resistance to change. A fixed, univocal past, satisfactory in its recorded permanence and unquestioned in its authority, needs no history.

Yet the very endurance of these ossified forms provides a concrete target against which history proper revolts, a kind of existential foil in which tradition can be characterized more easily as an insufficient mode of life that must be superseded. The very permanence that emerges from a will to closure provides potential traction for an attempt to rise above the traditional world. It provides traction for history itself, for "history represents a distancing from and a reaction against the period of prehistory; it is a rising above the level of the prehistorical, an attempt at a renewal and resurgence of life."[15]

It is thus to a great extent thanks to the ossified presence of the collective memory of the past, and thus a peculiarly visible ahistorical expression of life, that such a revolt is possible: historical life can now clearly demarcate what it is to free itself from, fix what it means to break from what has come before. As examples of the cultural and spiritual loci in which this revolt takes place, one might think here of the treatment of Homer (not to mention the pious Cephalus) in the first books of Plato's *Republic*, a sharply analytical affair far from any immersion in the mesmerizing song of the Homeric rhapsode. Another might be the complex relation of Greek tragedy, as much a manifestation of the new life of the polis in classical Athens as philosophy, and its relation to the Greek mythical tradition as a whole: here too a distance with the past is being orchestrated, through which a certain register of critical reflection is performed. Both philosophy and tragedy represent a complex, critical engagement with traditional ways of thought; both take place on a very public terrain shaped by the interplay of writing and performance; and both mark a distinct break with the past, which is no longer simply preserved but is being thought, re-formed, and subjected to increasingly explicit critique.

More generally, Patočka's thesis is that the organized life of the great ancient empires of the Near East, the preservation of its forms into an enduring, lasting traditionality, provided the opening of a horizon beyond mere existence or life, and thus the possibility of life for something more than life. Here Patočka again cites Arendt, in support of the idea of a properly political life as a rupture with the natural rhythms of the family, or again that distinction between *polis* and *oikos*, which is at the same time a tension and mutual exclusion.[16] This new, resurgent life of the political is not one of the acceptance characteristic of the will to preserve, but is instead driven by *initiative*, by the dynamics of what Arendt understood under the rubric of "acting in concert," which above all entails a conscious embrace of risk. For Patočka, the same also takes the form of an *upsurge*, an irruption of a new form of life:

> Something fundamentally different arises on this foundation, freeing humans from mere self-consumption and dissolution in transience—a life that freely defines itself so that it could define itself also in the future and in others, independently of that foundation. From that moment on this life is essentially and in its very being distinct from life in acceptation; here life is not received as complete as it is, but rather transforms itself from the start—it is an *upswing* [*vzmachu*].[17]

A life lived in the horizon of risk, guided not by what has been, but an initiative aimed at open possibility, in turn inaugurates the inception of a new way of *seeing*. It is a seeing that is no longer sheltered, but exposed to all that is. Life in this way becomes equally political, historical, and philosophical when risk is no longer embedded in a rhythm of acceptances, but embraces a free relation to contingency. Again, this is at bottom the figure of human freedom, or a life of undaunted freedom that Patočka sees echoed in the vocabulary of the earliest Greek thinkers: in the face of the night of existence, it is the lightning-flash (*keraunos* in Heraclitus) leading to wonder (*thaumazein* in Plato and Aristotle).

Patočka, here again citing Arendt and her discussion of the *bios politikos* in Aristotle, thus concludes that politics and philosophy share a common origin, with political life forming its first shoot: "political life at a stroke confronts humans with the possibility of the totality of life and of life as a totality. Philosophical life grafts itself to this trunk and brings forth what is enclosed within it."[18]

In a much earlier essay from the 1950s with the title "Time, Myth, Faith," which stands in remarkable continuity with the reflections found in the *Heretical Essays*, Patočka also describes the emergence of the possibility of history as a particular reshaping of our relation to the future in the form of an explicit rejection of the past.[19] A basic thesis of Patočka's philosophy of history finds one of its earliest expressions here: namely, the insight that time is not simply the phenomenon of the presence of the past, present, and future as indifferent, static dimensions of life, but is instead conditioned on the particular relations that humans assume, each characterized by a particular manner of being *in* time.

Accordingly, Patočka describes in this essay two general styles of grasping the meaning of temporal succession: the flow of time is either (1) grasped as a continuous modalization of what is "already there," thus appearing as a *repetition* of the past; or (2) it is grasped from a resistance to the "helplessness and surrender to an inaccessible past," and thus in favor of a future that has meaning precisely as the *overcoming* of the past, in rejection of its continuing dominance as repetition.[20]

These two styles of meaning are characterized in this early essay as bound together, just as prehistory and history will be some quarter century later in the *Heretical Essays*. The friction between them points to a profound shared dissatisfaction with time as raw succession, an unwillingness to simply accept the mere passage of time as a given. Each style of interpretation is in its own way an attempt to stamp time with a unifying sense: the first with the sense of the abiding of a past that is not gone but returns, and the second with the sense of a future that is not yet but is promised.

In this way, each meaning of time shapes the mere passage of time into the appearance of something that is anything but mere passage, and which in fact effectively lies beyond time altogether as its radical *other*, which thus emerges as a foundational moment in the human experience of time:

> A truly human reflection of time is not possible without the impingement, or better, the call of something that lies beyond our experience, that is, beyond the succession of time traversed by all reality. It is no paradox to say that the human consciousness of time essentially entails a relation to something outside the whole of the temporal world and of the temporal flow. The contact and the relation to this absolute alterity are characteristics of human time.[21]

It is important to emphasize that this relation to the wholly other (*to heteron*, in Patočka's phrasing) is not only true of the revolt against the past, but is equally true of the posture that seeks to repeat it, or to what Patočka in this essay describes as the basic meaning of time for mythical life: "mythical life is a living out of the past, out of that which already is: the past determines all becoming."[22] *To heteron* in mythical life is thus not the promise of the future as a release from time, but rather an expression of the divinity of its beginning. In mythical life, the wholly other marks time through an event, a decision, or an action that originally established the past as an absolute, divine order, and in this way gives the past primacy with regard to the meaning of time:

> Myth has its source in a conception of time that gives primacy to the past. The most general characteristic of myth, namely that it puts us under the absolute supremacy of one or more higher beings, is based on this orientation towards the past.[23]

If we were to recognize, as another option, the relation to the future as a rupture with the past, a revolt against its dominance, it is not one that breaks with a consciousness lost to its past, with no relation to a human meaning to time but pure animality. It is instead a rupture from one relation to what is other than time, which had originally mobilized the irreversibility of the past, for the sake of another relation to the same radical alterity, but now in a manner which mobilizes the potential for the *reversibility* of everything in the opening of the promised future.

Accordingly, the thesis of the rupture of history, so important in the *Heretical Essays*, is conceived in "Time, Myth, Faith" as the rupture of *faith*, or the belief in the eternal other as the truth of life:

> The conception in which the future takes priority can be realized only as *faith*. [. . .] Faith is essentially the belief in life. And to believe in life is essentially to believe in eternal life.[24]

In "faith" (leaving aside the question of whether or not to read the referent of this term as unproblematically religious) *nothing is irrevocable*, nothing need be accepted without question or recourse. This means that life can be redeemed, though not from out of its own immanent reality (this would be what Patočka in this period would call "titanism"), but precisely from out of a new relation to eternity. And this is in turn only because it is possible for human being to break free of itself, sacrifice itself and everything that would stand as a relative meaning or being; only in this way can "God and man act together in the redemption of man."[25]

In contrast to both of these, the modern, nihilistic embrace of relative meanings circumscribed within an indifferent now represents for Patočka a failed attempt to break from both myth and faith as possibilities of inhabiting time. Modern titanism has attempted to shape the dynamics of human openness exclusively in line with the demands of the present, inaugurating a human-centric perspective that seeks to break with eternity altogether, erasing any role of the *to heteron* in order to affirm the human as the ultimate origin and arbiter of meaning. This failure lays bare for contemporary humanity once again the basic existential possibilities of myth and faith:

> It follows that the dream of man's absolute "freedom" within the relative, a relative elevated to the human absolute, is a mere illusion: we are not and we will never be the masters of creation and the creators of meaning. What we can do at most is give meaning to our own life. We can, to be sure, always move further, extend and surmount our limitations, but at the limit of our possibilities we again find the very same possibilities with which man had been faced at the very beginning—the possibilities of myth and faith.[26]

What Patočka describes here under the heading of faith will be deepened and expanded in his account of the common origin of history, politics, and philosophy in the *Heretical Essays*. But equally important is his development in the same text, as well as in *Plato and Europe* and elsewhere, of the theme of myth and mythical life, precisely as a guiding clue to the essence of prehistory and its manner of conditioning the possibility of history. Before turning to a proper explication of the three movements, it is therefore instructive to consider Patočka's reflections on myth, for they provide an importance source of inspiration for the three movements of human existence that lie at the core of Patočka's philosophical anthropology.

The Mythical World

Patočka's reflections on myth are multifaceted and wide-ranging but can be characterized as oriented by two overall guiding theses. The first echoes a familiar trope of many histories of Greek philosophy, at least on the surface: namely, the idea that philosophy distinguishes itself in contrast to a mythical self-understanding, which it criticizes as falling short of the explanatory power that it alone is capable of achieving.[27] Often this opposition is presented in terms of the rise of *logos* at the expense of *muthos*, where the affirmation of the former as authentically rational is pitted against the inherent falsity or naivete of the latter.[28]

Despite obvious similarities, and at the risk of falling prey to an often misleading use of the distinction between *logos* and *muthos* in discussions of early Greek thinking, Patočka's aim arguably lies in a different direction, already signaled in the second thesis: namely, that philosophy as a distinct spiritual posture relies on an enduring mythical framework which, however transformed and rearticulated it may become in the wake of history, nevertheless remains as something existentially originary. Myth, in other words, is for Patočka not a mere transitory cultural form, and it is not at all the embarrassing irrationalism of an ancestral civilization often touted as the birthplace of reason; rather, it expresses something essential about the human condition that cannot be fully superseded, however powerful the contrast and critique of a philosophizing subject striving to break free from its influence.

In general, Patočka's reflections on myth can also be said to represent an interesting development of the problem of the "natural world," that remarkable mainstay of Patočka's thought that determines the trajectory of the development of his phenomenology. All the hallmarks of the natural world familiar from Patočka's phenomenological reflections will continue to play a role in his philosophy of history: its naivete and obviousness, belied by the hidden complexities of the human self-understanding at work within; the rootedness of the sense of the world in life as a movement projected in and among the things of our everyday existence; and finally the pre-givenness of the natural world as the dominant temporal form that gives shape to the universal horizon of experience.

Yet the mythical world is not simply identified with the natural world, but is a particular configuration of the same. Again, the early essay "Time, Myth, Faith" is useful in this connection, since it already contains a summary of what one might call the basic spiritual geography of the mythical world, which will be developed in Patočka's reflections on the problem in the 1960s and 1970s.

A key feature of this spiritual geography is that mythical life is not structured by explicit questions or clearly delimited concepts, but is instead dominated by "mysterious and monstrous images" whose visceral power is taken to be sufficient for the expression of meaning. Truth is present and given expression, but only as contained in metaphorical figures; imagination and reality find no clear separation, coalescing into a shifting whole that issues forth an almost endless wealth of allegorical representations of the human world. In this way, myth appears to be "made up of presentiments and suggestions; it does not say anything definite or universal,"[29] even if at the same time it gives expression to a profound, concrete relation to the whole. But perhaps most importantly—and this is a theme whose meaning will lie at the center of Patočka's later reflections on prehistory—myth expresses a profound sense of *helplessness* basic to the human condition: "Mythical wisdom is the wisdom of suffering that teaches men to endure their terrible, irrevocable, inescapable fate."[30]

Elements of this basic picture of myth are repeated later in *Plato and Europe*, but there the picture is arguably more positive, in that Patočka is keen to recognize what we might describe as the permanent contribution of myth to the spiritual articulation of the human condition, including the meaning of philosophy itself.[31] The reliance of philosophy on myth (and thus of *logos* on *muthos*) is not an accident of development, but belongs to the manner in which human openness lends itself to cultivation. This claim is a bold one: however much it may be the case that history seeks to renew life at the expense of myth, "myth is not something that mankind can shake off entirely and radically";[32] it remains in place as a primary if also suppressed and redirected articulation of the meaning of human existence. In short, "myth is truth," if also an unreflective, in the sense of unquestioned or unexamined, but for all that equally unshaken truth:

> And as long as a human being lives in truth—and it cannot be otherwise, because man is a creature determined by its structure through manifesting as such and manifestation—then that first, radical, and still-*unreflected manifestation* expresses itself *in the form of myth*.[33]

This mythical substratum of human meaning has a basic structure. Unreflected and unquestioned, the mythical dimension of life continues, however broken and intermittent, to articulate the life-space of humans in terms of a contrast between two poles: on the one hand, what is proximate, near, the inner core of life and its flame that carries the sense of safety, of sheltered existence which only lives; and, on the other hand, the distant, that which lies outside of the sheltering offered by others, outside of community and its limited success in the establishment of self-preservation, and which in turn threatens it.

The basic structure of the mythical world thus turns on an inner tension, originating in the fact that the presence of transcendence interpenetrates the sheltered core of immanence. The whole is something inescapable, something whose presence accentuates the finitude of human existence, thanks to which even the enjoyment of the relative safety and warmth of the fold of human care represents an implicit meditation on death, and the ultimate, inexorable breach of the dark outside. The outside, in which there lurk evils and dangers beyond what can be withstood, is present within as a constant, underlying anxiety, stamping even simple enjoyments and the sense of security with what Patočka describes as a certain *two-sidedness*, thus manifesting "the relation between these two terrible forces, between the power that accepts us into the world and the force that crushes and constantly threatens us."[34]

Two-sidedness need not entail a stark contrast between acceptance and threat. There are more subtle and enduring ways that various forms of this opposition remain a constant feature of everyday life, past and present. Patočka invites his interlocutors in *Plato and Europe* to recognize mythical two-sidedness as a familiar structure of everyday experience by citing the popular novel *Grandma (Babička)* by Božena Němcová, a beloved classic of nineteenth-century Czech literature.[35] Were his audience instead Anglophone, Patočka might well have referred to the character of Bilbo Baggins in J. R. R. Tolkien's *The Hobbit*, a novel which begins with a description of the Baggins' home that subtly echoes a variant of the same mythical two-sidedness:

> In a hole in the ground there lived a hobbit. Not a nasty, dirty, wet hole, filled with the ends of worms and an oozy smell, nor yet a dry, bare, sandy hole with nothing in it to sit down on or to eat: it was a hobbit-hole, and that means comfort.[36]

In Tolkien's novel, the character of Baggins carries this opposition with him throughout his adventures, equally comforted and disturbed at every turn, without ever fully being one or the other. A similar psychological profile of anxious comfort or threatened security is characteristic of Grandma, as Patočka emphasizes:

> Grandmother prays right from the first moment she wakes up. This means that from the beginning to the end, she always has this duality present in her mind, it is part and parcel of the elements of her life.[37]

Ancient examples expressing this two-sidedness abound, so for example in the *Iliad*:

> Calling her maids in waiting,
> she ordered a big cauldron on a tripod
> set on the hearthfire, to provide a bath
> for Hektor when he came home from the fight.
> Poor wife, how far removed from baths he was

> she could not know, as at Akhilleus' hands
> Athēna brought him down.[38]

The contrast between the desolation of the battlefield and "the far-away, precarious, touching world of peace" this passage evokes is an important strand of Simone Weil's remarkable reading of the *Iliad*. Commenting on this passage, Weil identifies this contrast as basic to the whole of Homer's epic:

> Far from hot baths he was indeed, poor man. And not he alone. Nearly all the *Iliad* takes place far from hot baths. Nearly all of human life, then and now, takes place far from hot baths.[39]

Mythical two-sidedness essentially expresses in metaphor and image the truth that humans are never truly at home in the world, but are always inwardly rent from the same, through a primordial violence that is both unfathomable and protean. As a result, humans do not dwell in the world, so much as blindly wander within it, to evoke a key metaphor of Patočka's in *Plato and Europe*. These wanderers have a world, revealed to them as a whole, but they do not understand this world in a coherent fashion. Neither the authors nor the competent caretakers of its manifestation, they blindly wander within it, caught between a tension of what is given as home and what breaks and disrupts the very possibility of home. Humans in this way are always in the grip of the possibility of a change of course towards the worse; there is a sense of aberrant contingency that haunts all human projects as that originary tension between good and evil:

> That means we feel in our revealing as people there is constantly the element of what can drive us from one path to the other [good and evil]. We are left to blind wandering. Our human revealedness is the revealing of the world in its whole, but within it there is at the same time this element and this strange awareness of *problematicity*.[40]

The two-sidedness of myth, Patočka argues, can also be discerned in the epic traditions of the great urban civilizations of Mesopotamia. Patočka takes it to be characteristic of the worldview of societies, such as ancient Babylon and Sumer, which had become not only settled communities with complex political forms, but increasingly organized structurally around the establishment of a material presence that, once set into place, required defense. For however great the accomplishment, there remains that all-too human sense of its fragility, the increasing potency of which, spurred on by the advancing success of human establishment in all its forms, leads to a profound awareness of the risk of death:

> In particular what becomes heightened is what characterizes mankind more than anything else: this consciousness of being threatened, a consciousness that while on the one hand we have much more that we can use and can therefore defend ourselves much better and, on the other hand, this very defense takes up so much space, that defense is to a large extent also offense, and this means that it constantly reminds us of the risk of death.[41]

Patočka sees in the epic of Gilgamesh, in particular the ultimately futile attempt of its eponymous hero to achieve immortality, an example of what he takes to be paradigmatic regarding the mythical understanding of death. There are two other examples Patočka cites that, each in its own way, are equally illustrative of how the awareness of death finds its essential expression in myth: the first is the biblical story of the tree of knowledge and the tree of life; the second Patočka describes as the Oedipal "myth of blind wandering" (*bloudění*).[42]

The biblical story receives the least attention in *Plato and Europe*, but it points to something important, namely the link between knowledge and eternity. Following an essay by Walter Bröcker, Patočka interprets the meaning of the two trees in the Garden, the tree of the knowledge of good and evil and the tree of eternal life, as the link between the knowledge of good and evil and the desire for immortality, but in such a way that also determines a certain dependence of the latter on the former: for only the tree of knowledge is guarded with the command not to eat. The implication is that there is desire for eternal life only if one has partaken of the knowledge of good and evil.

Death becomes a problem for humans—and thus release from death a genuine need—only once we grasp that, unlike things in general, we are not right, not in harmony with what is, which is precisely the knowledge of good and evil:

> All things are, and are in order. There is no division between them, no resistance against being, for within them is neither resistance nor non-resistance, within them is just so to speak mute agreement—from our point of view. But not so within ourselves, here there is this hard antagonism. What makes us what we are [knowledge of good and evil, knowledge of eternal life] at the same time excludes us from the rest of existence. We are a creature that is not all right.[43]

This "hard antagonism" within also manifests itself in the experience of work as a burden. Work, especially in its collective forms, is that paradox of realizing human possibilities while simultaneously exposing them to the risk of their being extinguished. Work is foundational for the collective experience of successfully building a world to "stand the test of time," perhaps the most powerful expression of which is the ancient city. Yet works also express a sense of their own futility, of the fact that whatever we build carries within itself the potential for its destruction, loss, and decay. The atrocity of the razing of a defeated city and the enslavement of its population, that sickening refrain in the historical record of the ancient world, follows the same logic: all that is made can be destroyed, all that is free can be enslaved. This hard logic takes hold the more that human communal existence relies on cooperative labor in the endless response to physical, bodily need, to the necessity of addressing material want in practices of procurement and consumption from which humans can never be wholly free.

For Patočka, at the root of all this is a negative awareness of human freedom. Work is experienced as a burden in the sense of being an *imposition* on a potentiality of free life that is expressed here only in its being *excluded*. The necessity of physical self-maintenance, whether in defense or consumption, takes humans away from themselves, from the full potential of their freedom, and it is experienced as such. Work accordingly comes to be experienced as a debilitating form of life that establishes itself only thanks to its being bonded to itself, a slave to life for the sake of life alone.

From the mythical perspective, to be able to act, to pursue the possibilities of life beyond the circumscription of the burdens of work, of life's bondage to itself, is accordingly to partake in something divine. Patočka here cites the Akkadian Atrahasis myth, with its story of the creation of humans to shoulder the burdens of work so that the gods may be free; likewise Gilgamesh who, two-thirds divine, is free enough to strike out into the unknown, in an attempt both to defeat evil and to overcome death itself, but who nevertheless remains limited, and human enough such that both attempts are ultimately in vain.[44] Behind all of this—the desire for an impossible immortality, the awe in the face of acts of freedom that can only be superhuman, the sense of being a freedom trapped by external necessity—is for Patočka the inner grasp of an existential situation of a being that is incommensurate with the world, that somehow is "not all right." The individuation of human existence does not introduce one into a harmonious order of a coordinated indifference of beings, but at best into a harmony characterized by tension, conflict, limitation, and burden.

Work, however, is not simply labor. Patočka's remarks on the establishment of writing in the early civilizations, already cited above, point to a form of "work" that is not easily characterized in the same terms as the burdens of labor. Following Arendt, one might trace here the thread of her distinction between labor as the endless cycle of the fulfillment of need, and that making which yields works, like writing and building (Gilgamesh is a builder of cities, of the great wall of Uruk), which preserve human presence as a kind of material memory, again along the lines already discussed. Equally important is the work of memory as a transformation of the meaning of death in ancestral cults: here a kind of finite immortality, conditioned by the memory of the generations that come after, is established for individuals. In the cult, individuation is no longer a merely physical, bodily affair, but takes on a spiritual dimension that begins to point to a potentiality for selfhood that transcends one's life, as a kind of life between life and death.

Myth itself as a body of representation, initially established within the proto-permanence of oral traditions and raised to a more secured form of concrete memory thanks to writing, belongs here as well. The work of myth expresses the order of things as present and established, according to which there is something like a highest, and with that an intimation, at least, of a relation to the whole, but in a way that folds it back into an apprehension of things as the repetition of a distant, and with that divine past. Moreover, the representations of myth fold virtually seamlessly into an orientation that has as its chief concern the continued maintenance of life, of securing shelter and sustenance. Whatever the whole means, it has to do mainly with the maintenance of those relations with the divine and the vagaries of material conditions that allow for this maintenance of human life within the modest confines of an accepted meaning. Early civilizations such as Sumer and Babylon, and their cousins further west such as Crete and Mycenae, are thus described by Patočka as "great households," *oikoi* firmly integrated into a cosmic order that includes semi-divine heroes, rulers who transcend the ordinary, approximating the power of the divine that far outstrips the common. Empire and cosmos are thus continuous in the mythical world, forming the landscape of beings that are anchored by the burdens of labor and who live within the tight circuit of their care for need.

In the work of myth, work as labor appears as the expression of the burden of life, of the necessity to submit body and soul to unfreedom, a restriction that equally intensifies the sense of one's own freedom precisely as what is being sacrificed for the life of all and the freedom of some. In this way, Gilgamesh as the great builder of Ur stands at the pinnacle of a hierarchy of human toil, occupying a space of freedom that virtually touches on the divine. Yet Gilgamesh is not in full possession of this space, for he remains mortal, quasi-divine at best: accordingly, the loss of his beloved companion Enkidu throws him off balance, and infuses him with a desire to possess what he does not have, immortality, a quest that ends in abject failure.

Gilgamesh's failure to secure immortality leads not to death, at least not right away, but instead back to the city wall, the human cloistering in that shred of what is possible: a life that oscillates between the burdens of labor and its periodic alleviations. The city in this way embodies a truth articulated by the divine Siduri ("the ale-wife, who lives down by the sea") in her attempt to persuade Gilgamesh of the futility of his quest, in a passage Patočka cites as emblematic of mythical self-understanding:

> Gilgamesh, where do you roam?
> You will not find the eternal life you seek.
> When the gods created mankind
> They appointed death for mankind,
> Kept eternal life in their own hands.
> So, Gilgamesh, let your stomach be full,
> Day and night enjoy yourself in every way,
> Every day arrange for pleasures.
> Day and night, dance and play,
> Wear fresh clothes.
> Keep your head washed, bathe in water,
> Appreciate the child who holds your hand,
> Let your wife enjoy herself in your lap.[45]

The two-sidedness of myth all but shines through in these words, as does its evident meaningfulness for the lot of finite humanity. All of life's joys, all the comfort of the proximate are laced with the hardness of the truth of human errancy, of homelessness. To be sure, Gilgamesh does not heed the words of the ale-wife and continues on his quest. Perhaps in doing so he steps beyond the constraints of mythical consciousness for the sake of a human individuality, a personal immortality that might be taken to emerge here as a possibility. But in the end, his failure quite literally re-envelops him in the sleep of mythical life, and immortality remains something irrevocably divine, out of reach of everything human.

There is a harshness to this, as Patočka emphasizes, a harshness that belongs to the openness of human existence as its irremovable nakedness:

> *Myth* is not any kind of consolation, it is not some kind of support, it is not any kind of irrational injection; this is harsh awareness, or if you like

harsh revealing of our revealedness/nakedness [*odhalenost*]. This is myth . . . it is without salvation.[46]

Gilgamesh is a wanderer, grasping at a security in life that continually eludes him, and ultimately lost in between a fragile reality constructed by human hands and a horizon of existence that belongs ultimately only to the gods. Oedipus, the hero of the third exemplary myth that Patočka considers in some detail in *Plato and Europe*, is also a blind wanderer. Patočka is likely alluding to Sophocles's use of the metaphor in the Theban plays, first at *Oedipus Rex* 726 when, at the decisive moment of his first realization of his crimes in the wake of Jocasta's revelations, Oedipus describes himself as set upon by a "wandering soul" (*psuchēs planēma*), and again at the opening of *Oedipus at Colonus* when Oedipus describes himself as a "wanderer," at this point one who is literally blind.[47]

It is important to stress that blind wandering is not a matter of complete ignorance; quite the contrary. Oedipus wanders in the horizon of his own wisdom, caught by that same two-sidedness that characterized, albeit in a different way, Gilgamesh's desire for immortality. Even a wisdom that seems to provide solid ground can always shift into its opposite; any success at having a grasp of things is in the end inexorably exposed to the consequences of its utter contingency, sometimes appearing almost as if nothing had ever really been known at all.

Yet there is more to this. Oedipus is not only shaken by a failed project, but destroyed by an act he could not have avoided, nor for which he can ever atone, and which strikes at the very foundation of his being in the world, and by extension that of the community he ostensibly leads. Oedipus is cursed, defined by an extreme limit of the tension that human existence can sustain within itself. "Home" for the one who kills his father and beds his mother becomes synonymous with crimes that render the very possibility of home impossible, thus hastening the necessity of his exile, and with that the symbolic affirmation of the utter homelessness that always lurks in the shadows of human life. Oedipus is in this way both sacred and damned, or sacred in his being damned, embodying the unapproachable in human existence as an expression of the absolute nullity that lurks in everything. Oedipus is in this way recognizable as an example, as Patočka notes, of the *bouc émissaire*, or the compulsion to maintain, through an act of violence, some balance between good and evil for the whole.[48]

The blind wanderer Oedipus thus expresses in a profound way the condition of not being originally at home in openness, yet at the same time manifest within it, present as something, though precisely in the mode of being out of joint. In this way human homelessness is not cut off from the truth, as if blind wandering were simple absence of understanding. It is instead a wandering within clarity itself, as something in which humans participate, but which is ultimately beyond their competence.[49] In short: "Clarity is the domain of the gods. Man has blindly wandered into it, and man blindly wanders within it."[50]

If the injunction to take refuge in the momentary shelter of everyday pleasures characterizes what one might call the wisdom of Siduri, it forms a coherent whole only when coupled with that of Silenus: for humans, it is best of all never to have been born, and if born, to die as soon as possible.[51] This combined wisdom cultivates a life that is ambitious—these are civilizations that built massive urban centers, achieved an extremely high level of culture, knowledge of mathematics and the natural world, and social organization—but at the same time holds back, retreats in dread of its own hubris that time and again reemerges to compel another impossible ambition of a Gilgamesh, or stumble blindly into another cursed monstrosity of an Oedipus. The meaning of existence cultivated here does not emerge as something autonomous, as the product of a free relation to the whole, however difficult to grasp; it instead emerges in the thrall of a sense that everything rests on a dark ground, one indistinguishable from the being of things, forming the limits of their individuation thanks to which they are encounterable at all.

In this way, mythical self-consciousness lives life in the mode of something like an ontological metaphor, as Patočka expresses it: the transcendent, the darkness that sustains the whole as a space of openness, is present, but only in the form of an inner mystery, expressed by an ultimate distortion of things taken up by an unsure imagination seeking to generate figures of limited, indirect comprehension. Blindness is thus something given, basic to the lot of humans; it itself is nothing inherently problematic, subject to a striving of life to overcome it, but is instead experienced as a recurring pull back to a darkness that is as inevitable as death.

If mythical life is unproblematic, it is so in a peculiar way. Problematicity is not experienced as a call, a challenge to transcend what is given, but this is not to say that such an existence is wholly at peace with itself, content in the dormancy of its freedom or the dream of its metaphors. To live life problematically is to live in the horizon of a search for meaning, for a questioning attempt at understanding; to live unproblematically is to defer the meaningfulness of life elsewhere, as out of reach, but still present in the form of a peculiar awareness of being blind. In unproblematic life there is still an understanding, even an ontological understanding, but one lived as if it were in the deferral of metaphor:

"Precisely because humanity here lives only in order to live, not to seek deeper, more authentic forms of life; precisely because humans are focused on the movement of acceptance and preservation, this entire life remains something of an ontological metaphor."[52]

As such, mythical existence is a form of *exposed* existence. Here finitude has a dark, terrifying significance of not only the inevitability of death, but of a fragility threatened by the arbitrary violence of divine anger that periodically lays waste to the human outpost in a world that is decidedly not its own. Patočka thus sees it as no accident that a version of the myth of the flood, terrifying not only to humans but even to the gods, finds its way into the Gilgamesh epic.[53] It is but one dimension of a sense of finitude not only as a set of limits within which life is possible and meaningful, but also as a relation to an impossible outside. Humanity here understands its limits in terms of the inescapable force of that which lies beyond it, threatening its integrity. Even the quasi-divine such as Gilgamesh, those who strike out the farthest into the realm of the impossible and, with that, into fantastic adventures in a world itself rendered fantastic, ultimately shatter themselves against the constriction of the possible that strikes finite existence at its very core of vitality and energy.

Myth, in a language appropriate to it, thus represents the expression of a definite way of inhabiting the openness of human existence, one that governs the way in which human being in the world is inscribed within a specific form of its unconcealment, its truth. Myth is understood in this way by Patočka as a drama of revealedness, unfolded as something inherently conflictual. For Patočka, this revealedness provides what he describes as the mythical framework for Greek philosophy:

> Greek philosophy arises from the very beginning from the *primeval situation of human revealedness*, from that, that man is the creature who lives within the revealedness of the whole. The uncovering of the whole world by Greek philosophy is the continuation of this myth.[54]

Philosophy is a continuation, but only insofar as it is also a transformation: "it [Greek philosophy] wants to penetrate behind the ordinary blind wandering, or behind the ordinary unclarity and unawareness in which we move."[55] In this way philosophy represents a countermovement to a mythical consciousness that itself represents a particular form of living in time, being in time, thanks to which a tyranny of the past conditions the potential for the other dimensions of time to harbor possibilities of meaning. To evoke the phrase that Patočka borrows from Otokar Březina,[56] if in myth the "answers precede the questions," in philosophy the attempt is to reveal the secrets hidden by this blindness, in order to rediscover the openness from which it and all human comportment draws its sense.[57]

For the mature Patočka, this implies, at least initially, a shift on the part of philosophy to the *present*, to beings in their presence. The correlate here is thus not the hope of faith described in the 1952 essay, a hope in something radically other than the given, that ancient domain of the tyranny of the past, but rather in the wonder that being "is," that there is anything at all. Yet like faith, philosophy as a turn to the present occurs in the experience of the failure of myth, the dawning realization of a fundamental decadence in which any attempt to experience time as something closed ultimately becomes mired, as if whatever has already revealed itself in time has exhausted all there is. The present, in other words, is already potentially incommensurable with the past; it itself represents the glimpse of a whole that stands apart from the multiplicity of things and their articulations, as an openness in the now, one that the past can never fully decide. If faith occurs in the wake of the failure of myth to acknowledge the incommensurability of received meaning with the transcendence of the wholly other, the *to heteron*, then philosophy discovers, in wonder, a glimpse of this otherness in the present, in the difference between things in their familiarity and comprehensibility and the sheer fact that they are at all.

The Basic Structures of Human Existence

Patočka's reflections on myth, and its contrast with philosophy that transcends it all the while continuing to rely on its basic framework, are part of a broader philosophical enterprise of elucidating the ontology of human existence in accordance with the philosophy of the body and movement that emerges from Patočka's phenomenological reflections.

The three movements Patočka describes in which human life unfolds the openness of manifestation are constituted in accordance with three basic attributes. The first is a characteristic *form* that serves to distinguish each movement from the other two; the second is an original meaning or organizing *ideal* unique to each movement; and the third is a specific *temporality* characteristic of each.[58]

As to form, Patočka divides the overall movement of existence into the movements of (1) acceptance, sinking roots, or anchoring; (2) defense, self-extension, self-projection, and everything that belongs to the sphere of human work and labor; and finally (3) truth, or "the movement of existence in the narrow sense of the word which typically seeks to bestow a global closure and meaning on the regions and rhythms of the first and second movement."[59] These three forms clearly interpenetrate, and are always co-present in some figuration or another in human experience.

As to meaning, in *Body, Community, Language, World* (where the entire enterprise is presented in the context of an appropriation of Heidegger's existential analysis of care) the three are likened to boundary situations in the sense introduced by Karl Jaspers: those encounters with fundamental dimensions of experience that fix the limits of possible existence.[60] Among other things, this entails that each movement not only has its corresponding ideal, or original life-wisdom that defines its horizon, but also a corresponding mode of non-understanding or the failure to understand, and thus a characteristic mode of the inauthentic or unfulfilled. Built into the existential structure of human existence is not only the recipe for success, but failure as well.

As to temporality, it has already been established above that human movement is for Patočka intrinsically *ecstatic*, standing out into time as a unity of self-temporalization, and thus is comprehensible only in accordance with the ecstatic modalities of past, present, and future. Each of the movements, as in Heidegger's temporal analysis of care, articulates the whole of this horizon, and is accordingly differentiated only by the relative emphasis on one modality over the other: "The emphasis laid now on the past (on what we passively accept as given), now on the present (which we actively modify), and now on the future (in regard to which the modifying takes place) is what gives each of the three movements its distinct sense."[61]

This temporal differentiation is not merely a question of presentation, but forms the basis for the realization of distinct human possibilities. The past corresponds to what has been established and set into place, allowing for those patterns of acceptance and bonding that are at the core of natality (to again borrow a felicitous expression of Arendt's); the future corresponds to "*that which is coming*," what "is" not properly but will be. This includes the possibilities of transcendence embodied explicitly not only in religion but in art, for this "on the way" is what "humans relate in image, dance, and song."[62] And the present, though in one sense the space in which the tension between the past and the future makes itself manifest, is also the place of engagement and disposal, of an intercourse with the material conditions of our existence as a plenum of entities to be manipulated, organized, and procured for the sake of our possibilities and overall posture towards both past and future.

Again, it is important to emphasize that the whole of temporality is articulated through the lens of each emphasis. The *ecstases* are not temporal strata that coexist in mutual indifference, but interpenetrating syntheses. From the perspective premised on an emphasis on the modality of the past, the future and the present take on the sense of a repetition, a passive reproduction of what is already given in which precisely its already having happened is the predominant mark of its phenomenality. Those possibilities rooted in this modality remain futural and present in turn, but only from a characteristic passivity lent to them by the dominance of an inviolable, irreversible past. In those comportments rooted in the temporality of the present, the mute passivity of the past is broken, and an active relation to things is predominant, yet even here human comportment remains "once more under the rule of the past—a hidden rule, no longer immediate but mediated by things."[63] The present in this perspective hews close to the immediacy of the past, even as it opens a tension with it, thus instituting a mediateness that enables its basic structure as retentional passage.

In the modality of temporalization represented by the future there is more, even radically more at play than a break from a mute passivity in favor of presence. Instead there unfolds here a break of a different kind, this time with the already existent in favor of what is not (yet), and thus "the possibility of not-being come[s] to the fore and sharpen[s] our eyes for that to which alone we can, and must, *give ourselves up*."[64] This remark from the 1970s again looks backward to the theme already met in the 1952 essay, namely faith as a belief in life, an embrace of the future through a relinquishing of all that binds humans irrevocably to a past which is ultimately not theirs even as it forms a basic parameter of their existence. It also looks forwards to central themes in Patočka's later thought such as care for the soul and, ultimately, sacrifice.

With these basic structures in mind, the next step is to turn to an explication of the three movements themselves.

First Movement: Anchoring

The first movement Patočka describes is one of sinking roots, of becoming anchored in the human world, understood in terms of something like an extended birth. Fundamental to all human life is its natality, to recall a central thesis of Arendt's. In Patočka, the emphasis is on natality as a beginning that necessarily takes the shape of an acceptance, a being gradually initiated into the openness of a world already prepared by others who are in a position to welcome the emergence of a new life.

For Patočka, this involves at its most basic level the concreteness of affectivity, and thus of the body, or better of the first emergence of the body as a comportment towards others and outwards into the world. Sinking roots thus means, among other things, the growing into one's own body, or the process of maturation that Patočka describes, somewhat elliptically, but accurately, as the progressive differentiation of life and its activity.

The affective body, however modified and suppressed it will eventually become, is always present in life as the primordial seat of all human activities and engagements with the world. Yet nothing corporeal is static or fixed; as already emphasized above, the body for Patočka is not "a changeless substrate but rather a chunk of lived-experiencing, which, like all experience, is itself a train of changes,"[65] and thus represents the dynamic core of all human unfolding, that thrust of bodily existence that is originally a taking-root in the world.

That the body is originally possible only as conditioned by acceptance means that this first movement of existence is something shared. The body emerges as a figure of human comportment only by first being provided a space in the world by others, those who share in the establishment of a vital core, a proximity of warmth and enjoyment. This vital core forms around what Patočka describes as an axis of *need* and *bliss*: natality unfolds primordially as a "radiation of neediness and the bliss of bonding,"[66] one that compensates radically for that chronic incompleteness constitutive of human animality. This primordial compensation at the core of natality, the triumph of survival in the bliss of acceptance and bond, reverberates throughout all subsequent relations to externality:

> Everything we do, our each and every function leads back and opens into life: every coming out of ourselves shows the way back, life's movement is a closed curve, and the blissful bonding which assimilates the outside without which we could not live is, in a way, a triumph over the incompleteness of individuation, over our sensed neediness.[67]

As can be expected from Patočka's phenomenology of the body, this first movement contains a referent to the earth, that from which the movement of human existence emerges and which remains present as a dark background to all natality, just as it does to all life. Accordingly, the earth always stands outside the limits of the horizon of the groundedness, the sinking roots of existence, but it also sustains and supports all bodily existence in its vital functioning. The earth is thus the indifferent immensity of the whole, as well as that which saturates human life, holds it inexorably from within. As suggested in the last chapter, the body, in its affectivity and the facticity of need and dependence, in this way bears within itself a cosmic significance.

The movement of anchoring, held inwardly and nourished by the earth, also provides a first and primordial relation to the whole of the world, making "this totality live, appear, become a phenomenon."[68] The world first emerges for humans as the phenomenalization of things "contained in the primal cell, in the acceptance of our own being by that which can hold sway over it, protect it, bring it to completion and fulfill it."[69] It is thus not simply the body as the engagement with motor-perceptual unveiling of things that provides the ground for manifestation, but the accepted, protected body, dependent on the other, ordered in such a fashion that yields the fundamental distinction of the "home/alien" as a basic dimension of the natural world.[70]

It is important to stress that even if this dynamic of acceptance, unfolding as what one might call the original body of human experience, first brings the whole into some form of manifestation, it nevertheless is only in the manner of a non-differentiated "outside" of what screens or shelters incipient life. For the world itself does not welcome a new life. This is something that mythical understanding, governed by the primordial structure of two-sidedness, understood on a fundamental level: only those who carve out a human, communal space within the indifferent and overwhelming immensity of the world can welcome a life:

> The world does not accept us in its immensity but rather in its human exponents: in the human micro-community, in human coming together, the world has thrown a span marking off something like an outer inwardness which screens the true figure of exteriority (which it fundamentally is), protecting the inside contents from the overwhelming force of the outside.[71]

This is the justification for Patočka's metaphor of *anchoring*: it is less of a taking possession, than a being given a *refuge*. "Human life necessarily drops anchor in the shelter of this span—it is under this factual and sense-giving condition alone that man can live, growing into individuation out of the bliss of its spanning, the warmth of which screens him from the icy breath of the universe."[72]

However successful the refuge, anchoring is nevertheless a fragile formation. Anchored, humans have refuge, yet remain exposed to contingency. Acceptance is a limited triumph over an incompleteness that remains susceptible to all the dangers that riddle its boundary-situation, defined here as a combined function of physical-biological limits, life-situations, individual capacity, and the fragility of everything made by human hands.[73]

Yet for all that, anchoring is a first taking hold of existence that in turn grounds the other two movements, which simultaneously move beyond it and remain bound to it. As already suggested in Patočka's descriptions of the two-sidedness of mythical truth, it is a shelter that is at once infused with what it shelters us from, for worldly rootedness in the end remains subject to the earth, or the "supremacy of *phusis* in the whole of our life," manifest in "this instinctive-affective prime motion, which constitutes so to say the ostinato of life's polyphony."[74]

In the *Heretical Essays*, Patočka relates this first movement of acceptance to a brief interpretation of the following fragment of Anaximander:

> The things that are perish into the things from which they come to be, according to necessity, for they pay penalty and retribution to each other for their injustice in accordance with the ordering of time [*didonai gar auta dikēn kai tisin allēlois tēs adikias kata tēn tou chronou taksin*], as he says in rather poetical language. (Simplicius, *Commentary on Aristotle's Physics* 24.18–21 = DK 12B1 + 12A9)[75]

Patočka reads this fragment not as an assertion about nature in the metaphorical obscurity of ancient physics, but from a human perspective. For humans, to exist is to be an imposition, and a wholly contingent one: to exist is to be a need one did not choose in circumstances one does not determine, driven by necessity to be addressed in one way or the other, met or ignored, in the course of time. This, Patočka tells us, is the meaning of Anaximander's *adikia*, or "injustice": it designates a being out of place that cannot remain unaddressed, an imbalance that must be bent towards harmony. Accordingly, *dikē* as the compensation for the *adikia* one is, can only be given by others; only the acceptance of others can provide the original amends that meet the demands of necessity and thus make individual life at all possible. Humans come to be in this way as a demand that has no right, and which finds a place in the world at all only thanks to those who set aside their own imposition on things in order to make space for the new. One arrives covered by others.

Though Patočka does not take this step, one might turn to the beginning of the fragment, though it is disputed, and extend the thought. "The things that are perish into the things from which they come to be" would perhaps mean: humans perish into that from which they arose, by making others in turn possible in the same way that they themselves had been welcomed into the world. Now standing on the other foot of natality, individuals in turn (and in time) set aside the *adikia* of others, in this way passing on the potentiality of an existence for which one has no right to others who erupt equally among things as moments of radical, contingent need.[76]

The first movement in this way renders the utter contingency of human natality into something viable, something abiding that is one's *own*, however otherwise unjustified, forming the foundation and condition to which the individual must bear responsibility:

> That we acquire, in the course of differentiated experience [i.e., being progressively more in control of body, of possibilities, inching towards the work-world], a situation which we have not chosen and cannot justify, yet which is nonetheless *ours*, and for which we bear responsibility—this is one of the fundamental characteristics of human finitude.[77]

The Anaximander fragment also points to something else, something that ultimately takes the reflection beyond the first movement. The others who set aside the *adikia* of individuation are themselves more than an inwardness of affective bonding, and must be so of necessity, precisely in order to be in a position to create that sheltering span between secured need and interactions with the outside. Others represent a kind of membrane that gradually, ineluctably draws one into the larger horizon of life, into a domain that demands everything from the beginning life that shelter had managed to establish, and often more. The first movement thus merges inevitably with another, equally corporeal comportment, one that lends itself to functions and differentiations which in turn threaten to unravel everything the first movement seemed to have accomplished. In the end, there is a futility to the bliss and the ecstasy of bonding as a response to radical need. As the dynamics of differentiation unfold, the original "primal cave" dissolves, and "we awaken from this dim slumber into equally vague antagonisms, jealousies, and hatreds."[78]

Each individual comes, in short, to slowly inhabit the lives of others, those who have accepted them, and whose own lives are not limited to the dynamic of this acceptance, but also exist in that broader horizon. All are pulled into this horizon, not only because the whole of the polyphony of human movement is a co-movement with others, but precisely because the original need for acceptance as an anchor of existence entails a fundamental primacy of the other. The "you" is that thanks to which the I, as its original object, is constituted from out of an acceptance that actively addresses a radiating need. In this way, the "you" is an inwardness that actively responds or rejects, in relation to whom one stands in utter dependence, and who remains a permanent beacon in all of one's life, expressed in simple yet profound gestures of human togetherness:

> If it is at all possible to understand this primacy of the *you* over the *I*, so often empirically observed and stressed, then it is only out of an understanding of the movement of anchoring, of its starting point in acceptance and being-accepted: in a gesture, a smile, a mimic, an act, there is an "I can," a control over what I feel in passive helplessness, which signifies a nucleus, a center, a living being.[79]

To be pulled into life is, however, to be pulled into a domain in which everything that belongs to this original affective sphere is, if not erased, nevertheless suppressed. To be pulled into life is in part to learn, out of the demands of material necessity, to suppress the life-giving sphere of acceptance and its affectivity, to act as if it did not represent the core of being, but something that, if not meaningless in itself, can and must be postponed and diverted. In this way the very tension between the first movement of an original anchoring and the second movement, the active engagement with reality, in which humans devote themselves to the tasks demanded of them in order to secure life and meet its needs, leads to a characteristic inauthenticity in which the living core of emotional existence is marginalized, and is taken to be something to tolerate at best but never as something capable of deciding in a fundamental way who one is.[80]

Yet for all its suppression and marginalization, affective life always remains, an ostinato that forever returns, however wide the other movements of life may depart from its basic rhythm. Even once one has become autonomous, seemingly no longer bound to others in a radical sense, but related to others in the world through diverse forms of cooperative action, there lingers that vestige of radiating need, that *adikia* that had inaugurated the movement of natality: "Individuated being does not cease to feel its incompleteness, it does not cease to understand its finitude, its being as a lack."[81] And with that, the other, that first accepting Other more basic than any cooperation or conflict, always stands in as the promise to mitigate this lack, to be the fulfillment of existence, and vice versa: "Precisely this mutual support, this overcoming of our exposure to the freezing cold of the alien throws the span by means of which the world—the other, that which I am not—answers the call of my deepest, of my total neediness."[82]

Moreover, the affectivity of human existence that is so radically shaped by the movement of acceptance and being accepted means that, despite everything, even despite the lingering sense of radical need that marks everything one does, that initial acceptance that makes each individual at all possible remains within. "Life has in it an overwhelming, irresistible moment of wholeness, a wholeness in unwholeness, everything in one instant, making up for all want, all separation and one-sidedness."[83] Affectivity carries, in short, its own unique ideal to which it endures as a lasting witness of its possibility; namely, an ideal that would embrace the immediacy of pleasure, of the happiness described mythically in the urging of Siduri for Gilgamesh to return to the simple love of his child and the arms of his wife. It is the ideal of that sudden oblivion of care in an unexpected turn of goodness erupting in the moment, that out-of-the-blue happiness of the trouble-free expressed in the German expression *Glück* and the Czech *štěstí*.[84]

Second Movement: Securing the World

The second movement—accompanying, in a co-original fashion, but at the same time disrupting the first—Patočka describes as the movement of self-projection, of being drawn into activities organized by possibilities that belong to things and cooperation with others. The second movement requires the affective basis of the lived body, gradually transformed into an original seat of action, but it does so in a way that realizes a potential for the free deployment of the body that disrupts the rhythms of the vital core of sheltered life, compromising the integrity of the closed circuit of need and satisfaction/enjoyment that defines the first movement.

Here the movement is one of giving oneself over to a task, a capacity for devotion that lies at the core of the phenomenon of work. This is also the realm of self-denial, of the experience of necessity met with the fashioning of the world of things and relations with others so as to be able to establish and maintain an environment that shelters and protects. The second movement is thus one of human making, of transforming the material world, bending it to the collective will in order to tend to the cares of life. It is the world of devotion to others, but also one that brings with it conflict and struggle, with regard to the contingencies of both material circumstances and the myriad complications introduced by the plurality of others. It is a world whose rhythm is no longer that of acceptance and the joyful meeting of need, but request and agreement, and their more troubled cousins command and submission, all animated by a debt, a guilt rooted in the hard reality of mutual dependence, with its continual demand for retribution that now takes the form of surrendering oneself to labor.

In this movement, human comportment takes the form of playing a role, assuming a function in a community oriented around the tasks of sheltering, sustenance, and defense. With that come the inevitable patterns of alienation, of being submerged in a social role, resulting in human freedom being subject to an ever more powerful bondage to particular forms of life. Here too humans prove to be earthlings, bound to the earth and ruled by *phusis* just as much as in the first movement; though now the rule of the earth is transformed into a bondage to the rhythms of cooperative action, the cultivation of things, and the demands put upon freedom to secure its earthly individuation.

Whereas the defining boundary situation of the first movement was the double contingency of biological limits and the frailty of the human artifice, here the boundary situation is the struggle, suffering, and guilt that define the extremes to which the world demands the devotion of our corporeal capacities.[85] And if the characteristic inauthenticity of the first movement was its marginalization, here it is alienation, the reification of self and others in accordance with the exigencies of struggle. "The reason is that existence in this entire realm is an *interested* one," Patočka argues, "this is the realm of the average, of anonymity, of social roles in which people are not themselves, are not existence in the full sense (an existence which sees itself as existence), are reduced to their roles."[86]

All of which can be expressed in terms of an ideal of asceticism, of self-denial as "overcoming instinctual, immediate desire"[87] precisely in order to attain the goal of successful action in the accomplishment of tasks. Accordingly, work stands at the very center of the second movement, organizing its rhythm and entire character as a movement of the self-organization of humans in the collective making of their world. Work in its most primordial form is inherently communal, attending to the needs of everyone; devotion here means to be pulled out of oneself so as to provide both for oneself and others. In this way, work also determines how the second movement stands in relation to the first, for only through work, in the existential form of that fundamental being at the disposal of others, can humans create the material space necessary for the acceptance, the welcoming of natality.[88]

Because work has its source in the mutual dependence and disposal of humans, in the bondage of life to itself that is organized therein, it is characterized by Patočka as a burden, that feeling of freedom frustrated from its being and sublimated into something other, giving work the living sense of an existence of dependence. "Work" is thus not understood in the sense of a wholly objective process of the transformation of things, one that would remain essentially the same were it to be performed by machines. Patočka instead describes work as an expression of the human ontological situation in the world: the situation of a freedom in bondage to that which makes its own existence and that of others first possible.

As already emphasized, work is an important theme in Patočka's reflections on prehistory. Central to both the organization and lived experience of the earliest civilizations, work expresses a life centered on consumption and self-preservation. The organization and intensification of work make something like a human world come into being as a work of freedom. Yet as a freedom only negatively expressed by its burdens, it remains an indirect, negative expression of openness, one that is in its essence not only non-historical but actually *anti*-historical: "If we understand work in this sense, then work proves to be not only a nonhistorical factor but actually one working against history, intending to hold it at bay."[89]

Arendt's basic distinctions in *The Human Condition* are instructive to recall in this context. She describes the structure of the *vita activa* as composed of labor, work, and action, each in turn corresponding to dimensions of the human condition: labor to life, work to worldliness, and action to plurality.[90] Arendt's project is to free the discourse of the *vita activa* from those traditional views that would conceive it from the perspective of the *vita contemplativa* (i.e., as its impediment). In this vein, she sets for herself the task of tracing the contours of the *vita activa* by way of a reflection on how, historically, polities have discriminated what should be visible in the realm of the *vita activa* and what should remain invisible.

Of particular importance for Arendt on this score is the manner in which the ancient *polis* defined itself in opposition to the household, the *oikos*, and thus what she takes to be the central role of the private-public distinction in the ancient articulations of political life.[91] And for Arendt, it is significant that work—in the sense of labor—is characterized consistently as a burden in the ancient world, one explicitly associated with pain and suffering. She offers some etymological evidence of this association that could equally be cited in support of Patočka's own depictions of the ancient experience of labor:

> All the European words for "labor," the Latin and English *labor*, the Greek *ponos*, the French *travail*, the German *Arbeit*, signify pain and effort and are also used for the pangs of birth. *Labor* has the same etymological root as *labare* ("to stumble under a burden"); *ponos* and *Arbeit* have the same etymological roots as "poverty" (*penia* in Greek and *Armut* in German).[92]

Yet Arendt also emphasizes a distinction that does not seem to play much of a role for Patočka. Burden and pain are associated with "labor" and its equivalents, namely anything having to do with securing the basic means for living, but this does not include "work" in the sense of fabrication or craftsmanship:

> Thus, the Greek language distinguishes between *ponein* and *ergazesthai*, the Latin between *laborare* and *facere* or *fabricari*, which have the same etymological root, the French between *travailler* and *ouvrer*, the German between *arbeiten* and *werken*. In all these cases, only the equivalents for "labor" have an unequivocal connotation of pain and trouble.[93]

For Arendt, this association correlates with a division in the kinds of things yielded by labor and work respectively: the products of labor are consumed, and are secured solely for the maintenance of life, for meeting its necessities; those of work are used, deployed in a milieu of worldliness irreducible to biological needs, thus constituting a distinctive dimension of human life. The former are marked by a characteristic impermanence, by the futility of meeting needs that soon resurface as if they had never been addressed; the latter are marked by their relative durability as components of what Arendt describes as the "human edifice."[94] The products of the third component of the *vita activa*, namely actions, stand apart from both: "Distinguished from both, consumer goods and use objects, there are finally the 'products' of action and speech, which together constitute the fabric of human relationships and affairs."[95]

This in turn yields an important distinction in Arendt between the human being as *animal laborans* and *homo faber*: the first represents life bound to the condition of necessity that is detrimental to freedom, while the latter life is dependent on the durability of the made as a condition of its humanity:

> Without taking things out of nature's hands and consuming them, and without defending himself against the natural processes of growth and decay, the *animal laborans* could never survive. But without being at home in the midst of things whose durability makes them fit for use and for erecting a world whose very permanence stands in direct contrast to life, this life would never be human.[96]

This distinction between labor and work is important for Arendt, and forms the framework within which she analyzes various historical phenomena, such as the institution of slavery. Yet it is also the fulcrum for emphasizing the role of other aspects of both labor and work; for example, the experience of alleviation and rest that alternate with the burdens of making and providing, offering in spite of all the toil and trouble an overall sense of satisfaction and a palpable sense of being alive. Patočka too emphasizes that the bondage of work is a suffering coupled with the possibility of relief, of the bliss of rest, and even of the erotic and the orgiastic as experiences of the release from pain and burden that are sometimes so powerful as to be associated with the divine.[97]

Even if an explicit distinction between labor and work plays no direct role in Patočka's reflections, it is hard not to speculate that his analysis is inspired by passages in *The Human Condition* such as the following, which describes with great elegance that same cycle of burden/alleviation whose importance Patočka is also often keen to emphasize:

> The fertility of the human metabolism with nature, growing out of the natural redundancy of labor power, still partakes of the superabundance we see everywhere in nature's household. The "blessing or the joy" of labor is the human way to experience the sheer bliss of being alive which we share with all living creatures, and it is even the only way men, too, can remain and swing contentedly in nature's prescribed cycle, toiling and resting, laboring and consuming with the same happy and purposeless regularity with which day and night and life and death follow each other.[98]

Such blessing and joy stand in direct contradiction to the other face of labor, its curse and despair. Together, *animal laborans* and *homo faber* not only represent the manifold ways humans are bound ineluctably to things, to their production and maintenance, but also how in the second movement humans can themselves be *made into things*. For to focus on things, on their manipulation in the moment in accordance with human interests, is also to discover the potentiality for becoming reified, in often extreme ways, in the roles humans assume in the procurement for life. There thus emerges in the second movement a peculiar circuit of function, one that pulls humans into the functionality of things such that they themselves become a function, bound ever more tightly to what gradually becomes a life of things: "on the one hand, we are that 'for the sake of' which the *pragmata* function, on the other hand, we ourselves exist solely for the *pragmata* to be able to function."[99]

Though an intrinsic limitation of freedom, work also amounts to an extension of the domain in which the body holds sway, in that it allows for the formation of something of a "non-organic body" that supplements the original body whose essential aspects had already been revealed in the first movement. In many respects echoing Hegel and the early Marx, Patočka understands alienation as the mechanism of human self-extension into nature, in which the world of work leverages possibilities "taken over from our anchorage," putting them in "the service of instrumentality, continuation, self-projection into things, and self-reification."[100]

If the second movement is not only a disruption but also an extension of the first, it is only at the cost of a reversal of its meaning: need is no longer met within an essentially asymmetrical movement of acceptance. Instead "the task of satisfaction, initially one-sided, now becomes reciprocal," for all are absorbed into the collective movement of labor, and in this way "we mediate for each other the outside which we put to use, while at the same time using one another."[101] This "community of mutually using users . . . imposed on us by life's bondage to itself"[102] is nothing less than the world of work taken as a whole, regardless of whether we view it from the perspective of *animal laborans* or *homo faber*.

This reversal in meaning illustrates the essential antagonism between the first and second movements: despite the fact that together they constitute the manner in which the earth rules within humans, and in this sense jointly form "our original world," each movement can only unfold at the cost of the other's retreat into its characteristic inauthenticity.[103] Just as with repression in the context of the first movement, so too reification, the reduction of oneself to a thing for the benefit of others, stands as a permanent threat in the second: the link to the outside, and the resulting bondage of life to itself, is ultimately a condition predicated on the suppression of freedom as a condition for the mass organization of the community.

Because humanity is always under this existential pressure to literally fashion itself into a world, thereby securing its existence in the face of the contingent material conditions it faces, freedom is in this way always open to exploitation: "man can be put to death," Patočka emphasizes, "life's bondage to itself can be exploited in order to shackle him to the task of mediating with things."[104] Situated, concrete freedom is never unmediated, never free from the possibility that the contingent exigencies of things and the demands of others would necessitate its submission. However decisive the successful securing of the world may be, it is always open to becoming undone, unraveled in a way that may potentially lead to disaster; this extends through all human relations to the very core of existence. However powerful the lord, however secure the situation of the free citizen, all the basic existential conditions that make slavery possible remain. The pressure of necessity ultimately renders everything contingent.

Another of Arendt's observations is germane to this line of reflection. For one might think that Patočka has in mind here political domination, at least in the primitive form of the rise of the master over the many. Yet it is important for Patočka to situate struggle on a plane that, even as it clearly relates to communal relations and thus ultimately to politics, is nevertheless for all that distinctly pre-political. For the violence implicit in the second movement is rooted not in some form of communal organization or other, but in life itself and its necessities. The roots of violence in human existence are thus deeper than politics, or as Arendt puts it: "Because all human beings are subject to necessity, they are entitled to violence toward others; violence is the prepolitical act of liberating oneself from the necessity of life for the freedom of world."[105]

Furthermore, for Arendt violence—again taken as a pre-political entitlement—is in turn operative in that agency of all reification, *homo faber*, for an "element of violation and violence is present in all fabrication, and *homo faber*, the creator of the human artifice, has always been a destroyer of nature."[106] Interestingly, this yields in Arendt's analysis a certain autonomy or mastery of *homo faber* in opposition to *animal laborans* and even the acting in concert of political life proper: for only those who fabricate use objects seem to be, at least potentially, the master of the beginning *and* the end of their products. *Animal laborans* is always subject to the rhythm of biological necessity, according to which there can be neither beginning nor end to one's labors, so long as one is alive; in the case of action, though one may have some control of the beginning, this does not extend to the end, for conditioned as they are by a dependence on plurality, the consequences and meaning of what one does are beyond reach. Only the maker is both origin and at least potential end, precisely because of the availability of a violence unmoored from physical necessity: "Alone with his image of the future product, *homo faber* is free to produce, and again facing alone the work of his hands, he is free to destroy."[107] In this way, in both the manipulation of the material world into an instrument for the satisfaction of interests and the reification of others, violence plays a fundamental and, at least originally, pre-political role in the constitution of the human community.

A similar line of thought, one that traces the origins of political phenomena to a pre-political realm, leads Patočka to distinguish work from struggle, though at the same time emphasizing their unity:

> The organized form of the movement of self-projection falls into the categories of *work* and *struggle*. Work and struggle are two fundamentally different principles: in work man confronts things, in struggle he confronts his fellows as virtually enthralled or enthralling. In practice,

the two principles combine: the organization of humanity for work is the result of a struggle, and is itself a struggle.[108]

It is important to emphasize that, just as the violation of making is not always aimed at the terminus of destruction, so too the violence implicit in struggle—and by extension its presence in the organization and intensification of the community of work—is not only the basis for exploitation, but also for self-formation, the shaping of an "ever more complicated social-natural body."[109] There is also violence in the manner in which, in self-projection, humans bend contingencies to their benefit, and in similar ways bend their own bodies to form together a more organized whole.

On the one hand, the self-projection of labor and work create the conditions for political life, or another permutation of free relation that is not predicated on reification. On the other hand, salient aspects of both, as in Arendt, actually form an obstacle to the emergence of political life. In Arendt, the ultimately inward orientation of *animal laborans*, consumed and limited by toil, stands as a bulwark against the free orientation of equals required for properly political life (in the ancient sense). However otherwise collective, *animal laborans*, "caught in the fulfillment of needs in which nobody can share and which nobody can fully communicate,"[110] is essentially "worldless," unable to form a clear awareness of a horizon of activity beyond animal needs and their satiation. Likewise, the reification of cooperative relations among humans, embodied in the reality of ancient communities (including the Greek polis as much as ancient Babylon) as essentially "consumption centers,"[111] not only helps to shed light on the dynamics that led to the virtual ubiquity of slave economies in the ancient world, but precisely defines the conditions that needed to be overcome in order for a properly political life of individuals acting in concert to be even conceivable. The slave, mired in the wordlessness of *animal laborans*, thus forms the ancient antipode to the life of politics: the slave represents the life that must be utterly rejected for political existence to be at all possible.

Patočka adds another element to this picture. Despite increasing organization, which is often a function of intensified violence and arbitrary authority, there remains an uncontrolled element in such prepolitical societies, or what Patočka describes as a "chaos inside and out." This chaos is predicated on what he calls the "absence of the essential" that characterizes the labyrinth of an ever more controllable and manipulable reality lost, as it were, in the untruth of its increasing reification.[112] By "absence of the essential" Patočka refers to the manner in which human openness, however in play it remains in the first two movements, nevertheless suffers a certain displacement, distortion, and exclusion in each. In neither does the openness of human comportment, much less the whole revealed in this openness, come to the fore as its own theme, or as a distinct parameter of human existence. If anything, each of the first two movements represents a turning away from the transcendence of the whole: the first movement, despite its cosmic resonance, is a being-given-over to the passivity of affect and the acceptance of proximate life in the intimacy of its individuation; while the second movement is the giving of oneself over to the regime of work and the exigencies of struggle, so bound to things so as in the end to become one.

The passivity of the first and the submission of the second movement stand as fundamental obstacles to the third movement, which is described by Patočka as the emergence of possibilities inherent not in the substance and permanence of human existence, but in its *meaning*, and in this sense to what is essential, and even *eternal*.

Third Movement: History and *Polemos*

The third movement is described by Patočka as the movement of existence "in the more narrow sense," that is, the movement within which existence itself is brought to manifestation as theme and problem. Accordingly, the third movement aims at the articulation of the meaning of the whole, from out of the possibilities inherent to the openness of human transcendence towards what is. With its very unfolding inherently frustrated and disrupted by the first and second movements, the movement of existence is disruptive in turn, seeking a freedom that breaks from the passive, monotonous bondage of life to itself, for the sake of an existence that is no longer mute, a freedom completely absorbed in things, whether in their affective or practical disclosedness. It is, in other words, an attempt to escape the inescapable, that domination of the earth that coalesces into the grip of finitude in the first and second movements of human existence.

Yet at the same time, this disruption of the first two movements in the third is also an attempt to inscribe the former within a meaningfulness that relates them to the whole, thus in this way revealing their reality, their fundamental human importance. The freedom germane to the third movement is an attempt to escape the domination of the concrete, but at the same time to illuminate all the dimensions of human existence in what is also their affirmation. The third movement, in short, is the attempt to give meaning to the human condition, for which meaning is not something ready made or given.

The boundary situation relevant to the third movement is finitude itself, the same finitude that is ever-present but never fully thematic in the first two movements.[113] Accordingly, its characteristic mode of inauthenticity is blindness before one's finitude, the ultimate nothingness of death.[114] It has already been shown earlier how this unfolds in the mythical representation of the world in the figure of blind wandering, epitomized in Oedipus, but for Patočka generalizable for the perspective of mythical life as a whole. On the one hand, myth represents a profound reflection on mortality, yet on the other hand it is this only in a way that falls short of the ideal of clarity and insight, which for Patočka will be paradigmatic of those historical attempts to break through the dominance of earth as a will to embrace finitude, and with that the human condition as openness.

Here it is helpful to come full circle, as it were, and return to Patočka's reflections on prehistory that open the *Heretical Essays*. It is important to emphasize that the third movement, as an inner relation to the truth of finitude, is not absent in prehistoric humanity, only occluded. Because prehistoric humans live in something like an ontological metaphor, where openness is not an explicit theme but is in a permanent state of deferral, the third movement is at most something implicit, hinted at in a world dominated by the first two movements.[115] Gods, heroes who straddle the abyss between divine and mortal, epic adventures that take place in far-flung, fantastic realms—all this gestures toward a domain or dimension of existence that is subordinated neither to the demands of acceptance nor of defense, thus hinting at something of the eternal. Yet for all that, prehistory for Patočka is defined by a sense of the presence of transcendence failing to form the horizon of a comportment that would belong essentially to human beings, thereby providing a point of departure from which to give shape to human life as a project of meaning.

Yet for all that, even as the movement of existence breaks free, in a limited sense, from the bondage of earthly life, it unfolds on the basis of its accomplishments. Here again one can point to the role of writing in the transmission of tradition, and by extension, as argued above, the entire sphere of what Arendt called the domain of *homo faber*: the whole gamut of the artifact world collectively provides a space within which the movement of human life gains permanence, substantiality, and with that a visibility that mere life as the natural rhythm of need and consumption fails to achieve. To be sure, this permanence is also fragile, its accomplishments temporary; at most it provides the traction for a reflection in which possibilities for meaning, or better for the explicit manifestation of the whole as a unity of sense or meaning, become actual or real. Writing in particular, both extending but also transforming more archaic modes of human preservation aimed at the possibility of meaning (such as oral traditions and ritual practices), thus serves as a basic presupposition for the development of those dimensions of human life in which articulations of a relation to the whole are established, reflected, but also transmitted trans-generationally, such as religion, art, and myth itself.

In order to better elucidate the dynamic of the third movement in relation to the other two, one can again turn to Patočka's conception, cited earlier, of history as comprised of three stages, roughly defined by the preponderance of one movement over the others, but importantly never at the exclusion or simple absence of any one of them. The first would be a "natural," non-historical humanity that cleaves close to the sphere of affectivity, but which has not yet unfolded the potentiality of memory and memorialization contained in the permanence of the human edifice. Here humanity takes the form of an unsettled roaming which, despite being in possession of language, is nevertheless blind to its own potential with regard to both the movement of self-projection as well as meaning. This is not because such possibilities are simply absent, but rather because humanity in this particular mode never embraces, so to speak, these possibilities in an attempt to assert its presence, to stake a claim for itself on the level of understanding.

Patočka tends to identify this condition, somewhat superficially, with so-called "natural" peoples, including ancient nomadic societies. Yet the basic point can be made even after a more nuanced understanding has been articulated with regard to the organizational possibilities, both social and material, realized by nomadic communities, thus avoiding the prejudice for properly settled, agriculturally based societies as the locus for the emergence of history proper. What is essential is not planting seeds and piling up stones, but creating a humanized landscape that is open for the progressive saturation of meaning. There is no reason in principle why this could not rely on the forms of tool-making, plastic arts, animal husbandry, writing, and the complex relations to land and sky characteristic of developed nomadic civilization.

The essential difference between non-history and the second stage of prehistory is the suppression of the instinctual, and thus a kind of self-inflicted violence that opens human beings to the self-transformative potentialities inherent in the other two movements of existence. Prehistory proper witnesses above all the flourishing of the second movement—here humans project themselves into the world based on the successful establishment of the material conditions that allow for denser concentrations of population, large-scale collective activity, and the social organization of making and fashioning. Paradigmatic for Patočka are again the great civilizations of the eastern Mediterranean, Sumer and Babylon, but also Egypt and Mycenae; many of his descriptions also find resonance in the examples of ancient China and other empires with a distinctive urban component, from Japan to the ancient empires of the Silk Road to ancient Mesoamerica. The center of gravity in this reading of history is the city, organized around the securing and sustaining of life; in this way these great urban centers of the ancient world embody for Patočka the productive potential of alienation and the mass organization of human activity.

In Patočka's historical reconstruction, blind wandering, though now transformed by writing and the emergence of a more defined experience of meaning, remains characteristic of these earliest civilizations. Here again the theme of the whole, the dynamics of reflection and the sense of the meaningfulness of all that is, does not find a free space to unfold, but is frustrated by its incorporation into a mode of life that is absorbed by an oscillation between the burden of work and its alleviation that represents a cyclical return to affective enjoyment. Meaning here is indeed present, finding its expression in myth, which means it is present but at the same time suppressed. An understanding of the whole infuses mythical expression as an inner rendering of particular things and personages as fantastic, as instances of worldly individuation that harbor a sense or meaning of the order of the whole within them, yet without giving way to their particularity and limitation. In this way the ontic, thus internally misplaced, marks the opening of a more universal meaning. The epic representation of heroes (more than human but human) traversing a terrain of the world both familiar and strange (mundane but more than mundane) serves to provide the articulation of a meditation on the meaning of the whole that has not yet broken free of the inevitable limitations put upon it by decidedly earthly existence.

Accordingly, meaning is present as if it were as pre-given as the earth itself, rooted in a past that has always already been decided, within a fold of acceptance in which "answers precede questions." If the third movement represents the upsurge of a new experience of meaning, the emergence of meaning as a problem of clarity and insight, it is only thanks to the *shaking* of this mythical meaning. The shaking of the meaning that life had always rendered in ways appropriate to its bondage to itself represents for Patočka the fundamental condition for the emergence of history—history in the sense of human standing out in separation from the past, even while at the same time experiencing the inevitable affirmation of its inescapability.

That shaking contains something positive; that it is not merely the experience of breakdown or an encroaching darkness; that within it humans grasp the possibility of being directed towards something of a fundamentally different character than the ordinary, rediscovering the entirety of human existence in a different light—this is what Patočka describes as an *upswing*, a breakthrough of life rising above mere life, above an existence that would remain bound within a relation to being that holds itself to the limits of the ontic.[116]

The beginning of history proper—and thus the third stage of history in the wake of the non-historical and the pre-historical—is first and foremost for Patočka the birth of political life, and the birth of philosophy as the reflective articulation of the possibilities of the same. Accordingly, given Patočka's unflagging emphasis on the central importance of the Greeks, the polis forms in his thinking the central motif of the life that breaks forth from the shaking of pre-accepted meaning. In the upswing of history from prehistory, the city is accordingly transformed from the site of human self-organization and preservation to a space of self-creation and action, or what Arendt describes as the "space of appearance" in which the words and deeds of individuals acting in concert become manifest and known.[117] For Patočka, the polis is also the space that allows for the emergence of an insight into what is that takes on a form essentially different from blind wandering: life is now something whose openness at least potentially lends itself to insight. What it is to be a human being as such is now the terminus not of a repetition of what has already been established, but of an accomplishment, a striving for a clarity that humans can claim as their own.

Patočka often relies on a decidedly Heraclitean formulation of this distinctive character of the life of the polis. He describes the unity of its being as something that lies in opposition, in the manner in which conflict, tension, in short *polemos* provides the ground for a unity in opposition. This unity not only allows for but demands the new discipline of insight, in the form of *phronēsis* as the practical capacity to read a situation in terms of the potentiality for action. The connotation of *polemos* as war and not simply strife (*eris*) is relevant here as well, in that the new life demands the fortitude of entering a space of risk *inter arma*.[118] *Phronēsis*, in Patočka's reading of early Greek thinking, is tied to a capacity to see, to judge things for what they are in the light of their *phusis*, which now means their *being*. To see is to see things as they emerge into openness, in this way tying *polemos* to openness and how humans stand in this openness.

This new world governed by *polemos* rather than by given meaning is a world of initiative; the time of life is now political through and through, a "time for . . .", its potential no longer limited to the maintenance of the ever-recurring cycle of want and procurement/consumption. Now humans engage their openness as the coming into presence of the most fundamental potentiality of human existence, the work (*ergon*) of the human being, to evoke Aristotle, whose fulfillment is expressed by the concept of *arēte*, human excellence.

Though such excellence will retain something of the divine, and carry forward in this way the framework of myth, it will no longer be the quasi-divinity of heroes such as Gilgamesh and Enkidu. Their divinity was pre-formed, given as decisively and incontrovertibly as their finitude, which means in turn that, however active and powerful the heroes of prehistory, they represent in the end a decidedly passive relationship to finitude, and thus ultimately an inauthentic form of the third movement. Life in strife, political but also philosophical life, is by contrast an active relation to finitude, an embrace of the risks of action and a new transcendence that carries with it a sense of the limits of sense, not as a fate to be passively accepted but as a challenge to push forward. Life in *polemos* is thus a life in risk, and as such brings with it a new form of shared existence, one now marked by what Patočka describes as the "solidarity of the undaunted": the new, now very political bond arising out of a willingness to risk everything for a life in the open.[119]

Patočka here by and large follows the European historical tradition in ascribing to the Greek polis an achievement unique in the ancient world.[120] The polis is understood by Patočka as a space of exception, a revolt against the futility of life summed up in that double wisdom of Siduris and Silenus described earlier. Yet at the same time, for Patočka this breakthrough of political life is never complete, least of all in the historical example of the polis. Existence remains a polyphony of different registers of movement, and one might argue that in the end Patočka's reconstruction of this very familiar story of the emergence of the polis in fact seeks to emphasize a fundamental continuity with other forms of urban civilization that preceded it, as well as the variety of departures from the ideal of the polis even in those historical moments that sought to articulate their self-understanding with an appeal to it directly or to its descendants (the Roman *res publica*, the Holy Roman Empire, the republicanism of the American and French revolutions). Ever co-present with the other two voices, the breakthrough of existence proper, in all of its particular historical manifestations, represents a new configuration that inevitably renews old problems, rediscovering a different voice from which to position oneself in the openness of existence.

One might understand this as a more nuanced formulation of a similar idea found in Arendt, who ranges labor, work, and action in a linear sequence within which each figure of conditioned existence poses a problem that is solved, or better "redeemed" by what follows. *Animal laborans*, "forever subject to the necessity of labor and consumption," is redeemed through the world-making function of *homo faber*; likewise, in turn *homo faber*, whose world is in the end meaningless, given "the impossibility of finding valid standards in a world determined by the category of means and ends," is in turn redeemed by the meaningful narratives of existence provided by speech and deed, memorialized in the living memory of the polis. It is as if, Arendt tells us, "from the viewpoint of *animal laborans*, it is like a miracle that it is also a being which knows of and inhabits a world; from the viewpoint of *homo faber*, it is like a miracle, like the revelation of divinity, that meaning should have a place in this world."[121]

The polyphony of Patočka's three movements has a somewhat different structure, given that it is not so much a linear progression as a threefold set of tensions. But for all that, the sense that each movement answers to a lack in another, precisely in a fashion that reveals for the latter some miracle of its own fullness, is certainly the case. The third movement thus comes into its own not merely with the representation of life in the meaningful stories of individuals who have decidedly entered a public sphere at the expense of the private, but with a transformation of the meaning of that struggle constitutive of the human community. *Polemos*, conflict, now takes on the role of origin: war is no longer limited to the protection of the already given, the security of those human things that are constantly under threat; instead, conflict becomes that space within which human beings come into their own as open to the spiritual potential that lies in the very contingency and risk of conflict. *Polemos* in this way emerges as the miracle of a deeper meaningfulness of finitude, of the very futility of existence that otherwise blinds humans in their wandering.

Philosophy thus begins as an experience of this shaking of mythical life, of this break with acceptance, or better: philosophy begins in an openness to the shaking of meaning with which history begins: "The point of history is not what can be uprooted or shaken, but rather the openness to the shaking."[122] What this means—what, born of risk, philosophy reveals about the new experience of meaning characteristic of properly political existence—will be the subject of the next chapter.

4

On the Care for the Soul

The Meaning of History

Karl Löwith, at the beginning of *Meaning in History*, notes that the phrase "philosophy of history" was coined by Voltaire, in an essay that marks the moment at which Western thought begins to break away from the dominance of a theological conception of history. Despite its radicality, Löwith explains, Voltaire's project falls well short of an outright rejection of the traditional idea of history itself, instead affirming its basic inspiration, even structure: his aim essentially boils down to replacing the will of God with the human will, Providence with Reason. This substitution is not a simple matter, however. Löwith characterizes this moment at the turn of the eighteenth century as a "crisis in the history of European consciousness," from which will eventually emerge the conception of history as determined by progress that would mark so indelibly the European self-understanding of the following centuries.[1]

The crisis was sparked by the reluctance to let go of a deeper conviction that there is something at all like an "end" of history, in the sense of a meaning: the waning of a faith in a providential purpose thus called for a substitution that would satisfy an enduring need for meaning. And in fact, this basic conviction is what Löwith takes to be determinative of any "philosophy of history" before or after the crisis of the Enlightenment, regardless of when the term was actually coined. Accordingly, a philosophy of history is "a systematic interpretation of universal history in accordance with a principle by which historical events and successions are unified and directed toward an ultimate meaning."[2] This idea of the course of history governed from within by an ultimate meaning—making its comprehension more than a mere explanation of events by way of their relation to local causes and conditions—Löwith traces to origins in Hebrew and Christian eschatology, and he follows its development through to its secularization in the modern idea of progress.

Löwith's thesis will be of interest in what follows, in part because it operates on the plane of the history of ideas in a manner that has much in common with Patočka's approach, but also because it offers a useful point of contrast. Patočka also takes up the question of the meaning of history in the third of his *Heretical Essays*, and it arguably functions as a central motif throughout his historical reflections. Patočka also develops a similar interpretation, broadly construed, of the respective roles of Christianity and secularization in the genesis of the modern understanding of history. Yet there are salient differences as well, which point to decisive elements in Patočka's mature conception of human historicity, as well as his diagnosis of the spiritual condition of contemporary humanity.[3] And above all, the contrast with Löwith will help clarify why the Platonic theme of the "care for the soul" comes to play such a prominent role in Patočka's late reflections on the philosophy of history in works such as *Plato and Europe* and "Europa und Nach-Europa."[4]

To bring out this contrast, and to prepare the ground for a discussion of Patočka's conception of the care for the soul, several aspects of Löwith's analysis are of particular significance. The first is his emphasis on the emergence of the philosophy of history as a decisive break with antiquity. For the ancients, the very idea of a "philosophy" of something that is in such a state of flux as historical events, Löwith argues, would have been nothing short of paradoxical: "To the Greek thinkers a *philosophy* of history would have been a contradiction in terms."[5] This is perhaps overstated, lending too much specificity to the concept of philosophy, and overlooks the ways in which a Thucydides or a Herodotus in fact participated in a shared set of concerns with philosophy, especially with regard to the task of understanding the human condition. The break in question has more to do with an attitude that is arguably more Christian in spirit, with its suspicion, articulated poignantly by Saint Paul, that worldly wisdom falls well short of being capable of comprehending what ultimately drives the course of events, much less determines their meaning.[6] Thus it is perhaps better to say, modifying Löwith's thesis, that the break with antiquity was not so much triggered by the inhospitable reception of the ancient perspective to a new idea of history, as it was by the deep dissatisfaction of the new consciousness of history with the putative authority of traditional modes of thought, including philosophy.

More important is Löwith's deeper point, that historical consciousness represents a break from the ancient belief in the cyclical character of time, the "eternal recurrence of the same" that backstops the role of fate and necessity in all things natural and human, in favor of the perception of events as a movement toward a specific, but as yet unrealized end (*eschaton*). Augustine is a good example of a thinker who not only represents but insists on this break, which he considers essential in order for the faithful to fully recognize the radical singularity of the birth and crucifixion of Christ.[7]

The ancient conception of the cyclical time of the cosmos minimized the significance of the future, whereas just the opposite is the case for an eschatologically oriented historical awareness, for which the future looms large as the object of hope. History has a meaning for the latter, to the extent to which it stands in relation to the promise of a fulfillment, the realization of a condition that is felt to be lacking. The singularity of events and the hope in a final fulfillment thus go hand in hand, forming the basic justification for a linear conception of history. This was a clear break from ancient expectations, ultimately mythical in origin, which were rooted in the belief that what has already been will be again, fate itself being that subsumption of the future to the past, as if the former were already present in the latter. Here it is not hope, but a mythical and, later, a tragic (or perhaps tragicomic) perspective that holds sway, expressing a fundamental sense of being trapped in time.

The rise of the new understanding, which Löwith traces to the Hebrew prophets and their Christian heirs, is tethered in this way to the positing of an explicitly transcendent meaning, thereby lending the future a measure of autonomy in the face of what has been.[8] The future thus becomes determined according not to the past, but to a hoped-for transcendence, and can be so determined only through such a transcendence.

It is difficult to underestimate the significance of this break with antiquity. Once it has taken hold, one consequence is that, absent the certainty of faith, whether religious or secular (such as the faith in progress, defined by an ideal state), the future in itself becomes radically opaque. And opaque in a way different from the ancients, as Löwith emphasizes: for them the future, precisely because it was predetermined, could in principle be known, even if humans often fell short of the insight necessary for it to be revealed, and were left to depend instead on the divination of mysterious signs.[9] If it has a meaning, then this meaning is precisely what it would mean to know the future as the present. For the new conception, however, it is transcendence or nothing; either hope is fulfilled in salvation, or the future brings nothing but arbitrary, empty meaninglessness.

This is a key point: the secularization of *Heilsgeschichte* into *Weltgeschichte* is not a return to the ancient conception of the order of time, in which the unforeseen mutability of fortune and the wheel of time are simply accepted as inherent to the human lot, whether in sadness or stoic withdrawal. For both Christianity and thinkers like Voltaire, the future is *provided*: it is provided by the will of God for the former, by human reason for the latter. This means that the collapse of faith, of hope in that which is to be provided, does not revert to the same kind of present future characteristic of the ancient wheel of time, but instead threatens the groundlessness of a "to come" that is no longer provided by either God or humanity.

Löwith speculates that the confrontation of these two principles—the cyclical time of the ancients and the linear time of Christian eschatology—seems to have exhausted the options for a functioning philosophy of history.[10] This is even true, Löwith argues, for someone like Jakob Burckhardt, who in his *Force and Freedom* (Löwith's first of thirteen case studies, following a reverse chronology) emphasizes in place of a properly eschatological end a linear, continuous conception of history, where "continuity as understood . . . is more than mere going on, and it is less than progressive development."[11] Continuity promises a kind of stability or endurance of meaning that depends neither on a philosophical principle nor an eschatological end, but on a consistent and comprehensible series of historical self-appropriations and interpretations sustained across generations toward the cultural achievement of what Burckhardt calls a "historical sense." This idea of historical sense seeks to split the difference, so to speak, between the constancy of the wheel of time and the fulfillment of an *eschaton*, without thereby providing a genuine third option.

It is instructive to emphasize that the history Löwith reconstructs—the history essentially of the philosophy of history—is marked by an inherent complexity, which in Löwith's treatment is the result of myriad attempts to reconcile the push and pull of these two competing conceptions of historical time. His reconstruction weaves together Augustine's conception of Providence anchored in a transcendent God, where meaning is revealed as Truth, and the future is the culmination of a transcendent purpose at the end of an irreversible and unrepeatable time; Vico's transformation of Providence into an immanent teleological principle of development, one wholly constructible in strictly empirical terms, even as it continues to bear the sense of the wholeness and finality of the original; Voltaire's attempt to displace all theological concepts with the principles of humanism, thereby enthroning humans as the new lords of history; and Hegel's Absolute cunningly appropriating limited, finite forms towards the development of its ultimate spiritual fulfillment.

At each moment in this history of the philosophy of history, there is often a contradictory mixing together of cyclical and eschatological conceptions of time. The most intriguing is perhaps Vico, for whom Providence is no longer bound to an absolute end, but is replaced instead by the give and take of progress and decadence within its overall horizon, or what Vico describes as the unending *ricorso* of downfall to the *curso* of progress.[12] Also of interest, given Patočka's understanding of these questions, is Nietzsche's Zarathustra, who *wills* eternal recurrence, as if the renewal of an ancient indifference to the very idea of historical ends could fulfill, against all expectations, the need for the fulfillment of precisely those ends.[13]

The complexity of this history of the philosophy of history, generated by the unstable mixing of ancient and modern conceptions, leads Löwith to one of his core insights:

> Modern man is still living on the capital of the cross *and* the circle, of Christianity and antiquity; and the intellectual history of Western man is a continuous attempt to reconcile the one with the other, revelation with reason. This attempt has never succeeded, and it cannot succeed unless by compromise . . . for how could one reconcile the classical theory that the world is eternal with the Christian faith in creation, the cycle with an *eschaton*, and the pagan acceptance of fate with the Christian duty of hope?[14]

Underlying this paradox is an abiding commitment to history itself as what Löwith describes as "the scene of man's destiny,"[15] which is precisely the commitment which leads Western humanity to turn again and again to the legacies of the cross and the circle, however ultimately disappointing such legacies turn out to be. The promise of fulfillment and salvation, the core gesture of *Heilsgeschichte*, retains its grip even after the rise of secularism precisely for this reason, and the mere recognition of this fact—which is the chief goal of Löwith's work—changes nothing. Löwith himself thus concludes that the philosophical importance of such reflections is not to somehow provide a solution to the contradictions, but rather to raise "the question of whether the 'last things' are really the first things and whether the future is really the proper horizon of a truly human existence."[16]

Patočka has an intriguing answer to just this question, but only if one first modifies several of Löwith's assumptions that brought him to pose the question in the first place. For Patočka has a very different account of the manner in which history becomes a problem of meaning, one that entails an emphasis on a different, if related set of spiritual themes whose origins can also be found in ancient thought, but which have to do more with the reconstruction of the history of philosophy than with the history of the philosophy of history.

Perhaps the most important assumption of Löwith's has to do with the operative sense of meaning when it comes to history. In the third of the *Heretical Essays*, "Does History Have a Meaning?" Patočka begins by evoking Frege's sense/reference (*Sinn/Bedeutung*) distinction, or the distinction between meaning as a way of conceiving something, and meaning as the establishment of an objective referent. Löwith arguably works within the horizon of the former: the issue has to do with ways of conceiving history as a meaningful whole, and thus its "concept" broadly construed as a "sense." Patočka's own approach operates with neither sense of "meaning," at least not unambiguously. It has instead to do with what he describes, evoking Heidegger, as "material intelligibility," or the meaningfulness that accrues to things thanks to the very manner in which humans comport themselves in the world, and which thus belongs to "that deeper background of living we have in mind when we speak, for instance, of the meaning of suffering, the meaning of anxiety, the meaning of corporeity."[17]

To illustrate this, Patočka turns to a consideration of the phenomenon of *value*. Value means that "being is meaningful," that it speaks to human beings thanks to their openness for such an engagement, or their concern with the significance of things. The fact that things are of value is ultimately rooted in the horizon of a fundamental non-indifference to things as a whole. Value expresses this dynamic as if it were something autonomous, an objective feature of things, but in fact it speaks to something deeper with regard to the possibility of an engagement with things at all:

> Value is nothing but the meaningfulness of what-is formulated as if we were speaking of something autonomous, as if we had to do with some "quality," as we used to call it, while in reality the point is that nothing can appear to us except in a meaningful, intelligible coherence, in the framework of our openness for the world, which means fundamentally that we are not in the world as indifferent observers, as witnesses, but that being in the world is the point of our being in its innermost sense.[18]

Meaning in the sense of value is something quintessentially concrete: as a value, being is meaningful as something affirmed in what it is, enduring even if not permanent. It maintains its integrity only so long as it is either experienced as a settled meaningfulness in itself, affirmed as non-problematic, or as standing relative to something else, identified in some way with what is experienced in itself as non-problematically meaningful—such as God, or a principle believed to be universal and sufficient. There is thus a fixity to value that entails a certain resistance to the need to question, an autonomy of the given as that towards which humans comport themselves.

Yet value and the establishment or justification of values do not exhaust the full horizon of what Patočka means by "material intelligibility." The meaning of meaning, so to speak, is also conditioned by fundamental experiences of the *loss* of meaning, of the disruption of precisely any apparent integrity of the fixed meaningfulness of value. The axis of this experience of loss is the same as its establishment, for meaning is nothing "for itself," but is instead rooted in human openness as the space of its discovery *and* loss. Accordingly, "we are no less open for the meaningful than for the meaningless," the stage on which the drama of each unfolds as inextricably entwined with the other.[19]

This drama of meaning and openness, of discovery and loss, is implicit in the third movement of human existence explored earlier, and gives expression to the shaking of meaning that lies at its core. Meaningfulness here encompasses a perspective on its own development, and that includes history as an emergence out of the shaking of pre-given meaning. At bottom this has to do with the question of the human relation to truth, to the openness of the whole; but it also has to do with the problem of the essence of human freedom. To be open to both the accomplishment and loss of material intelligibility is to be free, and in this way the question of the meaning of history, or the meaning of anything, must in the end be understood within the horizon of the problem of human freedom.

Nevertheless, while the meaning of history is for Patočka in an important sense the meaning of freedom, in an important sense it is not. This can be seen as a consequence of Patočka's elaboration of the three movements of human existence. Freedom in its most primordial sense is and always has been a part of human existence, even for those non- and pre-historical humans for whom history, in Patočka's account, remains effectively dormant. Freedom is built into the way in which human lives unfold as shared existence; it is interwoven with all the movements of human reality. The more humans comport themselves toward the revealed possibilities of their shared world, the more they discover and experience different forms of cooperation and harmony, but also domination and submission, success and failure. Something like this is obviously true of even animal life, and continues to be true for humans in the wake of the beginning of history: the struggle among those who would dominate and those who would liberate remains as if indifferent, at least on one level, to the advent of history proper.

Where freedom does not remain indifferent is the freeing in the wake of the third movement, and with that the breakthrough of history, of the problem of freedom precisely *as a problem*, and that means on the order of meaning and meaninglessness. Freedom becomes a problem in history on the order of significance within which the entire question of what it means to struggle is understood, and by extension what it means to be (to accept, to feel, to be happy, to labor, to live, to die), to again evoke the theme of *polemos* that closed the last chapter.

For Patočka, what emerges in the ascendancy of historical consciousness is thus not simply a new interpretation of history and human events in time, but rather the experience of a more demanding meaning,[20] one that can respond to the problem of freedom, thereby rendering intelligible even otherwise debilitating experiences of the loss of meaning. It is in and perhaps as this more demanding meaning that something like freedom comes into its own in a new way, thus indicating the sense that indeed the beginning of history is the beginning of freedom, or at least of a more demanding freedom whose meaning can no longer be deferred.

But this also comes with the profound risk that meaning, if not pregiven and present in the form of the already accepted, may not in fact be possible at all, that the shaking that propels the emergence of properly historical consciousness may in fact simply resolve into an empty meaninglessness. For if the self-understanding of the relation of humans to the whole as openness first becomes possible with the shaking or negation of meaning, then what if on the other side of this shaking is not a new meaning, but instead nothing like a "meaning" or a "sense" at all?

Accordingly, the first assumption of Löwith's that must be modified is that the two conceptions of time, the circle and the cross, operate solely on the level of the making sense of events, as if their contradiction were essentially one of competing interpretations over a common object. By contrast, if considered in relation to what Patočka describes as material intelligibility, then the implication is that their roots go far deeper, in that both are ultimately motivated by that drive for a more demanding meaning that would both affirm and address the problematicity of freedom, and in this way they belong equally to the horizon opened by the third movement of human existence.

The second assumption of Löwith's to be modified has to do with the role of philosophy. Philosophy for Löwith seems to be either an impediment to a robust philosophy of history, whether in the form of a putative ancient indifference to the idea of history being rational at all, or a more modern skepticism about the ultimate value of the future as the space for human existence; or else it is an ultimately quixotic attempt to provide a rational substitute for Providence as the ultimate end of history, thus appropriating the force of *Heilsgeschichte* by effectively transposing it into secularized form. In short, philosophy is either an unsupportable faith in some meaning or other of history, or it simply cedes the field.

Patočka's perspective is considerably more nuanced, in part because there is arguably much more at stake. As already seen, in Patočka's account there is a common genealogy shared by history and philosophy, and it turns precisely on the emergence of the problem of freedom. Moreover, the origins of historical consciousness and philosophical reflection are so intertwined, that it is impossible from Patočka's perspective to meaningfully disassociate philosophical reflection from historical concerns. Especially with regard to the problem of freedom, it is only by way of an embrace of philosophy as a proper historical problem that an understanding of its essence as human freedom can be ultimately understood. Philosophy and history stand or fall together.

Furthermore, the necessity of historical reflections is above all the case in the context of the discussion of the meaning of that understanding of philosophy that Patočka subsumes under the rubric of *metaphysics*. The problem of metaphysics plays a key role in Patočka's philosophical itinerary, early and late, and plays an outsized role in his understanding of the history of philosophy, as well as his approach to its central problems.

The problem of metaphysics takes center stage in his important 1953 essay "Negative Platonism: Reflections concerning the Rise, the Scope, and the Demise of Metaphysics—and Whether Philosophy Can Survive It." As the title already indicates, the essay is no mere historical exercise, but is framed by way of a diagnosis of the crisis of contemporary philosophy. Patočka begins the essay with the observation that one of the common features of the philosophy of the nineteenth century and contemporary philosophy is the sense that "the metaphysical phase of philosophy has come to an end."[21] The question, of course, then becomes "What is it that died?" True to form, Patočka surveys in broad but illuminating strokes some approaches to this question: there is positivism, with its claim that metaphysics represents a primitive, immature tendency to replace reality with simplified abstractions, ultimately to be replaced by rigorous science; and there is also Hegelianism, with its critique of the ahistorical character of metaphysical thinking, its illegitimate separation of infinite and finite, absolute and relative, in contrast to a proper historical-dialectical reflection. But in the end, Patočka's assessment is that these and other "critiques" invariably fall short, in that they all continue to bear something of the trappings of metaphysics, as if unwilling to break completely free of its influence:

> It is possible to reject a solution and to accept the question—that might be precisely the case of modern humanism. Might it not share the hope of traditional metaphysics for a factual, positive knowledge that would yet have a global significance? If so, then even a putatively antimetaphysical modern philosophy would still bear a metaphysics within it.[22]

Patočka's own approach is to engage in a historical reflection precisely in order to reconstruct the *question* that metaphysics attempts to address, and thus to assess its crisis in light of its original motivations and their abiding contemporary legacy. The project is thus critique in the sense of probing deeper into metaphysics, unearthing its originary problematic, in order to recognize what is genuine in its original philosophical motivations while at the same time searching for an alternative response, which is here understood explicitly as an alternative *historical* possibility.

It is only in the context of the reconstruction of this history that the role of philosophy in the various determinations of the meaning of history can be fully understood. The history of the idea of history, in other words, is not separate from the history of metaphysics, nor by extension the crisis of contemporary philosophy. They are inextricably combined. More, it is only the fate of the search for an alternative to metaphysics that will provide the basis for Patočka's answer to Löwith's question "whether the 'last things' are really the first things and whether the future is really the proper horizon of a truly human existence."

Socrates and Plato

Patočka's reflections in "Negative Platonism" and elsewhere on the origins of metaphysical thinking, though set in a broad historical perspective, center above all on the figures of Socrates and Plato. These reflections are intended to be historical in character and form, yet they are equally guided by Patočka's phenomenology and, in his later writings, by the philosophy of movement that represents its mature expression. Accordingly, the themes of manifestation, phenomenality, and being that organize Patočka's phenomenological thought come to play an important role in his historical reflections.

This path from phenomenology to ancient philosophy is of course well-worn. It is characteristic of Heidegger's thought, but also that of Eugen Fink, a friend and mentor of Patočka's and former collaborator with Husserl whose work provides a great deal of inspiration here.[23] An important point to make in engaging any of these thinkers is that it would be a mistake to take such historical reflections on early Greek thought as a series of philologically suspect phenomenological reinterpretations of ancient philosophy, at least if we understand by that the anachronistic application of themes and ideas alien to the latter. The premise instead is that one can and must work from a common ground, however obscure and in need of reconstruction.

If phenomenology takes any precedence in Patočka's historical considerations, it is only legitimate to the extent that it itself can be understood in terms of an attempt to rediscover the possible forms of life from which all philosophical activity ultimately draws. Patočka is convinced that phenomenology, construed precisely in this way, has a deep connection with philosophy in its very earliest forms. This is above all the case for him with regard to the ancient theme of the care for the soul: the idea of the soul as that which is capable of truth, the care for which is the cultivation of the original relation of life to the openness that forms the horizon of the world as something revealed to humans—all of this for Patočka has deep resonance not only with central phenomenological themes, but with the very spirit of the revolution in thought he believed Husserl and Heidegger to have initiated.

Still, an essay on Platonism, however convincing the idea that Plato (or better Socrates) embodies elements of a kind of proto-phenomenological thought, might seem indeed to be an anachronistic strategy, especially if it is intended to be a response to the contemporary crisis of philosophy. The cogency of the attempt stands on the assumption that the critique of modern metaphysics, articulated by Heidegger, brings phenomenology closer to the original questions and themes of Socratic thinking. It is Patočka's conviction that this is the case which draws him to Socrates, both in the 1953 essay and repeatedly thereafter.[24]

Inspired by Heidegger, much of this project is thus guided by the need to address essential characteristics germane to the specifically modern, technological reinterpretations of metaphysical themes, which Patočka believes have degraded the autonomy of philosophical thought in favor of a focus on power and the exploitation of the natural world. The most important of such reinterpretations is arguably the radical anthropological orientation of modern thought, in which the agency of thinking is no longer that of a contemplative soul open to the world, but the technical organization and mastery of things. This entails the transformation of essence into the secured representation of being in the form of a certitude that rests on the affirmation of the subject (which comes, as Heidegger puts it, to function as *subiectum*). It also entails the rise of a planetary thinking that exhausts the meaning of that which stands in the open, where this openness becomes "unworlded" to the point that transcendence itself no longer stands in any form of autonomy vis-à-vis human beings.[25]

That such a world, or an un-worlded environment of human domination, a fully humanized whole that anticipates all possibilities within an infinitely variable and flexible means of calculation, can be the source of unease, of anxiety and dissatisfaction, is for Patočka the contemporary version of the ancient sense of the state of the world as something in decline. And, with that, the story of Socrates—and of the task of understanding Socrates independently from the rise of the metaphysics that followed him—becomes poignant for contemporary thinking. It is not simply the fact that Socrates and Socratic thought engage themes germane to phenomenological philosophy that draws Patočka's interest, but that Socrates embodies an attempt to turn explicitly to the problem of the experience of truth as a response to the pressing sense of a world in decline. Socrates is important for Patočka, in other words, because he too was a philosopher of crisis, perhaps even in a paradigmatic way.

A philosopher of crisis, but one of a very particular kind, both with regard to motivation and method. The core motivation of Socratic philosophy is the need to spurn the decadent world in order to reestablish a bond with truth, affirming it as the ultimate guide in all human affairs and thought. This in turn expresses a unique response to the wonder of manifestation, itself a play of revealing and concealing, in its attempt to catch a glimpse of the eternal foundation of all that is. The manner of approach is everything: if Socratic thought is to fashion itself as a viable countermovement to decline, then the attempt to reestablish a bond with truth, to grasp the eternal, must take a specific form, one that (unlike myth) proceeds exclusively by way of the route of *justified* thought and speech, thus opening and establishing a uniquely *secured* path.

This partisanship of justification is accordingly identified by Patočka as the fundamental gesture at the core of Socratic philosophizing. As Patočka puts it in *Plato and Europe*:

> This *justifying* is the philosophical task that concerns us. To find something upon which stands the rest, and to find it in such a way that we might build in a solid, unshakable, tapped from the presence of existence itself, way everything that surrounds us, is the program.[26]

This program is not yet what Patočka understands by metaphysics, though it forms its fundamental presupposition, its basic horizon. Metaphysics is at root the attempt not only to renew an experience of truth through an ethic of justification, but to fix manifestation in a decisive, complete fashion, and with that to settle the problematic nature of what manifests. Metaphysics in its most raw form is thus a genuine, if also limiting species of a more original program of justification, in that it forces justification into a specific, ultimately constrained pattern of inquiry in its attempt to drive the journey to a final completion.

There is a fundamental contrast operative in Patočka's reconstruction of the rise of metaphysics between the potential for understanding justification as a posture within the horizon of an *embrace* of problematicity, and a sense of justification that understands its ultimate task as the *elimination* of problematicity. Patočka is tracing, in other words, what one might call the prehistory of the concept of *certainty*, understood, as it was in Heidegger, as a distortion of the original impulse of philosophical life.

It is easy to see why Socrates, who often frames even his most cherished convictions as questions, is fated to gain such prominence in Patočka's project, especially in the context of the "Negative Platonism" essay. Socrates in fact plays several roles. The first is the most patent one: Socrates has for Patočka virtually the status of an embodiment of Western philosophy in its earliest form, refracting in a single figure all the fundamental elements of the new way of life that had been signaled in the fragments of an Anaximander or a Heraclitus. As such, Socrates offers leverage with regard to Plato, in the attempt to recapture the basic themes and spirit of pre-metaphysical or pre-Platonic thought.

Socrates thus represents—perhaps even for Plato himself—a transitional figure between an originary proto-philosophy and the more theoretically systematic edifices of Platonic (and, subsequently, Aristotelian) metaphysics:

> It seems certain that in the figure of Socrates we have before us, in Plato's writings, a special active, anthropologically oriented version of this philosophical protoknowledge. Plato, the creator of metaphysics, remains rooted in this premetaphysical soil and seeks to capture and exploit it by describing the figure of Socrates.[27]

Second, Socrates stands for Patočka as a kind of "symbol of philosophy as such"—not just a particular conception of philosophy, but an allegorical expression of its original promise. This symbolism of Socrates is explicitly recognized as the result of a poetic expression, a product of Plato's literary genius: it is Plato's poetic representation of Socrates that we return to again and again, in order to interpret the very situation of philosophy itself. This is important to absorb: the richness of the literary figure of Socrates outstrips whatever content we might actually be able to historically confirm, for it is by way of the poeticized persona of Socrates that his thought came to stamp the history of philosophical discourse, endlessly priming the perennial reinterpretation of the meaning of philosophical life.

Third, Socrates for Patočka plays the role of orchestrating the problem of freedom. This is explicit: "Socrates' mastery" of dialectic, of questioning, "is based on an absolute freedom: he is constantly freeing himself of all the bonds of nature, of tradition, of others' schemata as well as of his own, of all physical and spiritual possessions."[28]

The freedom exercised by Socrates is remarkable for being a freedom from knowledge itself, or that knowledge of a different register than philosophy which, like value, gradually accrues to human experience in the course of dealing with things, or practical understanding writ large. Such knowing belongs to the rhythms of preservation, and imposes that limitation of the horizon of possibility characteristic of the second movement of human existence. The Greeks understood this domain as that of *technē*, and it is precisely this domain that is transformed radically by the new, audacious self-understanding embodied in Socrates:

> In appearance, it rests on the fact of purposiveness, on the model of *technē*, on the relation between means and ends with which ordinary, routinely practical human life operates. In reality, it uses this model for a leap into a space in which nothing concrete provides it with support.[29]

The kind of knowledge Socrates embodies is predicated on a renewed openness, based in turn on an inner transformation of what it means to know, one that, in breaking free from the rhythms of ordinary life, stands in the open, in relation to truth, in a new way. Socrates represents a countermovement to a more restricted mode of comportment in the space of transcendence, or the openness of human life, which for its part is represented not only by the domain of *technē*, but also by traditional opinions and attitudes about what is most important. The sense of being restricted, the yearning for a justification for what one thinks and believes, is what drives Socrates. This takes the form of a freeing of oneself from the perspectives of the given community in which one lives, but in an important sense it is also a freeing of oneself from oneself, from that familiarity of knowledge and accepted opinion that constitutes the very establishment of human life as the horizon of understanding into which one is born. This is what lies behind Socrates' rejection of his age: his dissatisfaction with respect to tradition arises from an experience of its hollowness and lack of living possibility, its failure to provide a compelling way of seeing things that would satisfy the need for a good life.

Fourth, Socrates inhabits an important structural position in Patočka's reconstruction of the rise of metaphysics. If he embodies protophilosophical knowledge, inwardly determined by a surge of freedom, according to which "the totality of things that are is to be transcended,"[30] it is only so *indirectly*, for it never escapes the circuit of problematicity. Hence the indeterminacy of Socrates, so important for Patočka, the intrinsic ambiguity of the freedom he represents. For genuine freedom in Patočka's thought is inherently problematic, its meaning is never something settled. On the contrary, freedom unsettles everything, including itself, in the wake of what is at first a challenging, ambiguous call for transcendence.

Socrates in this way comes to represent for Patočka the very problem that metaphysics attempts to address. Metaphysics is an answer to the problem of Socrates, to the quasi-anarchic, troubling and subversive character of the problematicity he embodies. Its fundamental goal is to determine a positive knowledge, in contrast to Socratic ignorance, that would articulate in a determinate fashion the realm of transcendence opened by freedom. In Plato, this gesture takes the form of the formulation of the doctrine of the Ideas, which will become in the tradition the very paradigm of eternally fixed meaning.

Yet while Plato's Ideas are explicitly metaphysical in Patočka's sense, they nevertheless continue to bear a "Socratic element," insofar as the Idea remains something towards which humans *strive*:

> Here *Idea* is understood as a unity over the many, anchoring the principle of a hierarchical order that makes a strict demonstrative method possible [thus serving as the basis for logic]. But *Idea* is also a goal and a model that confronts us—that is a Socratic element.[31]

Just as it is important not to overstate the "metaphysical" meaning of the Ideas, it is equally important not to overdetermine the association of Socrates with freedom. The story is, predictably, more nuanced in Patočka. Socrates does not represent an unambiguous break with the pre-shaken, traditional meaning that precedes the rise of philosophy, nor does he necessarily represent an alternative to metaphysics, at least not in the strict sense. As Patočka himself emphasizes, Socrates is in fact best understood as a defender of traditional life and values, but by other means.[32] Socrates seeks not a new morality, but another orientation with regard to the basic principles of the old one, aimed at rejuvenating a sense of the whole it reveals through insight rather than mere acceptance or naive ignorance. This is part of what informs his status as a transitional figure in Patočka's interpretation: Socrates is a new and unique kind of traditionalist, one who seeks to reestablish an older morality in the face of the shock of the political and social crisis of Greek life in the wake of the Peloponnesian War: "In this situation and this atmosphere, Socrates defends *with new methods* the old; he defends the thought that it is important not to harm, that it is better to undergo injustice than to commit it."[33]

This can be illustrated by the scene in the first book of the *Republic*, Socrates's discussion about justice with Cephalus, the patriarch of the household Polemarchus brings Socrates and his companions to after the oddly belligerent (but in a friendly way) encounter at the festival of Bendis in the Piraeus. Cephalus, the old man at the end of his life busily engaged with various religious rites in order to pay his dues, represents the old, fading traditional morality that is clearly losing any significant influence over the younger members in the company, especially Thrasymachus, who will shortly advance such an amoral conception of "justice" that he will emerge as the virtual antipode to the humble milquetoast religiosity of Cephalus. The latter of course is not quite a one-dimensional figure: a *metic* in Athens who sold arms during the Peloponnesian War, Cephalus played an active role in a world well on its way to ruining itself; if he still plays at being pious, it has already become a hollow gesture, far from embodying the ethos of traditional morality in any compelling way. If Socrates questions the meaning of the conception of justice operative in the ritual practices and traditional attitudes Cephalus plays, seeking its more precise definition, it is not in order to give a final kick to an already tottering edifice, but instead to rise to the challenge of finding a renewed foundation for the old morality. It is arguably Cephalus's grip on the meaning of what he does that is the issue for Socrates, not the meaning itself. And if Socrates employs methods similar to those of the more belligerently amoral Thrasymachus—who represents nothing less than the desire to finally break free of all impediments to unlimited power that the old, sick morality still manages to put in the way—it is not in order to embrace the heady impulses of a newfound freedom, but on the contrary, to expose the tyrannical tendencies of the same.[34]

In Socrates, the response to the world in decline is at first negative, grounded in a negative freedom that refuses to simply accept what is thought by the simple virtue of the fact that it is what one thinks. The demand for justification alone, and not the possession of the truth, is what forms the deceptively simple foundation of Socratic dialectic: that complex of ignorance and passion for inquiry so important to understanding Socrates. In this sense he is an enemy of all traditionality that would seek to remain unquestioned, unyielding to the demand for justification. Yet Socrates is equally the enemy of any cult of freedom or the will that would infer from the failures of tradition the license to break free of all limits, to allow for the unrestrained pursuit of desire and passion. As such, Socrates practices a willful ignorance, rejecting everything until the goal of justification has been met, until the demand for meaning has been satisfied.

Nevertheless, Socratic ignorance is also something positive: as a practice, it does not submit to, but actively cultivates non-knowing. Ignorance itself, not suffered, not feigned, but practiced, becomes the unexpected road to truth. Socratic ignorance is not a simple dead end or mute closure against which the desire to know rages, but on the contrary a radically open and questioning posture that seeks to grasp the known at the very root of its possibility. This is also what makes Socrates a distinctively pre-metaphysical figure, but at the same time, paradoxically perhaps, the origin of the "essential philosophical thrust" that will remain embedded in metaphysical thinking.[35]

This thrust is a facet of the peculiar experience of freedom, which hews close to experiences that are inherently non-objective, "negative," in a way that loosens the ties of our ordinary beliefs, right down to our trust in the objects given to us by our senses:

> Wherein does the experience of freedom consist? It is the experience of dissatisfaction with the given and the sensory, intensified by the growing awareness that the given and the sensory is neither all there is, nor definitive. For that reason, too, "negative" experiences are decisive for the experience of freedom, showing as they do that the content of passive experience is trivial, transient, and insubstantial. . . . It is these experiences that show that what initially appears as unreal, a matter of fantasy or a mere construct, can be more important, more significant than mere passive reality, that it can bestow meaning upon it.[36]

But what is this freedom itself? In the 1953 essay, Patočka's emphasis is on its intrinsic non-objectivity: freedom is not positive being, a something among somethings. From the perspective of metaphysics, it can only be negative, and with that dissatisfying, empty. Things given in perceptual experience are, by contrast, content-rich, they offer themselves as substrates for possible objective determinations. In freedom nothing is "given" in that sense at all, only freedom itself as the capacity for a peculiar negating separation with regard to all that is.

Metaphysics is the attempt to compensate for this nothing of freedom, claiming to discover in the horizon of its transcendence a determinability of a higher order, a kind of super-objectivity to counter the non-objectivity of freedom. Freedom itself, however, remains untouched:

> The experience of freedom contains no vision, no final terminus, which our activity, ever object-oriented, could grasp. The experience of freedom has no substrate, if by a substrate we understand some finite and positive content, some subject, some predicate, or some complex of predicates.[37]

In Patočka's reconstruction, what emerges in the history of metaphysics, beginning in earnest with Plato but already with roots in Democritus, is the gradual eclipsing of this "Socratic element," its occlusion in favor of a philosophy of the object, of what can be substantively secured by the intellect. This takes the form of the transposition of the searching towards the eternal, the nonobjective and thus open transcendent, in favor of the determinateness of the Idea, and with that the ossification of beings into a system of determinate unity governed by the image of the Unity, the One:

> Thus all those metaphysical disciplines... manifest the fundamental substitution of a transcendent, nonexistent Being for the perennial existents, a substitution bound up with the crucial conception of what-is as perennial. Thus the living force of transcendence is replaced by an image of reality which may be harmonious, "spiritual," but is rigid and lifeless; so in place of the living reality of Socrates' struggle against the degeneration of life we now have the imitation of the eternal world of *Ideas*.[38]

In Platonism, philosophy becomes determined both as an imitation of the Ideas, as "perennial existents," and as the instrument of education in the Ideas, in which truth is embodied in a "positive, objective, describable form."[39] This metaphysical impulse in Plato thus seeks to transform the negative movement of freedom: that towards which freedom strives, that towards which it projects a self-relation in transcendence, remains non-real or nonobjective when compared to the things of everyday experience, but only by also becoming a kind of hyper-reality, an absolute "thing" beyond the sensible realm. The Idea in this way becomes a fixed object of the ideal philosophizing gaze, an intellectual objectification of that thanks to which beings emerge from the ground of their possibility, and that towards which questioning and the desire to know must strive.

Yet at the same time, Plato for Patočka is himself a transitional figure; he is more than metaphysics. Plato's writings represent one of the earliest formulations of metaphysical thinking, but also its problematization. "Plato would not be Plato if he were not also more than Plato,"[40] as Patočka puts it. In "Negative Platonism," Patočka cites themes such as the inexpressibility of the matter proper to philosophical thinking in the *Seventh Letter*; the astonishing passage in the *Republic* when Socrates asserts that the Good, the ultimate terminus of Platonic striving, is "beyond being" or existence itself; and, finally, the separation or separateness (*chōrismos*) of the Ideas, which for Patočka continues to bear the mark of the Socratic perspective.[41]

The Platonic Idea, in other words, is in the end something double. On the one hand it is the inauguration of a radical, ideal objectification, the substitution of an ideal being for the openness humans inhabit only as a transcendence; on the other hand, it is "de-objectifying," holding fast a *chōrismos* between the Idea as a terminus of transcendence and the individual, finite existences that fall short of its perfection. The "negative Platonism" that Patočka proposes in the 1953 essay lies precisely in the attempt to wrest the latter function of the Idea free from the former, thereby reviving the proto-philosophical experience embedded in the Idea, at the expense of its metaphysical sense. Negative Platonism is thus a peculiar kind of counter-interpretation, disrupting the metaphysics that would avoid philosophy as a philosophy of freedom in favor of a philosophy of absolute objectivity, by activating the implicitly retained relation to the problem of freedom which, however neglected, remains essential for its functioning.

What emerges in Patočka's reading is thus not really a break from metaphysics *tout court*, but the sketch of a different mode of appropriating traditional metaphysical concepts. The counter-interpretation turns arguably on the theme of *chōrismos*, which Patočka argues is the one element of the Ideas that modern, principally neo-Kantian reconstructions of Plato's thought cannot reproduce. Or at least not once one resists the traditional interpretation of the metaphor as involving an objective separation between *things*, and instead recognizes its original Socratic inspiration, and with that its analogy to the phenomenon of freedom:

> We need to set aside one metaphor suggested by the label *chōrismos*, that of the separation of something from something, of two regions of objects. *Chōrismos* meant originally a separateness without a second object realm. . . . The mystery of the *chōrismos* is like the experience of freedom, an experience of a distance with respect to real things, of a meaning independent of the objective and the sensory which we reach by inverting the original, "natural" orientation of life.[42]

Moreover, *chōrismos* designates that sense of separation operative in rebirth, in initiation, all those forms of transcendence and the exceptional that are constitutive of the most fundamental experiences of religious, artistic, and philosophical life. *Chōrismos* understood in this way becomes the very "symbol of freedom," and in philosophy it designates that which prevents the philosopher from being absorbed back into the mundane naivete of established opinion.

Something similar is the case with the theme of the absolute. The Idea as absolute object bears a peculiar tension in Plato: Idea is Form, but "more basically than the seen, than the Form, it is what enables us to see, to behold."[43] If it is something seen, it is only because it is also what allows seeing at all to occur, like the sun which Plato in book 6 of the *Republic* uses as an analogy.[44] Whereas Heidegger emphasizes this same moment as the beginning of the ascendance of causality as a philosophical theme,[45] for Patočka the Idea is what allows us to see beyond the mere given, to recognize it as something incomplete, thus granting us a certain power of disassociation that represents "the power of liberation from the purely objective and given."[46]

This yields an interpretation of the Idea as that source of the very possibility of knowledge, the nonobjective ground towards which humans strive, thanks to a capacity to stand apart from the fixed reality of determinate being:

> Certainly, the *Idea* so conceived may not ever be seen itself; far from being the object-in-itself, it is only the origin and wellspring of all *human* objectification—though only because it is first and more basically the power of deobjectification and derealization, the power from which we derive all our ability to struggle against the "sheer reality," the reality that would impose itself on us as an absolute, inevitable, and invincible law.[47]

The inner secret of the hyper-real, in other words, is the power of transcendence, the liberation from the tyranny of the real as the objective absolute. It is in this sense that Patočka can sketch, reading Plato against Plato, an idea of a reorientation within metaphysics, within Platonism, in order to bring again this secret to the surface:

> In short, the *Idea*, as we understand it, is the only nonreality that cannot be explained as a construct of mere realities. It is not an object of contemplation because it is not an object at all. It is essential to understanding human life, its experience of freedom, its inner historicity.[48]

Democritus and Plato

The experience of freedom Patočka considers to be fundamental to the origin of philosophy is not, however, limited to the opening of transcendence alone, at least not if what is meant thereby is that towards which philosophical life strives. It is also about the kind of life characteristic of that striving itself. The problematization of freedom opens the horizon of the Idea, but it also serves as the catalyst for the articulation of a different kind of life, a different register of selfhood. Accordingly, coupled with the doctrine of the Idea is the central Socratic-Platonic theme of the "care for the soul" (*epimeleia heautou, epimeleia tēs psuchēs*).

Patočka's interpretation of care for the soul, which apart from the *Heretical Essays* is most prominent in texts such as *Plato and Europe* and "Europa und Nach-Europa," is both powerful and nuanced. It also brings with it a good dose of ambiguity. For what could be a more fraught concept today than that of the "soul"? From a contemporary perspective, the very term is vastly overdetermined by a complicated historical legacy arising from a myriad of crosscurrents of translation and interpretation, periodically infused with a dizzying array of the often contradictory experiences that the concept has been drawn on repeatedly to name.

The Platonic care for the soul is in fact the historical origin of one thread of this complexity, in that it introduces a fundamental modification of the archaic sense of the soul as a breathing, animate body into something very different, but without losing complete touch with its original association with biological life. Plato did not invent the concept of the soul, but he did leave an indelible mark on the philosophical legacy of the concept in the West, as well as other cognate notions such as mind, consciousness, person, and even human being. If nothing else, this complexity means that any historically oriented interpretation of "care for the soul" must pay particular attention to the semantics of the term specific to its usage at a particular historical moment.

This is clearly a necessity precisely in the case of Plato himself. For Patočka, the guiding clue for the interpretation of the concept in Plato is how human existence is conceived in his thought as a specific manner of being *in-between*: the soul stands on the one hand in relation to what is eternal, transcendent, all the while remaining bound in a relation to all that is changeable and individual, or what stands apart from the immutable Ideas even as it continues to participate in the same:

> What is the soul? The soul is the center mediating between principles and between principiates, between what is absolutely eternal and what is close to nothingness in all its character and all its stamp of being, to what, just about, does not exist. The soul is what is movable, but movable in the sense of lawful ordering and orientation to the higher.[49]

Patočka is emphasizing that description of the soul, familiar from Platonic dialogues such as the *Phaedrus*, as the self-moving being traveling between the visible and the invisible realms, between what truly is and what is only in a shadowy, incomplete, and imperfect sense, between the divine and the worldly.[50] This conception of the soul as a traveler between realms is not unrelated to the ancient understanding of the function of sacrifice, acts that mediate between the world of human care and the ancestral favor and divine forces upon which it remains forever dependent. As in the rituals of libation and sacrificial offering, in the Platonic conception the soul plays a cosmic function of holding the extremes of the world together—living and dead, divine and human—in a kind of harmony, as the mover that would weave together radically opposed beings as an expression of the unity of all.

What is new in Plato is the combination of the soul as mediator with a new ethic of *care* (*epimeleia*). Care has to do with the capacity of the soul to give itself form, the possibility of accomplishing an inner integrity, one that yields, as Patočka emphasizes, a heightened, more complete existence:

> The soul that is cared for *is* more, it has a higher, elevated being. This being is, so to speak, thickened, concentrated, it is always the same, it does not dissolve, does not blur.[51]

In short, thanks to the care for the soul, it does not wander—or at least it does not wander like Oedipus, lost in a world it only dimly comprehends, continuously disappointed by its false illusions of security.[52] Nevertheless, care for the soul does not replace an incomplete with a complete wisdom; human finitude remains paramount, and here finds expression in Socratic ignorance. Instead, care is the attempt to shore up the integrity of the finite soul thanks to a clear grasp of its own ignorance, to guard against the vicissitudes of those tendencies for dispersal and dissolution that plague all the dimensions of its existence. It is in this sense that care for the soul constitutes an idea of a heightened humanity, one that "is" more: care means no longer blindly submitting to the consequences of a partial understanding of things, but instead actively turning towards that glimmer of the eternal in itself, of truth, in order to work to shape itself into something more durable, more present, more focused.

The ethic sketched here is clearly one of self-discipline, but in a very specific sense.[53] If philosophy is to be a response to the shaking of meaning, one that attempts to regain some firm ground, then a certain strength and positing of oneself is required, and hence discipline. Yet it is not so much a discipline of self-control and obedience, as one of *wakefulness*. This is precisely that wakefulness characteristic of Plato's Socrates: to orient oneself as a whole towards the intellect (*nous*), towards insight and the potential for insight, is to be wakeful so as not to fall into the trap that oneself is—the trap of the human tendency to be caught in the dissimulating nets of semblance and opinion, dominated by desires and impulses, or seduced by the charisma of others.

The blind wandering of myth thus yields in this way to the wakeful wandering of philosophy, which is directed not only externally but inwardly, and seeks to bring into harmony the multiplicity of elements that make up the inner life of the soul, and in this way draw itself out of the decadent disarray of injustice into the harmony of a just life:

> The soul is just what is capable of taking care of itself, capable of drawing itself out of decline and forming itself into something solid, determined, precise, to find solid relations between each of its components. To establish such precise relations signifies justice.[54]

One is reminded of the advice Socrates gives to his companions at the beginning of book 9 of the *Republic*—the book which tackles the problem of tyranny—about how the philosopher prepares the soul for sleep, that dangerous state in which the soul is vulnerable to the inner dissatisfactions and uncontrolled desires that are normally constrained during the day. One should, Socrates instructs, first strive to satiate the desirous and spirited parts of the soul, within the limits of propriety, and then soothe the whole with "proper speeches," thereby convincing what is unruly in oneself, as much as possible, to be content with maintaining the order of the whole. Socrates seeks to promote in this way a certain habitual lingering of wakefulness even in sleep, extending the reach of rational self-reflection into that domain in which, quite often, what is in oneself but normally is not allowed to show itself in the light of day is given free rein, free license, compromising the peaceful integrity of the soul, like the monsters in Goya's etching *The Sleep of Reason Produces Monsters*. This little scene of the philosopher's bedtime ritual, apparently trivial, serves as a powerful introduction to the figure of the tyrant: for the tyrant is one who allows unlimited license to what lies in the soul that would destroy the same, effectively lacking that guarded wakefulness basic to the care for the soul *even while awake*.[55]

Following Patočka's reflections, the central role of Socrates in the articulation of the care for the soul suggests in effect that Plato's conception, however much it may be bound up with the metaphysics of the Ideas, expresses something basic to pre-metaphysical philosophy as such. Accordingly, it should come as no surprise that Patočka also credits to Democritus a role in the history of the concept, even if locutions of the phrase *tēs psuchēs epimeleisthai* do not appear in the fragments that have survived, and if also the conception itself is at bottom quite different.[56]

In both Plato and Democritus, Patočka argues, the discipline of the soul essentially amounts to a "morality of truth,"[57] a dedication to a life of wisdom. Both embody a spiritual commitment to an older order of things, but one that is marked distinctively by a peculiar blend of a sense of loss and the breakthrough of a new spiritual sensibility. The sense of loss expresses the recognition of the decline of the world, the folly of an order that is no longer possible, but with that not simply false. The power of a new sensibility takes the form of an experience of self as a free action, a choice of oneself in which the soul crystallizes around the necessity to forge itself in a project of self-responsibility.

To be sure, in the one there unfolds, in Patočka's terms, a "metaphysics from above," in the form of the transcendent Ideas, and in the other a "metaphysics from below," in the form of the immutable existence of atoms and void. At their core, however, is the common attempt to focus on what is present, or better, what counts as fully present, piercing thereby through the vagaries of illusion and the shifting fog of opinion. Here that ancient fascination with the contrast between what changes and does not change finds in both thinkers an original articulation: all that is, all the world of shifting and unreliable phenomena, "is" only as a reflection of that which does not change—whether it be the Ideas, or the eternal existents of atoms and void.

Plato and Democritus also share, as Patočka emphasizes, a common inspiration in mathematics as a model for thought. Mathematical form, such as number and figure, is that which gives order to things, which provides for the very sense of presence, allowing things to appear in their determinacy.[58] The inspiration of mathematical form is a key ingredient in the metaphysical gesture basic to both philosophers: in Plato it is the Ideas from above, as the archetypes or relations that definitively fix becoming in accordance with a proper measure (where the soul, as the being that measures or provides the measure, becomes that thanks to which the order of things becomes visible); in Democritus, the ultimate, eternal constituents of unchanging being (void and atoms) form the ultimate foundations for an understanding that reduces the confusion of the phenomenal world to an articulation of form that bears the mark of eternity. For both thinkers, the space of problematicity grounds the possibility for a traversal towards eternal being, and the care for the soul grounds the cultivation of the possibilities of an insight into the fixed and immutable with which to measure all that is.

Yet the difference between the two thinkers makes a difference. In Democritus, care for the soul is understood exclusively in terms of the formation of a capacity to understand, to pursue knowledge of what is fundamental in things, and in this way to bring life into relation with eternity. One thus perfects the soul in Democritus in order to know; in Plato, by contrast, one knows in order to perfect the soul. Knowledge in Plato is not itself the final end, but is ultimately instrumental in making the soul what it can be: "We do not care about the soul [in Plato] in order to understand, but rather we understand so that the soul *will become* what it is not yet completely, *what* it *can* be!"[59]

Accordingly, Democritus's understanding of the self-discipline of the care for the soul focuses on the cultivation of individual "cheerfulness," that constancy of humor necessary for the achievement of wisdom.[60] Plato, with his eye not only on truth, but on the project of improving oneself as a whole, calls on philosophy to provide a new foundation for practical life, understood in its specifically communal form. Accordingly, for Democritus the polis never seems to come into focus as a properly philosophical concern, while for Plato it becomes a central issue, and its reform becomes a fundamental goal of philosophical life.

This is why, in Patočka's reading, it is the Platonic articulation of the care for the soul that proves historically decisive: the care for the soul is understood in terms not only of the soul's relation to the cosmos, but to the polis as well. Justice is the ordering imprint of thought on the life of the soul within the community, the perfection of the self in harmony with others and with all that is, which, for Plato, expresses the ultimate desideratum of an ethics of truth.

Accordingly, Patočka summarizes the theme of the care for the soul in Plato as unfolding in three directions.[61] The first is "onto-cosmological," or the "general philosophical teaching that brings the soul into connection with the structures of being."[62] The already cited figures of the soul in Plato's *Timaeus*, *Phaedrus*, and book 10 of the *Republic* bear witness to this thread: interweaving mythical and cosmological images, the accounts of the soul in these philosophical/poetical masterpieces in which the soul is represented as engrained in the very order and operation of the universe are perhaps one of the most enduring and influential legacies of Plato's thought.

The second direction is Plato's teaching regarding the relation between the philosopher and the polis, where care for the soul plays the double role of envisioning how the state itself can be ordered, so as to be in harmony with philosophical life. This strand of reflection is perhaps most evident in one of the central organizing metaphors of the *Republic*, namely the analogy between the soul and the city: justice is germane to both, precisely because the being-together of the multiplicity that makes up the city is akin to the harmony of the parts of the soul, just as achieving the integrity and coherence of the soul is akin to the successful government of a city.[63] It is also exemplified in one of the fundamental guiding questions of the *Republic*; namely, that if a philosophical life is a properly just life, then what kind of community, organized according to what principles, would make such a life possible?

This second direction speaks, of course, directly to the question of the meaning of the trial and execution of Socrates. So does the third direction, in which the care for the soul is understood as "the teaching about the soul as the principle of individual life that is exposed to the fundamental experience and test of individual human existence, that is, death and the question of its meaning."[64] In the character of Plato's Socrates, this third tendency of the care for the soul—its relation to itself, its own interior reflection, problematized by the radical individuation of death—is in turn tied inextricably to the theme of eternity: not that of the immutable existences, but of the soul's *own* existence.

Here the ancient problem of the inconstancy of all things, the passage of time as the ultimate decay of all that is, becomes articulated in a particularly poignant form. For the question of the soul set into motion by the care for the soul has to do with the ultimate value of any resistance against decline, of all those attempts at constancy, unity, and heightened existence. All of this is at bottom nothing less than a grand "battle against time,"[65] a revolt against the inevitability of decline symbolized ultimately by death.

The ultimate meaning of the care for the soul, in other words, stands or falls on the problem of the human relation to eternity:

> In relation to it itself, the soul is the discoverer of eternity. It tends toward eternity, and its most proper problem—the problem of the status of its own being—is the problem of the relation to eternity; whether in its being it is something fleeting, or whether in its depths it is not something eternal.[66]

The problem of eternity—that peculiar intermingling of the experience of freedom and the horizon of otherness that embraces it—in fact runs through all three of these strands of Platonic reflection. The polis itself, conceived in the horizon of the unfolding of what we have seen Patočka describe as the undaunted life of free being, is coupled in this way with the theme of eternity, the imperishable origin of the meaning of all that is, that archetype in accordance with which the "painter of regimes" (as Plato describes it) crafts images of the state.[67] This idea of the soul intimately related to the eternal echoes the very beginnings of Greek philosophy in the thought of Anaximander and Heraclitus, with their evocation of the ground of all that is, *phusis*, in which, for Patočka, "eternity presented itself to philosophy first in the form of the imperishable wherein lies the genesis and perishing of all that is, its appearing, its waxing and waning, its fall into darkness."[68]

The problem of eternity also lies at the Platonic origin of metaphysics, which weaves these different signs of eternity together. For it is precisely the risk of political life, coupled with the palpable presence of the night of eternity, which yields that impulse toward a *decisive* bestowal of meaning that would, once and for all, resolve all the spiritual tensions inherent to the care for the soul:

> Philosophy, aware of its bond with the problem of the *polis* and sensing in the germ already its perils and perishing, was led by a striving for a definitive and new bestowal of meaning to see in that darkness only a lack of light, the night as a waning of the day. It was led to become, in the continuous clarity of definitive certainty that runs through all theory, a perception of being in which its meaning is exhausted in a new definitive statement.[69]

The problem of eternity also means that, in place of myth, and in response to its shaking, there arises in the ethos articulated by Plato not simply philosophy, but philosophy in the form of a *moral religion*.[70] Instead of the mythical framework that holds humans in a kind of "dream," an unreflected, seemingly permanent state, the moral religion of Platonic thought requires not only a demand for justification, but something like an act of faith. As an act, one in dialectic with justification, faith is alien to the passivity of the mythical world, and in this sense counts as one of the new children of freedom. Thus, even if there are clearly mythical elements in Plato's account of the care for the soul, the central axis of the problem of freedom, the freedom both to question and to believe, marks it off as something fundamentally different. Posited at the foundation of a moral religion, which is perhaps the epitome of the Platonic care for the soul, is precisely the necessity of a choice, a response to the moral demand to shape one's life in accordance with the demands of justification, but with that also a fundamental commitment to eternity.

Plato and Aristotle

Not even a cursory account such as given above of the rise of metaphysics would be complete without a discussion of Aristotle, and this is no less the case when exploring the ancient philosophical concept of the care for the soul. Specifically, Aristotle's fundamental revolution of philosophy, with its introduction of novel conceptions of nature, causality, and substance, impacts directly the three dimensions of the care for the soul that Patočka outlines in Platonic thinking.

This reshaping arguably proceeds virtually from the ground up, taking direct aim at what Patočka takes to be the original mathematical inspiration in both Plato and Democritus. Mathematics in Plato serves as a model for the construction of a hierarchy of being, in which Ideas take preeminence over the imitations of imperfect particulars. The ideality of mathematical form, announcing the sharp ontological differentiation of the Ideas from the objects of the senses, coupled with the capacity for the intellect to deal with such forms in an apparently non-sensory, immediate fashion, is an index for Plato of being in the superlative sense. Aristotle's rejection of the separateness of the Ideas, which in turn downplays the ontological significance of *chōrismos*, strikes at the very heart of that separation of the visible and the invisible so basic to Plato's hierarchy of being. Insight will continue to play a central role in Aristotle, as will a revised conception of a hierarchy or "great chain" of being, but only within the affirmation of an immanence that radically mitigates the separateness expressed in the metaphor of *chōrismos*, lending the being of the sublunary sphere an integrity that it did not have in Plato.

Ironically, this is carried out in Aristotle in such a way as to in effect downplay the role of materiality, at least with regard to the status of materiality as an active principle. As Patočka argues, in Platonic metaphysics the One is combined with the (material) principle of duality or indeterminacy: the One is what provides unity, while the *duas* or duality is what acts as a force of dispersion, unboundedness, of separation into the multiple. "Both of them *are effective*," as Patočka emphasizes. In Aristotle, by contrast, "material stopped being active, material is now mere possibility, only the essential substrate for its forming."[71]

In this way, the ontological basis of the need for something like the care for the soul, at least as it is understood in Plato, is trivialized if not negated altogether in one fell swoop. The whole drama of the soul struggling to maintain its integrity in the face of the active forces of its dissolution, embodied in the image from the *Phaedrus* of two horses pulling the hapless charioteer in two contrary directions at once, is no longer something clearly inscribed in the very order of being. Essence, form, and unity still remain of central importance, and with that the notion of care as self-realization and self-cultivation, but the resistance to the formation of the self no longer comes unambiguously from within, from one's own bodily materiality, which has effectively been rendered the passive vehicle for the expression of possible form.

Yet for all that the conception of the soul as movement, so central to Plato's account, is affirmed by Aristotle, even deepened.[72] It is deepened, paradoxically perhaps, in the wake of the limitation of the horizon of its onto-cosmological significance, or at least a peculiar modification of its universality. In Plato's *Timaeus*, the soul, as world-soul, is that thanks to which existence itself comes into movement: standing at the boundary between the invisible and the visible, the world soul is that which introduces movement into the very body of the world, animating it according to its comprehension of the eternal Same, quickening its participation in form.[73] In Aristotle, this psychic animation of the cosmos is replaced by a divine cause that itself does not move (and thus is without soul, in the Platonic sense). But for all that it remains the case for Aristotle that human life is movement, and on the intellectual plane of *nous* this movement takes the form of a comprehending-revealing of the development (movement) of all things. This renders humans not world souls, but still cosmic beings of a certain kind, for there remains a sense in which the "soul is all things": for as intellect, the soul is the place of all forms, that within which the essence of the all can be comprehended, and thus actualized in a unique fashion.[74] In Aristotle there is thus a transposition of the functioning of the soul, understood specifically as intelligence, from an animating principle of the whole of what is, to an intelligence that fills out and completes the order of nature as a whole.

Yet the most important reshaping of the Platonic legacy in Aristotle is arguably his account of the relation between the soul and the Good.[75] In the discussion of the good life in the first books of the *Nicomachean Ethics*, Aristotle explicitly adopts the Platonic version of the problem of the care of the soul, including its fundamental importance for political life, so standing on the side of Plato in contrast with Democritus on this point. The conception of a "function" proper to human beings, the central role of habit and education in the cultivation of human capacities, the positing of a life guided by the intellect and intellectual virtues as not only characteristic of a "higher" form of existence, but as something of intrinsic political value as well—all of this is characteristically Platonic.[76]

But in Aristotle, in Patočka's reading, the "good" in question, that in accordance with which the soul is to realize its potential for a higher existence, is not a given, standard measure. The good is not something established, at least not in the sense of an eternal unchanging basis from which to approach the task of one's existence, but is instead saturated with a basic indeterminacy that resists definition. If there is a good unique to human beings, it manifests itself only in a manner commensurate with the status of the human being as not-yet realized, as implicit, a "work" (*ergon*) to be accomplished, but all the while falling short of an explicit, objective determination. Virtue is not something mathematical.

The result, in Patočka's estimation, is that Aristotle in the end represents an important advance in affirming the original impetus of freedom at the core of the project of the care of the soul, precisely by managing to keep the sense of its inherent problematicity in view:

> Plato takes this problematicity away from man. For Plato, what is good is already here. The Good is written into the very last essence of things; the good is its first principle, from which entire existence follows and upon which entire existence hangs. To focus upon it and to direct one's attention to it means to constantly measure oneself with an absolute measure. The absolute measure says what is good. But human life is more problematic, and Aristotle sees it as such, as far more problematic. That is the new fundamental experience with which Aristotle goes to the problem of the care of the soul.[77]

If Aristotle does in the end preserve the idea of philosophy as in some sense divine, in touch with the eternal, nevertheless the human being as such is something decisively non-divine. It is this not only as falling short of divinity, but precisely as an other to divinity that harbors an independence, "a kind of amazing autonomy," as Patočka puts it, "because man is the 'finite creator,' man is the finite being which does that, which does not yet exist, and which does this according to principles that are not eternal, which it itself still has to constitute."[78] There is thus a certain kind of integrity ascribed to human being in-between, in-between the eternal and the mutable world of becoming, thanks to which the soul does not simply pose to itself the task of conforming to an already given, established model of truth, but opens itself instead to the question of what it means to stand in relation to truth at all.

The Antinomy of Meaning and Being

What is at stake in this history of the care for the soul is nothing less than the meaning of history itself, to the extent that this struggle with the problem of the self in ancient thought is a fundamental expression of the historicity of human existence, the necessity for all meaning to unfold historically. Whether history has a meaning is precisely the question of the meaning of human existence itself, or what it means to be that being who is open to being, to what-is. In Heideggerian terms, it is in and as history that *Dasein* relates to beings, to what-is, and in so doing brings beings into relation with their Being, including its own. Likewise in the case of meaning: *Dasein* relates beings to their "integral meaning," through an understanding that is not accidentally but essentially historical.

Yet for Patočka there is a paradox that must be faced, once the broad outlines of this perspective have been accepted, especially if Heidegger serves as a point of departure. For Heidegger argues that being is something humans have an explicit relation to only in the experience of the *loss* of meaning, a negative experience that is one of the fundamental possibilities of human openness. In Heidegger's thought, Being—or better, the human relation to Being, as something that can come to manifestation, as the "deep phenomenon" that emerges as the ground for the openness of human comportment as such—originally becomes manifest in phenomena such as the breakdown of the functionality of use-things and, more poignantly, in boredom and anxiety.

The worldhood of the world is given to *Dasein* in those states of being which emerge out of a sense of the breakdown or disruption not only of this or that meaning or significance, but in the emergence of the whole as that which resists significance, which remains reticent or withdrawn from the "world" as the context of interwoven significations.[79] If historicity is something basic to human existence, if it is that by which the understanding of humans with regard to their being is played out, then the implication of the central importance of such phenomena of breakdown for human disclosedness is that the meaning of historicity culminates in an openness not so much to the meaning of things, but to their meaninglessness, including that of human being itself.

To the extent that the shaking of meaning which lies at the origin of history has the same phenomenological content, revealing the same relation to Being, then one might conclude that history as such, understood as an original encounter with Being, has no meaning. Meaning and Being would in this way be mutually exclusive: to realize the potentiality of existing for the sake of the originary open disclosure of existence, to exist in this way "in truth," would be to turn one's back on meaning; vice versa, to demand something like a "meaning of the whole" would be to turn one's back on truth. There thus appears, Patočka concludes, to be a peculiar antinomy of meaning and being that problematizes the whole question of something like a "meaning of history."[80]

This represents an antinomy for Patočka, precisely because this apparent split between meaning and Being does not map out two existential options for human life, two autonomous forms of human existence that could be cleanly separated, like a forking path, each passage of which promises the integrity of a possible form of life. At most the difference is a tension, in which one pole or the other may exert dominance—whether as an interlude of meaninglessness that seems to irrupt in the midst of the world of sense, or a preponderance of coherence and comprehensibility that at least promises to fuse together into something settled once and for all. That each pole marks out an extreme form becomes more apparent given the influence of a need for a "more demanding" meaning, which feeds both on the program of the latter and the inevitability of the former.

In the *Heretical Essays*, Patočka somewhat confuses the point by embracing Wilhelm Weischedel's thesis that human beings can exist, even in a physical sense, only in a world that is determined by an absolute, non-relative meaning of the whole. A life in which one is convinced that there are only merely relative meanings, understood precisely to be such, is impossible for human beings.[81] This is what, for Patočka, seems to drive the antinomy of meaning and being: there can be no purely local, individual, and thus relative meaning that could stand as humanly self-sufficient; all partial meaning must entail the meaningfulness of the whole, and be carried by its force.[82] Human life as "dwelling in the world" is possible only given such a global meaning, inseparable from openness, thanks to which things speak to humans at all.

But this would seem to put humans at the mercy of an illusion they could not live without:

> The antinomy of meaning and meaninglessness, of meaning and being, seems so to suggest that life is only possible thanks to the perennial illusion of total meaning which certain experiences show precisely to be an illusion. Truth would thus prove fundamentally hostile to life, in an irreconcilable opposition and conflict with it.[83]

One might be tempted to mitigate the antinomy by suggesting that Weischedel's argument need depend only on a limited conception of absolute meaning, in which the absolute is defined as something that is not what it is out of a reference to something else. This sense of the absolute need not entail its infinity, nor even its transcendence or immutability. Perhaps a kind of epochal being, locally complete and closed and in that sense "absolute" at each given phase, would be sufficient to provide a non-relative referent for a finite humanity. Absolute meaning in this sense only needs to be something that has no local "outside," no other confronting it, apart from the absence of all meaning as such. The thesis would then be that human existence can only move, only be, within the immanence of a closed circuit of meaning, which would be equivalent to stating that humans can only move within a relation to the whole, even if the coherence of that whole is, from the perspective of the *longue durée* (that ether of unlimited historical awareness in which no one really lives anyway), finite and episodic (and hence "epochal"). The "truth" manifest in the experience of Being, then, is an index not of the incompleteness of the whole, so much as its radical finitude.

Yet this would only beg the question of precisely what manner of manifestation of the whole forms the foundation for the meaningfulness of human life. Patočka's real aim in embracing Weischedel's thesis might be better described as an attempt at a reversal of Nietzsche, who also posits a conflict between truth and life.[84] For Nietzsche, it is absolute meaning itself, not Being announcing itself in meaninglessness, that is hostile to life; the point is to affirm life at the expense of an absolute, global meaning that seeks to extinguish the radical individuality of creative existence in the form of the "truth" as the whole. What is to be affirmed instead is the relative, or that meaning which does not seek to become the whole, but to give creative form to a life expressing itself in the joy of self-creation.

As Patočka points out, Nietzsche essentially represents an embrace of nihilism, in the form of the destruction of absolute values in favor of the relative. Hence Patočka's interest in Weischedel's thesis in opposition to Nietzsche: "In its practical unfolding, life cannot rest on a relative meaning which itself rests on meaninglessness, since no relative meaning can ever render the meaningless meaningful but, rather, is always itself dragged into meaninglessness by it."[85]

In Patočka, this antinomy is resolved not by positing a meaning of the whole as something that is because it must be, but by recognizing that the experience of the loss of meaning precipitates a return to the world, and with that to meaningfulness, where life continues to be lived in a seeking for meaning inspired by the wonder, the mystery that being at all is. This brings us again to that Socratic moment so basic to Patočka's conception of the care for the soul: "the constant shaking of the naive sense of meaningfulness is itself a new mode of meaning, a discovery of its continuity with the mysteriousness of being and what-is as a whole,"[86] and again: "thus the result of the primordial shaking of accepted meaning is not a fall into meaninglessness but, on the contrary, the discovery of the possibility of achieving a freer, more demanding meaningfulness."[87]

The antinomy is perhaps thereby resolved, but only in a manner such that its tension is preserved, its richness mobilized for the ends of philosophy. It encompasses that Socratic-Platonic-Aristotelian embrace of problematicity for the sake of achieving a specifically human domain of meaning, which for Patočka refracts the original experience of the polis as an "autonomous, purely human meaningfulness, one of a mutual respect in activity significant for all its participants."[88] It is, from top to

CHAPTER 4

bottom, and in contrast to the efforts of a metaphysical tendency to resolve once and for all this tension, a life in accordance with and out of an embrace of the risk of meaninglessness, the experiences of which provide an ever-renewed impetus to the search for meaning.

One is perhaps now able to anticipate Patočka's answer to Löwith's question; that is, whether "the 'last things' are really the first things and whether the future is really the proper horizon of a truly human existence." Patočka's answer might run something like the following. The meaning of history both lies and does not lie in the *letzte Dinge* of death, judgment, heaven and hell. To the extent to which these "last things" bear *in nuce* the question of human finitude, the demand for justification, and the problem of the relation to eternity, they certainly are at work in the meaning of history. Nevertheless, such last things are not the first, if they are taken to be something external to the way humans strive for meaning, as if they have been taken up and swept unwillingly along by a tide of history whose end such things have come to inexorably define. Such a conception resonates more with the abiding remnants of the mythical world, with its characteristic sense of helplessness, than with an authentic affirmation of historicity. Such mythical remnants even occasionally influence the sense of history understood as providential, denaturing its original impulse to break free from fate. The meaning of historical existence, by contrast, is not the experience of the external pull of an inexorable future, but is something that hews close to the drama of human finitude, embracing it not as that in spite of which meaning is possible, but as the very condition for a free, demanding meaningfulness, one that saturates a life with risk to an extent greater than anything that came before:

> It is more full of risk because it draws all of life, both individual and social, into the region of the transformation of meaning, a region where it must wholly transform itself in its structure because it is transformed in its meaning. That precisely and naught else, is what history means.[89]

Contrary to Löwith, such a meaning is expressed neither in the form of a *Weltgeschichte*, if by that is meant a meaningfully coherent course of events, nor a *Heilsgeschichte*, that same course of events conceived in terms of a final end or purpose. Or at least it is not reducible to this opposition. The meaning of history stands instead as the condition of both conceptions, and is embodied in that form of life for which such conceptions can compete for attention. For both conceptions, world history and Providence, are attempts to respond to the need to explain what lacks explanation, to illuminate all that which remains obscure at the heart of human affairs, in order to fulfill the need for a coherent, universal sense of the whole. Both conceptions, in their own way, also threaten to obscure this common heritage, mistaking living problematicity for a problem that can and must be resolved.

The care for the soul, taken in its proper historical sense, is the fundamental expression of a need for meaning in the wake of the experience of meaninglessness; it is what is at stake in the rise and fall of the influence of eschatology, whether in its traditional Christian forms or its modern progressive permutations. The care for the soul is for Patočka not merely a stage in this history but, when seen as a response to the challenge of the shaking of meaning, an expression of its fundamental essence. It thrives when meaninglessness, the shaking of meaning and the decline of the age, yields to the industry of discipline and insight into the eternal of things; it suffers when discipline and insight no longer seem to have value, no longer seem to provide a bulwark against the nihilism of power that is always on the rise when the world is in decline.

Europe's Catastrophes

As the complex development of the theme of care for the soul reconstructed by Patočka shows—from its pre-metaphysical origins to its implicit expression in Democritus, explicit elaboration in Plato, and subsequent modification in Aristotle—the concept is rich but also fluid, drawing even in its earliest history from a wealth of spiritual themes that do not always stand in harmony. It is only as a deeply problematic ideal that the care for the soul forms the core of the ancient idea of philosophy as a way of life (and not a mere system of concepts). This problematic ideal comes to play an equally complex cultural, political, and social role in subsequent history, and is successively modified in the course of the myriad spiritual experiences and struggles that mark the ancient Mediterranean and early European worlds. Throughout, the care for the soul, however overtly influential at times it may have been and in whatever sense it remains recognizable, was for all that never for Patočka a cultural acquisition that was passed down by tradition as something that had a definite, repeatable form. The care for the soul is more the title of a problem, a task of grappling with promising hints of the possibilities of human existence, than a definite program or way of life settled in its essentials. If anything, the theme is continually renewed precisely by being chronically unsettled, demanding new articulations of its basic inspiration by those attracted to its promise, and in this way demonstrating the richness of a

CHAPTER 4

legacy that is as much one of dead-ends and failures as successes and advances. In short, the history of the care for the soul—or perhaps history as the history of the care of the soul—is fraught with transformations, shifts of emphasis, failed attempts at resolution, radical critiques, ambiguities, forgetting, collapses, and catastrophes. In short, it's a real history.

Patočka's reflections on this history are philosophical in both aim and tenor, but they are also guided by a narrative of empirical history that in many ways proves to be inseparable. This narrative can be gleaned from several sources, such as the fourth of the *Heretical Essays*, which traces the development of the history of the care for the soul from antiquity to the close of the nineteenth century; an important text on Czech history, "Was sind die Tschechen?"; "Europa und Nach-Europa," especially part 2; and a series of essays and contributions to intellectual history already cited above, ranging from extensive archival work on Comenius and Renaissance philosophy to Patočka's great work on the history of Aristotelianism.[90]

Patočka's empirical narrative of the history of Europe, while never free from possible criticisms, is both subtle and complex, but for all that not necessarily unorthodox, with perhaps the exception of his reading of the origins of the First World War in the sixth of the *Heretical Essays*. Its basic turning points can be summed up rather succinctly as follows. The history from which Europe as a spiritual complex emerges traces its origins to the Greek polis, which breaks in salient ways from the great proto-civilizations of the East, which nevertheless in essential respects provide the real beginnings of this history. The collapse of the Greek polis gives way to the rise of the Hellenistic and then Roman empires, each of which presents new spiritual challenges in response to which the insights and forms of Greek political (and philosophical) life are rearticulated in different ways, culminating in their absorption into Christianity. The medieval world that arises in the wake of the collapse of the Western Roman Empire and the barbarian conquests yields yet another rearticulation of ancient political and religious life, now within a social reality in which the state is increasingly reliant on theological justifications for its legitimacy, and which stands in existential competition first with the Eastern Roman Empire and then with Islam. The eclipse of the medieval European world in turn yields the establishment, and then the progressive weakening of the ideal of a "holy empire" as an attempt to preserve the spiritual and political legacies of the Middle Ages, an "empire" that stands in fundamental conflict with the emergence of a new, more practically oriented spiritual and political life quickened by European expansion as a global power. The rise of France after the Thirty Years War, which further weakens the Holy Roman Empire as the central axis of European civilization, is coupled with both the emergence of America as the outer periphery of European expansion and the rise of an imperially organized Russia to the east, which seeks to undermine or at least check European power and influence. The rise then of the Industrial Revolution, buttressed by the radical Enlightenment, refashions European spiritual life to fulfill the needs of the emerging capitalist economy, which is itself conditioned in turn by the exigencies that belonged to the rapidly expanding global power of Europe. The French and American revolutions are consequences of the spread of the radical Enlightenment and the conflict between emerging socioeconomic needs and interests and the sclerotic old social and political order. Europe's rapidly expanding technological and military development in the wake of the Napoleonic Wars raises it to a preeminent global power, but at the cost of an ever more entrenched spiritual crisis, which expresses itself in the revolutionary convulsions of 1848 and in the social and political tensions that marked the aftermath of the 1870–71 Franco-Prussian War, all of which set the stage for the darkness that would descend on Europe in 1914.

This itinerary is a familiar one, and in fact Patočka's purpose is neither to challenge nor essentially modify what one might call the conventional narrative of the history of the past several centuries in Europe, if such really exists. The real aim is philosophical, namely the need for a spiritual assessment of the legacy of this history; and here the fact that the history of the care for the soul is essentially a history of catastrophes is of central importance. For the implication is that, from the very beginning, the task of securing and keeping alive the inheritance of ancient philosophy has always been of paramount significance, to the point that its full force is best experienced precisely in those moments when it seems to be finished. Nothing brings philosophy to life more effectively than a good solid catastrophe.

If Patočka argues that the conduit of this history of catastrophes—from the collapse of the Greek polis, to the fall of imperial Rome, to the decadence of late medieval Christianity, to the rise of early modern science—constitutes the heritage of the modern world, even when it is no longer European, it is because the care for the soul never failed to emerge as an ever-renewed *living problem*. One could even say that what Patočka calls "Europe" as a spiritual reality is what it is only as a living problem: "In that way, through catastrophes, this heritage is kept alive, and that is why I suppose that perhaps it might be possible to dare suggest the thesis that *Europe*, especially Western Europe, but even that other one, arose out of *the care for the soul—tēs psuchēs epimeleisthai*."[91]

Relying on catastrophes as a lifeline to the heritage of the past is obviously an inherently hazardous affair, however one might choose to piece together the narrative. It is not simply a question of the chance survival of a healthy strand of the past that managed to escape disaster, remaining preserved in its essentials in the wake of radical change. Such a history is not so much one of preservation as one of compromises, of a continual struggle with the threat of decline, which is ultimately what sustains the care for the soul as a living problem. This means, however, that such compromises tend to simplify the whole at any given historical moment in favor of what seems to be the most solid, most compelling; in this way they progressively introduce a fundamental distortion, or a series of compounding distortions that saddle its inheritors with a thicket of ambiguities and unkept promises. Squeezed by the needs of a given moment, the living problem of the care for the soul becomes progressively convoluted and problematic for those who inherit its various permutations.

In the spiritual history of Europe, a long series of such distortions culminates in what Patočka describes as the "hypertrophy" of that side of the care for the soul that is practical in orientation, having to do with the shaping of the objective world of things and institutions, at the expense of "this other side, this fundamental side, of *forming of the self*."[92] Philosophy as a way of life, devoted not only to the reform of the community, but above all to the fashioning of the individual self, yields to a fascination with techniques for the organization and maintenance of social existence on the one hand, and the radical orientation towards objects and objectivity in the investigation of nature on the other. All those revolutions which transformed the sense of the project in the wake of the sequential failures of its past, any given one of which was necessary for the continuing legacy of the care for the soul, have ultimately left it unmoored from the roots of its original inspiration. Discipline has morphed into an ethic of technical mastery that no longer bears any coherent resemblance to the discipline of life so basic to the Socratic ideal. The trajectory of this unmooring is that of Europe's very decline, to the point which, as already noted above, Patočka declares to his companions in *Plato and Europe* that "Europe is dead."

Europe is dead, because its philosophical essence has invariably become either corrupt or dangerously ambiguous. One example of this Patočka points to is the legacy of Platonism with regard to the guiding concept of the state. Plato's idea of a polity fashioned along philosophical principles, exemplified by Socrates's "city in speech" in the *Republic*, was ultimately corrupted into a conception according to which the state was something that in itself belonged to the "true world," and thus bore in this way the mark of divine origin. Even after the death of the polis, Patočka argues, "the state will still remain something separated from the rest of the world by a sharp divide, for the state will belong to the context of the 'true' world and will derive the justification of its institutions and actions therefrom."[93] When and where the ethos of genuine attempts at rational justification weakens, the state nevertheless retains the authority of having been marked in some way by an association with the truth. In this way, the all-too-human power of the state becomes distorted by a prevailing political theology, whether in the figure of divine sanction or a diffuse sense of the mystery of state power that borders on the mythological.

Another example is how Plato's moral religion becomes absorbed and transformed by Christianity, and by extension how the ideal of a community in truth becomes a community organized according to a very different conception of faith than the Platonic, one that is no longer committed to the discipline of reason, but instead borders on the irrational. In the Christian reformulation of the care for the soul, human reason is in competition with, and is often eclipsed by, an order of love expressed in the conceptions of divine sanction and grace. Metaphysics itself is in addition provided with a framework of revealed truth that mitigates, even militates against all human susceptibility to skepticism, that which had once been the very opening for a free relation to truth.

Related to this, the collapse of the polis, Patočka argues, also inaugurates the collapse of any basic trust in philosophy and, more broadly, in the very order of things, that cosmos "which is both a part and an image of the *polis*,"[94] which had formed one of the sustaining inspirations for philosophy, and is one of the basic presuppositions of the Christianity of late imperial Rome after Constantine. In the wake of the crisis of the fall of Rome, the consequences of which were powerfully addressed by Augustine in the *City of God*, Christianity positions itself precisely as the rise of an alternative to Empire, one in which faith, as a relation to God, supplants the relation to the whole in the manner of the world, to the point at which both the "city of man" and the cosmos in which it is inscribed are taken to be "of secondary importance and ultimately as unimportant."[95] If Christianity nevertheless represents a decisive moment in the history of the care for the soul, it is marked by a profound discontinuity with philosophy, a rejection of any authority it might have once exercised, or hoped to.

Yet for all that, Christianity never breaks from the lure of Platonic *chōrismos*: God's meaning is from another world, wholly transcendent, in contrast with the poverty of meaning based on the merely human. From this transmission of a new meaning from the other side, coupled with a renewed Pauline mistrust of all worldly philosophy, there arises a form of community that is just as oriented to things eternal as was the Platonic city, but in a wholly new fashion:

It is not only a community of humans with each other, a mutual recognition in which they guarantee each other a spiritual perpetuation in the memory of glory. It is, rather, a community of humans with God who is their eternal memory and the perception of their essential spiritual being.[96]

The gradual collapse, beginning in early modernity, of this basic framework—in which meaning is determined and guaranteed by a sacred history of fall, salvation, judgment—leads to a reliance on secularized forms of the same, where humanity takes the place of God, and thus one finds in the scope of Patočka's historical reflections a basic agreement with Löwith's overall thesis.[97] The fragility of these substitutions underlies, in part, the spiritual condition of the modern age, that threat of despair in the wake of rapidly disintegrating forms of traditional self-understanding, and thus nihilism. This is, in addition, coupled with the degradation of nature resulting from the radical privileging of the relation to God above all else: once it is no longer God but humanity alone that stands as the guarantor of meaning, which in the end offers no guarantee at all, the way is open for the reduction of the natural world to mere resource and object of technical calculation.[98] The Christian conception of meaning in this way effectively nurtures a perspective that ultimately turns away from Christianity (in the form of sacred history), in favor of a pure naturalism for which the world, reality as a whole, is inherently meaningless: "Natural science thus becomes a nihilism of nature once it turns into a mere factographic discipline of unintelligible even though comprehensively manipulable data."[99]

Central to Patočka's account of the path of this history is that the various forms of the care for the soul—whether Platonic, Hellenistic, Roman, or Christian—were always shadowed by another fundamental spiritual tendency, itself arising out of the original shaking of mythical meaning: the care for power, for domination, for possession. The turning point for the radical ascendance of this tendency in European life was the sixteenth century, which for Patočka inaugurates the birth of European nihilism proper, but it was arguably already a distinct leitmotif in ancient thought. It is why the figure of tyranny stands at the heart of the Platonic problematic of the relation between the philosopher and the polis: the sense that the decline of the old order has released a powerful desire for unfettered power—power for nothing but power—haunts Plato's dialogues. And in fact, various projects in the pursuit of unfettered power continue to dominate the environment after the collapse of the polis as a viable political reality, leaving an indelible mark on the history of the care for the soul. One can refer here to the rise of the Macedonian empire, the conquests of Alexander that in turn expand the reach of Greek civilization whose political fortunes had been all but extinguished; likewise the expansion of the *imperium* of Rome, in which the embrace of the regime of order, both on the level of education (Greek *paideia* mobilized for the formation of the Roman citizen), as well as on the level of law, is expanded into a project of unparalleled domination, uniting the Mediterranean world and much of the western Eurasian continent. Even Christianity, nurtured in its infancy in both western and eastern Rome after Constantine, will forever bear the traces of this history in the very structure of the church's hierarchy and, later, in the notion of a *sacrum imperium*.

The rise of modern science—and more broadly the techno-civilization that provides the conditions for its flourishing in subsequent centuries, ultimately coming to dominate it spiritually—will realize one of the inherent possibilities of this dialectic of knowledge and power: instead of the meaning of the whole secured either metaphysically or through faith, philosophical or Christian, instead of a truth secured in the form of a transcendence that provides the whole of human life with its direction and sense, truth now becomes reduced to the capacity to manipulate, and the whole emerges in human experience as intrinsically meaningless. This turn to the domination of the inherently meaningless has its roots in the Renaissance challenge of early modern science and empiricism, which turns away from metaphysics as a mode of explanation in favor of a focus on local problems, culminating in a positivism that replaces the pretense of a knowledge of the whole with empirically secured knowledge of limited, particular things in aggregate. In this context there is a reemergence of the metaphysical impulse towards the whole in the form of a reorientation to the certitude of the subject. This new orientation, beginning with Descartes and culminating in Hegel, reasserts the metaphysical identity of thought and being, though now from the perspective of the subject, thereby enhancing the humanist-anthropological aspect of the metaphysical tradition even as it transforms it into something that would have been unrecognizable to a Plato or an Aristotle.

All of this represents a complex mix of spiritual themes that ultimately coalesce in the service of that drive towards acquisition that no longer shadows, but now displaces the care for the soul, taking the explicit form, in the late fifteenth and early sixteenth centuries, of European expansion and conquest: "The great turning point in the life of western Europe appears to be the sixteenth century . . . Not a care *for the soul*, the care to *be*, but rather the care to *have*, care for the external world and its conquest, becomes the dominant concern."[100]

It is no accident that the waning of the force of the heritage of the care for the soul accompanies the dramatic rise of Europe as a world power. Its expansion is not only driven by, but arguably defined by the care to have, and with such a brutal lack of constraint that wreaks havoc on world humanity. This thirst for conquest is a sign of something deeper, for the rise of the care to have inaugurated a Europe that essentially abrogates whatever universal bond it had cultivated as the heritage of earlier transformations of the care for the soul, in favor of a far more muscular, far more worldly universality in the figure of power itself. This new universality is first articulated forcefully by Francis Bacon, then by Descartes and others in the intellectual history associated with this shift, and it culminates in the revolutions and wars of the eighteenth and nineteenth centuries, with Napoleon in particular standing as the symbol of a new era of expanding power, one that dramatically sweeps away the old order in favor of a new conception of authority based solely on the material capacity for conquest:

> From that time on [the aftermath of the collapse of the Holy Roman Empire] the expanding western Europe lacks any universal bond, any universal idea which could be embodied in a concrete and effective bonding institution and authority: the primacy of *having* over *being* excludes unity and universality while the attempts to replace them with power prove vain.[101]

The shift from the care for being to the care for having is the shift from the pursuit of knowledge as the cultivation of the self to the pursuit of knowledge as the cultivation of a capacity to control and direct resources, natural and human. It inaugurates, in short, the rise of technocivilization, which in turn rearticulates the heritage of thought in accordance with the new value of practical mastery, all the while marginalizing and all but extinguishing the spiritual content that had once defined its center of gravity.

Here for Patočka the Enlightenment, especially in the form it took in England and France, paves the way for this new orientation of European life and mind; it is also the arena in which the new mentality competes with attempts to revive older spiritual forms. Kant's philosophy, and in general what Patočka in an earlier essay identified as the "German" Enlightenment,[102] is characterized by an attempt to revive the heritage of the care for the soul, to provide it with a renewed spiritual ground, by effectively ceding the understanding of nature to modern science (and by extension giving ground to the new orientation towards the mastery of nature), while establishing the moral and aesthetic domains as its proper field. Yet the fact that the Kantian tradition—and its successors in figures such as Fichte, Schelling, and Hegel—did more to contribute to national particularisms and the atomization of spiritual Europe than to provide a renewed sense of a universal bond, demonstrates for Patočka the extent of the disruption of the heritage of the care for the soul. One need only think of Fichte's role in the forging of a new German nationalism in the struggle against Napoleon, or the extensive influence of Herder's philosophy of language on the rise of nationalism in the late nineteenth century, to discern the extent of this failure.

The new orientation towards mastery, based on Enlightenment ideas that not only argued for the possibility of a mastery of nature but also justified it, is perhaps most poignantly attested to by the rationalization of the state as an organization of economic forces, a key element in the rise of global capitalism. There are of course contradictions—Patočka describes revolutionary tendencies of the new order emerging from the United States and revolutionary France in conflict with attempts to either preserve the old world, or to take the initiative in shaping a social transformation of the new political and economic order. Here the Enlightenment, itself arguably for Patočka a response to the technical needs of the expansion of European power that had begun with the expropriation of the non-European world, shows itself ultimately to be lacking in the spiritual resources needed to respond to the pressing social tensions of the late nineteenth century.

The result by the end of the nineteenth century in Europe is a state of spiritual crisis. It is a crisis that is both political and social, where the very ideas of the political and the social are in fact being forged by the experience of crisis, of a state of affairs in which conflicts and tensions within a globalized Europe are becoming too destructive and complicated to manage. Europe—the heritage of the Europe of the nineteenth century—is now for Patočka a peculiar blend of the development of an enormous capacity for the exercise of power, and with that of organization and the transformation of the world both natural and social, and an unsettling sense that everything is somehow without purpose or direction, that a great vacuum of values has taken hold, and is being filled with the brute exercise of power and the limitless accumulation of capital.

The destructive consequences of this complicated ascension of unlimited but also meaningless power become all too evident in the twentieth century, beginning with a new European Thirty Years' War and quickly evolving into the peculiar conflict of a global Cold War in which the very meaning of the care for the soul has either been rendered wholly impossible, or on the contrary once again set into motion as an existential possibility. For in this darkest of centuries, the philosopher has wandered into a world increasingly inhospitable to the very idea of a philosophical existence, and is haunted by the possibility of a care for the self that would unfold in ways other than those dictated by the regimes of power. If philosophy is to be at all possible post-Europe, it can only take the form of a resistance to the nihilism of the contemporary techno-civilization that has followed in its wake.

And in fact it is arguably the question of resistance that forms the crucial leitmotif of Patočka's understanding of the contemporary situation, taking three principal forms that will be the focus of the remainder of this essay: *sacrifice, hope,* and *dissidence*.

5

On Sacrifice

Winter

In the wake of the invasion of Czechoslovakia by the Warsaw Pact armies in August 1968, the reform movement initiated under Alexander Dubček was effectively over, but what exactly was to replace it would not be fully determined for some months. Initial civil resistance was peaceful but fierce, as spring gave way to a winter of discontent. Faced with early widespread opposition in the streets, the Soviets would allow a weakened Dubček to remain in office during this uncertain period, until Gustáv Husák took power in April 1969. A purge of reform figures in the government and in other leading political and cultural roles followed, inaugurating the policies of "normalization" that would characterize Czech public life through the 1970s, until Mikhail Gorbachev's *glasnost* in the 1980s would once again set into motion efforts towards its liberalization and democratization.

Discontent took sometimes dramatic forms. On January 16, 1969, Jan Palach, a history student at Charles University in Prague, set himself on fire in Wenceslas Square in front of the National Museum. Explicitly his demand was for an end to censorship and the distribution of the Soviet propaganda newspaper *Zprávy*, but implicitly it was in protest of the encroaching public resignation that was eclipsing the initial revolutionary mood of August. Palach's was the first of more than two dozen attempted acts of protest by public suicide that would follow, resulting in several more deaths.

The shock of the twenty-year-old student sacrificing himself in such a brutal fashion roused the conscience of the nation, much as the self-immolation of the Buddhist monk Thitch Quang Duc in Saigon in 1963 drew attention to the corruption and injustice of the Diem regime in Vietnam, and the cynicism of the American policy supporting it. In the Czech context, the act of "Torch #1," as Palach referred to himself, invited comparison to Jan Opletal, another student martyred in protest of another foreign occupier thirty years before. In some eyes it even invited comparison to Jan Hus, the Bohemian proto-Protestant reformer who had also lost his life to flames in the fifteenth century, galvanizing an armed resistance to another empire of another time and ideology. Whatever the comparisons, the outpouring of public reaction to Palach's act of self-sacrifice was immense, the massive turnout for his funeral counting as one of the formative experiences of a generation, offering a taste of resistance and national solidarity that would prove to be a portent of the events of 1989. In fact, it would be the thirtieth anniversary of Palach's self-immolation that would serve as the catalyst for the opening salvo of public protest that would lead to the Velvet Revolution.[1]

Palach's act and its complex resonance in the social and political context of the months following August 1968 and the subsequent years of normalization would also, if not openly acknowledged in his writings, have a marked influence on Patočka's philosophical reflections in the 1970s. This is perhaps above all the case in the *Heretical Essays*, in which the theme of sacrifice plays a critical role in the context of Patočka's reflections on the First World War. It is equally true of several lectures and private seminars from the same period, in which sacrifice is interwoven with themes fundamental to Patočka's thinking. Together, these otherwise scattered and largely undeveloped engagements with the theme of sacrifice show Patočka being drawn to the conviction that the phenomenon expresses something essential about the times, encapsulating a truth about the awful legacies of a world that had been indelibly marked by war and revolution.

The question of sacrifice in Patočka is thus not limited to echoes of the historical moment, but emerges in a fashion that is inextricably bound to his philosophical development as a whole.[2] One might go so far as to argue that the concept of sacrifice came to play a systematic role in Patočka's late philosophy, fusing two central strands of argument that had become central to his reflections on human existence and the meaning of history. The first strand is the thesis, following Heidegger, that technology represents an essential determination of the modern age, and by extension the metaphysical character of a civilization that has become defined by technology; the second is the contention that historicity, in the form of that explicit orientation of human life to open possibility that had been definitive of the care for the soul, is something inherently at risk, and that the burning question of our times is how to respond to the forces that threaten its disintegration.

Still, it is important not to lose sight of the historical echoes in Patočka's writings. Patočka's explorations of sacrifice in conjunction with these two essential themes—the essence of techno-civilization and the meaning of human historicity—are orchestrated on a level of abstraction that belies the resonance they would have had among the participants in Patočka's private seminars. For in the context of Prague in the 1970s, the thesis Patočka sought to advance, namely that self-sacrifice constitutes an act of resistance against the spirit of an age that would reduce life to its bare maintenance, could not fail to evoke the memory of the young idealist Palach, dousing himself with petrol and setting himself ablaze in a bid to shake the conscience of others.

This inexorable association of Palach that accompanies Patočka's reflections also serves to highlight the problematic, even disturbing character of the former. This is for the simple reason that the use of suicide for political ends is not morally unambiguous. The memory-image of Palach's sacrifice, though today as enshrined in Czech national consciousness as Patočka's own sacrifice in 1977, is not free of a lingering tinge of unease. As with any use of suicide for ends religious or political, the meaning of such an act is inevitably haunted by a sense of waste, of a suspicion of a death too quick to express anything more than a moment of despair, or perhaps a misguided expectation, whatever the context of its motivation may be—whether the desire for political change, or the hope for spiritual elevation.[3]

However powerful its symbolic valence, Palach's sacrifice did not spark the revolution he might have intended (at least not in 1969); the path to normalization continued to be pursued successfully by the authorities in the weeks and months that followed, seemingly ending forever the hopes of the Prague Spring. By the time Patočka takes up the theme of sacrifice some five years later, at a point where he is himself once again in exile from university teaching and marginalized by the politics of exclusion at the heart of normalization, its failure was complete, morphing imperceptibly into the hopelessness and malaise of the Brezhnev era. If there was any moral resistance to the regime during the years between 1968 and 1989—and there certainly was—it had retreated into the more moderate forms of dissidence. If the memory of Palach continued to play any role, it was only as a complicated mix of moral admiration and tragic sense of failure.

"Waste" and "failure" are of course loaded terms. They challenge with the thought that perhaps a loss need not have occurred at all, that there were other ways that would not have been so costly. At a minimum, to hazard the description of any sacrifice as a waste suggests something ambivalent about the loss it entails, a doubt that it must be seen as somehow necessary, as if it were required. In the case of Palach, this is the doubt that it was necessary for him to sacrifice himself either for the explicit political ends he cited in his demands, which were oddly modest, or in a deeper sense for the satisfaction of the basic need for human dignity, which he ultimately came to represent.

The question of waste is not tangential. It is precisely the specter of waste and failure, that problematic emptiness haunting the image of

Palach's sacrificial act, that arguably conditions Patočka's engagement with the general problem of sacrifice.[4] To understand what this might mean, however, first requires a closer look at Patočka's diagnosis of the spiritual context in which Palach's sacrifice was performed, or what for Patočka was the meaning of that long winter that had renewed its hold on central Europe in 1969, despite all the hopes of so many for a thaw.

Dangers of Technology

The texts in which Patočka develops his reflections on sacrifice are few, and taken together they are more suggestive than comprehensive. But they do lay the foundation for a coherent approach to the problem of sacrifice. Apart from the sixth of the *Heretical Essays*, "The Wars of the Twentieth Century and the Twentieth Century as War," there are two additional texts of particular importance for any reconstruction of this approach. The first is a lecture, "The Dangers of Technization in Science according to E. Husserl and the Essence of Technology as Danger According to M. Heidegger," part of which Patočka presented at the 1973 World Congress of Philosophy in Varna, Bulgaria. The second, "Séminaire sur l'ère technique," is the transcript of a recording of three sessions of a private seminar held soon afterwards in Prague that was devoted to a discussion of the Varna lecture.[5]

In all these texts (the lecture, the seminar, and the essay), the theme of sacrifice is situated, with some variation, in a more general reflection on the essence of contemporary techno-civilization. In the Varna lecture, the focus is initially on the contrast between the respective analyses of technology found in the writings of Husserl and Heidegger.[6] This contrast serves as an introduction to Patočka's own position, which in turn differs from both Husserl and Heidegger in salient ways, even if it is fair to characterize it as essentially Heideggerian in inspiration and tone.

On Patočka's account, Husserl's approach to the question of technology emphasizes the phenomenon of a forgetting of origins. The forgetting of origins is an essential hazard that emerges in the movement of the development of scientific understanding, from its foundations in the lifeworld to the formations of rational idealization characteristic of the theoretical constructs of modern mathematical physics and, by extension, modern science generally. The methods of ideal mathematization inaugurated in the Renaissance, in which more and more of the manifold of the natural world is brought under the umbrella of predictive calculation, eventually transforms scientific activity itself into a radical program of technization.

Patočka understands Husserl's critique of technology (or better, techno-science) as essentially turning on the identification of an obfuscation. The technization of scientific method covers over, distorts human understanding as that web of meanings and structures of comportment that constitute the matrix of the human world of life. Meaning, reduced to predictive calculation, is governed ultimately by methods of mathematical idealization; the full panoply of the lifeworld is thereby truncated into ever more precise reconstructions of phenomena into discernible effects of force. In this way, the mathematical turn in scientific thought obscures not only nature, but the living sources of validity for scientific understanding itself, thereby rendering the origins of the otherwise obvious accomplishments of science ultimately incomprehensible from a broader human perspective.

For Husserl, however, this obfuscation does not undermine the abiding integrity of the lifeworld as a living horizon of meaning. A reorientation of scientific thinking away from the "garb of ideas"[7] resulting from the myopia of overinterpreted mathematization always remains possible, at least in principle. Husserl's response to the "crisis of the sciences" is accordingly a philosophical project of recovery, of rediscovering the thread of understanding that would lead thinking to again embrace the full life of insight. Husserl thus sets out to renew a fuller sense of the comprehension of things in their truth, their being, in a way that breaks free of the limitation of the understanding to techniques of technological mastery.

Husserl's fundamental conviction, which is in turn his grounds for hope, is that there remains a virtually inviolable reserve of possible understanding that is indifferent to our repeated failure to embrace it, or even pursue it. This reserve of meaning, indifferent to any project of methodological reductionism predicated on the willful blindness to its presence, represents the lasting possession of a possible course of a more thoughtful, more responsible existence. Philosophy becomes, in short, for Husserl a project of not only self-reflection (*Selbstbesinnung*) but the renewal (*Erneuerung*) of a life in reason.[8]

Heidegger, Patočka argues, formulates the problem of technology in a more radical fashion. For Heidegger, technology is more than a shift in understanding, a self-distortion that obfuscates the original motivating sense of thought. Technology represents instead a radical transformation of meaning itself. Meaning, or rather the meaning of what it is to be, has become reduced to *position* (*Stellung*), to a role in processes projected by technical manipulability, according to which things and persons exist within the circumscription of "being-on-order" (*Ge-stell*). In this way (according to Patočka), "apparently autonomous units are integrated into a vast network of relations in which they function rather than dwell, have an effect rather than repose, though in this sense they are: the very meaning of their being has been transformed."[9] What for Husserl had been a mirage of mathematical idealization, for Heidegger becomes a defining event in the history of the meaning of being, determining the condition of the truth of being itself, of the manner in which all things are manifest. Technology does not obscure a world that would nevertheless remain as a ground for renewal, but transforms its essence from within.

Unlike the Husserlian problematic of origins, in Heidegger this transformation of being entails not only a crisis in self-understanding but also a peculiar danger, one that emerges both within and against the existential human relation to truth. In the Varna lecture, Patočka fully endorses this basic leitmotif of the late Heidegger: how human beings stand in relation to truth, which for Patočka as it was for Heidegger is definitive of human existence, is not only obfuscated in technology, but threatened by an inner transformation of being itself, one that risks the suspension of all access to being as an originary uncovering or manifestation of things. For the meaning of being in the age of technology threatens to become something wholly univocal, a static background that fixes beings in place as available nodes for the projection of force. If part of the experience of meaning is a consciousness of the ground of meaning, of the open existence that gives meaning its life, then techno-civilization represents a way of being in which this consciousness is not only restricted, but potentially closed off, replaced by a rigidity of sense that radically ossifies the movement of human existence as a life in the openness of truth.

This, for Patočka, is where Heidegger's diagnosis of technology moves decidedly beyond Husserl. It is one thing to experience the withering presence of meaning in modern technology, but still have a sense of the exigency of meaning in general, of the human need for meaning as a basis from which to resist a perfectly self-enclosed nihilism of power and its management. This had defined the extent to which Husserl recognized the danger, but also the potential limits of his vision. At most, the threat for Husserl is the generational possibility of missing an opportunity for self-reflection and renewal, but by no means the radical loss of the existential ground for renewal itself, that inviolable bond of life and meaning that Husserl never ceased to affirm. Heidegger's claim is that the problem is precisely the latter, for it is quite something else for meaninglessness to arise from an eclipse of the very experience of the exigency of meaning itself, in the wake of which not even its loss can be registered. Hence Heidegger's dark thought: with the rise of technology, humans face the possibility of the very loss of possibility as a generative source of meaning, and this implies nothing less than the loss of truth as that open space of encounter. Accordingly, Husserl's is a diagnosis of the spiritual condition of the age that reserves the concrete possibility of philosophical critique, while Heidegger's is one that raises the specter of the erasure of its very possibility, and with that of the end of philosophy as such, along with the mode of humanity it embodies.

Effectively embracing what he sees to be the more radical perspective of Heidegger, Patočka argues that technology is more than a mere means for manipulation, that it is itself a manner of human existence that closes access to the very ground for an experience of truth, of the uncovering of beings. Technology is that paradoxical uncovering of truth or movement of manifestation that threatens to block access to the very uncovering that nevertheless serves as its own ground:

> And therein precisely lies the danger. The uncovering that prevails at the essential core of technology necessarily loses sight of uncovering itself, concealing the essential core of truth in an unfamiliar way and so closing man's access to what he himself is—a being capable of standing in an original relation to the truth.[10]

It is important to recognize the paradoxical character of the task of responding, philosophically, to this peculiar danger of closure. It amounts to nothing less than a revolt against truth, against the specific epochal form of its manifestation. For technology is again nothing less than the manner of uncovering, of the disclosure of being that determines the age of techno-civilization; it is neither false nor an obfuscation, at least not in an unambiguous sense. To respond entails the difficult pursuit of an insight into that which, in the sway of technology, makes the very being-sense of humans, as those beings who stand in an original relation to truth, something unfamiliar and alien, a vanishing point of indifference—it is like trying to catch, consciously, and hold the moment of losing consciousness.

What is paradoxical about such a revolt (apart from the notion of a philosophy formulated against truth, for the sake of truth) is that the point cannot be to regain a familiarity thanks to which humans would somehow once again be at home with the truth. This would be more germane to Husserl's way of thinking the matter. Instead, Heidegger strives to discover, as the secret at the heart of the very unfamiliarity revealed in the technological age, a familiarity of *another kind*. That which has closed off one manner of experiencing the ground of truth potentially opens another; the eclipse of meaning in the age of technology is at the same time the ground for the emergence of the truth of meaning as something other. The alienation of technological civilization does not in this way take humans away from themselves, but paradoxically brings them closer to that nullity of existence, that nothingness which remains, in a way still to be understood, the most important thing for understanding human being.

Appropriating Heidegger, this peculiar nullity at the core of the relation to truth will be the axis around which the theme of sacrifice will play itself out in Patočka's own thinking.

"Das Rettende"

In "The Question Concerning Technology" Heidegger famously posits, by way of some lines from Hölderlin's apocalyptic poem "Patmos," a "saving" (*das Rettende*) that is at play at the extreme closure of technology.[11] The poetic figure of this saving, Patočka emphasizes, indexes the role of the problem of historicity in Heidegger's text, the question of whether and how humans can embrace their historical essence in the decadent age of contemporary civilization.[12] Truth and history come together in the ground of manifestation, which is ultimately that in which the very threat of technology plays out as the potential to extinguish the meaning of both.

Commensurate with its unfamiliarity, this ground is implicit, and is present within existence determined as *Ge-stell*, but only in the manner of a peculiar reticence. "That ground refuses to yield to us," Patočka tells his listeners, "yet it is already present in the way it resists us."[13] Thus again the paradoxical character of philosophical reflection in the age of technology: caught by an insight into a sense for what is implicit in the being of truth and the inherent resistance of the same to yield to thought, philosophy finds itself grappling with the ambiguities of a response that seems to amount more to an expression of unsettled disquiet than an illuminating exposition and discovery of the ground of things. The philosopher proper—that ideal type of insight, reflection, illuminating speech and thought—is left grasping at the outer fringes of this "saving" that may or may not be preparing itself in the ground of meaning. Critique here becomes more akin to hope than either analysis or justification, much less renewal.

In the Varna lecture, however, Patočka is also preparing a certain parting of ways with Heidegger, and precisely with regard to the problem of the philosophical response to the danger of technology. The split occurs in reference to Heidegger's suggestion, at the end of his technology essay, that art represents a potential point of departure for an appropriate questioning of truth. In fact, the citation of the lines from Hölderlin occurs precisely in the context of Heidegger's attempt to gesture towards art as that domain within which a philosophical questioning can find traction. Heidegger:

> Because the essence of technology is nothing technological, essential reflection upon technology and decisive confrontation with it must happen in a realm that is, on the one hand, akin to the essence of technology and, on the other, fundamentally different from it. Such a realm is art. But certainly only if reflection on art, for its part, does not shut its eyes to the constellation of truth after which we are *questioning*.[14]

Art, in both its historical and essential bond with ancient *technē* as a mode of revealing, shares with technology a constitutive role in the movement of manifestation. Yet art, in its essentially modern uselessness, also lies outside of what can be fully in the grip of manipulation and control. In this way it promises the possibility of a posture from which humans may sound out the saving that remains inherent to the truth of technology, to the danger of its closure. "The more questioningly we ponder the essence of technology," Heidegger claims, "the more mysterious the essence of art becomes";[15] that is, the more important the essence of art becomes for the posture of a thought open to the turning of another relation to truth, and with that another possible destiny.

Patočka finds this turn to art unsatisfying, not so much because it is mistaken, but because it is not radical enough, as he suggests in the Prague seminars.[16] The root of Patočka's dissatisfaction is the fact that what saves, what potentially turns from one relation of truth to another, is for Heidegger something wholly other than the human subject, and in relation to which the only meaningful response seems to be a certain passive thoughtfulness. The implication is that the openness of human existence should not be conceived as something conditioned by an effort on behalf of a responsibility to what such an openness entails, but *given* by the essence of truth itself, by that which gives or allows beings to become manifest. If the essence, the ground of truth withdraws and in that way becomes danger, if that which gives (*es gibt*) retreats in the wake of the manifestation of beings it makes possible, then what "saves" can only lie in the finitude characteristic of that withdrawal or danger itself. The possibility of a different sending of truth is preserved (*wahren*) only in the fundamental historical character of the withdrawing gift of openness, untouched by all human decision or decisiveness. "When the turning comes to pass in the danger, this can happen only without mediation," as Heidegger puts it elsewhere.[17]

All this feeds a strong tendency in the late Heidegger to describe the condition of truth, and of the human relation to it, in wholly passive terms, something that Patočka rejects fundamentally in the Prague seminars. A related criticism can be found in *Plato and Europe*, one levied by Patočka against Heidegger's contention in "The End of Philosophy and the Task of Thinking"[18] that we can only acknowledge the fact of past philosophies, and never enter into a relation of genuine evaluation of them, given that we do not and cannot be in possession of the appropriate measure for such a task. For Heidegger, any such measure must be immanent to the finite movement of thought that is determined by the experience of a given epoch, outside of which can be given only as an individuated otherness in relation to which one must remain wholly passive. One pretends to measure past philosophies only by way of a certain violence against this otherness, thus in a manner that is not only illegitimate but ultimately incomprehensible. "We simply have to acknowledge the fact that a philosophy is the way it is," Heidegger proclaims, "it is not our business to prefer one to the other."[19]

Patočka will have nothing of this. He sees in this gesture of Heidegger's a fundamental retreat into non-philosophy, one that abrogates the original and abiding impulse of Greek thought as a living affirmation and reaffirmation of a life in truth. Indifference, which differs little in the end from sophistry, is not an option:

> This entire article [i.e., "The End of Philosophy and the Task of Thinking"] about the end of philosophy is defeatist. How, for example, does the entire problem of philosophy, as it is indicated from the classical epoch look from this point of view? What do Socrates and Plato want? To live in truth—that is their own definition of philosophy. Now we have gotten there, where the sophists were.[20]

Heidegger's appeal to art as a context for establishing the passive posture of thoughtful questioning, like his insistence on neutrality in the face of the inner epochal necessity of a given historical figure of philosophy, belies for Patočka a deeper sense in which the danger of technology manifests originally as a *tension* within being, a *conflict*. It is a conflict that unfolds for Patočka not in our remaining passively borne along by the inner movement of open possibility, but through an experience of active strife, of *polemos* as a call to confrontation. It is, in other words, that tension of non-indifference which had once underscored the entire project of the care for the soul, and which in the end is arguably what is again at stake here, even if not explicitly expressed in either the Varna lecture or the "Séminaire."

Certainly, Patočka can be said to be in effect reading one Heidegger against another, marshalling the earlier account of *polemos* as confrontation in Heidegger's *Introduction to Metaphysics* against what one might call the temptations of quietism that emerge in the later essays.[21] Accordingly, at the end of the summary of his own position in the first of the four seminars held in Prague, Patočka evokes, as he does repeatedly in these years, Heraclitus's dictum: *"polemos* is the father of all."[22] What is preserved of possibility in the danger of techno-civilization, what "saves," will be inextricably bound up for Patočka not with passivity, but with resistance and confrontation.

The Ambiguities of Sacrifice

It is in connection with this parting of ways with one Heidegger in favor of returning to another that sacrifice is first mentioned in the Varna lecture. It is introduced as a possible alternative response to the danger of the metaphysical closure of technology, with its peculiar double reality as the danger of loss that at the same time prepares a saving preservation.

Yet its introduction in this context is also a poignant expression on the part of Patočka of the painful awareness that sacrifice has been ubiquitous in the experience of the wars and revolutions of the twentieth century, and so once again a certain historical echo can be heard in Patočka's text. The meaning of these myriad experiences of sacrifice is however articulated in unabashedly metaphysical terms, according to which sacrifice represents a marked resistance against the danger of technology, and with that a fundamental disruption of its hold on meaning. For Patočka, the fact that we find ourselves talking about sacrifice at all, in its double sense of victim and offering (*oběť* in Czech, like *Opfer* in German, means both), problematizes any suggestion that it could be merely another figure of the technical mastery of the real, of the management of humans as material on demand.

If Patočka thus turns from the question of technology to a reflection on sacrifice, it is thanks precisely to what he sees to be a basic incomprehensibility of sacrifice in terms of the dominant metaphysics of the age:

> Can we, however, understand this great upheaval which, historically, manifests itself in the readiness of ever so many to sacrifice themselves for the sake of a different, better world simply in terms of a will to arrange oneself within what is manageable, within our power and calculation? Is it not a misunderstanding to explain this upheaval with the help of the conceptual apparatus of the technical, as an anticipatory grasp of what is to be managed?[23]

And again a few pages later:

> It is a fact nonetheless that countless people have willingly entered into such conflicts, offering themselves as instruments of the accumulation, escalation, and discharge of power, fully aware that thereby they either sacrifice themselves or are sacrificed in it. What does sacrifice mean here, and why are we speaking of sacrifice at all and not simply of resources, of their utilization and consumption?[24]

It is important not to assume that these questions are merely rhetorical, but to take seriously an inherent ambiguity in the concept of sacrifice that they express. This ambiguity turns on a basic question: Is sacrifice just a function of the myriad ways in which the world makes use of human beings, of their bodies and lives as just so many resources, where even the willingness of the sacrificed is ultimately understood in terms of its instrumentality, and with that valued in terms of the nobility or goodness of its end? Or is something else preparing itself, not so much in victimhood as in the willingness to sacrifice emphasized here by Patočka, namely a potential reversal with respect to how human beings relate to the very order of things?

If the former, if the meaning of sacrifice turns on its relation to the attainment of ends, then it is clear that sacrifice would be only one mode among others of the subsumption of human life to the technical order of things, and with that to the dynamics of techno-civilization and its mode of revealing being. Sacrifice would be all about what kind of work it can do, what kind of effect it can have. But if it is the latter, if sacrifice is instead inscribed in the tension or strife that Patočka seeks to affirm at the core of the human relation to openness, then its meaning would amount to something very different, and with that inaugurate a very different figure of understanding.

Yet, again following Heidegger, sacrifice in this second sense would not amount to an instance of a rediscovery of a capacity for insight, or even of a renewed incorporation of insight as a fundamental dimension of human self-understanding, as it was in Husserl. Sacrifice does not reveal anything, it does not yield any insight into the meaning of things. If instead the understanding it embodies were to follow the track of the figure of saving (*das Rettende*) that Patočka appropriates from Heidegger, it would entail a kind of reversal, one ontological in character, that would amount to a turning away from the manner of one meaning of being to another. It would be the turning from a meaning of being in which the human relation to truth is absorbed in and extinguished by the ordering of beings, to a meaning of being that reaffirms the position of human *Dasein* as that being who stands out into the horizon of the uncovering of being. It would be an act of resistance to the one, in open comportment towards the other.

If Patočka embraces sacrifice as a saving resistance in this sense, it is not because sacrifice unproblematically disrupts the hegemony of *Ge-stell*. The ambiguity of sacrifice is instead constitutive. On one level, sacrifice fits perfectly into the machinations of total mobilization, and thus symbolizes precisely the status of human life as just so much reserve made available for the expenditure of power. If there is nevertheless a deeper meaning to sacrifice, a hidden saving potential, then it is only because the very tendency of technological civilization to an ever-greater accumulation of force, and with that the intensification of conflict demanding more and more sacrifice, leads inexorably to a sense of something mysterious at work. For like art, sacrifice seems to stand apart: "the readiness of ever so many to sacrifice themselves for the sake of a different, better world"[25] seems to problematize the logic of those deployments of resources and the institution of patterns of manipulation constitutive of techno-civilization. The phenomenon of sacrifice is not just a fact of use and being used; the *readiness* to sacrifice, the *willingness* to give unconditionally, seems to offer a *fil conducteur* to a plane of existence that stands in tension with anything that would be exhaustively defined by assigned roles and functions, means and ends.

But again, not unambiguously. If sacrifice seems to be more than a phenomenon dominated from within by the logic of calculation, then it is only so thanks to a sense in which human being is somehow *drawn back* from its own inexorable deployment, setting it into relation with that within which anything appears at all:

> And yet perhaps precisely here a transformation of our relation to what is primordial may be being prepared, because a sacrifice means precisely drawing back from the realm of what can be managed and ordered, and an explicit relation to that which, not being anything actual itself, serves as the ground of the appearing of all that is active and in that sense rules over all.[26]

This passage is both suggestive and precarious. Doubts abound: Why do those who sacrifice begin "to sense that this lack opens access to what is richest, to that which bestows everything and presents all as gift to all"?[27] Above all, why is this so if, as Patočka himself takes pains to affirm, sacrifice as a ritual exercise in spiritual elevation in an ontic sense is a dead letter? The act of sacrifice can no longer promise access to another, sacred dimension standing in contrast with the present, for it remains "indebted to the technological world in this sense"—that is, precisely a world in which something like "metaphysics," in the sense of the positing of a "true world," is no longer possible.[28] There is no hint here of sacrifice being capable of renewing that ancient sense of a hierarchal world in which the divine transcends the secular, in which a higher power would function as a uniquely autonomous court of appeal. At most, as the site of the final demise of metaphysics, technology for Patočka (as it did for Heidegger) brings closer what metaphysics had always kept at a distance—the primordial ground of manifestation and not some projection or other beyond it—though at the same time it also puts contemporary humanity face to face with the danger of losing it forever.

Hence the precariousness of the suggestion. A sacrifice can draw back from "the realm of what can be managed and ordered," but only by also heightening the sense of the reticence of being that lies at its innermost core. Sacrifice draws back from its utility only into the void of a withdrawing essence of truth. At most, sacrifice can exacerbate the potential for an experience of a new manner of transcendence at the extreme closure of meaning, but it cannot, out of mere willingness alone, provide for a new order of being. Sacrifice remains, in an unavoidable sense, suspended over an abyss.

The Sacrifice of the Front

If techno-civilization is the paradoxical horizon for the kind of saving potential Patočka seeks to identify in sacrifice, it is because of its unique embrace of force as that which determines all of reality. Techno-civilization is in its essence an expansion, an unlimited increase in power and calculation; it is that in which power is gathered as a manner of being in its own right. The inherent necessity of escalation for techno-civilization means that it necessarily takes the form of conflict: "The most powerful means of its escalation proved to be contradiction, dissension, and conflict."[29] This, for Patočka, is the fundamental truth revealed by the wars of the past century: they show incontrovertibly that humans have become fully subsumed to an order that manifests itself in the mass violence of planetary conflict, thanks to which "it becomes especially clear that man as such is not understood as dominant but is included as something that is 'on order.'"[30]

This means that, perhaps more than anything else, for Patočka it is in the horizon of the modern experience of war that the question of sacrifice is to be posed in its most radical form. In modern war the self-loss, destruction, and erasure basic to sacrifice have come to express the fundamental appropriation of human existence in its entirety for the sake of the discharge of power. The very willingness of the participants only underscores the inherent ambiguity: sacrifice does not represent a moment of exception to such domination, an escape from its grasp. Quite the contrary: it is also a fundamental expression of the same.

This is the driving thesis of Patočka's lines in the dark final essay of *Heretical Essays* on the meaning of the front-line experience in the First World War. The total mobilization of modern war represents the limitless reduction of everything human to the expenditure of force, and the gesture of sacrifice, whether one throws oneself on the fire or is thrown by someone else, is no exception. The logic of sacrifice germane to the regime of peace turns on the necessity to fight, to die, so that others may be secure in their lives, that the viability of the whole would be secured from want: "Peace and the day necessarily rule by sending humans to death in order to assure *others* a day in the future in the form of progress, of a free and increasing expansion, of possibilities they lack today."[31] Sacrifice according to this logic is purely instrumental. It is meaningful only to the extent to which it secures a future, which means it is meaningful in the end for the sake of those who benefit, or for those who use the sacrifice of others to secure a goal, as a necessary price paid for progress.

Yet implicit even in the depths of this use of sacrifice—again following the dynamic of the inherent ambiguity of sacrifice—is the glimmer of another possible meaning, one that is not governed by the idea of sacrifice as an exchange or price to be paid, but rather by an original relation to the finitude of life. This is a darker meaning that stands in contrast to the logic of the day: "Of those whom it sacrifices it demands, by contrast, *endurance* in the face of death," Patočka emphasizes, and "that indicates a dark awareness that life is not everything, that it can sacrifice itself."[32]

This counter-possibility yields a kind of double logic, one rooted in the existential ambiguity of sacrifice. On the one hand, when understood as a price to be paid for . . . , sacrifice is relative, and with that it is fully absorbed into the machinations of the day. On the other hand, Patočka argues, sacrifice is something absolute, an experience of non-relative freedom. Sacrifice means that a life is capable of providing everything, giving what it cannot give and still be, in return for nothing. Sacrifice in its most radical expression is in this way the shedding of its relative sense, revealing something autonomous:

> The front-line experience . . . is an *absolute* one. . . . the participants are assaulted by *an absolute freedom*. Freedom from *all* the interests of peace, of life, of the day. That means: the sacrifice of the sacrificed loses its relative significance, it is no longer the cost we pay for a program of development, progress, intensification, and extension of life's possibilities, rather, it is significant *solely in itself*.[33]

Just as the front line represents the height of the power of the day, of its unlimited capacity for human bondage, for the submission of life and death in the organized reality of total mobilization, so too does the front line represent for Patočka the experience of an absolute that represents a transcendence of that very reality of force: "The motives of the day which had evoked the will to war are consumed in the furnace of the front line, if that experience is intense enough that it will not yield again to the forces of the day."[34] Such an experience of the front represents accordingly a fundamental shaking of the given meaning of the day (the ideals of progress, the value of future life), leading to the emergence of a perspective from a peak of existence that yields "an image of the cosmic and the universal to which humans attain by the absolute sacrifice of themselves and of their day."[35]

Absolute sacrifice strips itself of all roles, of any future projected by the day, including the call to peace, and in this way represents a fundamental overcoming of the regime of force. As such it paves the way for a peculiar spiritual response to the experience of modern war. It is a response that seeks to embrace a dark positivity, to which the meaning of everything must now be related, and thus tethered to the radical touchstone of authenticity represented by absolute sacrifice. In this way, and in direct contrast to the logic of sacrifice for the purposes of power, absolute sacrifice beckons an authentic trans-individuality, binding individuals not to the de-individualizing machinations of power, but to the common nullity at work in their essential relation to truth.

Sacrifice in the absolute sense is thus not an affirmation of a given bond of life, but constitutive of a radical new bond outside of the grip of life itself. What binds here is not interest, not that of the power of the day or the interests of peace, but rather "the solidarity of the shaken for all their contradiction and conflict"—a phrase that, to avoid gross miscomprehension, ought to be understood from "contradiction and conflict" to "solidarity," and not somehow the other way around. For, as Patočka puts it:

> The most profound discovery of the front line is that life leans out into the night, into struggle and death, that it cannot do without this component of life which, from the point of view of the day, appears as a mere nonexistence; the transformation of the meaning of life which here trips on *nothingness*, on a boundary over which it cannot step, along which everything is transformed.[36]

The hope borne by such a response does not lie in the potential for a new force-configuration that one must struggle to achieve in order, for example, to forge a durable peace through mutual security. From a metaphysical perspective, "security" is merely a euphemism for a figure of renewed domination of life bound to itself. *All* such configurations serve the purposes of the day, *all* project the horizon of conflict in a way that instrumentalizes relative sacrifice for the sake of the domination of the real. Rather, the hope Patočka places in the solidarity of the shaken lies in the continued existence along a front line of inner resistance to the day, bound together by an experience, shared by the shaken, of the utter nullity of existence, the experience of a world tripping on its own unsurpassable nothingness.

The significance of this is that for Patočka the modern meaning of sacrifice as a fundamental experience of the ground of existence is not predicated on an interruption of war, whether real or hoped for, nor is its full significance grasped from a distance secured by the withdrawal of war. Solidarity here does not indicate some interpretive heuristic for coming to terms, from the perspective of peace, with war as a state of exception. It is for this reason important for Patočka to draw a contrast with the pacifist call to mobilize against war, as found in figures such as Henri Barbusse.[37] The point for Patočka is not to cast the fallen as heroes in their willingness or as victims in their suffering, either for the purposes of mourning or for marking the transition from war to peace (or back again). Instead, sacrifice for Patočka forms the core of the event of the front line of war itself, it encapsulates the strife of existence as its most profound experience, and can only be understood either from the front line directly, or from some analogue in times of supposed peace.

It is thanks to solidarity in light of this "profound discovery" that one is called to side with the front line, to join its protest against the lies of a peace that serves only the same ends of power as did the destruction of war. The shaken find their solidarity only in their being fully conscious of the inner meaning of war, thanks to which they, as those who understand, forge an inner bond with the very nullity of human finitude, consciously embracing sacrifice as an expression of the rule of the Night. The solidarity of the shaken articulates in this way the existence of a combatant who never leaves the line, never abandons the meaning it offers as a perspective on what has become the endless reality of war.

The Inscrutable Non-Indifference of the Shaken

In the Varna lecture, Patočka takes pains to disassociate the novel sense of sacrifice he is seeking to articulate from older, more traditional or even archaic conceptions. Myth once again plays a central role in his thought, with its blurring of ontic and ontological expressions. Sacrifice in its traditional mythical-religious sense, Patočka explains, involves the binding of a higher being to oneself and one's interests through a process of exchange. In this sense of sacrifice, one orchestrates a loss, but only in order to gain something else from somewhere else—something ontically specific for oneself, or for the community, from an equally ontically specific deity or sacred power. This act of voluntary loss makes sense only if something like a relation to some higher being or domain of existence has been established in some fashion and can be relied upon to make sense of the act. Sacrifice in its mythical form thus establishes a basic conduit of signification that builds meaning into an act that would otherwise amount to mere destruction or waste.

Yet any putative relation to a higher domain of being or beings is precisely what, in the wake of the metaphysics of techno-civilization, has been rendered effectively impossible. In the modern world, Patočka emphasizes, "there really are no distinctions in the order of being; rather, all hierarchy is arbitrarily subjective, and practically there are only quantitative differences of power." Older forms of sacrifice are rendered obsolete, their performance in this context impotent and hollow, for they no longer have an anchor in the order of things. "From this viewpoint," Patočka concludes, "to continue speaking of sacrifice is an inconsistency and a prejudice."[38]

To be sure, such inconsistency and prejudice are only evident from the sober perspective of rational assessment. The lingering symbolic forms of archaic notions of sacrifice remain as cultural and psychological survivals, and are often appropriated to great effect for the ends of power, as the familiar loathsome operetta of modern war propaganda all too amply demonstrates. In effect, to speak of sacrifice, again from the point of view of sober assessment, risks complicity in propagating a myth that has been cynically instrumentalized for the purposes of mobilization. For there is no longer any discernible hierarchy in contemporary reality that sets humans in relation to a higher power of appeal. The age of techno-power has essentially leveled everything to that which is on demand, capable of being organized in accordance with the prevailing needs of conflict and escalation. Sacrifice is either an empty euphemism for resource consumption, or it is a ruse using traditional symbolic forms that continue to bear some psychological efficacy in order to wed individuals ever more tightly to their roles. Or it is inscrutable.

It is perhaps best to characterize Patočka's position as the argument that sacrifice has become all three of these things at once, but with an emphasis on the philosophical significance of its inscrutability. This inscrutability from the predominant perspective of the day represents for Patočka an index of resistance. Sacrifice expresses an inner reticence of humans to being deployed nakedly as a resource, insisting that there is a difference between the use of life and its inner meaning, between a role assigned by the community and the life that lives in its performance. Sacrifice expresses the reality that humans are not mere things, that lives are not merely disposable, and it shows this precisely where humans have been made into things and disposed without any apparent reserve or restraint. Sacrifice hints that even in the most extreme reification of existence in the brute exercise of force, such as modern war, there still resides a problematicity, a sense that there is an inherently indeterminate remainder that recedes from absolute consumption by the will to domination that characterizes the age.

It is important to emphasize that sacrifice expresses this reticence, this reserve, not necessarily because it affirms anything like an inherent value to human life, such as a right to ultimate possession of oneself that would somehow provide a properly moral reserve for resistance. It does not deny the moral value of life, but neither does it rely upon it, as if moral value alone counted as a liberating force. This is due to the simple fact that there is no *effective* resistance to techno-civilization. All value, even the most cherished values of the spirit, is ultimately complicit, for value as such manifests in this world only as force, if it manifests at all. The resistance of sacrifice does not consist in the limiting or expanding effects of value, but only in an ontological strife within the openness of existence itself, an implicit clamoring of problematization inwardly troubling the machinations of total power.

Yet for all that, Patočka still claims that "in a sacrifice ... the idea of a difference in order is contained in the true sense of the word."[39] The break from older, mythical or religious senses of sacrifice is not a rejection of this difference, but its transposition from the idea of an ontic order between the sacred and the profane to that of an ontological order between beings and the Being of beings, between what it means to be and the originary uncovering from which this meaning emerges. Sacrifice, in other words, must be conceived in a demythologized form. Demythologized, ontologically oriented to the ground of being instead of an ontically determinate presence of the sacred, sacrifice in this sense does not, and cannot in the age of technology, manifest itself in mythical-religious terms. It cannot fit into any distinct ethical, theological, or cosmological profile of a relation between beings; it is a difference in order that refuses to be captured by a metaphorical contrast between different *kinds of things*. Hence its inscrutability, and with that its proximity to a certain register of mystical experience.

The primary mode of the manifestation of demythologized sacrifice is arguably on the order of mood. Sacrifice is borne by the mood, or perhaps better the attunement, of the care of non-indifference, for "a person does not sacrifice something that is indifferent to him, something that does not concern him."[40] Non-indifference, heightened into the resolve of an act of destruction and refusal, solidifies the sense of a difference in order, and with that the appeal of meaning to the ground of meaning; it stiffens in this way against the leveling indifference of techno-civilization, disrupting its metaphysical closure. As a mood, sacrifice is an attunement not to the ordering power of a hierarchy of values or beings, but to the rumbling of a deeper conflict below the surface of the ordering of life, to the tension in being itself, which Patočka in the "Séminaire" does not hesitate to call "divine."[41]

The non-indifference of sacrifice, however embedded in a reality of force and violence it may otherwise be, renders sacrifice irreducible to the utilization and consumption of resources, which obeys only the anonymous logic of increase, escalation, and expansion. Expenditure in the case of sacrifice cannot be exhausted by the indifferent forces in bondage to which it may be otherwise deployed. However bound with the fate assigned to it by the forces of the day, sacrifice remains reticent. It remains above all immune to that blind indifference of the old man in Wilfred Owen's "The Parable of the Old Man and the Young," which renders the story of Abraham as having him refuse the ram offered by the Angel as a substitute for the sacrifice of the son:

> But the old man would not so, but slew his son,
> And half the seed of Europe, one by one.[42]

This cold modern Abraham is deaf to the entreaty (or better, the command) of the ethical being called out to him by the Angel. Sacrifice continues unabated in the form of an indifferent transposition of one thing into another, of life into death, according to the pitiless logic of the increase and expansion of power alone. But this is only on the surface. Inwardly, the slain harbor a secret inner resistance to the prevailing indifference, thanks to which sacrifice does not merely add to the pile. A sacrificial victim is not simply used up; the act of submission of the seed of Europe described by Owen is not reducible to the old man's mechanical pulsion of death, "one by one." Sacrifice in its inscrutable inwardness, founded in the non-indifference of care, affirms despite everything that a price is borne and not merely extracted, a cost is shouldered and not merely expropriated. The old man, indifferent to all this, is both deaf to the ethical and blind to the existential drama of atonement written on the palimpsest of the history he believes to be composed by power alone.

In this fashion there emerges a double meaning, however ambiguous and inscrutable, to those grim expenditures of the conflicts of the twentieth century, according to that same double logic of relative and absolute sacrifice that Patočka articulated in the *Heretical Essays*:

> Revolutionary and war-like conflicts of our century were born of and borne by the spirit of a technical domination of the world; but those who had to bear the cost were in no case a mere store of disposable resources, but something quite irreducible to that. That precisely comes to the fore when we speak of sacrifices.[43]

Strikingly, for Patočka, when one today speaks of sacrifices, this "we" is not limited to those who have directly experienced the front line, such as Ernst Jünger or Teilhard de Chardin, those literary witnesses of the "life at the peak" called upon to such effect in the *Heretical Essays*, or to those who have suffered comparable extremes.[44] In some fashion the meaning of sacrifice belongs, in different registers to be sure, to the common horizon of contemporary existence. To some extent all of life has become inscribed in an order of things dominated by the grammar of violence and the indifferent machinations of power. Accordingly, the wars of the past century are significant, in that they distill for Patočka something essential to the modern condition as a whole, in such a way that humans can be said to always find themselves enmeshed in some form of war, enduring the strife of one of its myriad theaters, whether hot or cold, global or local, patent or latent.

For this reason, it would be a mistake to read the sixth of the

Heretical Essays as if it were focused exclusively on the First World War, its meaning encapsulated in the particularities of the front-line experience as described by Jünger or Teilhard de Chardin. If contemporary humanity continues to live in the horizon of the truth of existence which those experiences so forcibly bring to the fore, it is only because this same truth can be seen expressed in different forms, including those that belong to an oppressive peace in which the front line continues to rage.

In the end, it is arguably not the First World War that is Patočka's real subject, but the reality of the Cold War that is both its legacy and fulfillment. The Cold War is a reality for which the front line continues to be present as an inner movement of existential resistance, the drama being played out at the heart of a world wholly consumed by force:

> Currently war has assumed the form of that half peace wherein opponents mobilize and count on the demobilization of the other. Even this war has its front line and its way of burning, destroying persons, robbing them of hope, dealing with them as with material for Force being released. The front line is the resistance to such "demoralizing," terrorizing, and deceptive motifs of the day. It is the revelation of their real nature, it is a protest paid for in blood which does not flow but rots in jails, in obscurity, in life plans and possibilities wasted—and which will flow again once the Force finds it advantageous. It is to comprehend that here is where the true drama is being acted out; freedom does not begin only "afterwards," after the struggle is concluded, but rather has its place precisely within it—that is the salient point, the highest peak from which we can gain a perspective on the battlefield.[45]

This "perspective on the battlefield," and the front line of resistance to the deceptions of the day on which it rests, endures, but is not for all that something stable or reliable. However much it may belong to the existential dynamics of the age, it is not something which by virtue of its mere expression yields a transformation of the whole. If anything, the existential residence of the solidarity of the shaken is shrouded in an atmosphere of failure, of waste. Patočka is thus at pains in the *Heretical Essays* to acknowledge a failure to realize what is implicit in the front line experience, a failure to unfold its meaning in a way that would lead humanity out of the monotony of repeated devastations and the darkness of moral resignation:

> Why has this grandiose experience, alone capable of leading humankind out of war into a true peace, not had a decisive effect on the history of

the twentieth century, even though humans have been exposed to it twice for four years, and were truly touched and transformed thereby? Why has it not unfolded its saving potential?[46]

Patočka's conception of the solidarity of the shaken is meant in part to formulate a response to this failure. Yet it is important to emphasize that the solidarity of the shaken does not reverse the failure, it only refuses to accept it as conclusive. The solidarity of those who have been exposed to the truth, to the peak of existence experienced in acute confrontation from which a will to self-sacrifice emerges, is in the end not a solution, but the indication of a continuing struggle in the face of the fact that "we continue to be fascinated by force, allow it to lead us along its paths, fascinating and deceiving us, making us its dupes."[47] Humans remain, despite the shocks of the experiences of the twentieth century that have repeatedly put them face to face with the truth of themselves, the dupes of raw power, at best dissidents in a world all are powerless to change.

From Naive Resistance to Critical Protest

In all of Patočka's engagements with the figure of sacrifice, from his reflections on the metaphysical essence of techno-civilization to the experience of modern war, the memory of Jan Palach is not far from the surface. Palach's self-immolation can be taken to illustrate Patočka's portrayal of sacrifice as inwardly meaningful, if also outwardly futile. It expresses the same attunement of non-indifference, the same resistance to the hegemony of power, as well as the same preserving inscrutability of sense that Patočka seeks to describe. Though he does not do so explicitly in these pages, Patočka provides the means to interpret Palach's self-sacrifice as a radical act of refusal, a pulling back of life itself from all that would seek to submit it to an external bondage, and in this way as representing an expression of a quintessential freedom.

At the same time, Patočka's reflections hardly quell doubts one might harbor regarding the meaning of Palach's sacrifice, doubts that it was more than a waste of a life still full of the promise of youth. Such doubts apply equally to the loss of a generation in 1914–18, and have been repeated in the efforts to extract some meaning from the subsequent paroxysms of war, revolution, and holocaust ever since. There is always something of a misdirection in using the very language of sacrifice, something of a failure to take full responsibility for the utter meaninglessness that haunts any attempt to come to terms with things with which no one in their right mind could possibly come to terms.

If anything, such doubts are exacerbated by Patočka's reflections. Why did Palach's sacrifice have such resonance, why did it move so many? That it did so is beyond doubt. But why would the willful forfeit of one's own life seem to speak louder than other, less wasteful but equally genuine articulations of conscience, even of protest? Had some hard conviction taken hold, perhaps as a result of so many catastrophes and so much death, to the effect that the world had become so deadened, so exhausted, that something as shocking as burning oneself alive in public had become necessary, as visible proof that at least someone is still alive, someone who can still feel, who can still care about life? And if Palach is not an isolated phenomenon, but symptomatic of the human condition in the contemporary age, is the conclusion, then, that nothing short of the sacrificial embrace of death is required to be heard across the wasteland of force to which the world has been abandoned by history?

Even if one were to be convinced that sacrifice in this sense captures something essential about the spiritual situation of the age, it is hard to miss a certain irony here. Part of what drives all this is a sense that life and death have become routinized, fitted within a calculation that seems to demonstrate nothing less than the utter meaninglessness of both, that both life and death are determined solely by force alone and are thus stupid. Suddenly, despite all its trappings of futility, sacrifice seems to rob life and death of their calculability, not by giving one or the other incalculable value, but by forcing a contrast between the inscrutability of sacrifice and a life no longer worth living, and with that somehow succeeding in the expression of something fundamental about human freedom.

At one point in the Varna lecture, Patočka sallies a distinction that is fraught with peril, even if it is also demanded by the logic of his thought. He distinguishes between what one might call naive sacrifice and critical sacrifice (the latter is not Patočka's term, but it is consistent with his reflections). The former is that willing sacrifice out of the mood of nonindifference already described above; the latter is an expansion of willing sacrifice into an explicit consciousness of what is existentially at stake, and thus "critical" in the sense of raised to a higher, more philosophical level of reflection. The first encompasses all those who have sacrificed themselves in the conflicts of the age, in its wars and revolutions: they have sacrificed willingly, out of genuine non-indifference, but at the same time naively, without full awareness or understanding of the relation to truth at work in the inscrutability of their actions. In the second, Patočka understands those "who have undertaken the repetition of the experience of the sacrificial victim, thereby prying it out of forgetting,"[48] that is, those who make explicit what had been only implicit in the first, "naive" form of sacrifice:

> The repetition of sacrifice presupposes a voluntary self-sacrifice, just as in the case of the naive sacrifice, but not only that. For if in this repetition the central point is the overcoming of the technical understanding of being which is the basis for the nonacknowledgement and vanity of sacrifice, then the naive stance with respect to sacrifice will no longer do at all.[49]

This revealing, and in that sense critical, repetition transforms naive sacrifice from an unreflective *resistance* inscrutable to techno-rationality into a reflectively determined *protest* directed against the dominant understanding of the age: "The entire mode of acting needs to be understood as a protest, not against individual concrete experiences but, in principle, against the understanding by which they are borne."[50] In repetition, the non-indifference native to naive sacrifice is thus leveraged into a thinking that seeks to make visible what has become unfamiliar in technology—the human relation to truth, to the manner of its unveiling as retreating ground.

A living sense of problematicity, again rooted in *polemos*, constitutes in this way for Patočka a basis for protest; moreover, it represents an immanently concrete impetus, as a mood of non-indifference expressing itself in practical action. Sacrifice is thus a genuine phenomenon of active resistance and protest, one that is explicitly determined according to the dynamics of the existential movement of truth. More basic than either idea or purpose, sacrifice in this way comes to represent, in Patočka's reflections, a fundamentally human act of freedom, one that perhaps presages a new form of the care for the soul.

Yet at the same time, neither the naive act of sacrifice nor its critical repetition in the form of explicit protest against the mentality of the age has any content for Patočka. This thesis is perhaps the most difficult aspect of Patočka's conception. However reflectively determined, there is no positive idea at the core of sacrifice, no call to arms for a new principle of the organization of reality. There is at most only a peculiarly self-conscious relation to one's own finitude. Sacrifice points in this way to a relation to existence that is effectively unreal, wholly empty from the perspective of a human project that would seek to mold what is in accordance with an ideal, some highest good as a future happiness in exchange for present suffering. Evading any association with a logic of exchange, Patočka here formulates the striking idea of a sacrifice that falls completely outside of any logic of determination; sacrifice here is not only *for nothing*, but for *no one*, at least "no one" seen from the point of view of those who as individuals would demand a right, a value, a life:

> In this way, sacrifice requires a remarkably radical and paradoxical form. It is not a sacrifice for something or for someone, even though in a certain sense it is a sacrifice for everything and for all. In a certain essential sense, it is a sacrifice for nothing, if thereby we mean that which is no existing particular.[51]

The Lure of Religion

In the closing paragraphs of the Varna lecture, Patočka suggests, rather surprisingly, that this conception of a sacrifice for nothing is not new, but arguably lies implicit in the Christian conception of sacrifice, discoverable once it has been stripped of its mythological expressions. The suggestion is that the essence of Christianity, its *evangelium*, is at its core a turning towards the divine as something that falls outside of the world as a field of force, of manipulation and domination, not as a transcendent deity but as an originary relation to openness.

This thread of reflection represents one of the most intriguing engagements in Patočka's writings with the question of religion, and it has accordingly attracted the attention of several prominent commentators.[52] It is also a puzzling turn. How, in the face of the diagnosis of techno-civilization and the regime of force that dominates existentially the modern age, can religion resurface in any form as a viable human experience?

Perhaps it can emerge only as a figure of protest, an insistence on an exception, one that seeks to lodge itself decisively within the human relation to truth that holds sway in technological civilization. The "demythologized Christianity" Patočka gestures at in the Varna lecture would then be the rediscovery of the original radicality of historical Christianity, that impulse that had driven a revolt against the very reality of the ancient world. But now it would presumably be a revolt for the sake of something that belongs not to a new truth, but to the essence of truth, and which accordingly can only take the form of a nullity, one that is wholly lacking in content. In this way, religion might surface as a protest that finds traction by embracing that historicity of the giving of truth which lies ultimately at the origin of the present, but which technology as a mode of being fundamentally threatens with the closure of indifference. The repetition of sacrifice, as the core dynamic of a demythologized religiosity that would activate what had otherwise remained "unthought," would be aimed squarely at this threat, in this way effectively retracing the being of force to its ontological origin, seeking to inwardly transform this origin into a renewal of the essential non-indifference thanks to which a human relation to truth is originally constituted.

This renewal, this "saving," would not occur through the discovery of a hidden, overlooked power for the sake of the good, the true, that somehow continues to be woven into the human frame. As we have seen, the power to preserve for Patočka is something entirely different, something that in the end rests on the same existential dynamics of the world determined by force, and thus lies implicit in the human experience of power. A demythologized religiosity is thus not a counterpoint to the age of technology, an opposition of the truth of the one with the falsity of the other; both emerge from the same openness, both are turns within the same dynamic movement of truth:

> For, considered in itself, the ground of understanding is no force; it is, quite the contrary, something like a light or a clearing which makes manifestation possible. However, in man, whose being is essentially elevated by this ground, it does become a force and, as the essential core of technology shows, an immense and terrifying force, which, though, might be transformed into a saving one through sacrifice.[53]

Christianity, too, had sought to discover in the meaning of sacrifice a "saving" power, one that broke away from more archaic ideas of sacrifice that understood it as a means for forging a bond with the divine. Sacrifice is transformed in Christianity from a burden, from a necessity for repeated enactments of reconciliation in the face of permanent guilt, into a symbolic opening of salvation in which the relation to the highest as a power is denuded of its violence, resulting in a transvaluation of the bonds of submission, obligation, and the unfreedom of life's burdens.[54] This is for Patočka what Christianity represents in its core, and is the possibility which he strives to evoke in the idea of a demythologized Christianity: it is the possibility that the relation to the divine as power can be taken as a metaphor for the ontological relation of humans to Being.

Patočka's reference to the problem of Christianity here also resonates on another level. For the relation to Christ, to the divine as unfolding within the horizon of a sacrifice, also represents the fundamental transformation of the meaning of death. The point here is in part historical. Christianity triumphed over the ancient power of empire not by escaping the death it threatened, but by transforming it, resisting the systematic use of death as a means to enslave life by turning the self-abandonment to death into an act of love and radical atonement. The cross, a machine of torture and the power of death over life that had been a symbol of Roman domination, is transformed through a radical act of transvaluation into the symbol of a love that disassociates death altogether from power, in such a way that even brings the necessity of sacrifice itself in its mythical-religious sense to a decisive end.[55]

Here once again the importance of Socrates, once shorn of the positive metaphysical associations in Plato, can also be glimpsed. For Socrates as well, existence was not a mere function of life, reducible to its desires and needs and thus unlimited in its vulnerability; the entire effort animating the care for the soul aimed at the orchestration of a surplus of sense that would embrace finitude as a positive project, refusing passive submission to the demands of desire and need. Likewise, for Socrates, the meaning of death was not reducible to that which threatens life, but was what ultimately makes freedom possible, and with that responsibility.[56]

Patočka's description of the repetition of sacrifice in the technological age can thus be conceived as a kind of repetition of these two ancient attempts to overcome a death that binds humans to life, and in turn to servitude. Together Socrates and Christ—the former in a sense perhaps serving as a fulcrum for the demythologization of the latter—yield a conception of transcendence that represents a freedom not *from*, but *for* death, where a gift of death would once again establish the motivation for the upsurge of a renewed life, and with that the focus of a renewed responsibility.[57]

Parentheses

Whether or not Patočka's conception of sacrifice might be germane to the modern problem of religion, and in general to questions of European decadence, it clearly resonates with the political act of Palach and others. This is no accident. Patočka is arguably seeking in these brief engagements with the problem of sacrifice to grasp precisely the meaning of such extreme acts of protest, interpreting their excess as expressing something fundamental regarding the human condition.

Yet can one ascribe to Palach those motivations and that awareness that Patočka details under the rubric of the repetition of sacrifice, described above in terms of a species of critical self-awareness? Perhaps, but only if one can assert with confidence that Palach's act did not arise from a sense of arbitrary futility, that it was instead predicated on an awareness of the saving potential of an extreme freedom, one that ultimately has no content apart from the fundamental relation of humans to the nullity of their finitude. If, in other words, one can distinguish meaningfully between an act of nihilistic desperation, and an existential responsibility grounded in a freedom for death.

It is one thing to make this distinction in the abstract, and quite another to make it from the position of external witnesses to the life of an individual human being. The latter is an ambiguous affair at best and should be approached with a measure of discretion. When is it appropriate to recognize a concrete act of self-sacrifice, not only that of Palach but of the many others who have turned to sacrifice before and since as a form of protest and resistance, as genuine expressions of human freedom and spiritual sensibility that are somehow uniquely appropriate to a post-metaphysical age? Is it a matter of evidence, a chance turn of biography that, once discovered, could be relied upon objectively, or is there something inscrutable here that will always engender doubt?

Perhaps one should be wary of trying to come to any firm conclusions. There is arguably a consistent mix of doubt and conviction, of failure and promise that characterizes what might be called the modern history of sacrifice that unfolds in the course of the twentieth century. Patočka's most difficult thought, arising from the appropriation of diverse Heideggerian motifs that take on a unique constellation in his own thinking, is perhaps a case in point. Patočka seeks a radical conception of sacrifice singularly appropriate for the spiritual challenges of an age of power and domination, one that would free humans from the bondage to life, but precisely by having no content, seemingly turning the very emptiness of nihilism against itself. His insight is that the nothingness inherent to human finitude forms an axis of orientation thanks to which a radical need for meaning basic to human existence, whose affirmation is the mainstay of Patočka's philosophy, can be addressed—not by way of its satiety, but through the affirmation of the need itself in the very depths of its utter abandonment, as something thanks to which one is able to remain fundamentally human in an increasingly inhuman world.

This thought clearly disrupts the more traditional logic of an understanding that would insist that sacrifice ultimately affirms forms of a *given* meaningfulness of life, whether on the level of national existence, the community of religious conviction, or the love for others for whom one will always be willing to give until one can give no longer. Nevertheless, it should be acknowledged that this logic has a powerful hold on human understanding. It could be argued that, regardless of its cynical deployment in propaganda, sacrifice is traditionally evoked precisely in order to reject claims of the utter meaninglessness of loss, and therein finds its abiding purpose. A call to honor the sacrifice of others remains central to the effort to resist a defeatist nihilism that would declare everything in vain, pointing in despair to the hopeless fragility of human meaning under repeated assault by the absurdities of modern existence.

There is thus a tension characteristic of this modern history of sacrifice, one that is perhaps most acute in discourses, moral and political, regarding the meaning of the wars of the past century. The interpretive poles of such discourses can be quite extreme. Sacrifice is either condemned as a cynical ruse that ultimately rings hollow, or is embraced as an almost divine expression of a commitment to the affirmation of the meaning of collective existence. It is difficult to not be pulled to one or the other of these poles, and it is impossible to reconcile them. A peculiar prism thus doubles events and experiences that would otherwise seem to be so decisive as to be univocal. The carnage of Gallipoli represents both the very epitome of the absurd waste of modern warfare, and acts as the catalyst for Australian national self-awareness; the battlefield graves of the Somme represent both ground hallowed by the heroic sacrifices of the dead, and ground cursed by the enormity of the crimes of war and the waste of so many for nothing. In the cultural history of these wars, this conflict is expressed perhaps most poignantly in competing discourses surrounding the monuments to the Unknown Soldier,[58] or poetically in Owen's bitter clash with Horace's *dulce et decorum est.*

What is perhaps unique to Patočka's reflections on sacrifice is that they arguably embrace precisely this doubling of meaning, in a way that affirms the irresolvability of the contradiction. These reflections recognize both the moral necessity of stepping back in horror in the face of senseless waste, and the unavoidable significance that is nevertheless laid bare by the same. Patočka does not explain sacrifice, so much as render its paradoxical place in the modern world more visible, submitting the question to the standards of a clear-sightedness, and even an intellectual courage, that renders his account all the more compelling.

Nevertheless, there is another set of doubts that arise when attempting to understand the significance of Patočka's reflections on the wars of the twentieth century, those vast experiments in human sacrifice that for many seemed to have brought the very world to the brink of destruction. They have to do with the specificity of time and place, and above all with the atmosphere and psychological pressures arising from the wrenching experiences of normalization that characterized post-1968 Czechoslovakia. More than a collapse of hope, it was also the harrowing experience of a society in the process of betraying itself. Václav Havel, in a conversation with Adam Michnik, expresses this point well:

This was a time of breaking spines that was worrisome and painful and which furthermore had arrived remarkably quickly. Only in this context could one understand the self-immolation of Jan Palach. It was an extreme expression of the tension in a society in which cleansings and amazing turnabouts by many people had started—when one who'd been known as a person of the Prague Spring yesterday became a dedicated "normalizer" today who fired people from their jobs.[59]

Something similar can be said with regard to Patočka's reflections on sacrifice, though arguably the frame of reference is broader. For Patočka, reflecting on the state of humanity in the 1970s, war had become something permanent, something definitive of the meaning of being that defined the age. Not just the wars of the twentieth century, but the twentieth century *as war* was for Patočka the inevitable background against which were set all acts of protest, of conscience, of the universal struggle with alienation. This is affirmed to such an extent in the *Heretical Essays* that it seems to render the reconciliation of homecoming—and with that the wars of the twentieth century finally coming to an end— effectively impossible, so that the conditions that call for sacrifice, or at least provide the concrete horizon in which such acts have valence, have become permanent.[60]

The very extremity of this assessment draws much of its force from the context of 1970s Czechoslovakia, understood in turn as the culmination of the collective destruction of Europe that began in 1914, leading to the question of whether such an assessment is itself not subject to the invariable vicissitudes of history. Does Patočka's description of the age as one of permanent war prove commensurate with contemporary experience, with the spiritual condition of the world some half-century later, which has seen not only the end of the Soviet Union, but the emergence of a world no longer polarized by the confrontation between two massive machines of total war?

How one understands the legacy of Patočka's reflections on sacrifice ultimately depends a great deal on this question, whether or not it is posed explicitly. And perhaps it is a question that is often settled too quickly, in the interest of preserving the philosophical power of Patočka's insights despite the presence of nuances and perspectives that have become increasingly alien with the passage of time. The world may very well still remain in the throes of a myriad of conflicts both social and political, racked by wars and even the rivalries of superpowers, but it nevertheless falls well short of the devastation of the world wars that had always remained Patočka's point of reference. The extent to which the danger of technology and the whole problematic of "civilization" that Patočka associates with it still finds resonance today is, as a result, at least open to question.

If one is to come to grips with the complex legacies of the twentieth century, it is probably necessary to adopt a certain optics of distance, one that puts both then and now, to use the phrase of David Jones, "in parenthesis":

> This writing is called "In Parenthesis" because I have written it in a kind of space between—I don't know between quite what—but as you turn aside to do something; and because for us amateur soldiers (and especially for the writer, who was not only an amateur, but grotesquely incompetent, a knocker-over of piles, a parade's despair) the war itself was a parenthesis—how glad we thought we were to step outside its brackets at the end of '18—and also because our curious type of existence here is altogether in parenthesis.[61]

Perhaps such a "space between"—between the wars of the twentieth century and one of its most profound of contemporary philosophical responses, as well as between the latter and current efforts to understand what it might mean today—is the best place to situate all philosophical-historical reflection. This does not mean rejecting the fact that the past is a part of the world in which humans now live, that there is a continuity with the past thanks to which its legacy must be recognized as constitutive of the present. The parenthesis is instead a marker to remind one that the past is not reducible to the inheritance of the present, that the meaning of those wars, and the philosophy that emerged in their wake, tends to slip ineluctably from one's grasp, the more one attempts to pin it down and claim it for oneself. For as Jones describes, in the passage of time human beings wander out of one parenthesis into another, and with that become subject to a peculiar lability that makes the spiritual conditions of the past century shift between a certain familiarity and a certain strangeness, both of which challenge philosophically.

6

On Hope

Titanism and the Problem of Faith

By any reasonable measure, Patočka's *Heretical Essays in the Philosophy of History* represents the crowning achievement of a lifetime of philosophical reflection. Virtually all the principal motifs of Patočka's thought find unique and powerful advancement and expression in these essays: the natural world, the three movements of human existence, human historicity, the care for the soul, the problem of Europe. It is difficult to resist the temptation—and the present study is no exception—to anchor any serious reading of Patočka firmly in the *Heretical Essays*, interpreting everything that came before it as trial and preparation for the many components of its complex argumentation, as if the guiding genius of this work had been present embryonically since the very beginning of Patočka's *floruit*.

The *Heretical Essays* is also a very dark text, thanks principally to its culminating essay on the century of war, with its quasi-mystical descriptions of the front-line experience and its call for the austere "solidarity of the shaken," though not for those alone. The text as a whole possesses a certain unsettling beauty, which Paul Ricoeur in his preface to the French translation of the *Heretical Essays* likens to "that dense beauty of certain figures of Rembrandt, emerging out of the vibrant obscurity of the background," captivating the reader in the gathering of an atmosphere that turns decidedly alien, with its "frankly shocking passages about the dominance of war, of darkness and the demonic at the very heart of the most rational projects of the promotion of peace."[1] Both beauty and shock make the *Heretical Essays* a compelling read, all the more cementing the impression that it represents the very key to Patočka's philosophy.

At the same time, it would be a mistake to take the *Heretical Essays* to be the last word in Patočka's thinking, or the solidarity of the shaken its final message, even if one were to focus exclusively on the later writings. The *Heretical Essays* should instead be read in conjunction with another late text—in fact one of the last Patočka composed, right after the *Heretical Essays* and just months before his death in 1977—that is equally powerful, but far less dark, and even hopeful in contrast: namely, the *Two*

CHAPTER 6

Studies on Masaryk, especially the second study, "Masaryk's Philosophy of Religion."[2]

This title might strike the reader who has just finished the essay as somewhat misleading. Masaryk's ideas on religion take up very little of Patočka's discussion, which is by and large devoted to a reading of Dostoevsky, Kant, and Nietzsche, the center of gravity being Dostoevsky. When Masaryk is engaged at all, it is only as the target of some rather severe criticism, above all with regard to what Patočka perceives to be his failure in understanding several basic theses of Kant's moral philosophy. One might wonder, in short, why Masaryk is even mentioned in the title at all.

This perplexity is to some extent justified, yet at the same time Masaryk does help illustrate the central problem Patočka addresses in the essay. This is even more evident when one surveys several earlier engagements with Masaryk that one finds in Patočka's writings.[3] More broadly, there are also biographical and historical reasons why Masaryk plays an important role in this and earlier essays. Masaryk was a key figure for Patočka throughout his life, both politically and intellectually. On one level, the elder philosopher often provided something of a conservative foil to Patočka's attempts to articulate his conception of the task of philosophy, while on another, more political register, Masaryk provided a lens through which to engage the myriad challenges facing contemporary humanity from a specifically central European perspective.

This can be illustrated with a brief look at two of Patočka's early essays, both of which appeared some four decades previously, in 1936. The first is "Titanism," which is ostensibly a review of Václav Černý's *Essai sur le titanisme*, but can equally be read as a critique of part 3 of Masaryk's *Modern Man and Religion*. The second is "Masaryk's and Husserl's Conception of the Spiritual Crisis of European Humanity," which was written apropos the occasion of Husserl's visit to Prague in the fall of 1935 at the invitation of the Cercle philosophique.[4]

Both essays reflect the debate about the sources of modern nihilism already underway at the end of the nineteenth century and which quickened considerably in the aftermath of the First World War. Masaryk was deeply engaged in this debate, having published a sociological study on suicide in the years before the war, and following this up after the war with a series of reflections on war and revolution.[5] Masaryk had been a direct participant in this history, and a key figure in the founding of the modern Czechoslovak state in the wake of the collapse of the Austro-Hungarian Empire in 1918. Masaryk was active in the formation of a Czech government in exile during the war, including the formation of Czech military units that had fought on the side of the Allies in the last days of the conflict. He was not only instrumental in successfully lobbying the Allied powers for postwar Czechoslovak independence, but later also became the first president of the new democratic state.[6]

Politics and philosophy found in Masaryk a unique symbiosis. Before entering the political sphere—Masaryk was a Czech representative to the Austro-Hungarian Reichsrat and the Bohemian Diet in the early 1890s, and became one of the founders of the Czech Realist Party in 1900—he had a substantial career as a professor of philosophy at Charles University since 1882, and was the founder of the critical journal *Athenaeum* in 1883. Masaryk's increasing involvement in party politics, war, and revolution that came to a head with the formation of the Czechoslovak state in October 1918 hardly diminished his commitment to the life of the mind, and in many ways, in fact, gave it its focus and final purpose. To the end, he counted among his duties as a politician the articulation of a modern democratic ethos in direct competition with what he saw as the spiritual crisis of the times, a crisis that had led to the destruction of war and social upheaval, and which continued to threaten the postwar hopes of the young Czechoslovak (or Czecho-Slovak) nation. Masaryk arguably not only articulated such an ideal but embodied it, and with that the hopes of a generation seeking to regain its footing after the catastrophes that had inaugurated the century.

For Masaryk, the central cause of the crisis of Europe, of which the marked statistical increase in suicides and the mass devastation of the First World War were symptoms, was the dramatic decline of religious faith as a result of the domination of materialism and atheism that had become characteristic of modern Europe.[7] "Titanism," as Patočka emphasizes, was Masaryk's term for what Dostoevsky understood under the heading of nihilism: it designated an attempt to deify the human through a radical embrace of "subjectivity" or "subjectivism," in short, rationalized secular humanism.[8]

Metaphysically, for Masaryk, titanism represented the revolt against the idea of a transcendent, objective world order; morally, it represented an unconstrained egoism and indulgence freed of all effective normative constraint. The two are linked: the lack of faith in an objective order sustaining the world, providing things with a coherent meaning and purpose, and thus the collapse of an objective morality, opens the way for the excesses of a humanity that seeks to usurp the role of the guarantor of the order of things, a vain claim to authority that leads invariably to the destruction of oneself and others. As Patočka writes:

> According to him [Masaryk], the Titans seek in vain to storm Olympus, in vain do they stress their moral autonomy, in vain do they demand the right to live their own life, in conformity with their own free nature; they

will never achieve that and will end by destroying their own life and the life of others; their strivings lead to immeasurable cataclysms which threaten the very life of Europe.[9]

In "Titanism," Patočka seeks to defend modern subjectivism—or better, modern philosophy—against Masaryk's critique. Patočka's claim is that Masaryk fails to grasp the phenomenon of the modern turn to the subject radically enough, and essentially reduces it to a straw contender pitted against a traditional religious perspective that is almost scholastic in its presentation. Yet at the same time, Patočka seeks to credit Masaryk with bringing consistently to attention the legitimate problem of faith in the modern world. The value Patočka finds in Masaryk does not necessarily lie in the success of the latter's argument, at least not in terms of its theoretical evaluation (here Patočka is invariably critical, sometimes brutally), but rather the manner in which the philosopher-president gave expression not only to the continuing relevance of but a genuine need for religious faith.

Masaryk in fact embodies both the relevance and the need for such a faith. "Masaryk's religion," Patočka emphasizes in the second of the essays from 1936, "is the central axis of his thought. It sets the tone of his entire life."[10] Masaryk's religion is not a facile ideology, but a sensibility. Behind the affirmation of a divine moral order guiding history is a fundamental trust in things, regardless of whether they are in any way under human control. Such trust represents an expression of the enduring presence of hope, in a time marked by an increasing hopelessness. The fate of this sensibility is the problem of religion, of faith, for in its essentials "religion is a trust and a hope," as Masaryk puts it in *Conversations*, and "the stance of hope is the essence of religion."[11]

Not only Masaryk's unwillingness to yield to modern secularism, but his ability to resist, his continuing insistence on the central role of religiosity in human existence, is precisely what draws Patočka's interest: faith not as an argument, but as an enduring hope that motivates arguments, and with that continues to provide a ground from which to articulate a sense of the whole:

> Faith in the sense of an absolute trust is not a theoretical standpoint, but far more a practical one, a matter of a personal decision which does not follow from theories or rest on arguments, but rather leads to them and explicates itself in specific views of the world-all.[12]

If in Masaryk's thought faith leads him to a rejection of modern titanism—and if by "titanism" one means a radical claim to individual moral autonomy, rooted in rationality and an attempt to free oneself from the tutelage of traditional religion—Patočka's defense of the same will not turn on a rejection of faith per se, but rather on the argument that a proper understanding of the essence of faith need not lead us to reject these central aspects of modern consciousness. On the contrary, Patočka's critical engagement with Masaryk will point the way to the articulation of a fundamental philosophical task, namely one in which the aim is essentially to embrace titanism, or at least the phenomenon it is meant to describe, as a basis for precisely the rediscovery of faith as a central element of human existence. The task, in other words, is not one of rejecting modern subjectivism, as it was in Masaryk, but carrying it through to its logical extreme, in order to affirm a version of precisely what Masaryk believed it to deny.

The itinerary required to fulfill this task sketched in the "Titanism" essay traces a route through the problem of theodicy, or rather the problem of the moral impossibility of theodicy for titanism. "Titanism stems from the impossibility—the *moral* impossibility—of resolving the problem of theodicy positively," states Patočka, in his gloss of Černý's argument, and "that is why the titan revolts against the order of the world and seeks to substitute for it one of his own, a new, human one."[13] The moral impossibility of theodicy stems from a shift in the understanding of the problem of evil, one that crystallizes around the demand for rational moral justification in the wake of the experience of evil. Subjectively, the experience of evil is an incontrovertible reality, which within the parameters of titanism can no longer be explained away by reference to some order or purpose of the whole that transcends subjective experience. Absent the crutch of faith, and abandoned to the limits of reason alone, the experience of evil can only lead to an affirmation of the moral impossibility of making any sense of a world in which evil is allowed to play a role. Theodicy for the titans effectively collapses into meaninglessness; once faced with the experience of the utterly fortuitous destruction wreaked by evil, the modern subject is besieged by its utter incomprehensibility. The only possible moral response is to reject any claim to the necessity of evil, or by extension the rejection of any order of things that would claim any harmony with its efficacy: either the world is incompatible with evil, or the world is immoral.

From the "objectivistic" point of view (again in Masaryk's sense of trust in a given moral order, one that is justified in itself), by contrast, "theodicy is easy": evil is at most an expression of the finitude of things, of their falling short of being, thus of a nothing that has no meaning "in itself" apart from the fallenness of the world. The being of the world as a whole renders evil a "nothing," a mere privation. The objective meaning of the whole, in itself an expression of God's infinite wisdom and goodness, thus diminishes the problem of evil to the point of utter nullity. Once this support gives way in the modern dissolution of faith and religious morality, once the suffering of evil becomes an incontestable reality, a "being" that is fundamentally unjustified and unjustifiable, the revolt of the titans seeking to overthrow the false legitimacy of Olympus becomes inevitable, and chaos ensues.

For Patočka/Černý, to the extent that the modern impossibility of theodicy is rooted in a distinctively moral sensibility, Masaryk's contention that titanism represents moral decadence is either misleading or altogether untenable. Titanism, in other words, cannot be reduced to the dissolution of the moral integrity of the self into egoistic indulgence and excess. The phenomenon is more complicated. If titanism is a revolt, then it is so only out of indignation at a faith that would console itself with trust in an objective, given order that escapes all understanding, an empty credo of endless tutelage to a higher power whose very existence is doubtful at best. Titanism is thus not a revolt against morality for the sake of immorality (even if its agonies might nevertheless lead to similar results), but is originally motivated by the attempt to address a moral sensibility rocked by the outrages of evil, searching for a consolation in a meaningfulness that flows directly from human reason itself.

Titanism, in short, represents for Patočka an original moral experiment of freedom:

> Titanism is, in sum, a transition from a traditional, synthetic, and theocentric perspective to a modern, open, and personalistic one; it is an emancipatory phenomenon, a moral experiment in human freedom, a test whether the meaning of life can be found in life itself and under what conditions.[14]

Modern titanism is thus not so much a condition, illuminated by a sociological diagnosis of the age, as it is an experiment, the very experiment of the Enlightenment itself. As such it remains indeterminate, its success or failure at best inconclusive. Accordingly, its cultural proponents (Černý's focus is the Romantic poetry of the nineteenth century, including Goethe and Alfred de Musset, who also figure prominently in Masaryk) tend to waver between bold assertions of ultimately superficial rationalism and relapses into traditional religious symbolism. The result—and Patočka is again following the lead of Černý here—is an "inner instability of titanic conceptions: their subjectivism is too matter-of-fact, too rationalistic, not nearly radical enough."[15] In short, the rationalism of these titan-poets fails to address the deep spiritual needs it has putatively been marshalled to satisfy, resulting in an aborted revolution. If "titanism" represents a possible point of departure for deeper philosophical reflection, it will only be once this tendency has been shorn of these limitations, once its radical core has been revealed and understood in its essence. Once, as Patočka puts it, humans accept their "solitude amid the cosmos" as their destiny.[16]

And such acceptance is precisely what Patočka calls on his readers to ponder at the end of "Titanism," and which, some forty years later, will again provide a basic leitmotif of the essay "Masaryk's Philosophy of Religion": "Out of that nothingness man must first create his world, not by refusing modern subjectivism but by passing through it to its very end, to the point at which it becomes the source of moral strength."[17]

The Hope of Moral Theology

Kant plays a notable, if also brief role in the 1936 "Titanism" essay. He is the thinker who perhaps articulated most thoroughly and consistently the impossibility of a rational theodicy—Patočka cites Kant's 1791 *Miβlingen* essay[18]—but he is also important as a transitional figure. For Masaryk, here perhaps inspired by the anti-Kantianism of Brentano, Kant had been exemplary of titanism, arguing for a morality unmoored from traditional foundations, based instead on a purely, and ultimately insufficient, subjective reason. "The *Critique*," Masaryk declares at one point in *Modern Man and Religion*, "is a philosophical *Faust*."[19] Patočka counters this assessment with a very different characterization of Kant, according to which he falls well short of titanic aspirations: hardly an apologist for pure subjective relativism, Patočka's Kant instead consistently emphasizes the limits of the human faculty of reason, and with that its ultimate incapacity to make definitive pronouncements on ultimate things.

Accordingly, as Patočka emphasizes, with regard to the problem of evil, Kant represents an important defender of the tradition precisely in the midst of titanic hubris:

> For Kant, evil in the world represents a warning to reason not to transcend its own finite boundaries; therein Kant is a defender of tradition: man for him is a finite intellect which cannot penetrate the metaphysical mystery of evil. In that respect, titanism goes beyond Kant as a more radical humanism and rationalism.[20]

If anything, in Patočka's eyes, Kant represents the attempt to preserve the basic impulse of metaphysics in the face of the rapid dissolution of its traditional forms when confronted by the rise of modern natural science. Where Masaryk all but misses the point of Kant's famous declaration that he had to "deny *knowledge* in order to make room for *faith*,"[21] Patočka effectively seeks to emphasize its central importance, by understanding how Kant's critical philosophy delivered the death-blow to rational metaphysics, while at the same time attempting to set its most basic convictions on a new foundation.

Patočka in "Masaryk's Philosophy of Religion" makes the important observation that, given the contemporary identification with modern science and the naturalism that defines its basic orientation, one tends to overlook the important role played by rational theology and rational metaphysics in early modern philosophy. Above all, one tends to overlook the hope they represented for an intellectual culture that, despite all of its differences with the medieval perspective, was still deeply invested in a harmony between science and religion, and thus the possibility of a new, rationally justified reconstruction of the relations between humans, God, and world. The hope was for a modern *praeambula fidei* no longer determined by the old dogmatism, but rejuvenated by a new constellation of faith and knowledge consistent with the truths of religion and the methods of the new science.[22]

It didn't work out. The collapse of rational theology—or rationalist metaphysics in general—threatened the collapse of any confidence in the legitimacy of human reason to pronounce basic truths about the most fundamental things. The existence of God, the ultimate reality of the world, the immortality of the soul, all revealed themselves to be undecidable with regard to what can be known. The revealed truth of religion, to put the point differently, does not and cannot form an organic whole with human understanding; truth here can only mean a sense of mystery, not a supplement to a project of reason that would pretend to articulate what otherwise eludes its grasp.

If it was Kant who did the most to hasten the demise of rational theology, it was also Kant who led the search for new grounds for the hope that it had embodied. This is evident throughout the *Critique of Pure Reason*. The systematic limitation of the pretensions of reason throughout the transcendental dialectic (paralogisms of rational theology with regard to the substantiality of the soul, antinomies of rational cosmology with regard to the totality of the world, the ideal determinations of rational theology with regard to God as *ens realissimum*) is coupled consistently with repeated affirmations of the legitimacy, and even the necessity of the interests that human reason has in attempting to transcend its sensible limits in response to fundamental questions of immortality, the coherence of the world, and God.[23]

Among such interests figure practical considerations, whose perceived decisiveness will ultimately lead Kant to seek their satisfaction not in reason's pursuit of knowledge, but in the rational determination of action or human freedom. Accordingly, morality for Kant is not based on the objective knowledge of human freedom, but is rooted in the capacity—at once subjective, but universal for all subjects, and thus in a sense "objective" as well—to act on principles, or in accordance with reasons that are able to ground or justify an action. Freedom, not as something known but as a will whose action is determinate out of an autonomy of the free self-legislation of reason, thus comes to the fore as the only possible ground for morality: "What speculative philosophy could not succeed at," as Kant puts it in a note to the section on the clarification of the cosmological idea of freedom in the *Critique*, "practical reason is able to do, namely, giving an existence that is not sensible, [and] through laws that are grounded on reason. This is morality, if one admits it through freedom."[24]

Patočka's focus in his remarks rests squarely on Kant's doctrine of the postulates of pure practical reason.[25] The postulates are something of a supplement to morality, a set of theoretical theses that delimit rationally justified hope, yet which can make no claim to representing instances of justified knowledge. As rationally motivated, they possess a certain subjective necessity, but are not themselves assertions of a self-legislating reason. For Kant, morality itself is grounded on the law established by the categorical imperative, the guiding principle that determines the rightness of action from out of a rational reflection on the form of the maxim adopted. Here morality is justified within and as a striving for universality, for bringing that for whose sake one acts, the reasons for one's actions, into conformity with the drive of reason for completeness of systematic determination—and thus reason precisely in a categorically determinative sense, and not merely a hypothetical, instrumental sense. The incentives that Kant considers to be sufficient for this striving for universality, however, are minimal: they amount to a reverence for the law, a sense of its superiority over the claims of the passions. Respect flows directly from the self-consciousness of a free reason, but only, as it were, congealing around its minimal expression.[26]

For this reason, respect for the moral law, a feeling that for Kant has an intellectual origin, promises little in the way of defending the integrity of the actual morality of a concrete human being from the inevitable onslaughts of doubt. Inevitably, the Kantian subject is always faced with the anguish that, however right and true it may be to strive to live in accordance with the demands of morality, such a life will always be haunted by the thought of futility, that all of this is in vain. Hence the harshness of Kantian duty, the asceticism it demands. There is no guarantee, in the form of something that one can *know*, that being moral will result in any increase in happiness, or that, at the end of the day, it will have any meaning beyond the limited, subjective satisfaction of having done what was right, or having at least attempted to live in accordance with the demands of duty.

For the sake of at least some mitigating balance to this harshness, Kant's practical postulates—that there is a wise architect of the world, that the soul is both free and in possession of sufficient time to perfect itself—articulate the hope that moral action and happiness will nevertheless find an ultimate harmony, a condition that Kant describes as the "highest good."[27] It is the hope that moral worth makes one worthy of concrete happiness, that what is rationally moral is actually possible, and not empirically futile. It is the hope, in sum, that God guarantees the happiness of the just, that the striving to fulfill the task of morality is not in vain, given the finitude of the moral subject, but is sustained by a power that secures its concrete possibility. "And so practical reason," Kant declares, "gives us a pure moral basis for assuming this cause (since we can do so without contradiction), even if only for the sake of avoiding the risk of [having to] regard that striving as wholly futile in its effects and of therefore allowing it to flag."[28]

The postulates do not, however, substitute for the moral law, as if they revealed its real secret. The highest good, understood as a concrete empirical condition, cannot serve as a pure determination of the will, or even its real incentive. The moral law itself, as Kant expresses it in the second *Critique*, always remains the sole *determining* ground of morality, for "if one assumes any object under the name of a good as a determining ground of the will prior to the moral law and then derives from it the supreme practical principle, this would always produce heteronomy and supplant the moral principle."[29] There is thus an essential conceptual order that determines the highest good as an object of morality, but which nevertheless presupposes, and does not determine, the moral law itself. Kant in this way attempts to conjoin to the categorical imperative a special, supplemental imperative to realize the highest good, without suggesting that the latter is somehow the secret ground of the former, as if happiness, even a worthy happiness, could ever represent the ultimate meaning of morality.

This does not, however, diminish the necessity of the highest good. For Kant is convinced that human beings are incapable of acting on what is concretely futile, whatever the moral value of a given action may be.

Another aspect of finitude expresses itself here: the moral law may determine right, but that is not sufficient to satisfy the rational need for right to stand in at least a postulated harmony with the whole of existence, which for humans can only be a question of happiness. For this reason, Kant is convinced that the interests of reason give rise to an idea of a world, and a special imperative for its realization, in which any futility of morality is effectively superseded.[30]

Another way to articulate the hope expressed in Kant's postulates is that it amounts to the faith that *the whole is meaningful*, that it relates to humans in such a fashion that provides a basic comprehensibility with regard to the significance of what one does and what becomes of one. Patočka in fact begins "Masaryk's Philosophy of Religion" with the question of meaning, again evoking the thesis articulated in the third essay of the *Heretical Essays* that humans require meaning, a non-relative total meaning, in order to live at all. Kant's moral theology is accordingly presented as a contribution to the modern philosophy of meaning: the affirmation of the interests of reason in the questions of the immortality of the soul, the existence of God, and the finality of the world-whole amounts to the assertion of their meaningfulness, in spite of their theoretical insolubility. Their truth cannot be known, but nevertheless the ideas themselves continue to be meaningful, and it is precisely their articulation in terms of this meaningfulness—their subjective force in the context of moral existence—that constitutes the program of the postulates.

As Patočka emphasizes, Kant himself never makes "meaning" in this sense and in this context an explicit theme. His contribution to the philosophy of meaning is thus oblique, but nevertheless it is important, and precisely in the way in which Kant's thinking also falls short. Kant's language is one of purpose (*Zweck*) and purposiveness (*Zweckmässigkeit*), of ends and their realization as what organizes motivation and action. Accordingly, the postulates are meant to articulate a conception of the world as the context in which moral life unfolds, thanks to which, given its inherent purposiveness, such action is not in vain. There is an author of things; the world has a moral purpose that is ultimately compatible with human happiness; the soul will ultimately be able to reach the object of its striving. Everything here moves within the domain of the ontic: all meaningfulness is encapsulated in deliverable ends, however delayed in their consummation; all motivation issues from specific needs and terminates in determinable objects.

The hope of moral theology is thus in a world delivered, an ultimate reward for which human beings are morally worthy. It is rooted in a vision of a consummation, a moral purpose that gives meaning to history itself. And it is precisely this hope of moral theology, Patočka argues, which forms the target of a powerful critique from a perhaps unexpected source: the fiction of Fyodor Dostoevsky.

Ivan's Rebellion

Patočka's rather risky claim at the heart of his reading of Dostoevsky in "Masaryk's Philosophy of Religion"—at least if one is being cautious about ascribing to Dostoevsky views that he actually held—is that the story of the brothers Karamazov dramatizes the implicit contradictions of the moral theology of Kant's postulates, with each brother illustrating in different ways the human tragedy of attempting to live in the world they describe. Inspired by the study of the Russian philosopher Iakov Golosovker, Patočka argues that Ivan's moral failings and spiritual contradictions, above all his inspiration of the murderer Smerdyakov and his inability to act decisively in the drama of his accused brother Dmitri, are the effect of being unable to escape the contradiction between the thesis of an objectively closed moral world order, and the antithesis of an open horizon of relative meaning. Ivan, ever the philosopher, "plunges violently into the embrace of the antithesis, yet *in practice* is unable to give up the thesis," thus proving unable to reconcile the need for harmony with the ultimate impossibility of confirming that harmony is in fact possible. Dmitri, the very epitome of passionate recklessness, "unknowingly fuses" the thesis and the antithesis, throwing all cares to the wind while at the same time experiencing profoundly their draw and claim on his soul, and like Ivan he is "consumed in the blaze of the antinomy."[31] Even Alyosha, apparently embracing the thesis with a simple and pure conviction of the heart, and in this sense emerging as the most Christlike of all the characters of the novel, is not unscathed: profoundly disappointed at the failure of the death of the Elder Zosima to yield a miracle, the young acolyte is thrown into despair over the conflict of his inner need for proof and the outer refusal of the world to provide it to him.

The focus of Patočka's reading is the "Rebellion" chapter in *The Brothers Karamazov*, which is part of a sequence of chapters in which Ivan and his brother Alyosha are having a long conversation over dinner. Ivan is at pains to explain that he makes no claim to be able to adjudicate fundamental questions, such as the existence or nonexistence of God. His "Euclidean mind," as he puts it at a prior point in the conversation, is just too weak: "all such questions are completely unsuitable to a mind created with a concept of only three dimensions."[32] Yet at the same time,

Ivan cannot be indifferent to the demands of morality and religion; he *believes*, and cannot honestly turn his back on belief even if he does not *know*, in part because the very meaning of the world is clearly at stake. This is where the problems begin, and the theme of futility, which, as already adduced above, motivates Kant's theory of the postulates, plays a central role here.

Futility, one might say, in a double sense. The first sense echoes precisely the underlying problem that the postulates in Kant are meant to address: futility threatens because the pure incentive for moral virtue, respect for the moral law, is too minimal; respect alone offers little in the way of defending the practical integrity of subjective motivation from the inevitable onslaughts of doubt. Respect alone can never relieve one of a sense that, however right and true it may be to act in accordance with the demands of morality, there is no guarantee that being moral will have any meaning beyond an all too limited, subjective satisfaction of having done what was right. The postulates are meant to articulate a perspective on the world in which it is rational to hope that such action is not in vain, yet such hope seeks at most to leverage a potential implicit in an unknown future in order to buttress a rational incentive for living a moral life, and in this way open the path for the special imperative of the "highest good."

There is a second sense of futility, however, which the postulates do not and cannot address, given their dependence, as Patočka emphasizes, on a conception of the moral subject as essentially closed in a circuit of rational ends and self-love. The moral subject here is "closed in on itself" precisely because rationality in Kant is something ultimately constituted by the subject, both articulated and recognized as its own.[33] To extend the immanent articulation of the interests of reason into the realm of hope in effect calls on the subject to constitute its own faith, to create, out of its own earthly, "Euclidean mind" a bulwark against despair. In short the subject must, by its own devices, decide whether the world is worth it, whether it has any ultimate moral meaning at all.

In Ivan, this bulwark built from the resources of reason alone proves to be woefully inadequate, yielding him little but torment. Rational hope at best posits God's justice at some distant point, unknown in its ultimate content, perhaps even to infinity, leaving the contingencies of the moment, the particularities of concrete existence, all the more trenchant. Armed as he is only with the categorical imperative and the thinnest of rational justifications that the world is in the long run of moral value, the existence of evil, whose violence and depravity are inescapably present and overwhelmingly real, becomes for Ivan an obsession, one that undermines his rational ability to hope.

For Ivan, the hope that "the whole offensive comedy of human contradictions will disappear like a pitiful mirage" at some distant point, "that ultimately, at the world's finale, in the moment of eternal harmony, there will occur and be revealed something so precious that it will suffice for all hearts, to allay all indignation, to redeem all human villainy, all bloodshed,"[34] would seem to demand that, *right now*, one must accept the concrete evil experienced in the moment, the evil that one *now* witnesses and suffers, as if it all somehow played a role in an order of things arranged by Providence. Forcing the postulates in this way to play the role of theodicy effectively overloads their capacity to convince, since such a theodicy can only be stitched together out of the thin weave of incentives spun from rational hopes, and not firmly established by either a subjective certainty or an openness to the experience of grace. The Kantian moral subject is neither certain, nor open, and thus remains distinctively vulnerable to suffering in acute abandonment.

Ivan's rebellion—explicitly against God, but following Patočka/Goloskover, implicitly against the Kantian conception of moral theology—is deeply rooted in the experience of an abhorrence of evil, of a sense of its utter meaninglessness, which Ivan condenses in his description of the suffering of children in a string of truly shocking stories that he recounts to his increasingly horrified brother Alyosha. The moment of theodicy, or rather the moment of its failed intervention, takes the form of precisely the desire for the redemption of the world: its realization will redeem all that came before, giving meaning to the apparent meaninglessness of human suffering. More, it is the hope that not only is this going to happen, but it is going to happen *for us*:

> I want to see with my own eyes the hind lie down with the lion, and the murdered man rise up and embrace his murderer. I want to be there when everyone suddenly finds out what it was all for. All religions in the world are based on this desire, and I am a believer.[35]

This is where Ivan strikes: "But then there are the children, and what am I going to do with them?"[36] What justification could such a world ultimately have that would require the suffering of the innocent as some kind of price to pay for happiness?

In Patočka's reading, Ivan's posture here is again an embodiment of Kantian rationality, in that he rejects fatalism, and instead insists that all action is ultimately in a sense free, even and perhaps especially those actions that are presumably determined categorically by the moral law. For even actions determined by the law presume that one would choose to act at all, to freely assume participation in a life, in a world, that would have consequences such as the suffering of the innocent—again this is nothing but the consequence of the self-constitution of reason. And in fact, Ivan makes a key distinction that echoes this: he does not abhor suffering in general, for it is perfectly reasonable to hope that the suffering of those who act, who have lived their lives and with that essentially chosen to be in the world as it is, as it is given, will be expiated eventually in the course of the world as it unfolds. But to accept the sacrifice of those who have not chosen, who face the full brunt of human depravity naked of responsibility, is a price, Ivan tells us, he is not willing to pay—"the whole of truth," as he puts it, "is not worth such a price."[37] A postulated harmony in the face of such evil simply fades into the futility that it was supposed to avoid:

> I don't want harmony, for love of mankind I don't want it. I want to remain with unrequited suffering. I'd rather remain with my unrequited suffering and my unquenched indignation, *even if I am wrong*. Besides, they have put too high a price on harmony; we can't afford to pay so much for admission. And therefore I hasten to return my ticket. And it is my duty, if only as an honest man, to return it as far ahead of time as possible. Which is what I am doing. It's not that I don't accept God, Alyosha, I just most respectfully return him the ticket.[38]

Alyosha at this point drops his eyes and says softly "That is rebellion." It is that indeed, but a peculiar one. The respect accorded to God, the faith Ivan professes, is not empty cynicism, but drives the entire demonstration. If there is any cynicism here, it is in Ivan's project to tempt Alyosha, to pull him away from the Elder Zosima. But this does not explain a commitment to God which remains at the core of Ivan's rebellion. It is a rebellion that affirms a commitment to the moral ideal, the moral purpose of the world, but which recoils in the face of the price of responsibility that must be paid for this purpose to be realized. The situation is not only antinomic but self-destructive, in an existential sense, as Ivan makes quite clear: the fact that one lives and has embraced life—or "eaten the apple," as Ivan puts it, and "still go on eating it"[39]—subjects one necessarily, and justly, to the imperative to realize its ultimate aim; but it also exposes one to the necessity to affirm that one is willing at all to continue to embrace such a life, and with that the world.

This is where for Ivan the suffering of children, and his indignation that it is necessary at all for such suffering to occur, that it belongs to the history of an unfolding harmony and is thus *morally meaningful*, becomes unbearable. It strikes at his very willingness to be a part of that history at all, to act at all, to pursue anything. Such is the crux of this particular expression of Ivan's peculiar moral immobility: embracing life, inwardly rebelling against its embrace, Ivan is caught in a pattern of inner and outer destruction he cannot escape.

Underground

Patočka cites Ivan as an example of what Dostoevsky elsewhere explores under the heading of the "underground man."[40] At first blush this might strike one as unconvincing. The (unnamed) narrator of *Notes from Underground*, which is clearly the reference here, is far more unstable than Ivan. The underground man is a tormented soul utterly incapable of sustained social interaction, constantly pulled into a spiral of self-destruction and torment, often at the expense of others (such as the prostitute Liza) who are victims of his increasingly wild antics. Ivan's edges are smoother, thanks perhaps above all to the influence of his brother Alyosha, and overall the sense of acute spiritual hopelessness characteristic of the underground man seems to be lacking, at least at first. Ivan is clearly struggling, yet the extent to which he is lost is not altogether clear. The narrator of *Notes*, by contrast, is not only completely lost, but perversely proud of it, forming in this way a perfect, if also deeply disturbing literary counterpoint to N. G. Chernyshevsky's utopian vision of the rational egoist devoted to the progressive perfection of self and world.[41]

Yet Ivan also has his moments of madness: the feverish hallucination of his often comic dialogue with the devil, the intervention in Dmitri's trial, the result of which leads to Ivan being literally hauled away as a madman, are obvious cases in point.[42] One could also cite the recklessness of Ivan's moral corruption of Smerdyakov, the root cause of the murder that lies at the narrative heart of the novel, and even his attempt to entice Alyosha from his faith, which culminates in the famous Grand Inquisitor chapter: each recalls the compulsion to manipulate and torment others, if not the perverse pleasure in the same, that is characteristic of the narrator of the *Notes*.

These factors are, however, only effects of a deeper similarity. Both Ivan and the unnamed narrator of the *Notes* are fundamentally alienated, caught in a cycle of repeated experiences of the emptying of meaning, to the point where alienation itself has crystallized into something of an identity, a distinctive mode of self-awareness and self-understanding. In Ivan, this alienation expresses itself as an effect of a moral conscience that is both unmoored and aimless, but for all that more than a mere game. Ivan's rebellion is not a forsaking of such conscience altogether, the embrace of "everything is permitted," but instead an affirmation of morality, even faith in God, that nevertheless recoils from within, succumbing to a growing sense of its utter meaninglessness.

In general terms, the alienation of the underground man can be described as threefold. As an inveterate materialist, he is alienated from things, which represent for him the mere instruments of practical existence unworthy of serious attention (the narrator of the *Notes* lives in poverty, Ivan in the practical limbo of an underemployed intellectual); he is alienated from others, who are reduced to their use in the limited pursuits of meaningless advantage, and who in turn use him in a similar fashion, all in a common world of reticent monads that manipulate one another for ends that are ultimately without any lasting value; and, most importantly, he is alienated from himself, his own projects and hopes, his own beliefs and desires.

Alienation here is not simply a passively experienced condition, but something that has become a constitutive principle, one that drives the intensification of a sense of one's own utter nullity. This takes the form of a hypersensitivity, a peculiar self-loving (*amour propre*—the narrator of *Notes* uses, naturally, the French expression) in which one also continuously debases oneself, caught in the contradiction of loving a self that is invariably affirmed in its unlovability:

> The underground man is "terribly self-loving." He is infatuated with himself, irritable and irascible, immeasurably over-sensitive with respect to himself, even though this self is false, paltry, entirely determined by this constant competition.[43]

On the one hand, the underground man throws himself into a cycle of suffering and agony over how stupid everything is, but on the other hand, he also experiences a perverse sense of superiority. The underground man is a nullity, but so is everyone else; what is different is that the underground man is *conscious* of his nothingness, and experiences it in a manner that is authentic, in contrast to the empty-headed superficiality of the dull-witted who live a life of decadence, but think they are healthy and full. Suffering is here instituted, intensified, and perpetuated by an addiction to the consciousness of its utter emptiness, even to the point where consciousness itself is condemned. "I am strongly convinced," exclaims the narrator of *Notes*, "that not only too much consciousness but even any consciousness at all is a sickness."[44]

The underground life is a life that eats away at itself, devaluing everything on course to a boredom that infuses existence with a meaninglessness in the face of which the underground man becomes increasingly sensitive, sensitive to the inherent absurdity of an existence becoming ever more insufferable. Boredom both marks an inherent indifference to meaningless suffering and propels the underground man into ever more suffering, in order to act out, to feel emotions and passions that he cannot genuinely feel. "And you ask why I twisted and tormented myself so?" the narrator of the *Notes* explains: "Answer: because it was just too boring to sit there with folded arms."[45]

In Dostoevsky's literary explorations of this psychology, the only response—and a response there must be, since the experiences of alienation being described are not instances of a passive emptiness, a momentary boredom that one can just allow to pass, but spur one to act, imparting an urgency towards running through boredom to its very ground—is either suicide or murder. Each response finally brings this twisted pathos of conscious emptiness to a resolution, a point of decision that promises to transform a slow, open-ended destruction into a decisive annihilation, thus expressing its inner truth.

The "thoughts" of a materialist who "committed suicide out of boredom" described by Dostoevsky in "The Sentence"—a story that also echoes Ivan's critique of the fundamental unjustifiability of an eventual happiness of humanity predicated on so much misery—sum up this double nihilism almost in the form of a mathematical proof. Here the narrator speaks from a boredom encapsulating a moral subjectivity closed in the circuit of its own perverse *amour propre*, letting drop its sentence from the position of both plaintiff and defendant:

> Therefore, in my incontrovertible capacity as plaintiff and defendant, judge and accused, I condemn this Nature, which has so brazenly and unceremoniously inflicted this suffering, to annihilation along with me. . . . Since I am unable to destroy Nature, I am destroying only myself, solely out of the weariness of enduring a tyranny in which there is no guilty party.[46]

The Conversion to Life

Notes from Underground has no ending, at least not in the sense of a resolution of the existential paradoxes its strange narrator describes. The text of the narration simply breaks off; Dostoevsky, in his own voice, indicates that the sufferings the notes express, and with that their literary articulation, continue: "the 'notes' of this paradoxicalist do not end here. He could not help himself and went on."[47] The reader is left with the sense that the condition of the underground man is inescapable, short of the acts of murder and suicide.

Nevertheless, Patočka argues, Dostoevsky believed in a way out, in an alternative to murder and suicide as an escape from the underground condition. This alternative is modeled, in a way, on the figure of passing through all the phases of nihilistic self-destruction to the "end," to the final consummation of its inherent tendencies, and in this sense it runs parallel to the experiences of the unnamed narrators of both the *Notes* and "The Sentence." To the very end, but now in a fashion that does not result in the closure of annihilation, but instead what Patočka describes as a "conversion to life," an unexpected affirmation that unfolds in a drama enacted at the outermost extreme of alienated existence. In "Masaryk's Philosophy of Religion," Patočka elaborates this conception with an interpretation of Dostoevsky's 1877 short story "The Dream of a Ridiculous Man," which he cites as the "key" to Dostoevsky's conception of a conversion to life.[48]

"The Dream of a Ridiculous Man" is the story of another underground type on the brink of a decision with regard to the meaning of his own meaninglessness. In this case, it is to be suicide, which is decided upon, though in a manner that at first lacks any real motivation, any genuine catalyst for the act to occur at all. Like other examples of the underground man, including Ivan Karamazov, the character in this story is plagued with a peculiar immobility: he is virtually incapable of carrying through with any action in a deliberate, non-arbitrary fashion, including the very suicide on which he has resolved himself, even going so far as purchasing a revolver for the purpose.[49]

The particular form of alienation that plagues this character is a heightened sensitivity to his own "ridiculousness," precisely in the eyes of others, as Patočka describes: "he *is* as he is seen, he sees himself, he lives his life as the victim of others, the victim of ridicule."[50] Fully convinced of his own absurdity, wholly absorbing the ridiculed self afforded by his alienation from others, the ridiculous man counters his abasement not with a feeling of the superiority of the consciousness of his nullity and that of others, but with a false veneer of pride behind which he *hides*.

In this particular configuration of the underground condition, in Patočka's reading, boredom comes to particular prominence, as a kind of defensive reaction to the harbored secret of the ridiculous man's self-consciousness of his absurdity. The profound indifference of boredom is a response of his soul to the unsustainability of hiding himself, behind his pride, from the ridiculed self he has become in the eyes of everyone, including himself:

> Once the unsustainable is reached, sensitivity becomes replaced with its opposite, absolute brutishness, profound boredom, indifference. There is no other defense against this agonizing hypersensitivity other than absolute apathy without limit, sheer boredom.[51]

The nature of this boredom is central to Patočka's interpretation of the story. On one level, its significance lies in a sense of release, one that results from a short-circuiting of the mental anguish that plagues the ridiculous man. "For some reason I became calmer," the ridiculous man tells us, "even though with every year I became more and more aware of my awful quality."[52] It is not a release that brings any peace or repose—the ridiculous man continues to "ache," to be tormented by the "conviction that everywhere on earth *nothing mattered*"[53]—yet nor does it, as was the case with the narrator of the *Notes*, hurl the ridiculous man back into the ferment of passion and suffering, orchestrating all the feelings of life but with the cynicism of "folded arms" born from the consciousness of their meaninglessness.

Boredom here has nothing to do with anything in particular, either with regard to origin or outcome. It is instead, Patočka argues, an example of that profound boredom of which Heidegger speaks, quoting the following passage from the latter's 1929 "What Is Metaphysics?":

> Such boredom is still distant when it is only this book or that play, that business or this idleness, that drags on and on. It irrupts when "one is bored." Profound boredom, drifting here and there in the abysses of our existence like a muffling fog, removes all things and human beings and oneself along with them into a remarkable indifference. This boredom manifests beings as a whole.[54]

A certain innovation of the Heideggerian account of boredom, at least as it appears in the text Patočka quotes, should be noted. This can be done by a look at what Heidegger writes just before the passage quoted by Patočka:

> No matter how fragmented our everyday existence may appear to be [i.e., in the sense of being preoccupied with particular things], however, it always deals with beings in a unity of the "whole," if only in a shadowy way. Even and precisely when we are not actually busy with things or

ourselves, this "as a whole" comes over us—for example, in authentic boredom.[55]

Hence the innovation: instead of the "whole" overcoming one unawares, catching one in moments in which immersion in the particular matters of existence (others, oneself, one's activities) flags, as a kind of unanticipated attunement to what always lies just beyond the sway of the world, the ridiculous man is overcome by boredom as a result of being stripped, rendered defenseless given the absence of any such connection to the meaningfulness of things. Boredom is for him, as he recoils from the world of involvements whose meaninglessness causes him nothing but nausea, something that cannot be avoided, or put to sleep: it is profound by default.[56] With the lure of things all but extinguished in himself, boredom emerges as an uncanny experience of the whole, or the whole as the nothingness of existence: "I began to sense and feel with all my being that *nothing existed around me*."[57]

Beset in this way by profound boredom, the ridiculous man is rendered immobile. The loaded revolver, ready for the deed, would remain in its drawer were it not for purely contingent events that finally spur him on to the decision: a lone, tiny star against the ink-black of the heavens that despite his indifference strikes him, in a way that lifts him out of his lethargy and again resolves him to suicide ("why the tiny star gave me that idea I don't know");[58] an encounter with a little girl in distress that, again despite a feeling of no connection with anything, elicits in him a pity that throws him into a rage, brutishly pushing away the child in need.

Yet before the act of suicide itself, the ridiculous man pauses. Again, that immobility of the underground, though here the catalyst is the memory of the little girl, or better: the anguish of pity that he feels despite being unable to credit it with any meaning. Sluggish with refreshed immobility, sitting at the table with his revolver, the ridiculous man falls asleep and has a dream.

The ridiculous man dreams that, as planned, he shoots himself. His acute alienation renders the act of self-destruction utterly effortless, there having remained no meaningful ties whatsoever to the world that would somehow stay the hand, refuse the movement towards being cut off from everything. After the sudden flash of pain, and the initial experience of a cold grave into which his body is abandoned, he is thrown into darkness. It is a tomb-darkness of a now complete, fully alienated limbo, its utter sense of abandonment, without any hope of resurrection, evocative of Hans Holbein's *Dead Christ*.[59]

Yet this nothingness into which he slips is *positive*. The grave opens, signaling a break even from the abandonment of his own alienation that had been given such a decisive form in the complete suffocation of the grave. The something positive in the subsequent nothingness does not emerge as a ground, as a basis upon which to stand, but as a horizon, an ether of separation in which one can *fly*:

> Flight means that the heart, existence itself, being-in-the-world as such, has been *detached*. It has been detached from things, from its separation, and from its false being that had opposed it to others in the name of "otherness."[60]

Patočka suggests that we think of the flight of the ridiculous man—in which he is borne by a dark companion who reveals nothing in the nothing, yet mysteriously penetrates the ridiculous man to the core of his being—as the uncovering not of some dimension or kind of being, but of Being itself as that ultimate horizon in which life unfolds and things are encountered at all. It is a horizon which is itself nothing, in the sense of no-thing, but for all that does not lack in positivity, for it is the pure possibility of life that is not bound to any of its forms or permutations. It is a positivity thanks to which indifference, absurdity, nothingness, alienation in all its forms, however extreme, never ultimately break from life and its living. There remains in all these forms of alienation, down to the suicide lying in his cold grave broken by the overwhelming indifference of boredom, a silent relating to . . . : to oneself, to things, to others. This silent relating, present even in utter detachment, is neither disrupted nor negated by the meaninglessness of the contingent forms that such relations otherwise take in life. It is as if on the other side of meaning—of meaning in an existential sense, of the play of meaning and meaningfulness, comprehensibility and absurdity, seriousness and ridiculousness—life remains as the ineradicable open of the possible.

Patočka discerns in this positivity of nothing a nascent conception of *love*, and if he accordingly interprets the dream of the ridiculous man as the story of a conversion to life, it is on the basis of love as a union with Being that has, despite the nullity in which it announces itself, turned towards all in the profound gathering of love:

> This opening up of the whole, just at the moment where *nothing* remains of the initially isolated "why" and "wherefore," shows what *always still remains*, what always again opens up the present and, with it, all of what can be gathered, which leads us toward this whole. This wonder, due to which we are no longer among tools, instruments, equipment (*Zeug*), but among *being*, is a union, an opening up that one may thus designate with

the word "love." Being is turned toward us, as if it had returned—and it has gathered us to itself, to others, to things, to ourselves.[61]

There are, of course, other echoes of this figure of love in Dostoevsky's fiction, and they are not always related to the condition of the underground man. One example from the *Brothers Karamazov* is the story of the Elder Zosima's conversion experience before the duel; another is Alyosha's speech at the stone after the funeral of the boy Ilyushechka that closes the novel.[62] Love in these cases is not a movement towards a love-object, and in that sense nothing specifically goal-oriented, but operates at best at the apparent periphery of a life that would otherwise define itself in terms of such ends. It is not the love of this or that, but instead the secret movement, incomprehensible in itself, of that which *gives one to love*—gathering each into the love of others, the love of self, of beings, not out of some ultimate purpose (moral or otherwise), but merely out of its own inexhaustible affirmation.[63]

The rest of the dream of the ridiculous man replicates the trajectory of the biblical story of the fall, casting it as a movement away from a giving love that, paradoxically, makes the movement away from Being possible in the first place. From his flight of detachment the unseen power sets the ridiculous man on an island paradise, where he encounters children of the sun living in a world infused with love: "their faces radiated wisdom and a consciousness that had attained serenity, but their faces were happy: the voices and words of these people rang with childlike joy."[64] Paradise is that original state of love as a being given over to . . . , which in its innocence, or rather in its beginning from the opening of the pure possibility of life, traces the figure of a being-in-the-world characterized by a sympathetic understanding, a non-alienated togetherness in pure openness to all that is.

The fall takes the form of a tendency inherent to this openness itself, even in such a way that traces its genesis in the love that gives one over to the open. For love is ultimately a giving over to separation, to all that individuates life, and everything that comes with it. The guilt inscribed in the origin of the fall is thus not something discrete, a sharp break fixed by a definable act of transgression, but an inexorable tendency of selfishness, of the closure of the self, one that has been set into motion by separation. If so, Patočka argues, then no one is "guiltless": guilt belongs to individuation, not as its first or most primary act, but as its invariable consequence, and thus to the after of the open or fundamentally to time. It is present in its most poignant form not in looking at the group, at the whole, but precisely in the self that stands both apart and in relation—and in fact, as the narrator of Dostoevsky's tale confesses, "the fact is that I . . . I corrupted them all!"[65]

How, of course, he has no idea; it may have even begun *innocently*. And it would never have happened, had the innocent been incorruptible, but that is precisely what is not the case, for all who are given by love over to individuation are guilty—not only for themselves, but for everyone. This universality of finitude is not an expiation, an excuse, as if guilt evaporates when there is no longer anyone who is innocent, or only one who is guilty. That "all are guilty for all" is meant, instead, to be an intensification of the experience of guilt, a fault whose recognition is liberating, as experienced by the Elder Zosima in his conversion before the duel.

Here the Heideggerian theme of "wanting to have a conscience," embracing a call that comes from the very depths of one's own limitedness and thus nullity, has particular resonance: guilt, a sense of fault, is built into the very individuation of the individual, and serves as a touchstone for authenticity.[66] What Patočka adds to this, as a result of his reflections on Dostoevsky, is the affirmation of love complicit with the original upsurge of this wanting to be guilty. Wanting to have a conscience refers to love in its very essence, or to love in the sense of that which gives one over to love. Called to this favor of Being, gathering at the very root of *Dasein*'s care, human beings *want* conscience, because for a separated being conscience provides the countermovement to the alienation and self-loss of separation, to the night of selfishness.

The story of the ridiculous man is accordingly that of a conversion to life from out of a movement that traces an arc from the extremity of individuation, its oblivion as the consummation of the tendency of its own nothingness, through the affirmation of what makes life possible at all, and finally flowing again into an individuated existence conscious of its guilt for everyone. The possibility of this conversion, for Patočka's Dostoevsky, lies at the core of radical nihilism, and is discoverable through those fundamental limit experiences that follow nihilism through to its very end.

The idea of such a conversion contains—or rather circles—a moment of sacrifice: conversion to life is the sacrifice of selfishness, of the tendency in oneself for individuation, for the sake of the affirmation of an openness to being given-over to things. This is the core of Patočka's reading of the biblical epigram to *The Brothers Karamazov*: "Unless a grain of wheat falls into the earth and dies, it remains just a single grain; but if it dies, it bears much fruit":

> "If we do not die . . ." We know that finitude, death, is not an end in the objective sense, an end that one may experience. Death is the extreme

possibility that can only be seized by each individual alone, in such a way that, from something remote and abstract, it grows into that great presence of the event that shatters everything hitherto significant on the side of things and of one's own self: every hope, every desire, every rejecting resistance. Meaning reveals itself in relation to this, not as a gift sent to humans from above, not as a reward for merit, not as retribution and compensation for offenses.[67]

Death here is the death of selfishness, not in a pejorative but in a natural sense: the selfishness that always lives towards itself as a future, where the future is always something at least in part "for me," for the "me" who hopes for rewards, for compensation and retribution. To experience this death of selfishness is to experience the futility of meaningfully hoping for a world that would settle all accounts in such a way that everything was not in vain, yet for all that might still love. "I'll say even more," the ridiculous man tells us at the end of his tale, "suppose this never comes to pass, suppose paradise never is realized (that much I do understand, after all)—well, I shall still go on preaching."

"And I've found that little girl . . . And I shall go on! Yes, I shall go on!"[68]

Wandering

Is this nothingness of Being, the positive nullity that gives one to love, and with that to life, the same nothingness over which humanity trips on the front line, described so poignantly in those lines in the *Heretical Essays* that Ricoeur finds so shocking? Is it the same nothingness that governs the sacrifice "for nothing" that Patočka posits as the source for resistance against the cynical tyranny of techno-civilization? And is the "conversion to life," to the conscience that returns from nothingness in the grip of a being-guilty for all, a new, modern figure of the ancient theme of the care for the soul?

Perhaps, though one should always be wary of crediting a promising line of reflection, however profound it might seem, with more than what it actually establishes. Patočka's philosophy is not complete, nor for that matter is any philosophy that is worth its while. That in one of his last writings Patočka turned to a reflection on Dostoevsky in his attempt to think nihilism through to its end, a task he had set for himself as early as 1936 if not before, shows that the brief allusions to the problem of religion in the *Heretical Essays* in fact signal a potentially significant shift in his thinking, one in which the quietism of Heideggerian thought would be significantly transformed, not only through the adoption of a more activist posture, but also by an existential philosophy of love. That the old, all but surpassed engagement with Masaryk is again rehearsed at the very end of his philosophical itinerary, stands perhaps as a sign of Patočka exploring once again his most fundamental philosophical commitments, searching for sources of renewal.

What attracts Patočka to Dostoevsky's philosophy of love is the promise of a sense of meaningfulness that is premised neither on subjective affirmation, nor on the rational agreement of the Kantian moral subject, nor on a faith in a given order of meaning to which humans are subject, but rather out of meaning that is experienced uniquely as a gift. It is a gift not from a will to lead, emerging either from a transcendent will or from the will of human beings, but is rather the gift of finitude, sustained by nothing, promising nothing but itself, the gift of Being as the site of an encounter with the truth of things. "The underground man does not have the final word," Patočka declares at one point, nor do any of us:

> Is it even possible to say that Truth dwells inside man, that it is human in nature? For the light did not initially reveal itself *in* man, but *above* him. Man is not the creator of Truth, but someone who is abandoned to it or immersed in it . . . there where he is capable of renouncing all he clings to as his own.[69]

Is there not as a result of all this an intimation of a certain kind of *wandering*? Not the blind wandering of Oedipus, but rather the wandering of an authentic freedom caught up in the experience of the nullity that gives it over to what it is? The wandering, in other words, not of a mythical humanity in the thrall of its own ontological metaphor, and with that of everything worldly to which it clings, but of *insight*, and thus in ultimate conformity with the promise of humanity articulated in the ancient ideal of the care for the soul? Insight not as something one can own or even achieve, but which illuminates the landscape of human existence as being open to the world, to one another? A wandering insight, a living questioning after a truth which is not and can never be one's own, as the only possible philosophical response to the nihilism of modern existence?

7

On Dissidence

Absurd Power

"I am a man who has a strong sense of the absurd," Václav Havel once said of himself in a conversation with Adam Michnik.[1] This sense of the absurd was of course more than a contingent character trait, as Michnik himself argues in his essay "When Socrates Became Pericles," given that the playwright Havel was in fact a professional absurdist:

> The theater of the absurd, he [Havel] later explained, is neither pathetic nor didactic. It tends to be "decadently joking in tone," but is not nihilist. It "does not offer us consolation or hope. It merely reminds us how we are living: without hope. And that is the essence of its warning."[2]

The sense of the absurd, along with irony, its joking companion in a troubled world, found ample opportunity to express itself in the post-1968 atmosphere of normalization in Czechoslovakia. There was a surfeit of performative opportunities, and not only for those who would come to be known as "dissidents" (there is a story of Havel bringing out hot grog on a cold winter night to StB agents surveilling his home), or involved in what Ivan Jirous described as the "second culture" of the music underground (a vibrant community that would come to play an important role in the politics of the 1970s and beyond).[3] The journalist Jaroslav Putík describes a scene during the initial Soviet invasion that captures well both the spirit and the circumstances of the absurd that would for many characterize the years that followed:

> A scene from Wenceslas Square. A taxi rides in and out among the tanks that have overwhelmed the whole square. A young man is leaning out of the window from the waist—and playing the violin. He is playing for the tanks; he is playing to enrage those horrible anti-muses: it's a challenge, it's beautiful, I rub my eyes, pinch myself, I can't believe what I see, but the taxi surfaces again and again and the man plays some kind of devilish czardas.[4]

It is important not to trivialize the warning at the core of such gestures. It is a warning to not let wane the sense of the hopelessness they express but also to guard against its corrosive nature, and to acknowledge the need to respond in some way other than submissive silence. It is also important to keep in mind that memories of the repression and violence of Stalinism were at the time still palpable for many, and though the coming years would not see a repeat of the same extremes, this was by no means a foregone conclusion for Putík's taxi violinist, not to mention the dissidents who would eventually coalesce around the Charter 77 initiative, among whom Patočka would figure prominently. The joking companions of irony and the absurd were always shadowed by fear, like revelers in Renaissance paintings by skeletons of the plague.

The rise of Charter 77 would be followed by the introduction of more severe police methods, including an increased reliance on physical intimidation and violence, but the situation was for all that a far cry from the police torture and forced-labor camps of the 1950s. The mechanisms of repression adopted by the regime were overall more moderate, a kind of "civilized violence," as the Slovak philosopher Milan Šimečka would describe it, adding all the more to that feeling of disjointedness basic to the absurd.[5] Normalization was more insidious than catastrophic, its effects more gradual than immediate, always avoiding the outright disruption of normalcy, even as it was being degraded from within. "The political crackdown of the 1970s should not be seen as a portcullis slamming shut," as John Bolton puts it, "but rather as a blanket of snow settling slowly over a landscape, with familiar landmarks still occasionally peeking through."[6]

This atmosphere of slow-motion repression, with its blend of fear, absurdity, and irony, is also registered in Patočka's writings from this period, though often only indirectly. One example is a distinct shift in tone that can be discerned when comparing a lecture Patočka gave abroad in 1968—the leadup to the Prague Spring not only brought Patočka the chance to lecture at the university for the first time since 1949, but also the opportunity to travel more freely—which was expanded and published in early 1969 under the title "The Intellectuals and Opposition,"[7] with his texts from the 1970s that touch on the political, such as the *Heretical Essays*. In the first version of the 1968–69 text, Patočka effectively embraces the possibilities implicit in the political thaw under the Dubček regime, and speculates on the potential for intellectuals as an emerging class to provide direction in modern mass politics. Here one discerns the echoes of the hopes and promise of the youth movement that was such an important part of the experience of 1968, and not only in Czechoslovakia. Patočka saw the significance of the mass movements that were everywhere rocking the political and social scene not so much in terms of a radical revolution that would overthrow ossified and illegitimate authoritarian structures—like many even in the Czech youth movement, Patočka harbored a skeptical attitude toward any "radical" solution, violent or nonviolent, that would promise an all-too-easy ushering in of a new reality—but rather as an impulse, an energy, to move towards an internal reform of existing state and political structures, and above all towards the cultivation of a moral awareness attentive to and engaged with modern mass politics.

This even included at least a tentative embrace of the project of reformed Communism, as indicated in the last lines of the published essay:

> The significance of the Czechoslovak events in 1968 is that, for the first time, the possibility of a new free society is taking shape, based on the transformation of the working class—within socialism itself—into a class which has intellectuals at its core, a core which is capable of introducing society to a new productive and historical era. This society, despite the incomprehension and the pressures to which it has been subjected by the old-style socialism, has not let itself be persuaded by the suggestion that it represents merely a liberal reaction but has insisted, despite everything, on the validity of its own principles for socialism.[8]

There still seemed to be some vestiges of hope in January 1969, when these lines appeared in print, for salvaging the situation. It was not long-lived. Patočka would cut this passage from another iteration of the essay that appeared later that same year, and generally his assessments of the current situation, glimpsed in *Plato and Europe* and powerfully expressed in the two concluding essays of the *Heretical Essays*, would be far darker.[9]

This shift in expectation would also bring a transformation, one that would have profound consequences, and not only for Patočka the person. After having spent a lifetime avoiding any direct political activity, even when he had been directly affected, largely negatively, by the painful twists and turns of decades of complicated central European history, by the mid-1970s Patočka would become intimately involved in the initiative of Charter 77 as one of its principal spokespersons.

And it would begin with an engagement with something akin to the sphere of the absurd, in the guise of the Czechoslovak underground music scene. The development of a robust counterculture had accelerated during the relative thaw of the Prague Spring, and in the 1970s the Czechoslovak government decided that it was a threat to the state, and began to harass the community, breaking up concerts and targeting individuals. In 1976, authorities orchestrated several trials against figures in the underground, including Jirous. These trials quickly became a *cause*

CHAPTER 7

célèbre among the intelligentsia, many if not most of whom—including Havel—had had very little contact, or even sympathy for the rebellious, long-haired musicians who indulged in often vulgar exhibitions ("primitivism" was an important trend) that strained what many (and not only the authorities) considered to be "art."[10]

Patočka was sympathetic to the accused, and signed with other intellectuals an open letter to Heinrich Böll, appealing for him to join them in protest of the actions of the government against the music underground.[11] He even circulated a short text apropos the trials, some of the defendants of which belonged to a popular band that called itself The Plastic People of the Universe, known for covering material from Lou Reed's Velvet Underground, and another group called DG 307, named after a psychiatric diagnosis that exempted one from military service.[12] Patočka's text, "On the Matters of the Plastic People of the Universe and DG 307," offers a retelling of the Dostoevsky story "The Dream of a Ridiculous Man," which had played such a prominent role in his late essay "Masaryk's Philosophy of Religion," and indeed could be read as something of a coda to the same.[13]

Patočka's sympathy does not reflect any real familiarity with the underground scene, but then again, neither did many of the literati and intellectuals who had rallied to its support. The central theme of his short text on the Plastics and DG 307, circulated among friends and students, is the universal hope in youth, in the generational introduction of at least the chance for something like an uncorrupted innocence shifting the course of a doggedly corrupt world. The picture Patočka paints is a far cry from the often subversive, pointedly acerbic and often just plain loud raucousness of the underground music scene, not to mention the tension with the reality that its members were far from being universally young (Jirous, the artistic director of the Plastics, was in his thirties, and Egon Bondy, the dominant muse of the Plastics and to some extent the scene as a whole, was in his forties), and far from innocent. But that is beside the point. Patočka's sympathy lay squarely with those who were forging spaces of free expression and life in the increasingly grey, fear-ridden, conformist world of 1970s Czechoslovakia.

Yet at the same time, Patočka's support was more than a mere expression of general solidarity with the victims of an oppressive regime. It was an acknowledgment of a shared dissatisfaction with the superficiality, and even outright mendacity of a public culture that would refuse even the limited space needed for a rock concert (not to mention long hair). Patočka shared with his underground counterparts like Jirous and Bondy a common indignation, laced with a sense of despair and hopelessness. Not the despair and hopelessness that comes in the wake of war and chaos, but new forms of discontent arising from a shared experience of the suffocation of public life both political and spiritual, a leaden existential dreariness that had settled into the general ethos at the time. And so, while "it would be as difficult today for some phenomenologist to go to a rock concert as for the members of this rock group to go to his lecture," as Havel notes, the absurdity of the climate in 1976 put the phenomenologist and the underground rock musician on the same wavelength.[14]

A classic, more patently political document of what one might call the spiritual condition of normalization is Havel's manifesto "The Power of the Powerless" (1977).[15] Havel's essay echoes much of Patočka's philosophy, taking up the themes of life in truth and the problem of human existence with an explicit emphasis on their political significance in the moment. The essay as a whole can be adduced as evidence of Patočka's intellectual influence on Havel and, by extension, the direction of Charter 77. This was especially true in the years that followed Patočka's death, which saw Havel's interpretation of the initiative gain broad acceptance, not least given the influence of that very essay. Perhaps more significantly, Havel's essay also expresses a self-conscious reserve with regard to just what is or is not possible in the current situation, a reserve, one might suggest, that is tempered by that warning of hopelessness at the heart of the absurd.

Havel's essay is, famously, organized rhetorically around the story of an ordinary, everyday greengrocer who receives from the center, along with tomatoes to put in his window for sale, a placard bearing the slogan "Workers of the World Unite!" The greengrocer proceeds diligently to place the placard in his window, along with the tomatoes. He does this not because he believes in the slogan, nor as a response to any explicit threat, but simply in order to avoid trouble. He doesn't even really think about it, thereby becoming a quite witting organ of propaganda in the form of a protagonist who just wants to get it over with and be left alone. This, in effect, is the extent of his "message" in putting the sign in the window. As Havel puts it,

> Verbally, it might be expressed this way: "I, the greengrocer XY, live here and I know what I must do. I behave in the manner expected of me. I can be depended upon and am beyond reproach. I am obedient and therefore I have the right to be left in peace."[16]

Propaganda like this, as Havel understands it, is an instrument of ideology, which he goes on to define as a kind of excuse that allows for a constructed, false harmony in the absence of actual conviction. In this way ideology avoids the question of not only one's complicity in power, but occludes the very sources of that power itself. Ideology understood in this sense is an example of collective bad faith. "Ideology is a specious way of relating to the world," Havel claims, "it offers human beings the illusion of an identity, of dignity, and of morality while making it easier for them to *part* with them."[17]

Ideology is also a two-way street. It allows the government to claim that its propaganda expresses the will of the people (after all, they are hanging the signs), and thus enjoy a legitimacy that is not genuinely affirmed by anyone involved, just as the greengrocer is allowed the illusion of a normal life lived in accordance with a measure of self-respect and social coherence. All of this is secured effectively by an instrument, the performative lie of hanging an empty slogan in the window, which essentially deflects attention away from the question of belief or responsibility, leaving our greengrocer alone to sell his tomatoes in peace.

The greengrocer is a metaphor for a more complicated regime of mechanisms of collective bad faith which, Havel argues, has become dominant in what he calls "post-Communism" or "post-totalitarianism" (contrasting the Communist world after 1968 with the revolutionary Communism of the 1940s and '50s, both with regard to forms of action and, at least implicitly, ideology). This regime has become so pervasive that power itself seems to have come to serve ideology, and not the other way around:

> Reality does not shape theory, but rather the reverse. Thus power gradually draws closer to ideology than it does to reality; it draws its strength from theory and becomes entirely dependent on it. This inevitably leads, of course, to a paradoxical result: rather than theory, or rather ideology, serving power, power begins to serve ideology.[18]

The "normal" of normalization is a kind of lie, one bought with a near universal abnegation of responsibility to reality, and with that a loss—or at least confusion—of real power. It takes the form of the collective construction of one Potemkin village on top of another, not as a face-saving show for outsiders, but as an absurd reality in which one *lives*. Such a life has strict, ritualistic rules for social expression. In this "dictatorship of the ritual,"[19] appearances of legitimacy, of the faith of the people, of the purposiveness of politics, are orchestrated in order to fortify a bond to an all-justifying ideology, one that demands nothing more (or less) than to remain within the confines of its "correctness": everything must conform to its logic, to its principles, to its legality.

It is important to stress that the main point of Havel's essay is not to emphasize that such a regime, or set of social practices, amounts to a suppression of human freedom, individual or collective. This is obvious, and almost beside the point. More problematic and difficult to understand is the mass participation in post-totalitarian societies ruled in this way by ideology; or, if it must be about freedom, how it is that free beings have precisely the capacity to essentially live a lie. This is the deeper philosophical question animating Havel's essay. It emerges from the recognition that the regime is sustained not simply by imposing conformity on individuals from above, but from the practice of the ubiquitous, even anonymous rituals of ideology, such as placing that placard in the window; avoiding persons or activities with an overt political meaning; repeating when asked empty propaganda slogans; voting in elections everyone knows are a farce; and reading newspapers no one believes. These are rituals that the vast majority of the population, whether their hands happen to rest on actual levers of power or not, whether or not they are members of the Party, comes to practice in one form or another. "By pulling everyone into its power structure, the post-totalitarian system makes everyone instruments of a mutual totality, the auto-totality of society."[20] In such a world there is no easy distinction that one can make between rulers and ruled that would go beyond determining whether or not one holds a given office (and even this would not get one very far); all individuals are, to varying degrees, of course, victims of the system as well as complicit in it. Individuals are effectively split within themselves between a self that performs the rituals demanded by the integrity of the system, and a self that remains unspoken, and betrayed.

Havel juxtaposes living the lie with living in truth—here evoking Patočka explicitly, if not in name, then in conception. Havel draws this juxtaposition with an important nuance: it is not as if these amount to two lives, one in truth and the other in lie, each running separate and parallel to the other. For each presupposes the same existential terrain, the same core of authentic humanity with regard to which each represents a decision, and which each inevitably carries within it:

> Individuals can be alienated in themselves only because there is *something* in them to alienate. The terrain of this violation is their authentic existence. Living the truth is thus woven directly into the texture of living a lie. It is the repressed alternative, the authentic aim to which living a lie is an inauthentic response.[21]

Living in truth reveals what the lie covers over, that part of oneself betrayed, and with that the original demands that human life cannot compromise with and still remain morally stable. The converse is also true: living in truth is constantly haunted by the possibility of the lie, hovering in wait, anticipating the exhaustion of a life in truth. The captive mind is thus caught between the inherent difficulty of truth, thus its vulnerability to ideology, and the impossibility of giving up on it altogether.

Havel's point is ultimately a moral one, but one existentially articulated. Living the lie is a distortion of one's being, a self-contortion of consciousness in order to secure safety in a world that has been built almost exclusively on mechanisms of conformity. The lies of this world shape life, and thus have existential consequences. To live the lie brings a price, that expense of living in denial of one's innermost identification with one's possibilities. The reaction against the lie is understood in equally existential terms, implicating both world and self: to revolt against the lie undermines, almost magically, the mechanisms of post-totalitarian ideology, taking unexpected advantage of the always provisional, always contingent force of falsity. The revolt against the lie also creates a renewed human space of possibility, and with that a resurgence of an integrated self-identity, even if (or perhaps above all when) it takes place solely on the level of the individual. In the lie, one lives a life one can never recognize as one's own; in the truth, one lives a life by bearing its responsibility, attempting to close the circle of the question one always is for oneself.

Havel's essay is a classic in dissident literature, and though its luster has perhaps faded over the past half-century, along with the memory of the post-totalitarian society it describes, it continues to be essential reading for anyone interested in the history of late Communism.[22] The essay also figured prominently in discussions, just after 1989, of the nature of "civil society" as an attractive explanatory construction for the transformations of the Communist world that had taken virtually everyone by surprise—above all perhaps Havel himself. Or at least the 1977 author of the "Power of the Powerless." For the essay arguably makes no sense unless one exercises its basic assumptions about how the world is put together; namely, that the system is for all intents and purposes permanent, that it may perhaps evolve into something more sensitive to the moral needs of human existence, but for all that, the basic political parameters of the present will extend indefinitely into the future.

This sense of constraint, of the need for low expectations, animates the appeal, late in the essay, for what Havel describes as an "existential revolution." Here the call is not so much for political transformation as it is for a transformation of the ethos of society as a whole, even the world-community, one that would aim for the "rehabilitation of values like trust, openness, responsibility, solidarity, love."[23] Havel is asking his readers how to envision, within the constraints of an oppressive reality that shows no sign of change or changeability, a genuine moral awakening, one that finds its sense of purpose not in the utopian promise of a future, but in the way we comport ourselves in our everyday life. How to envision power, in other words, which has been present all along in our powerlessness, an absurd power that lies implicit in life, despite all evidence to the contrary, as a kind of future present:

> For the real question is whether the "brighter future" is really always so distant. What if, on the contrary, it has been here for a long time already, and only our own blindness and weakness has prevented us from seeing it around us and within us, and kept us from developing it?[24]

Charter 77

Any reflection on the political meaning of Patočka's philosophy, writ narrowly or broadly, invariably finds its way to a consideration of the implications of the final days of the philosopher's life as one of the spokespersons for Charter 77. The manifesto was written in late 1976 by a group of intellectuals, including Havel, in the wake of the trials of the music underground, and through creative clandestine methods was initially signed by a loosely associated group representing a relatively wide cross-section of the intelligentsia. The central demand of the Charter was deceptively simple, even anodyne: it called on the Czechoslovak government to honor the guarantee of human rights that had been articulated in various formal treaties and agreements of which it was the signatory, above all the Helsinki Accords of 1975.[25] Not exactly the stuff of haunting specters.

This public reminder of the government's own sworn obligations was not welcomed by the authorities, and was interpreted as a direct challenge to the authority of the Communist state. And, in fact, Charter 77 was meant to be just that. Couching the text in terms that conformed to the letter of the law was a tactic that played on the ritualistic legal conformity that characterized the post-totalitarian state, even when it came to police oppression. Nevertheless, the official and unofficial response of the regime was as harsh as it was swift: the text of the Charter was suppressed, and its signatories were publicly attacked and systematically persecuted in an attempt to crush the movement.[26]

The Charter was an unusual document, and Patočka an equally unusual choice for spokesperson. Not exactly formulated as a manifesto, the text of the Charter called for no action other than diligent monitoring of the law, and affected a combination of legal formality with a certain naivete that cloaked the more radical motives of its framers. The drafters and targets for initial signatories included poets, writers, various species of academics, religious leaders and thinkers, and even reformist Communists who had been expelled from the party after 1968. Havel was chosen as a spokesperson, largely based on the idea that a younger writer would represent an important group within the initiative, and likewise the former foreign minister Jiří Hájek in order to represent the reformist Communists. The literary historian Václav Černý and Patočka were the two choices considered for the third spokesman, based on the idea that an elder figure with significant scholarly stature was necessary, and the two were the most obvious candidates at the time. The relatively apolitical, modest Patočka was chosen over the more openly political Černý, who was well known for taking aggressively polemical public positions (and often suffering as a consequence). After some hesitation, and assurance that his role as spokesman would be endorsed by Černý, who was perhaps the more obvious choice, Patočka agreed.[27]

Patočka thus came to play an active role in the history of political dissidence in central Europe during the Communist period, due, at least in part, to his long history of relative political inactivity. Combined with his stature as an international philosopher, the fact that Patočka was not easy to pin down politically represented, ironically, a tactical advantage in this context.

This perhaps explains why Patočka was approached by the Chartists with the request to be one of their spokesmen, but it does not explain why he agreed. The motivations behind an individual's involvement in any political movement, or for that matter any movement at all, remain more often than not very difficult to untangle and bring into focus. This is especially true when, as was the case with Charter 77, participation risked almost certain persecution. Why expose one's self, family, friends, and colleagues to the dangerous consequences of an action that will almost certainly result in failure? It is one thing for circumstances to pull one into the fray, but to choose to step into it is another dynamic entirely.

There is almost never just one answer to such questions. One should be wary of generalizing from the expressed motivations of one individual to those of everyone involved, just as one should avoid drawing from the general import and meaning of a movement too many conclusions about what might have brought any given individual to take the risk. Things become arguably even more complicated in the case of a philosopher such as Patočka, for whom political life represented not only a field of action and expression, but also an object of properly philosophical reflection. Fundamental questions of the meaning of responsibility and personal risk are woven through virtually all of Patočka's major philosophical writings, making it difficult to avoid the conclusion that his thought is both deeply ethical and political at once.

For this reason, philosophy arguably belongs just as much to that complex of motivations that led Patočka to embrace Charter 77, as do his moral, personal, and political beliefs. And in fact, Patočka's philosophical thought is palpably close to the surface in two texts that he circulated in conjunction with the public release of the Charter. The first, "The Obligation to Resist Injustice," appeared on the same day as the Charter itself (January 3, 1977), and the second, "What We Can and Cannot Expect from Charta 77," was written in the hospital just before his death.[28] The critique of modern technological civilization, so central to Patočka's understanding of modern humanity, provides a central frame for each text; likewise, his ideas about the centrality of responsibility and moral existence as a whole provide much of the content. The result is that it seems obvious that we have here an instance of a philosopher who has been driven by his ideas to confront the patent injustice of the situation in which he finds himself, and that this confrontation will take the explicit form of a powerful appeal to the conscience of both those who perpetrate injustice and those who have chosen to be passive witnesses.

And furthermore, it seems obvious that this appeal in turn strives to speak to basic human truths expressed by the concept of human rights. Consider this passage from "The Obligation to Resist Injustice":

> The idea of human rights is nothing other than the conviction that even states, even society as a whole, are subject to the sovereignty of moral sentiment: that they recognize something unconditional that is higher than they are, something that is binding even on them, sacred, inviolable, and that in their power to establish and maintain a rule of law they seek to express this recognition.[29]

This apparently seamless continuity between the thought of a philosopher and a political act of protest is potentially misleading, however. First of all, Patočka was not a moral or political philosopher in the sense of someone who labors to produce theories of the state, political rights, or sovereignty in order to provide an understanding and justification for adjudicating a given set of readily identifiable and familiar moral and political commitments. Even if one finds in these two texts on Charter 77 a clear expression of the values of democratic liberalism in a more or less familiar form, it is far more difficult to identify examples in Patočka's philosophical writings in which the same ideas are expressed in the fashion of such an unequivocal endorsement.

On the contrary, the philosophical texts of Patočka offer, as explored throughout this book, overwhelming evidence of a complex, deep, and even troubling thinker of the human condition. The more politically oriented of these texts, such as the *Heretical Essays* but also *Plato and Europe*, clearly consider the liberal democracies of the West, with their pursuit of the technological domination of the planet and embrace of consumerist culture, to be just as inhospitable to authentic existence as the world of the authoritarian regimes in the states then under Soviet domination. Patočka, one might say, would just as likely have been a critic of the system had he lived in 1970s London or New York, those epicenters of a crude consumerism cloaking itself in the ideals of liberal individualism. It so happened he lived in Prague, and that it was the politics of that particular time and situation that fixed the immediate parameters of his struggle.

This is not to suggest that Patočka did not act out of the moral and political convictions expressed so powerfully in the two texts from 1977. He most certainly did, at considerable personal risk, and ultimately at the cost of his life. Yet the individual person who acts and makes choices at a particular moment in life, and the philosopher who follows a lifelong path of thinking, are not quite the same thing, though of course they are not completely different either. The result is that, looking at the two Charter 77 texts through the lens of the way in which the nature of the political is articulated within his phenomenological philosophy, it is difficult to avoid the impression that Patočka could have said much more, that there is a wealth of questions and issues left unspoken, perhaps for the sake of rhetorical brevity, and certainly out of the interests of political calculation.[30]

What was left out, however, is important to consider, not only to help untangle the specifically philosophical motivations that led Patočka to his involvement with Charter 77, but also to help free a reflection on Patočka's thinking about politics from the oversimplified ideological labels that his contemporary status in political memory as a dissident-intellectual threatens to accrue. The triumphalist narrative that took hold in the West after 1989, with its proclamation of the inevitable world domination of democratically governed liberal societies, not to mention capitalism, would have us see in Patočka an important intellectual proponent of the justice of its cause. This perception of Patočka's significance is not wholly false, but it does obscure significantly the nuances of the complex philosophical perspective Patočka developed over the course of a fascinating and productive intellectual life, one that spanned virtually all of the significant events in the history of the twentieth century. For Patočka's thinking on the nature of political existence is much richer than the labels commonly deployed when reconstructing the politics of the Soviet era can capture, even if at the same time it is also often ambiguous and perplexing.

The Space of the Political

> The distinction between the sociopolitical sphere of state power and the moral sphere, which we noted above, demonstrates that Charta 77 represents no political act in the strict sense, that it constitutes no competition or interference with political power in any of its functions. Charta 77 is neither an association nor an organization; its basis is strictly personal and moral, and so are the obligations it entails.
> —Patočka, "Obligation to Resist Injustice," 341–42

Commentators on Patočka's two Charter 77 texts often emphasize his tactic, like that of the Charter itself, of emphasizing the personal, "nonpolitical" character of the initiative, in order to avoid arrest and prosecution under the anti-sedition laws of the state.[31] This was, as already suggested above, a tactical ruse of affected naivete. The pressure of conscience—despite Patočka's protestation that Charter 77 has no interest in being the conscience of the state—is being deployed here in a decidedly political fashion.[32] The subsequent persecution of those involved would show that this was precisely the interpretation adopted by the authorities.

Yet this implicit agreement between Charter 77 and its opponents regarding its ultimate political meaning does not really address the question of just what actually constitutes an explicitly "political" act. If it is not definable in terms of a division between private expressions of belief and conscience and the exercise of public instruments of power, then what does define it? More to the issue at hand, what is the nature of that space in which a formally apolitical expression of moral conviction can take on the valence of the political, or where the naked violence of an authoritarian regime could conceivably be deployed to lay claim to a monopoly of all things political?

As explored earlier, one of the most interesting aspects of Patočka's philosophy of history is his understanding of the nature of the historical emergence of political life. For Patočka, how politics comes into history is an essential element in understanding its nature and defining characteristics; it is also, by extension, essential to understanding what it means to live and move in an environment such as post-totalitarianism, in which the very domain of the political has been fundamentally distorted, but for all that remains recognizably "political" in nature.

It is helpful here to again rehearse some of the basic gestures of Patočka's philosophy of history. One such gesture has to do with the claim that politics, or the political proper, emerges against the background of, and in fundamental opposition to what Patočka describes as the mythical world of pre-historical humanity. This distinction between mythical and post-mythical existence implies that political life is not simply one form among others of the communal organization of human beings (like the family, or religion); it is instead a distinctive manner of being, one that makes its appearance at a particular point in human history, before which it makes little sense to talk about "political existence" as such. The emergence of the political inaugurates in this way the emergence of a new kind of *world*: political life is not something that overlays a neutral, apolitical existence, but is itself the emergence of a worldly existence of a different register.

All human worlds for Patočka, whether historical or pre-historical, political or apolitical, can be understood as a permutation of the fundamental openness to the world and things that defines human life existentially. As has been explored in earlier chapters, Patočka articulates human openness as a threefold movement, or a threefold unfolding of the manner in which life opens up a space of encounter in which humans relate to things and to one another. The first of the three movements Patočka elaborates is that of rootedness, of being born into a concrete situation that initially opens existence onto the plenitude of being; the second is the movement of defense, of the sheltering and protecting of what is essentially an exposed and contingent irruption of existence into the world. And finally, the third is the movement that illuminates an implicit ordering and order present within the otherwise raw contingency of human effort at self-preservation in the wake of having been born. This final movement draws humans back from their immersion in things and orients them toward an insight into the essence of their lives as openness, thus fashioning that very openness in such a way that provides the possibility of something like understanding and truth.

Everything turns on the relative weight that life gives to truth. This weight of truth is not something given but is accomplished, and in such a way that involves a fundamental decision about the meaning of existence. The mythical, pre-historical and pre-political world exhibits the threefold movement in a particular way, one that establishes a priority of the first two movements, those of rootedness and defense, over the third movement with its implicit promise of a relation to truth. Accordingly, in the case of mythical humanity, the past, as something closed and in that sense already decided, is given priority; meaningfulness, whatever it may otherwise be, is ultimately grasped in the form of a repetition of what was. Here life lives out of a pre-given understanding of itself, following tracks of meaningfulness long since laid down, and which always remain impervious to human insight—not so much because they are obscure and difficult to comprehend, but because they are not approachable at all as problems of comprehension. Such a world is thus "pre-historical" not because there is no memory, but because historical consciousness has not yet taken root as an organizing mode of life. Human beings are always historical to the extent to which their lives are the movement of openness, but they only *exist historically* when history is embraced, when there is an explicit taking up of the fundamental movement of openness as that which guides the order of meanings, or the world as a horizon of manifestation.

The great cities of the early Bronze Age are for Patočka emblematic of this pre-historical mode of being in the world. The city is a concentration of human existence, the original space of its manifestation gathered together into a unique, concrete expression, one that reveals the manner in which humans exist in the world, and in this sense it embodies their self-awareness. Yet the ancient city remains oriented around the priorities of rootedness and defense; it also represents both the endurance of the past and a sense of the sacred as both guarantors of life and the source of its ultimate fragility. The ancient city is, so to speak, a primordial expression of that basic orientation to the truth of human existence that holds sway for mythical humans: their fundamental subjection to power, whether that of the gods or the demigod-like great among humans, and the inviolable necessities of sustenance and self-preservation. The city as a space of manifestation, as the being of a deeper openness that is not reducible to the particular individuals and forces that compose its individuality, is fused with those same individuals and forces. The relation to truth, to openness as such, is not absent here, but latent.[33]

For Patočka, the twin emergence of political life and philosophy—the two being for him inextricable—can be understood as a temporal and existential reorientation to a meaning of truth determined by an explicit embrace of this latent openness. It represents, as it were, the rebirth of the primordial ancient city in the Greek polis, an event that for Patočka marks a fundamental, if not wholly clean break with a past indifferent to both the historical and political potential of human existence. Unlike the ancient city, the polis is no longer the site of an accepted submission to a power virtually indistinguishable from divinity or the cosmos. Power is now something *contested*, and with that perennially open to unexpected results. In short, with the rise of the polis, power and rule are now uniquely open to their own future, and thus are historical through and through.

Accordingly, Patočka in the *Heretical Essays* characterizes the polis as a life of initiative, or "a life in active tension, one of extreme risk and unceasing upward striving in which every pause is necessarily already a weakness for which the initiative of others lies in wait."[34] The political and the philosophical thus differ from the mythical with respect to the manner in which human possibility is made manifest in an essential sense. The polis is not so much the birth of a new world, as if it were some kind of alternate reality of action wholly transcending pre-historical existence, as it is a shift in the way that human beings pursue themselves, their possibilities and futures. Human life, whether mythical or non-mythical, is always a pursuit of the possible, always a movement; but to pursue beyond the limits of the given, beyond the patterns of pre-formed existence, is to unfold possibilities in the form of transformations, or fundamental changes that are pursued in full consciousness of what is at risk: "Here life is not received as complete as it is, but rather transforms itself from the start—it is an *upswing* [*vzmachu*]."[35] Here the course of time no longer takes the form of a repetition, or of an expression of settled meanings; the future is instead decoupled from the past, at least enough so that something like a decision can be made with respect to the meaning of each.

That something like a decision is at all in play on the order of time, regarding how humans comport themselves in time, implies that political life is a pursuit of human possibility that is itself without foundation—it is a decision in the sense of a gamble, a grasp at what is not secure or coupled with an expectation of security. As such it is a life that is not simply exposed, and hence fragile relative to the forces that dominate the world (that *are* the world); it is also a life that is actively risked and precarious, a life that "does not stand on the firm ground of generative continuity, it is not backed by the dark earth, but only by darkness, that is, it is ever *confronted* by its finitude and its permanent precariousness of life."[36]

In the upswing of history, human finitude gains a different sense: humans are no longer the lesser powers in a hierarchy of being, though they have not become the most powerful either. Their existence marks instead the space for a promise of something *new*, to evoke an important theme from Hannah Arendt.[37] Yet just what the new entails is not, in any given case, clear from the beginning. If the mythical, the pre-historical, is characterized by a certain kind of unconsciousness, expressing itself through images relative to which it has no interpretive distance, then political existence, however "conscious," is nevertheless beset by a certain characteristic darkness. And for Patočka this darkness is ontological.

Historical in its essence, this darkness takes the form of an experience of the rootlessness, the groundlessness of existential possibility.

The meaning of this groundlessness, and the question of whether to embrace it or, on the contrary, to reject it in favor of the apparent values of stability and coherence, is one of the core themes of Patočka's philosophy. And it is something that haunts the two texts on Charter 77. For it implies that, beyond any structural distinctions between those who are authorized to fulfill public functions and those who are forbidden a role in determining how those functions are to be carried out, or the difference between those who are allowed to speak and those who are only allowed to be spoken to, to act or to remain passive, there is a more primordial space of political existence understood as a *common problematicity*. "Political" action in this philosophical sense is the pursuit of the possibilities opened by this problematicity—it is the pursuit of possibilities inherent to a consciousness of the promise implied by the difference between the meaning of the past and the future, and the guiding sense of being those who are situated at a moment in which the decision of this meaning is in play.

Accordingly, what constitutes a "political act" is an act that has a decision about the status, the significance, and the force of human problematicity as its guiding *daimon*. Such an act can occur only in a horizon, a space of the political, in which human freedom finds itself face to face with its own promise, however much it might otherwise seek to hide.

Strife

> For all these reasons, we consider a time when it became possible to sign a Declaration of Human Rights a new historical epoch, the stage for an immense outreach, since it represents a reversal of human consciousness, of the attitude of humans to themselves and to their society. Not simply or primarily fear or profit, but respect for what is higher in humans, a sense of duty, of the common good, and of the need to accept even discomfort, misunderstanding, and a certain risk, should henceforth be our motives.
>
> —Patočka, "Obligation to Resist Injustice," 342–43

Perhaps the most perplexing of those parts of Patočka's philosophical writings that touch directly on the theme of political life is the central role played by the concept of *polemos*.[38] The thought is a difficult one, and seems hardly compatible with even the spirit of the two Charter 77 texts being considered here. For what does it mean to argue that strife—even war (*polemos*)—is not the exception, but is central to political life, rooted in its very origin? Is Patočka, in texts such as the *Heretical Essays* and elsewhere, committing himself to a conception of human communal life that is fundamentally agonistic, saddled with inevitable irruptions of conflict, violence, and destruction? Is the subtle evocation of "discomfort, misunderstanding, and a certain risk" at the end of the passage quoted above meant to signal the possibility that the new epoch, the "reversal of human consciousness" heralded in the first lines, will more than likely unravel, throwing the world back into a state of devastating conflict that agreements such as the Helsinki Accords were putatively meant to prevent?

It is thus important to consider again Patočka's interpretation of the concept of *polemos* in his reconstruction of the origins of political life and philosophy. Its root significance has to do, as with virtually all things political in Patočka's thinking, with the problem of human finitude. Discomfort, risk, misunderstanding, and likewise all the varieties of strife and conflict in which they are embedded, have their ground in relations conditioned by human finitude, the limitations of understanding and action, and ultimately death. Accordingly, the origin of political existence in Patočka's account is in its fundamentals the emergence of a distinctive relation to finitude and death; yet at the same time it is a new relation that remains, at bottom, a modification of a very old one. The point is not to argue that somehow in prehistory mythical humans were unaware of their finitude, or even that they gave death a different, false meaning that had become ripe for being replaced by a "true" account offered by philosophy and the founders of the new humanity of the polis. If this was to some extent the case in at least some part or other of the world, it is beside the point. Nor is the point that with the rise of political life death had suddenly taken on a distinctively moral significance, or was freed from superstition and tied to individual conscience or responsibility. Again, this might to some extent be the case for some, but more fundamental than all these phenomena is the radical experience of finitude that for Patočka comes to determine political life writ large: to embrace the historicity of existence is nothing less than to understand human life as something that emerges from its own groundlessness, its own brute problematicity, and in that sense from *nothing*.

Once again, the question of nothingness has to be acknowledged as central to Patočka's reflections. In the context of historical consciousness, and by extension political life, this nothing is not a simple absence borne or weathered, but something cultivated. Nothingness is the origin of a sense of the promise of freedom, and it takes the shape of an insight into the groundless meaning of the being of all that is, of all that can be said to be. What is "higher in humans" (to again echo the passage from "The Obligation to Resist Injustice" quoted above), what remains standing when everything else seems to be lost, is precisely the obscure terminus of this groundless, essentially wandering life of insight. Patočka's descriptions of the beginning of history thus focus on the beginning of a form of life that reorients itself as capable of seeing across the landscape of beings in their emergence; it is a life that exists in being cut by the tension between what shows itself for what it is, and what refuses and recedes into a nothingness that remains implicit in all striving, all fixing and determining of things for what they are.

In other words, the emergence of history is the emergence of a specific form of *seeing*, one oriented by both clarity of understanding and the experience of its dark ground. It is a seeing that strives to grasp things for what they are, or that is taken up by the problem of orienting oneself towards this "as they are." Not the past, but the present of life is now the axis of attunement, and it is an attunement to the manner in which things emerge into presence, into manifestation.

And furthermore, it is the presence of emergence in the specific form of that which is contested and in conflict, and thus within the dynamic of individuation inextricably woven with the nothingness of finite being. It is this strife-ridden, tension-filled emergence that, Patočka argues, one finds articulated in the theme of *polemos* in the extant fragments of Heraclitus.[39] *Polemos* is at once a power that binds all to all, the strife (*eris*) that lies within the inwardly stretched, tension-ridden harmony of manifestation. Yet it is also at the same time the manner in which all that exists is understood and grasped in insight, in *logos*:

> The power generated by strife is no blind force. The power that arises from strife is a power that knows and sees: only in this invigorating strife is there life that truly sees into the nature of things—*to phronein*. Thus *phronēsis*, understanding, by the very nature of things, cannot but be at once common and conflicted. To see the world and life as a whole means to see *polemos*, *eris*, as that which is common; *xunon esti pasi to phroneein*: "insight is common to all."[40]

Passages such as these in the *Heretical Essays* are strongly reminiscent of Heidegger's reading of Heraclitus in his 1935 *Introduction to Metaphysics*.[41] For Heidegger as well, Heraclitus's *polemos* is tightly bound up with *logos*, and above all with *phusis*.[42] *Phusis* on Heidegger's account means emergence, manifestation, appearing: "The roots *phu-* and *pha-* name the same thing. *Phuein*, the emerging that reposes in itself, is *phainesthai*, lighting-up, self-showing, appearing."[43] What emerges is manifest as something set apart, within limits that are animated by a confrontation with what distinguishes it from other things, thanks to which it becomes fixed within its *logos*. To "see" (or to understand, in the broad sense of *phronēsis*) what is in accordance with its *logos* is thus to track its emergence as *phusis*; it is to witness the event of its strife, and thus to "be" or exist in the event horizon of a conflict, of the emergence of a being into the open landscape of beings.

It is in this sense that *logos*, *phusis*, the world opened by strife, is something "common" (*xunon*). This commonality is in turn for Heidegger, now turning to Heraclitus's fragment 114, something in play at the very core of what it is to be a polis. The polis is not merely a collected manifestation, an acquired achievement of organization that provides an indifferent platform for human speech and action; it is a collected manifestation as the dynamic event of being, which means that it is a unity held together in tension. The "common" here thus does not indicate some abstract, universal principle but the commonality of a finite bond, a hold on oneself and on things, which is always coupled with a seeing thanks to which what is, what exists, is gathered together into the bond of its *logos*.

In the polis, this commonality of the *logos* takes the form of the unity of *nomos*, or "law," as a specific face of collected presence constitutive of the being of the city. Again Heidegger:

> The *eon*, the being, is according to its essence *xunon*, a gathered coming to presence; *xunon* does not mean the "universal," but rather what gathers everything together in itself and holds it together. For example, according to fragment 114 such a *xunon* is the *nomos* for the *polis*, ordinance [positing as placing together], the inner composition of the *polis*, not something universal, not the sort of thing that floats above all and seizes none, but the originally unifying unity of what strives in confrontation.[44]

Heidegger repeatedly emphasizes this figure of the originary unity of confrontation (*Aus-einander-setzung*), of what is set in a tension apart, as being at the core of Heraclitus's thinking, and it is that which, for Patočka as for Heidegger, governs the operative meanings of *polemos* in Heraclitus's fragments 53 and 80. The concept thus expresses an original ontological signification of war. *Polemos* so conceived also represents in this way a properly historical form of Patočka's third movement: *polemos* marks a moment in which openness, both to what appears, what becomes manifest, and to the appearance of what refuses to appear, becomes an explicit theme of human comportment and thereby determines its specific form.

Polemos thus describes a figure of human comportment, one inwardly determined by a seeing that is at once in tune with the darkness and the light of things.[45] Conflict sums up the essential determination of being as the groundless initiative to grasp and pursue the possible as it is illuminated by the insight, the seeing of *polemos*. Insight is in turn anything but disinterested contemplation, it is the life of an understanding experienced on an explicitly ontological plane. If so, as Heidegger also emphasized, then Heraclitus's *polemos* cannot mean war in a sense limited to an exchange of blows on a battlefield in competition for a particular prize. Just as little can this conception of *polemos* ultimately be understood from the perspective of its utility for the satisfaction of human desires, as seems to be the claim in book 2 of Plato's *Republic*. For neither Patočka nor Heidegger does the polis emerge out of *polemos*, as if it were a solution. Yet neither does *polemos* emerge from the interests of pursuing war or peace, narrowly understood as the conquest of wealth and property. *Polemos* and the polis are instead co-constitutive; and here both thinkers brush up against the possibility that violence is older than either politics or war, with roots in human existence deeper than insight itself.

In Patočka, the result is that the emergence of *polemos* as a figure of thought in Heraclitus must be understood to be intrinsically political, but not in the sense of the reduction of being to primordial violence. *Polemos* in Heraclitus instead signals a profound transformation in the meaning of the violence of war: no longer merely the work of destruction necessary for preservation, war now becomes an essential dimension of the pursuit of the possible in a new and open horizon of the significance of what it *means* to fight. Again, the contrast with the established, non-problematical meaningfulness of the mythical world is central to Patočka's analysis:

> Warriors prior to the emergence of political life find their support in a meaning woven into the immediacy of life, fighting for their home, family, for the continuum of life to which they belong . . . in contrast to that stands the goal of a *free* life as such, one's own or that of others; it is, essentially, an unsheltered life.[46]

Once history begins, how humans fight changes, and how they comport themselves "*inter arma*"[47] provides a powerful symbolic instance of who they have become, as political beings. Battle as a political phenomenon is inscribed in the wake of that fundamental shaking, so important to Patočka's account of the origin of philosophy, of the pre-given meanings of pre-historical existence. A properly political existence entails that this shaking is embraced and affirmed in the form of risk, of the groundlessness of pure initiative in a world of possibilities cut by the movements of strife and confrontation. The commonality of the polis, then, the existential rhythm of a properly political existence, is no longer the mere fact of belonging together as a repetition of the past; it is now a being together in solidarity, facing the consequences of a collective gamble. This solidarity was expressed in ancient Greek political life by the rigid formation of the hoplite phalanx, the act of standing shoulder to shoulder and shield to shield in a *harmonia* of mutual effort; accordingly, the phalanx served the Greeks as a visible symbol of the polis, expressing its spirit, not of conquest, but what Patočka calls the "solidarity of the undaunted," a unity of existence that is "perhaps the only mode [of being human] that offers hope amid the storm of the world."[48]

This reflection is not far from that which subsequently yields Patočka's conception of the "solidarity of the shaken," and in fact they are intimately related: the solidarity of the shaken, arising out of the traumas of the wars of the twentieth century, is in effect the rediscovery of the fundamental existential roots of political life generally, and with that its inner relation to human historicity.

Human Bondage

> We are convinced that no one fails to realize that the Helsinki agreements must be accepted if we are to break free of the bondage of wars and near-wars and that no one fails to recognize that such acceptance will call for many concessions.
> —Patočka, "What We Can and Cannot Expect," 345

The discussion of *polemos* at the end of the second of the *Heretical Essays* signals the essential role of an embrace of risk, of an insight into the constitutive movements of tension and conflict; it further signals the role of problematicity, that mainstay of Patočka's thinking, as a fundamental orientation of human beings, and not a contingent stage of inconvenience that will eventually pass in the march of human progress. And it also, as Patočka indicates in the following passage from the *Heretical Essays*, signals the enduring importance of the Greek experience for contemporary humanity—in particular given the apparent unwillingness of the latter to exist historically:

This beginning [of history] then reaches out to future attempts at historical resurgence, especially by teaching what humankind does not wish to comprehend, in spite of all the immense hardness of history, does not want to understand, something that perhaps only latter days will learn after reaching the nadir of destruction and devastation—that life need be understood not from the viewpoint of the *day*, of life merely accepted, but also from the view of strife, of the night, of *polemos*. The point of history is not what can be uprooted or shaken, but rather the openness to the shaking.[49]

To understand life from the "viewpoint of the day" means to take life as a given positivity, one that can either be augmented or destroyed; it also means to take given life as the ultimate basis, the ultimate good that stands as the absolute justification for all that is. It entails, in this sense, a form of bondage: there is nothing other or more than life, only its mere absence as a brutal shock of the exception, an affront to what ultimately can only have value—one's continued existence as a living being. Accordingly, the "day," in Patočka's idiom, is that which bonds human beings to preservation, and with that to perspectives that cleave close to their relation to things, to the world as an aggregate of objects and the potential energy for their production and destruction. The day in this way shapes the care for being into a care for things; it emphasizes the need for safety, for shelter and sustenance, and for an undisturbed health. And with that the day motivates a turn away from anything that unsettles, that forces the groundlessness of existence into experience. The day, in other words, unfolds as a refusal, a resistance to any *letting go* of things.

In the *Heretical Essays*, Patočka sketches a complex history that leads to the dominance of the day, one that informs in salient ways his diagnosis of the contemporary situation, and which again lies palpably beneath the surface of his two Charter 77 essays. Both the history and the current situation are constituted in accordance with a complicated set of spiritual themes. One part of this set has to do with the nature of knowledge, its gradual shift away from the figures of insight and wisdom to the modern figures of the predictive methodologies of science and technology. The latter coupled together express the interest of the day in the manipulability of things, the possibility of capturing their essence in terms of an ability to predict their behavior under precisely defined conditions. "Knowledge" is thereby transformed into a powerfully radicalized potential for material and spiritual organization. Another group of themes has to do with the relation of the human being to power, or rather how human existence has fashioned itself into a force. Here the interest of the day in security and preservation takes on the form of a will to have, to possess and thus humanize all of being in terms of a fundamental acceptance of only that which can be controlled and dominated. The two sets of themes work together: knowledge as the grasp of the manipulability of things supports and makes possible the dominance of the relation of possession, of a mastery that solidifies the hold of the day.[50]

The result of this development is yet another shift in the very meaning of war. Part of this shift is material in nature. Based on the success of modern natural science, the human capacity for destruction has increased exponentially: the more humans understand things in terms of how they can be manipulated, the better they are positioned to orchestrate their destruction. Likewise, the more humans become invested in things, in their accumulation and increase within the dynamics of the modern will to have, the more the sphere of human existence becomes a mass of positivity ripe for destruction. The more that human reality is experienced as a mass of forces, the more that change and action can only mean the rearrangement of these forces in response to a greater, overwhelming force.

In this way the *night*, that reserve of the exceptional, of what lies outside of the techno-economy of the day, itself becomes pressed into the service of the day. Wars are fought to destroy what are perceived to be the sclerotic structures of the concrete world that hold humans back from acquiring *more*, whether more wealth or more security or more freedom. The night of finitude, the darkness that remains an irremovable dimension of human affairs, becomes embodied in "the bondage of wars and near-wars," and in turn in the enormous *instrumentum* of destruction that has been amassed by human beings.

One should not forget that in the background of the Helsinki Accords, and by extension Charter 77, was the collective sense of the moment that the planet had just managed to pause before settling the issue of who would command the future by means of a global nuclear holocaust. How to manage the competition of the superpowers, the basic premise of which was the possibility of mutual destruction, determined the fundamental existential question of the age, one that was, from Patočka's point of view, understood wholly in terms of the logic, or the economy of the day, with its paradoxical bondage to the threat of a war that it cannot fight. To break this logic, and with that free humanity from its bondage to things, entails—for Patočka the philosopher, who remains at least partially out of sight in the two Charter 77 texts—embracing the hidden exception of a night shorn of its role in destruction, for a renewal of a life in risk, together in solidarity.

Heresy

> In sum, what we expect from Charta 77 is that it will introduce a new ideal orientation into our lives. . . . It is a new orientation to basic human rights, to the moral dimension of political and private life. The Charta will unceasingly remind us how far we fall short of those rights belonging to our citizens by law; it will not cease to remind both our and the foreign public of it, regardless of the risks of such activity.
> —Patočka, "What We Can and Cannot Expect," 347

Patočka's philosophical challenge in the *Heretical Essays* is to shift from an orientation of the day, in its modern form of a will to have and a knowledge to manipulate, to one of the night, of *polemos* as an existence together in risk, a solidarity of the undaunted, of the shaken.[51] It is a challenge, a heresy, that again haunts the two Charter 77 texts. It is a challenge at once philosophical and political, and it introduces a tension into almost every line. The call to *polemos* sounds in the repeated admonition to accept the risk of resistance, to move beyond the calculations of "fear and gain,"[52] even if at the same time it speaks from a fundamental commitment to peace, and with that to the hope of a world without war. The call to *polemos* underlines the questionability of all the evocations to a moral sense of purpose, inwardly problematizing the otherwise clear moral tonality of each text.

Coming to these texts fresh from Patočka's philosophical writings—even those written within months of the two Charter 77 texts, such as "Masaryk's Philosophy of Religion," with its project of thinking nihilism through to the positivity of the nothingness at its ground—the reader can't help but ask: What is the true nature of this moral dimension Patočka seeks to evoke, from where does it receive its orienting force? Is it a promise of reason, of the construction of a society governed by the principles of justice, or the hope of religious faith in a world that, at the end point of history, will redeem the good and punish the evil? Or on the contrary, is it a morality shorn of the imprimatur of reason, and even more generally of a commitment to a world in which everything already has a meaning, in the form of a defined purpose and end? What, in other words, is behind this faith in humanity that is so powerfully expressed here?

Such questions lend a distinctive heretical dimension to these two texts on Charter 77, written so close to the philosopher's death. This dimension remains invisible if they are read in isolation from the rest of Patočka's reflections on history, politics, and philosophy; and likewise, if they are taken uncritically as accurate summary conclusions of the same. Virtually all the principal theses of the Charter texts function as markers for a more probing questioning. In a world in which morality seems to be in decline, Patočka's text calls for a recommitment to a very Kantian moral vision of the world—yet at the same time it is questionable whether Patočka means a return to traditional conceptions of what is highest in humans, or on the contrary, a far more radical embrace of that which transcends in a darker, more unsettling fashion. In a world threatened by nuclear destruction, Patočka's text calls for a change of perspective, for a reorientation that would save humanity from the threat of war and near-war, thus situating itself solidly on the side of the party of peace—yet at the same time his continuous evocations of the necessity of risk, of accepting and embracing risk as a fundamental commitment, point to a conception of solidarity that is ruled not by peace, not by the interests of the day, but by the night of *polemos*.

Some might take all of this as evidence of inconsistency. This would be a mistake, though perhaps a forgivable one. The inner drive of all philosophy, as Patočka understood it, is to strive for justification in clarity, in insight; and this means to be able to give an account of oneself, of why one comports oneself, whether in action or in thought, in the way one does. This is the inner telos of the care for the soul, and for Patočka the very meaning of European civilization. Yet this does not preclude a certain modality of wandering. For the inevitable lesson for all philosophy, and perhaps its hardest-won insight with regard to its own possibility, is the inchoate nature of the life from which this striving emerges, its utter dependency on its own facticity, and with that the nullity of free existence.

The balance between the two, between the ends of clarity and harmony towards which the philosopher strives and the conflicted groundlessness of the human condition on which all such striving ultimately rests, was the ultimate desideratum of Patočka's thought, and forms the motivating inspiration for some of his most brilliant philosophical writings. The two texts here under consideration reflect the moral ideal Patočka sought to embody in his public involvement with Charter 77; they also hint at a deeper truth with regard to the meaning of such ideals, that they are ultimately not so easily achieved, nor even comprehended. They hint, in other words, at the drama of human existence that finds a broader, more complete expression in Patočka the philosopher, even if at the same time they figure prominently as documents of that same drama being played out in Patočka's own life.

Conclusion

Legacies

The Death of a Dissident

In "The Power of the Powerless," Havel cites from one of Patočka's two Charter 77 texts a sentence that would become something of a slogan for the movement: "There are some things worth suffering for."[1] When Patočka wrote this sentence, he was already suffering. Not in the best of health for some years, the pressures of being a spokesperson for the Charter brought on a serious case of bronchitis in February, confining him for a time to bed. Breaking his needed rest to accept an invitation to visit the Dutch foreign minister Max van der Stoel, Patočka was further rocked by a visit from the police on March 1 and again on March 2, followed by an all-day interrogation at the police station on March 3. The next morning, he woke with distressing heart palpitations, and went to the hospital, where he composed "What We Can and Cannot Expect from Charta 77" as well as written responses for an interview with the German newspaper *Die Zeit.*

Though initially he seemed to be responding well to medical treatment, the philosopher's health took a rapid turn for the worse, and Jan Patočka died of a brain hemorrhage on March 13, 1977.[2]

The Legacy of a Philosopher

In a short autobiographical text from 1976, Patočka tells the story of receiving from Husserl in Christmas 1934 the gift of a small, portable lectern that Husserl in turn had received in 1878 from Masaryk in Leipzig, on the eve of his departure, on the advice of Masaryk himself, to attend Franz Brentano's lectures in Vienna. "And so I became the heir of a great 'tradition,'" Patočka notes, "for which I have never felt worthy enough."[3]

The tradition Patočka has in mind is considerably broader than phenomenology, and coincides with some of the most basic philosophical trends of the Enlightenment in central Europe. Both Masaryk and Husserl had articulated a conception of the life of the mind that was devoted above all to reason, to the ideal of a scientific culture and mentality, standing in direct opposition to proponents of authority and legitimacy who would appeal to tradition over inquiry, mystery over argument. For Husserl, this devotion expressed itself in the program of "philosophy as a rigorous science," an embodiment of the guiding ideals of reason that would serve as a countermovement to the relativistic influence of a narrowly conceived historicism and naturalism.[4] For Masaryk, it expressed itself in the affirmation of what he took to be the fundamental human ideals of self-determination and freedom, guided by insight and self-understanding, free from the pernicious effects of prejudice and a perverse need to be ruled. Yet at the same time, both philosophers were deeply critical of a scientific culture that was increasingly indifferent to what they believed to be the fundamental moral needs of humanity, including questions of faith. Both philosophers saw themselves at odds with a modern nihilism that would sacrifice living reflection on the altar of facticity or, in its most extreme forms, power. If for both thinkers, modern science represented the legitimate heir to the ideals of the Enlightenment, it was only on the condition of a renewal of those same ideals, whether in the context of a reflection on the foundations of science as in Husserl, or in Masaryk's defense of a rational democratic liberalism.

By the time Patočka inherits this tradition in 1934, it is under increasing strain on virtually all fronts imaginable. On one front, the rationalism of the nineteenth century, with which Husserl could still identify comfortably, even to some extent in its positivist guise, had become almost completely supplanted by the rise of a scientific rationalism wholly indifferent to the ideal of universal self-responsibility which Husserl considered essential to philosophy. If the ideals of the Enlightenment continued to influence contemporary philosophy, it was no longer in the foundationalist mode of a philosophy as rigorous science, but more on an ethical or social-political register that no longer sought common cause with modern natural science. On another front, the political and social ideals of Masaryk, embodied in the experiment of the new state of Czechoslovakia, would soon be in tatters after the shock of Munich four years later. At best they would come to express the naive perspective of another, simpler time, wholly eclipsed by the experiences of war and revolution that would render the hopes embodied by the philosopher-liberator all but obsolete. If Patočka, "the man whose lot it was to be the philosopher of a time without hope," as Erazim Kohák puts it,[5] was the inheritor of the Enlightenment legacies of Husserl and Masaryk, it is hard to avoid the impression that by the end of the 1930s this bequest was of rapidly diminishing value, and Patočka had little more to look forward to than the pauperism of philosophy.

Patočka was in turn a consistent critic of this very tradition. In the history of phenomenology, he contributed one of the earliest and, in the tradition of Heidegger and Fink, one of the most compelling critiques of Husserl's Cartesianism, opening the way for a rejection of idealism for the sake of a phenomenological ontology that would speak more directly to the richness of human experience in all its forms. Patočka's reconfiguration of the existential structures of care along the lines of the three movements of human existence provides not only a powerful expression of the promise of the project of phenomenological ontology, but in turn yields the foundations for both a compelling philosophical anthropology and the basic framework for a philosophy of history that is by and large free from the vestiges of theology.

Patočka also offers, in his trenchant critique of Masaryk, a conception of the task of philosophy in the modern age as not simply a defense of reason and the ideals of freedom, but as a commitment to the articulation of human freedom shorn of the positivism and naturalism that he believed compromised Masaryk's views from within. An unquestioned naturalism led Masaryk's thinking into the ambiguity of at once affirming both the essential meaninglessness of the natural world articulated by modern science, and the deep need for meaning expressed in the ideals of political freedom and the positivity of religion. Patočka's lifelong ambition can be likened to an attempt to provide a compelling analysis of the problem of nihilism represented by the former, while pursuing the insights of phenomenological philosophy in increasingly profound ways to reveal the fundamental truths of the latter.

Patočka thus seeks to fundamentally modify from within the tradition he inherits, submitting its Cartesian and positivist elements to a thoroughgoing critique, in order to preserve its fundamental Enlightenment affirmation of the ideals of human freedom and rational self-understanding. If Patočka is the thinker who bears witness to the end of a Europe that had once been motivated by the ideal of the care for the soul, he is also in an important sense the philosopher who continues to embody its promise in dark times.

Yet it would be misleading to reduce Patočka's relation to this inheritance to the mere preservation of cultural capital, however modified by critique. To be content with a simple assessment of whether or not what Patočka inherited was of any real value, or whether he was able to keep the flame alive in the darkness of the twentieth century, would ultimately prove to be too limited an approach. This is not to say that such an assessment is unimportant. The enduring force of ideas is a vital element in collective self-understanding, and part of Patočka's legacy is the role he played in twentieth-century thought, especially in the context of central

CONCLUSION

Europe, as a conduit for the transmission of what Masaryk would have called the "ideals of humanity" at a time and a place that had become increasingly hostile to the same. Patočka was in fact a keeper of the flame, above all for those who still yearned for its light among the dislocated intelligentsia in the Czechoslovak context, but arguably for Europe as a whole as well.

But Patočka was more than this, in such a way that perhaps he wasn't even really this at all. For there is something deeper at work in Patočka's philosophical legacy. He not only kept the faith that philosophy mattered, he showed that it was at all possible. The preservation of tradition, especially when under assault, is often a very conservative affair: the instinct is to cloak a truth with inviolability, defend it against heretics, and for this reason the task is often best performed by dogmatists, for whom "critique" is at most a pedagogical technique for shoring up flagging conviction. When not under assault, the most effective practitioners at preservation tend to be those who exude an optimism that opens itself to all questions and doubts, confident that in the end the truth will prevail, that it need not be protected so much as given a chance to shine. Patočka was neither a dogmatist under siege nor an optimist with the confidence to roam. What "reason"—or better, the care for the soul—is to mean after the death of Europe was for him a question far more open than would be acceptable to any dogmatist; likewise, the risk implicit in opening unadorned truth to the onslaughts of doubt was never, for Patočka, assumed with an air of any absolute confidence as to what the outcome might in fact turn out to be.

What Patočka showed, in other words, is not that it is possible to preserve intellectual traditions in times of crisis, holding together a community of the faithful, and allowing for a generational transmission of the spiritual insights of the past. There were many who did this, and still do, in a world that has never been anything but ambivalent when it comes to the legacies of the Enlightenment, or the history of ideas writ large. Instead, Patočka showed that, in an environment increasingly inhospitable to the very practice of philosophy, whether due to official censure or to a culture turning increasingly away from the life of the mind, hostile to both its apparent moral authority and inaccessibility, it is still possible to dedicate oneself to the rigors of questioning. This suggests that self-understanding is not simply a matter of a commerce with traditions, whether preserving or contributing, ignoring or criticizing them; it also has to do with living the very questions that such traditions reflect, questions that remain in force even when traditional means for their articulation stumble: what it means to be born, to be dependent on others and others dependent on you, what it is possible to see, to understand, the mystery of death and the surprise of love. The common cultural heritage of human beings, that non-system of the expression of human life of which Europe is in the end only a ripple in the stream, invariably provides powerful means for posing and addressing such questions, but the catalyst is always and only can be the concrete life one lives. Ultimately, all humans are wanderings in-between—in between the truth experienced in the questions of life and the contingent, fallible expressions each life offers that give temporary form to human existence.

Thus on a deeper level, Patočka's philosophy is best conceived as an expression of a fundamental devotion to human wandering, not as a lot or burden, but as a source of inspiration in a time of hopelessness, for orientation in a time of disorientation. It is a philosophy of the affirmation of meaning in the face of a loss of meaning, of a situation in which meaning is nothing that humans can claim for their own. The meaningfulness of which Patočka's philosophy speaks is one that humans neither create nor inherit, but to which they can open themselves, offering themselves as a space in which it can take root:

> Man faces a tremendous challenge, namely not to claim meaning for himself, not to attempt to lay hold of the meaningfulness of the universe for his own benefit but, on the contrary, to comprehend *himself* as a being existing out of meaning and for meaning, living for what gives rise to a world full of meaning, sacrificing himself so that the meaning whose foundation "is" outside of beingness can take root, make a home, and grow in him.[6]

The Legacy of a Teacher

Václav Havel tells the story of how, around the age of seventeen, somewhere in what he describes as "the deep fifties," he met Jan Patočka through a book, *The Natural World as Philosophical Problem*, at the library of Charles University in Prague. There was a complication: it was one of those books that were at the time deemed "not for lending," so it took some convincing on the part of the young Havel before the university librarian agreed reluctantly to loan him what was not for lending. The experience was profound. The aura of books (Havel in this connection also mentions a collection of Jiří Kolář's poetry) is an important part of any intellectual coming of age, and those that strike most powerfully

CONCLUSION

early on serve time and again to reconnect with that magic that had once guided one's first steps in the world of ideas.

In the deep fifties, the aura of such books in the countries of central Europe could take on an especially vivid character. "These books," Havel writes, "their magic spell further strengthened by their suppression, meant the world to me—truth, genuine culture and inspiration—and for a long time remained the only thing in modern Czech culture that truly spoke to me and that I considered worth reading (again and again)."[7]

Ideas are central for philosophy, but philosophy is not a life limited to ideas alone: there is always a personal dimension. Part of the aura that surrounded Patočka's work was a function of the suppression of what it represented. Phenomenology had become, in the estimation of official Marxist ideology, associated with conservative bourgeois decadence, and was thus something of a *philosophia non grata*, its proponents frozen "under the ice of time," to borrow Havel's borrowed phrase from Boris Pasternak. Few things attract our interest more than the rumor of riches kept hidden from view. This of course comes at the cost of being put on ice. For Patočka, this involved being excluded for most of his career from professional teaching, along with restricted travel and publishing opportunities. Yet these personal constraints seemed not only to have galvanized Patočka, but to have provided conditions for the cultivation of a powerful pedagogical persona, adding to the aura of the forbidden a tincture of authenticity. By the time of his death Patočka had become a kind of legend, though in a sense far from any cult of personality. Authenticity flowed instead from the person of Patočka, with his blend of generosity, quiet seriousness, and genuine concern for the spiritual well-being of those who came to philosophize with him.

And, ultimately, later in life, Havel did come to philosophize with the author whose books were not to be loaned. He describes how his initial shyness, arising from his reverence for the philosopher, finally dissolved, to be replaced by a hunger for the activity of discussion that was going on in Patočka's unofficial seminars, often held in his living room or other temporary venues such as the Theater on the Balustrade, where Havel first met him in person. Patočka offered these seminars in part in order to allow students banned from the university to continue their studies, but they also meant much more, certainly to those like Havel and other artist-intellectuals who were hungry for any opportunity to think in speech with someone they trusted. For these seminars were, in a deep sense, a coming together that made philosophy itself possible in impossible times:

Listening to him was a delight: he spoke slowly, sometimes even pausing for a long time to find the right word, but he talked with enjoyment, engagingly and with inner passion, and even the actors listened attentively. The strength of his expositions lay not only in all he knew and in his ability to penetrate unswervingly below the surface of phenomena and relations but in his whole personality, its genuineness, modesty, and humor. And through these unofficial seminars we all were carried into the world of philosophizing in its authentic, original sense. No pulpit boredom, but an absorbed and alive searching for the meaning of things and an illuminating of oneself, of one's own situation in the world.[8]

The legacy of these seminars, and of Patočka's influence as a teacher, is evident not only in the example of Havel himself but reaches more broadly, arguably contributing to the formation of a generation of intellectuals in the lands of the former Czechoslovakia and beyond. All of this is better documented and analyzed by intellectual historians. Here the intent is only to emphasize the importance of something more ephemeral, if also evident and attested to by many, including Havel: the ethical resilience that enabled Patočka to preserve the practices of the life of the mind—serious scholarship, open discussion, intellectual curiosity and, perhaps most important, honesty.

All this regardless of conditions, even to the point of holding an impromptu seminar in a prison waiting room between police interrogations, as Havel recounts in a text that was itself written from prison:

> It was during my last encounter with him that I comprehended all of this most clearly; he and I, together with a third accomplice, were spending the last break between interrogations in the Ruzyně Prison waiting room for "interrogees" philosophizing. At any moment they would come for any one of us, but that did not matter to the professor; in his impromptu seminar on the history of the notion of human immortality and human responsibility he weighed his words as carefully as if we had unlimited time at our disposal.[9]

Socrates, too—or so a poet of another age tells us—philosophized about death and responsibility in between phases of a process that would end in his own death. And like that scene, the meaning of Havel's last discussion with Patočka is not so much about ideas as it is about those ethical bonds that human beings rely upon in order, together, to face their fears, to face what threatens them in both body and soul. Such bonds are among the principal reasons for the turn to ideas at all, and in a way, philosophy amounts to a play on this paradoxical experience of the thinking of abstract things bringing lives closer together, helping to weave them into a common reality of wandering together in a world pregnant with meaning.

Epilogue

At the beginning of his history of Prague, describing a love-hate relation to his native city, Peter Demetz cites a poem of Franz Kafka's, in which he "speaks of walking across the Charles Bridge and softly resting his hands on the old stones, *'die Hände auf alten Steinen.'*" It is an image evocative of both old Prague and Kafka's iconic position in it, the mystery of the one and the magic of the other. Yet like all things Prague and Kafka, there is an element of the tragic involved. "I always believed," Demetz continues, "that he tried in that gentle gesture to keep the blood of many brutal battles from oozing out."[1]

I often think of this passage when remembering the way Krzysztof Michalski used to tell the story of his visit to Prague in the 1970s as a graduate student from Warsaw. He went to meet Patočka to discuss his dissertation on Heidegger, and the philosopher gifted him with an extensive walking tour of the city. The older Michalski described, many years later, what a privilege it was to have as a guide someone of such deep learning, who was fully at ease with the intricate complexities of historical Prague—that baffling medley of Přemsyl kings and Holy Roman emperors, scientists and alchemists, poets and musicians, and the often tortured but sometimes peaceful multiethnic coexistence of Czechs, Slovaks, Germans, Jews, Ruthenes, Hungarians, and Roma. And of course there were the brutal battles Demetz alludes to, the inter-ethnic violence of pogroms, wars secular and religious, and the forced expulsions of minority populations, but also more recently the less violent trend toward political homogenization along ethnic lines that would ultimately lead to the breakup of the Czechoslovak state itself, long after Michalski's visit.

The younger Michalski, in his correspondence with Patočka around the time of their meeting, hints at an even more profound experience:

> My visit with you very much mobilized me; it was one of the greatest experiences of my life. I feel extremely grateful and indebted—and I believe that the best way to pay this debt is by intense work. And I cannot wait to begin.[2]

The correspondence suggests that the two men talked about much more than history, or at least the kind of history one would offer to a curi-

EPILOGUE

ous tourist on a walking tour. It suggests they talked about the situation of post-totalitarian states, as Havel describes them, in particular the views of young Polish intellectuals, many of whom had fled abroad after 1968, but some, like Michalski, who remained behind. This correspondence also suggests that the groundwork was laid during that visit for Michalski's subsequent invitation to Patočka to write an article on "phenomenology and history,"[3] a project that would rapidly blossom into the *Heretical Essays*.

This story of the utterly contingent origin of the *Heretical Essays*, a text that plays such a profound role in any interpretation of Patočka's life and philosophy, invites some reflection. One often looks at the work of a philosopher as a body of interlocking achievements, each somehow born out of a vision, conceived wholly in the abstract, of what preceded it and in anticipation of what follows. This synthetic perspective is a natural consequence of the interests of scholarship, in which reflection on contingent particulars tends to be relegated to the responsible bookkeeping of sources, in order to favor the development of definitive readings that posit an interlocking whole that is both transparent and comprehensible. One thus tends to underestimate the role of chance encounters, unplanned conversations, or the sheer contingencies of an occasion as the catalyst for what one chooses to write and when.

These contingencies are ultimately opaque, slipping past our notice by being apparently too unimportant to remember. Whatever Michalski actually discussed with Patočka—one can imagine it was about the respective political situations of Poland and Czechoslovakia, about the Prague Spring and the disappointments of 1968; or perhaps it was about the meaning of Europe, what it means to exist historically, the importance of phenomenology for contemporary philosophy; it is hard to know where to stop, or to begin—it was also only a moment in time, of which there is little documentation and very little living memory.

This brief visit of only a few days quickly vanished in the undertow of events in the lives of both philosophers. Within three years Patočka would embrace the role of dissident, promoting the program of Charter 77 and perishing as a result. Michalski's path from that moment would be longer, beginning with several opportunities to establish himself abroad as a professional philosopher, and by the early 1980s leading the foundation of a research institute in Vienna dedicated to exchanges between intellectuals from both the East and the West. Michalski would also subsequently experience another version of post-totalitarianism, one that would significantly modify the horizon of possibility even imaginable during his walk with Patočka across Charles Bridge in May 1974, whether they rested their "*Hände auf alten Steinen*" or not.

The reason why I think of Demetz's allusion to Kafka in connec-

EPILOGUE

tion with Michalski's story of his visit is my conviction that Patočka—and Michalski for that matter—did not have any illusions about history. If both of these philosophers remained dedicated to the ideal of Europe, or perhaps some ideal or other that is recognizably "European," it was conditioned heavily by an acute awareness of the disasters of its history, and the burdens that belong to its legacy. Both thinkers were, in any case to my mind, driven by a deep suspicion that guarded them from idealizing distortions that would seek to disguise the horrors felt to be always just beneath the surface, and the threat of a renewed wave of hopelessness those horrors represented, ready to burst forth whenever given the opportunity. This suspicion informs much of the tone of their writings, whether or not it is given express articulation. Perhaps it represents an example of what Havel describes as a certain skeptical reticence of central Europeans, born from so many failed springs, that "strange, almost mysterious horror of everything overstated, enthusiastic, lyrical, histrionic, or overly serious."[4]

Can we perhaps add a suspicion, a skeptical reticence regarding philosophy as well? For Michalski this is perhaps the case, or at least I would feel more confident in making the argument for this. Part of this skepticism had to do with his oft-expressed distaste for academic hubris, with which I have always found myself sympathetic, despite my own tendency to lapse into the same. Students flush with the excitement of the fresh discovery of the wonders of ideas always found their enthusiasm parried with gently mocking remarks punctuated by eyebrows well-practiced in the arts of ironic emphasis. Part of it had to do with his devotion to religion, a calling I do not personally share, but which over the years I have come not only to respect but to recognize as a rich source of inspiration for Michalski's philosophical thought.

Michalski in the end was an intellectual only partially dedicated to professional philosophy, and he endeavored to maintain a certain independence from its institutions, even as he worked to contribute to their formation. Perhaps this had to do with a certain ironic skepticism regarding the very vocation of the philosopher, but it was also coupled with a palpable drive to engage a broader intellectual terrain. It was as if fully committing himself to the life of the mind would for Michalski risk failing to fulfill a wider set of responsibilities both political and intellectual. At least in part, for there was also a distinct restlessness to the man that could never be tamed into satisfaction with what he always perceived to be the dry rituals of academic life.

Patočka is a different matter. His writings speak to a powerful dedication to the idea of philosophy which, however open it also proves to be, shows little trace of real uncertainty. His reticence is of a different kind than Michalski's, and is tempered by a devotion to philosophical renewal that never really flags. The entire figure of "Europe is dead," playing as important an organizing role as it does at the beginning of the presentation of Patočka's thought offered earlier, is in the end something like the gun Chekhov warned against, that never goes off.[5] Patočka is eager to carry the heritage of Europe into its own post-European future, however paradoxical a project this might be, even on his own account. It may be apt to describe Patočka as a philosopher in times of despair, but it is difficult for me to conclude that he himself ever succumbed to the times, or accepted with any finality the death of those traditions of which he always saw himself to be an heir. Which is part of what makes him so elusive a thinker, and fascinating.

Yet in the end, Patočka for me belongs to another place and time, with which I am familiar only from very far away. The most I can say is that I am convinced that, for those of us who seek to understand what philosophy means, and who ask ourselves why there are philosophers at all,[6] the life and thought of Jan Patočka cannot fail to draw our attention and inspire our wonder. In a world beset by a myriad of crises and the perennial problems of freedom, the thought of this Socrates of Prague continues to resonate, as I expect it will for some time to come, in ways I do not pretend to be able to predict.

Notes

Introduction

1. See Jan Patočka, "Curriculum vitae (1968/1969)," in *Texte, Dokumente, Bibliographie*, ed. Ludger Hagedorn and Hans-Rainer Sepp (Freiburg: Alber, 1999), 457–59.
2. Jan Patočka, *Body, Community, Language, World*, ed. James Dodd, trans. Erazim Kohák (Chicago: Open Court, 1998), 179–83 ("Translator's Postscript").
3. Jan Patočka, *An Introduction to Husserl's Phenomenology*, ed. James Dodd, trans. Erazim Kohák (Chicago: Open Court, 1996).
4. See Jan Patočka, "An Attempt at a Czech National Philosophy and Its Failure," trans. Mark Suino, in *T.G. Masaryk in Perspective: Comments and Criticism*, ed. Milič Čapek and Karel Hrubý (SVU, 1981), 1–24.
5. Jan Patočka, *Heretical Essays in the Philosophy of History*, ed. James Dodd, trans. Erazim Kohák (Chicago: Open Court, 1996).
6. Jan Patočka, *Plato and Europe*, trans. Petr Lom (Stanford, CA: Stanford University Press, 2002), 1–14.
7. For an account of the "underground university" during the normalization years, see Barbara Day, *The Velvet Philosophers* (London: Claridge, 1999).
8. See Donella Meadows, Dennis Meadows, Jørgen Randers, and William Behrens, *The Limits to Growth* (New York: Universe Books, 1972).
9. Eugene Ionesco, *Discourse d'ouverture du Festival de Salzburg 1972*, ed. Fritz Wotruba (St. Gallen: Erker-Verlag, 1976).
10. See Tomáš Masaryk, *Suicide and the Meaning of Civilization*, trans. W. B. Weist and R. G. Batson (Chicago: University of Chicago Press, 1970); and Max Scheler, *Späte Schriften*, ed. Manfred Frings (Bern and Munich: Francke Verlag, 1976).
11. Patočka, *Plato and Europe*, 8.
12. See Edmund Husserl, *The Crisis of European Sciences and Transcendental Phenomenology*, trans. David Carr (Evanston, IL: Northwestern University Press, 1970), §§1–7; and Edmund Husserl, "Fünf Aufsätze über Erneuerung," in *Aufsätze und Vorträge (1922–1937)*, ed. Tomas Nenon and Hans Rainer Sepp, *Husserliana: Edmund Husserl Gesammelte Werke*, vol. 27 (Dordrecht: Kluwer, 1989), 3–93.
13. On the history of the "*Cercle philosophique de Prague pour les recherches sur l'entendement humain*" and Patočka's involvement, see Hans-Rainer Sepp, "Patočka und der Cercle philosophique de Prague," in Patočka, *Texte, Dokumente, Bibliographie*, 176–257.

14. Edmund Husserl, "The Crisis of European Humanity and Philosophy," in *Crisis of European Sciences*, 269–300. For the text of the Prague lectures, see Edmund Husserl, "Die Psychologie in der Krise der europäischen Wissenschaft: Die Prager Vorträge (November 1935)," in *Die Krisis der europäischen Wissenschaften und die transzendentale Phänomenologie: Ergänzungsband: Texte aus dem Nachlass 1934–1937*, ed. Reinhold Smid, *Husserliana: Edmund Husserl Gesammelte Werke*, vol. 29 (Dordrecht: Kluwer, 1993), 103–39.

15. Husserl, "Crisis of European Humanity," 270.

16. See Rodolphe Gasché, *Europe, or the Infinite Task* (Stanford, CA: Stanford University Press, 2009); and Denis Guénoun, *About Europe: Philosophical Hypotheses* (Stanford, CA: Stanford University Press, 2013).

17. Husserl, "Crisis of European Humanity," 274.

18. Husserl, "Crisis of European Humanity," 274.

19. Husserl, "Crisis of European Humanity," 291.

20. Husserl, "Crisis of European Humanity," 275.

21. Husserl, "Crisis of European Humanity," 276. See Robert Bernasconi, "*Krimskrams*: Hegel and the Current Controversy about the Beginning of Philosophy," in *Interrogating the Tradition*, ed. C. E. Scott and John Sallis (Albany: SUNY Press, 2000), 189–206.

22. Husserl, "Crisis of European Humanity," 286.

23. Denis Guénoun, "On the Figure," in *About Europe*, 7–23.

24. See Gasché, *Europe*, 124–25.

25. Husserl, "Crisis of European Humanity," 288.

26. Husserl, "Crisis of European Humanity," 281.

27. Husserl, "Crisis of European Humanity," 280.

28. Husserl, "Crisis of European Humanity," 281–82.

29. Husserl, "Crisis of European Humanity," 279.

30. Husserl, "Crisis of European Humanity," 283.

31. Husserl, "Crisis of European Humanity," 283.

32. Patočka, *Plato and Europe*, 9.

33. Patočka, *Plato and Europe*, 89; see also 10.

34. See Martin Heidegger, *Introduction to Phenomenological Research*, trans. Daniel Dahlstrom (Bloomington: Indiana University Press, 2005).

35. See Jan Patočka, *Komeniologické studie*, in *Sebrané spisy Jana Patočky*, ed. Ivan Chvatík and Pavel Kouba (OIKOYMENH, 1997, 1998, 2003); and Jan Patočka, *Aristote, ses devanciers, ses successeurs: Études d'histoire de la philosophie d'Aristote à Hegel*, trans. Erika Abrams (Paris: Vrin, 2011).

36. See Jan Patočka, *Kunst und Zeit: Kulturphilosophische Schriften*, ed. Klaus Nellen and Ilja Šrubař, *Jan Patočka: Ausgewählte Schriften* (Stuttgart: Klett-Cotta, 1987); and Jan Patočka, *Schriften zur tschechischen Kultur und Geschichte*, ed. Klaus Nellen, Petr Pithart, and Miloš Pojar, *Jan Patočka: Ausgewählte Schriften* (Stuttgart: Klett-Cotta, 1992).

37. It used to be routine to remark that Patočka was little known outside of eastern Europe, especially in the Anglo-American philosophical world. Fortunately, this is no longer really the case, thanks principally to the efforts of Erika Abrams, who has translated into French a large number of Patočka's most impor-

tant works. In addition, numerous essays by Ludger Hagedorn, Ivan Chvatík, Francesco Tava, L'ubica Učník, James Mensch, and many others on virtually all aspects of Patočka's work have appeared in both English and German (among other languages) over the past several decades. For some of the more notable monographs that attest to the richness of Patočka's thought, see Sandra Lehmann, *Der Horizont der Freiheit: Zum Existenzdenken Jan Patočkas* (Würzburg: Königshausen & Neumann, 2004); Karel Novotný, *La genèse d'une hérésie: Monde, corps et histoire dans la pensée de Jan Patočka* (Paris: Vrin, 2012); and Renaud Barbaras, *L'ouverture du monde: Lecture de Jan Patočka* (Chatou: Les Éditions de la Transparence, 2011).

Chapter 1

1. Jan Patočka, *The Natural World as a Philosophical Problem*, trans. Erika Abrams (Evanston, IL: Northwestern University Press, 2016), 6.
2. See Patočka, *Introduction to Husserl's Phenomenology*, 3.
3. Plato, *Theatetus*, trans. Harold Fowler (Cambridge, MA: Harvard University Press, 1987), 155d; Aristotle, *Metaphysics*, trans. Hugh Tredennick (Cambridge, MA: Harvard University Press, 2003), 982b.
4. Patočka, *Introduction to Husserl's Phenomenology*, 6.
5. Patočka, *Introduction to Husserl's Phenomenology*, 6.
6. Patočka, *Introduction to Husserl's Phenomenology*, 7.
7. Patočka, *Introduction to Husserl's Phenomenology*, 10–11.
8. Patočka, *Introduction to Husserl's Phenomenology*, 10.
9. Patočka, *Introduction to Husserl's Phenomenology*, 11.
10. See Immanuel Kant, *Critique of Pure Reason*, trans. Paul Guyer and Allen Wood (Cambridge: Cambridge University Press, 1998), A805 / B833ff.
11. Patočka, *Introduction to Husserl's Phenomenology*, 15.
12. See Richard Avenarius, *Der menschliche Weltbegriff* (Leipzig: O. R. Reisland, 1905), 3.
13. See Edmund Husserl, *Ideas for a Pure Phenomenology and Phenomenological Philosophy: First Book: General Introduction to Pure Phenomenology*, trans. Daniel Dahlstrom (Indianapolis, IN: Hackett, 2014), §§27–30 (henceforth cited as *Ideas I*); and Husserl, *Crisis of European Sciences*, §§28–34. It should be stressed that Husserl's earlier concept of the "world of the natural attitude" and the later "lifeworld" are not equivalent—the former is constructed around what Husserl calls the "general thesis of the natural standpoint," while the latter is built around more complex forms and structures constitutive of intersubjective life—though the emphasis on pre-givenness remains essential to both. Of more interest here, as was the case with Patočka, is the later conception of lifeworld or *Lebenswelt*.
14. On Avenarius, see Edmund Husserl, *The Basic Problems of Phenomenology: From the Lectures, Winter Semester, 1910–1911*, trans. Ingo Farin and James Hart (Dodrecht: Springer, 2006), §10. See also Manfred Sommer, *Husserl und der frühe Positivismus* (Frankfurt am Main: Suhrkamp, 1985); "Einleitung des Herausgebers," in Edmund Husserl, *Die Lebenswelt: Auslegungen der vorgegebenen Welt und*

ihrer Konstitution: Texte aus dem Nachlass (1916–1937), ed. Rochus Sowa, *Husserliana: Edmund Husserl Gesammelte Werke*, vol. 39 (Dordrecht: Springer, 2008); and Patočka, *The Natural World*, 138–39.

15. See Husserl, *Ideas I*, §§70–75.
16. See Wilhelm Dilthey, *The Formation of the Historical World in the Human Sciences*, trans. Rudolf Makkreel and John Scanlon, *Wilhelm Dilthey, Selected Works*, ed. Rudolf Makkreel and Frithjof Rodi, vol. 3 (Princeton, NJ: Princeton University Press, 2002).
17. Husserl, *Crisis of European Sciences*, 110.
18. Husserl, *Crisis of European Sciences*, 113, translation modified.
19. Husserl, *Crisis of European Sciences*, 118.
20. Husserl, *Crisis of European Sciences*, 104.
21. Husserl, *Crisis of European Sciences*, §32.
22. Husserl, *Crisis of European Sciences*, 122.
23. Husserl, *Crisis of European Sciences*, 125.
24. Husserl, *Crisis of European Sciences*, §34e; see also 138fn.
25. Husserl, *Crisis of European Sciences*, 131.
26. Husserl, *Crisis of European Sciences*, 140.
27. Husserl, *Crisis of European Sciences*, 146; see also Husserl, *Ideas I*, §§30–32.
28. Husserl, *Crisis of European Sciences*, 148.
29. Husserl, *Crisis of European Sciences*, 152.
30. Husserl, *Crisis of European Sciences*, §43; see also Edmund Husserl, *Cartesian Meditations*, trans. Dorion Cairns (The Hague: Nijhoff, 1977).
31. Husserl, *Crisis of European Sciences*, 153.
32. Husserl, *Crisis of European Sciences*, 166.
33. Husserl, *Crisis of European Sciences*, §49.
34. Husserl, *Crisis of European Sciences*, 169.
35. Husserl, *Crisis of European Sciences*, §51.
36. See Edmund Husserl, *Phänomenologische Psychologie: Vorlesungen Sommersemester 1925*, ed. Walter Biemel, *Husserliana: Edmund Husserl Gesammelte Werke*, vol. 9 (The Hague: Nijhoff, 1962).
37. Jan Patočka, "Afterword to the First French Translation (1976)," in Patočka, *The Natural World*, 181.
38. Husserl, *Crisis of European Sciences*, 6.
39. Patočka, *The Natural World*, 9.
40. Patočka, *The Natural World*, 10.
41. Patočka, *The Natural World*, 11.
42. Patočka, *The Natural World*, 3.
43. Patočka, *The Natural World*, 20.
44. Patočka, *The Natural World*, 20.
45. Jan Patočka, "Supplement to the Czech Edition (1970): 'The Natural World' Remeditated Thirty-Three Years Later," in Patočka, *The Natural World*, 127.
46. See Husserl, *Cartesian Meditations*, §11.
47. Jan Patočka, "The 'Natural' World and Phenomenology (1967)," in *Jan Patočka: Philosophy and Selected Writings*, trans. and ed. Erazim Kohák (Chicago: University of Chicago Press, 1989), 239–73.

48. See Martin Heidegger, *History of the Concept of Time. Prolegomena*, trans. Theodore Kisiel (Bloomington: Indiana University Press, 1985), §25.
49. Patočka, "The 'Natural' World (1967)," 250–51.
50. Patočka, "The 'Natural' World (1967)," 251.
51. The image is from Patočka's 1971 Warsaw lecture: "Edmund Husserl's Philosophy of the Crisis of the Sciences and His Conception of a Phenomenology of the 'Life-World,'" in Kohák, ed., *Jan Patočka*, 233.
52. Husserl, *Ideas I*, 89.
53. Patočka, "The 'Natural' World (1967)," 253.
54. Jan Patočka, "Text Nr. V [Phänomenologie als Lehre vom Erscheinen als solchem]," in Patočka, *Vom Erscheinen als solchem: Texte aus dem Nachlaß*, ed. Helga Blaschek-Hahn and Karel Novotný (Freiburg: Alber, 2000), 133–134.
55. "Apriori ist also nicht das Subjektive, sondern das auf das vorgängige Ganze Gehende und das Rein-generelle," Patočka, "Text Nr. V," 134.
56. Patočka, "The 'Natural' World (1967)," 253.
57. Patočka, "The 'Natural' World (1967)," 253.
58. Husserl, *Crisis of European Sciences*, 143.
59. See Edmund Husserl, *Experience and Judgment*, trans. James Churchill (London: Routledge, 1973), §29.
60. Husserl, *Crisis of European Sciences*, 143.
61. See, for example, Jean-Luc Marion, *Reduction and Givenness*, trans. Thomas Carlson (Evanston, IL: Northwestern University Press, 1998).
62. See Patočka, *Body, Community, Language, World*, 106–7.
63. Patočka, *The Natural World*, 127.
64. Jan Patočka, "*Epochē* and Reduction: Some Observations," trans. Matt Bower, Ivan Chvatík, and Kenneth Maly, in *Asubjective Phenomenology: Jan Patočka's Project in the Broader Context of His Work*, ed. L'ubica Učník, Ivan Chvatík, and Anita Williams (Nordhausen: Traugott, 2015), 51.
65. Edmund Husserl, *Logical Investigations*, ed. Dermot Moran, trans. J. N. Findlay, vol. 2 (London: Routledge, 2001), 335–48; see also Franz Brentano, *Psychology from an Empirical Standpoint*, trans. Antos Rancurello, D. B. Terrell, and Linda McAlister (London: Routledge, 1995), 59–77; and Jan Patočka, "The Concept of *Phenomenon*," in Patočka, *Introduction to Husserl's Phenomenology*, 57–70.
66. Jan Patočka, "Husserl's Subjectivism and the Call for an Asubjective Phenomenology," trans. Ivan Chvatík, Matt Bower, and Kenneth Maly, in Učník, *Asubjective Phenomenology*, 28–29.
67. Patočka, "Husserl's Subjectivism," 31.
68. Patočka, "Husserl's Subjectivism," 32.
69. Patočka, "Husserl's Subjectivism," 32.
70. Patočka, "Husserl's Subjectivism," 33.
71. Patočka, "Husserl's Subjectivism," 38; see also Martin Heidegger, *Being and Time*, trans. John Macquarrie and Edward Robinson (Oxford: Blackwell, 2001), §2.
72. Patočka, "Husserl's Subjectivism," 38–39.
73. Patočka, "*Epochē* and Reduction," 47. See also Husserl, *Ideas I*, §§27–62.
74. Patočka, "*Epochē* and Reduction," 47.

75. See also Husserl, *Ideas I*, §§44, 46, 54–55.
76. Patočka, "*Epochē* and Reduction," 47.
77. Patočka, "*Epochē* and Reduction," 48.
78. Patočka, "*Epochē* and Reduction," 49.
79. Patočka, "*Epochē* and Reduction," 50.
80. Jan Patočka, "Was ist Existenz? (*Co je existence?*)," trans. Peter Sacher, in *Die Bewegung der menschlichen Existenz, Phänomenologische Schriften II*, ed. Klaus Nellen, Jiří Němec, and Ilya Srubar, *Jan Patočka: Ausgewählte Schriften* (Stuttgart: Klett-Cotta, 1991), 230–56.
81. Yet see Husserl, *Ideas I*, §§70–75; and Martin Heidegger, *The Basic Problems of Phenomenology*, trans. Albert Hofstadter (Indianapolis: Indiana University Press, 1982), 172ff., where the evocative power of fiction is clearly recognized as a resource for phenomenological thinking.
82. Patočka, *Body, Community, Language, World*, 58–59.
83. Patočka, *Body, Community, Language, World*, 59–60.
84. See Edmund Husserl, *Ideas Pertaining to a Pure Phenomenology and to a Phenomenological Philosophy: Second Book: Studies in the Phenomenology of Constitution*, trans. Richard Rojcewicz and André Schuwer (Dordrecht: Kluwer, 1989), §§22–29, pp. 54–61 (henceforth cited as *Ideas II*).
85. Patočka, " Supplement (1970)," 117.
86. See Patočka, *Body, Community, Language, World*, 165: "Husserl's phenomenological reduction, cast as an absolute reflection, will not do as a viable philosophical idea for placing philosophy on a solidly experiential rather than a speculative footing. Husserl lacks a *theory of reflection* itself." This last sentence is, of course, *prima facie* false, but that is beside the point: the real issue for Patočka is how to break out of a conception of reflection limited to its function as an indifferent psychological capacity of objectification, in order to grasp reflection in its essential role in human life, as he goes on to indicate in the rest of the passage: "We need to conceive of reflection as a vital act, placing it in the context of an existence on the way to itself, seeking itself, understanding itself, that is, understanding its possibilities." Patočka, *Body, Community, Language, World*, 165–66.
87. Patočka, "Supplement (1970)," 118.
88. Patočka, "Supplement (1970)," 118.
89. Patočka, *Body, Community, Language, World*, 65.
90. Husserl, *Ideas I*, §§77–78.
91. Patočka, "Supplement (1970)," 118.
92. Patočka, "Supplement (1970)," 120.
93. Patočka, "Supplement (1970)," 120.
94. See Husserl, *Ideas I*, §77.
95. Patočka, *Body, Community, Language, World*, 84.
96. Husserl, *Cartesian Meditations*, 49.
97. Husserl, *Ideas I*, §§67–71.
98. Patočka, *Body, Community, Language, World*, 101.
99. Patočka, *Body, Community, Language, World*, 93–94. See also Patočka, "Supplement (1970)," 124.
100. Patočka, *Body, Community, Language, World*, 95.

101. Patočka, *Body, Community, Language, World*, 95.
102. Patočka, *Body, Community, Language, World*, 97.
103. Heidegger, *Being and Time*, §§39–42.
104. Patočka, *Body, Community, Language, World*, 100.
105. Patočka, *Body, Community, Language, World*, 100.
106. Patočka, "Supplement (1970)," 126.
107. Husserl, *Ideas I*, 43.
108. There is, however, arguably ground in Husserl for a certain relativization of self-givenness by way of a broader conception of originary givenness indicated in §67 of *Ideas I*: "We do not identify *'given as itself'* [*das 'selbst-gegeben'*] with *'given in an originary way'* [*dem 'originär-gegeben'*], 'in person' [*'leibhaft'*]. In the specifically designated sense, 'given' and 'given as itself' are one and the same, and the use of the latter, overloaded expression should only serve to exclude *givenness in the wider sense*, in terms of which it is said of whatever is presented that it is given in the presentation (but somehow 'in an empty way')." Husserl, *Ideas I*, 122. See also the discussion of the "principle of all principles" in Patočka, *Vom Erscheinen*, 135–38.
109. Patočka, *Body, Community, Language, World*, 102.
110. On Husserl's conception of the philosopher as "disinterested observer" (*unbeteiligte Zuschauer*), see Husserl, *Cartesian Meditations*, §15. Also see the discussion in Patočka, *Vom Erscheinen*, 227–30.
111. Patočka, *Body, Community, Language, World*, 111.
112. Patočka, "Supplement (1970)," 152.
113. Patočka, *Body, Community, Language, World*, 119.
114. The early Heidegger, of course, argues along similar lines in his own critique of Husserl. See Heidegger, *Introduction to Phenomenological Research*, §§48–50.
115. Patočka, "Supplement (1970)," 127.

Chapter 2

1. Husserl, *Ideas I*, §77.
2. See Edmund Husserl, *Phantasy, Image Consciousness, and Memory (1898–1925)*, trans. John Brough, in *Edmund Husserl Collected Works*, ed. Rudolf Bernet, vol. 11 (Dordrecht: Springer, 2005).
3. See Aristotle, *Physics*, trans. C. D. C. Reeve (Indianapolis, IN: Hackett, 2018), III.1, 201a5. See also Jan Patočka, chapter 1, "Les débuts de la mathématisation du mouvement et le rôle d'Aristote dans sa development," in Patočka, *Aristote, ses devanciers, ses successeurs: Études d'histoire de la philosophie d'Aristote à Hegel*, trans. Erika Abrams (Paris: Vrin, 2011),
4. Aristotle, *Physics*, II.1
5. See Aristotle, *Physics*, III.1, 200b15, and VI.4.
6. See Henri Bergson, *Time and Free Will: An Essay on the Immediate Data of Consciousness*, trans. F. L. Pogson (Mineola, MN: Dover, 2001), 100–101.

7. Patočka, *Body, Community, Language, World*, 144–45. See also Aristotle, *Physics*, III.1, 201b5–15.
8. Aristotle, *Physics*, III.1, 201a 10; see also 201a25.
9. Martin Heidegger, *Basic Concepts of Aristotelian Philosophy*, trans. Robert Metcalf and Mark Tanzer (Bloomington: Indiana University Press, 2009), §§25–28.
10. Aristotle, *Physics*, I.7, 190b1–3.
11. Patočka, *Body, Community, Language, World*, 146–47.
12. Heidegger, *Being and Time*, §§67–71.
13. Patočka, "Supplement (1970)," 153.
14. Patočka, "Supplement (1970)," 155.
15. Husserl, *Ideas II*. See also Patočka, *Introduction to Husserl's Phenomenology*, 140ff. The distinction between *Leib* and *Körper*, or more precisely between *Leibkörper* and *Körper* which are not *leiblich*, occurs frequently in Husserl's writings before *Ideas II*, but is arguably sharpened considerably in the course of the long history of the composition of *Ideas II* from roughly 1912 through 1928. See "Translator's Introduction," in Husserl, *Ideas II*, xi–xv.
16. Husserl, *Cartesian Meditations*, 97; Maurice Merleau-Ponty, *Phenomenology of Perception*, trans. Colin Smith (London: Routledge, 1978), 92.
17. Husserl, *Ideas II*, §§41–42; Patočka, *Introduction to Husserl's Phenomenology*, 142.
18. Husserl, *Ideas II*, 167 (translation modified).
19. Husserl, *Ideas II*, §60; Patočka, *Introduction to Husserl's Phenomenology*, 143.
20. Patočka, *Introduction to Husserl's Phenomenology*, 144.
21. See also Patočka, *Introduction to Husserl's Phenomenology*, 145.
22. Patočka, "Supplement (1970)," 155.
23. Patočka, *Introduction to Husserl's Phenomenology*, 147.
24. Patočka, *Introduction to Husserl's Phenomenology*, 147.
25. Patočka, *Introduction to Husserl's Phenomenology*, 147.
26. Patočka, *Introduction to Husserl's Phenomenology*, 147.
27. Husserl, *Ideas II*, §64; see also Patočka, *Introduction to Husserl's Phenomenology*, 148; and Patočka, *Body, Community, Language, World*, 44.
28. Patočka, *Introduction to Husserl's Phenomenology*, 148.
29. Patočka, *Introduction to Husserl's Phenomenology*, 148.
30. Patočka, "The 'Natural' World (1967)," 255.
31. See Martin Heidegger, "Building, Dwelling, Thinking," trans. Albert Hofstadter, in *Poetry, Language, Thought* (New York: Harper and Row, 1971), 143–62; and Edmund Husserl, "Kopernikanische Umwendung der kopernikanischen Umwendung (1934)," in *Raumtheorie: Grundlagentexte aus Philosophie und Kulturwissenschaften*, ed. Jörg Dünne and Stephan Günzel (Frankfurt am Main: Suhrkamp, 2006), 153–65.
32. Patočka, *Introduction to Husserl's Phenomenology*, 145; see also Patočka, "The 'Natural' World (1967)," 256.
33. Patočka, "The 'Natural' World (1967)," 256.
34. Patočka, *Introduction to Husserl's Phenomenology*, 154.
35. Patočka, "The 'Natural' World (1967)," 258.

NOTES TO PAGES 75-87

36. Compare Heidegger, *Being and Time*, §§21–24; Husserl, *Ideas II*, §§50–52. See also Jan Patočka, "Der Raum und seine Problematik," trans. Maria Maier, in *Die Bewegung der menschlichen Existenz, Phänomenologische Schriften II*, ed. Klaus Nellen, Jiří Němec, and Ilja Srubar, *Jan Patočka: Ausgewählte Schriften* (Stuttgart: Klett-Cotta, 1991), 63–131.
37. Patočka, *Body, Community, Language, World*, 148–51.
38. Patočka, *Body, Community, Language, World*, 31; see also 57.
39. Patočka, *Body, Community, Language, World*, 36.
40. Patočka, *Body, Community, Language, World*, 36.
41. See Heidegger, *Being and Time*, §§29–30, 68; and Edmund Husserl, *Studien zur Struktur des Bewusstseins: Teilbände I–IV*, ed. Ullrich Melle and Thomas Vongehr, *Husserliana: Edmund Husserl Gesammelte Werke*, vol. 43 (Dordrecht: Springer, 2021).
42. Patočka, *Body, Community, Language, World*, 137–38.
43. Patočka, *Introduction to Husserl's Phenomenology*, 148.
44. Patočka, *Body, Community, Language, World*, 138.
45. Patočka, *Body, Community, Language, World*, 158–59.
46. See Edmund Husserl, "Phänomenologie und Anthropologie," in *Aufsätze und Vorträge (1922–1937)*, ed. Thomas Nenon and Hans Rainer Sepp, *Husserliana: Edmund Husserl Gesammelte Werke*, vol. 27 (Dordrecht: Kluwer, 1989), 164–81.
47. See Heidegger, *Being and Time*, §10.
48. Patočka, *Body, Community, Language, World*, 169.
49. Patočka, *Body, Community, Language, World*, 178.
50. Patočka, "Supplement (1970)," 159.
51. Patočka, "Supplement (1970)," 160.

Chapter 3

1. Patočka, *Heretical Essays*, 6.
2. Patočka, *Heretical Essays*, 8.
3. Patočka, *Heretical Essays*, 9.
4. Patočka, *Heretical Essays*, 9.
5. Patočka, *Heretical Essays*, 9.
6. See Heidegger, *Being and Time*, §28, 171.
7. Martin Heidegger, "On the Essence of Truth," trans. John Sallis, in *Pathmarks*, ed. William McNeill (Cambridge: Cambridge University Press), 145.
8. Patočka, *Heretical Essays*, 10–11.
9. Patočka, *Heretical Essays*, 14. See Hannah Arendt, *The Human Condition* (Chicago: University of Chicago Press, 1958); and Aristotle, *Nicomachean Ethics*, trans. Terence Irwin (Indianapolis, IN: Hackett, 1999), book VI.
10. Patočka, *Plato and Europe*, 51.
11. Patočka, *Heretical Essays*, 25.
12. See Arendt, *The Human Condition*, 170, on the example of poetry.
13. Patočka, *Heretical Essays*, 35.

14. Patočka, *Heretical Essays*, 35–36.
15. Patočka, *Heretical Essays*, 36.
16. Patočka, *Heretical Essays*, 37; see also Arendt, *The Human Condition*, chapter 2.
17. Patočka, *Heretical Essays*, 38 (translation modified).
18. Patočka, *Heretical Essays*, 40.
19. Jan Patočka, "Time, Myth, Faith (1952)," trans. Ludger Hagedorn, in *Religion, War, and the Crisis of Modernity: A Special Issue Dedicated to the Philosophy of Jan Patočka*, ed. Ludger Hagedorn and James Dodd, *The New Yearbook for Phenomenology and Phenomenological Philosophy*, vol. 14 (London: Routledge, 2015), 5.
20. Patočka, "Time, Myth, Faith (1952)," 4–5.
21. Patočka, "Time, Myth, Faith (1952)," 5–6.
22. Patočka, "Time, Myth, Faith (1952)," 6.
23. Patočka, "Time, Myth, Faith (1952)," 7.
24. Patočka, "Time, Myth, Faith (1952)," 9.
25. Patočka, "Time, Myth, Faith (1952)," 10.
26. Patočka, "Time, Myth, Faith (1952)," 11.
27. For a sophisticated representative of this tradition, see Jean-Pierre Vernant, *The Origins of Greek Thought* (Ithaca, NY: Cornell University Press, 1982); and by the same author *Myth and Society in Ancient Greece*, trans. Janet Lloyd (New York: Zone Books, 1990).
28. The contrast has its origin, of course, in ancient Greek philosophy itself. See Aristotle, *Metaphysics*, III.iv, 1000a11–20; and the discussion in Vernant, *Myth and Society*, 210ff.
29. Patočka, "Time, Myth, Faith (1952)," 8.
30. Patočka, "Time, Myth, Faith (1952)," 8.
31. Patočka, *Plato and Europe*, 42.
32. Patočka, *Plato and Europe*, 43.
33. Patočka, *Plato and Europe*, 43.
34. Patočka, *Plato and Europe*, 44–45.
35. Patočka, *Plato and Europe*, 44.
36. J. R. R. Tolkien, *The Hobbit, or There and Back Again* (New York: Ballantine, 1973), 15.
37. Patočka, *Plato and Europe*, 45.
38. Homer, *Iliad*, trans. Robert Fitzgerald (New York: Anchor, 1974), 529 (book 22, lines 385–450).
39. Simone Weil, "The Iliad, or the Poem of Force," in Simone Weil and Rachel Bespaloff, *War and the Iliad*, trans. Mary McCarthy (New York: New York Review Books, 2005), 4.
40. Patočka, *Plato and Europe*, 45.
41. Patočka, *Plato and Europe*, 46.
42. Patočka, *Plato and Europe*, 46.
43. Patočka, *Plato and Europe*, 47. See Walter Bröcker, "Der Mythos vom Baum der Erkenntnis," in *Anteile. M. Heidegger zum 60* (Frankfurt am Main: Vittorio Klostermann, 1950), 29–50.
44. See "Atrahasis" and "The Epic of Gilgamesh" in *Myths from Mesopotamia:*

Creation, the Flood, Gilgamesh, and Others, ed. and trans. Stephanie Dalley (Oxford: Oxford University Press, 2009), 1–153. For a perceptive discussion of Patočka's reading of Gilgamesh in the context of his philosophy of history, see Nicolas de Warren, "He Who Saw the Deep: The Epic of Gilgamesh in Patočka's Philosophy of History," in *Thinking after Europe: Jan Patočka and Politics*, ed. Francesco Tava and Darian Meacham (London: Rowman and Littlefield, 2016), 135–60.

45. "The Epic of Gilgamesh (Old Babylonian Version)," in Dalley, *Myths from Mesopotamia*, 150; see also Patočka, *Heretical Essays*, 20.

46. Patočka, *Plato and Europe*, 48.

47. The theme finds further use by Sophocles throughout the play, so for example at lines 50, 205, 305, 445, 565, 1090, and 1685. For both plays, see *Sophocles I*, ed. and trans. David Grene and Richard Lattimore (Chicago: University of Chicago Press, 1954). The metaphor also appears in Parmenides' proem, describing the road of opinion (*doxa*), and is further echoed in Plato's *Republic*. See Richard D. McKirahan, *Philosophy before Socrates* (Indianapolis, IN: Hackett, 2010), 146; and Plato, *The Republic of Plato*, trans. Allan Bloom (New York: Basic Books, 1991), 479d. If the characterization of the human being as a wanderer is arguably a part of the mythical framework of ancient Greek philosophy, perhaps something similar could be said of ancient Chinese philosophy as well, so for example in the writings of Zhuangzi. See *Zhuangzi: The Complete Writings*, trans. Brook Ziporyn (Indianapolis, IN: Hackett, 2020), 3–10.

48. Patočka, *Plato and Europe*, 49; see also René Girard, *The Scapegoat*, trans. Yvonne Freccero (Baltimore, MD: Johns Hopkins University Press, 1989).

49. Patočka, *Plato and Europe*, 53.

50. Patočka, *Plato and Europe*, 56.

51. Patočka, *Plato and Europe*, 52. See also Sophocles, *Oedipus at Colonus*, in *Sophocles I*, ed. Grene and Lattimore, lines 1223–26; and also Friedrich Nietzsche, *The Birth of Tragedy*, trans. Ronald Speirs, in *The Birth of Tragedy and Other Writings* (Cambridge: Cambridge University Press, 1999), §3. The wisdom of Silenus is not unrelated to Solon's claim in book I of Herodotus that the happiness of a life cannot be judged until it is over, a claim which Aristotle takes up at *Nicomachean Ethics* 1100a10. For both (Silenus and Solon), the idea is that only once the obscurity of our individuation has run its course (or in the case of Silenus, prevented our emergence) can calling a life "good" find any real referent. See Herodotus, *The Histories*, trans. Tom Holland (New York: Penguin, 2013), 17.

52. Patočka, *Heretical Essays*, 29.

53. See "The Epic of Gilgamesh," in Dalley, *Myths of Mesopotamia*, 109–15; see also "Atrahasis," in Dalley, *Myths of Mesopotamia*, 29–35.

54. Patočka, *Plato and Europe*, 49.

55. Patočka, *Plato and Europe*, 50.

56. Patočka, *Plato and Europe*, 51.

57. Patočka, *Plato and Europe*, 52.

58. Patočka, *Heretical Essays*, 29.

59. Patočka, *Body, Community, Language, World*, 148.

60. Patočka, *Body, Community, Language, World*, 143–62; see also Karl Jaspers, *Psychologie der Weltanschauungen* (Berlin: Springer, 1960), 229–80.

61. Patočka, "Supplement (1970)," 164.
62. Patočka, *Heretical Essays*, 33.
63. Patočka, "Supplement (1970)," 164.
64. Patočka, "Supplement (1970)," 164.
65. Patočka, "Supplement (1970)," 165.
66. Patočka, "Supplement (1970)," 166.
67. Patočka, "Supplement (1970)," 166.
68. Patočka, "Supplement (1970)," 166.
69. Patočka, "Supplement (1970)," 168.
70. Patočka, "Supplement (1970)," 168.
71. Patočka, "Supplement (1970)," 165–66.
72. Patočka, "Supplement (1970)," 170.
73. Patočka, *Body, Community, Language, World*, 150.
74. Patočka, "Supplement (1970)," 165.
75. In McKirahan, *Philosophy before Socrates*, 43. Rather than cite the English translation of Patočka's Czech translation from the Greek, reproduced here is an English translation close to the spirit of what Patočka is trying to convey. See also Patočka, *Heretical Essays*, 30; *Plato and Europe*, 60–61.
76. See Martin Heidegger, "Anaximander's Saying (1946)," in *Off the Beaten Track*, ed. and trans. Julian Young and Kenneth Haynes (Cambridge: Cambridge University Press, 2002), 242–81.
77. Patočka, "Supplement (1970)," 167.
78. Patočka, "Supplement (1970)," 167.
79. Patočka, "Supplement (1970)," 168.
80. Patočka, *Body, Community, Language, World*, 150.
81. Patočka, "Supplement (1970)," 169.
82. Patočka, "Supplement (1970)," 170.
83. Patočka, "Supplement (1970)," 170-1.
84. Patočka, "Supplement (1970)," 170; see translator's note 33 at Patočka, 213. See also Patočka, *Body, Community, Language, World*, 158–59.
85. Patočka, *Body, Community, Language, World*, 150–51.
86. Patočka, *Body, Community, Language, World*, 151.
87. Patočka, *Body, Community, Language, World*, 159.
88. Patočka, *Heretical Essays*, 31.
89. Patočka, *Heretical Essays*, 16.
90. Arendt, *The Human Condition*, 7.
91. Arendt, *The Human Condition*, 28–29.
92. Arendt, *The Human Condition*, 48 fn. 39.
93. Arendt, *The Human Condition*, 80 fn. 3.
94. Arendt, *The Human Condition*, 94–95.
95. Arendt, *The Human Condition*, 94–95.
96. Arendt, *The Human Condition*, 135.
97. Patočka, *Heretical Essays*, 31.
98. Arendt, *The Human Condition*, 106.
99. Patočka, "Supplement (1970)," 172.
100. Patočka, "Supplement (1970)," 172.

NOTES TO PAGES 117-128

101. Patočka, "Supplement (1970)," 173.
102. Patočka, "Supplement (1970)," 173.
103. Patočka, *Body, Community, Language, World*, 158.
104. Patočka, "Supplement (1970)," 173.
105. Arendt, *The Human Condition*, 31.
106. Arendt, *The Human Condition*, 139.
107. Arendt, *The Human Condition*, 144.
108. Patočka, "Supplement (1970)," 174.
109. Patočka, "Supplement (1970)," 174.
110. Arendt, *The Human Condition*, 118–9.
111. Arendt, *The Human Condition*, 119, citing Weber. See Max Weber, "Agrarverhältnisse im Altertum," in *Gesammelte Aufsätze zur Sozial- und Wirtschaftsgeschichte*, ed. Marianne Weber (Stuttgart: UTB, 1988).
112. Patočka, "Supplement (1970)," 174–75.
113. Patočka, *Body, Community, Language, World*, 159–60.
114. Patočka, *Body, Community, Language, World*, 151.
115. Patočka, *Heretical Essays*, 33.
116. Patočka, "Supplement (1970)," 175.
117. Arendt, *The Human Condition*, 199–200.
118. Patočka, *Heretical Essays*, 40–41.
119. Patočka, *Heretical Essays*, 43.
120. Compare, for example, Vernant, *Origins of Greek Thought*, 49–68.
121. Arendt, *The Human Condition*, 236.
122. Patočka, *Heretical Essays*, 44.

Chapter 4

1. Karl Löwith, *Meaning in History: The Theological Implications of the Philosophy of History* (Chicago: University of Chicago Press, 1949), 1, 104. The essay in question is Voltaire's *Essai sur les mœurs et l'esprit des nations*, 2 vols., ed. René Pomeau (Paris: Garnier, 1990).
2. Löwith, *Meaning in History*, 1.
3. And in this way Patočka arguably offers an interesting riposte to the Löwith-Blumenberg debate on the legitimacy of the modern age. For an interesting reconstruction of this debate, see Peter Gordon, "Secularization, Genealogy, and the Legitimacy of the Modern Age: Remarks on the Löwith-Blumenberg Debate," *Journal of the History of Ideas* 80, no. 1 (January 2019): 147–70.
4. See Patočka, *Plato and Europe*; and Jan Patočka, "Europa und Nach-Europa: Die nacheuropäische Epoche und ihre geistigen Probleme," in *Ketzerische Essais zur Philosophie der Geschichte und ergänzende Schriften*, ed. Klaus Nellen and Jiří Němec, *Jan Patočka: Ausgewählte Schriften* (Stuttgart: Klett-Cotta, 1984), 207–352.
5. Löwith, *Meaning in History*, 4.
6. Compare 1 Corinthians 1:20: "Has not God made foolish the wisdom of

the world?" and Colossians 2:8: "See to it that no one takes you captive through philosophy and empty deceit, according to human tradition, according to the elemental spirits of the universe, and not according to Christ." *The New Oxford Annotated Bible*, ed. Bruce Metzger and Roland Murphy (New York: Oxford University Press, 1994).

7. Augustine, *City of God*, trans. Henry Bettenson (New York: Penguin, 1972), 488–89.

8. Löwith, *Meaning in History*, 6.

9. Löwith, *Meaning in History*, 10.

10. Löwith, *Meaning in History*, 19.

11. Löwith, *Meaning in History*, 21. See Jakob Burckhardt, *Force and Freedom: Reflections on History*, trans. James Hastings Nichols (New York: Pantheon, 1943).

12. Löwith, *Meaning in History*, 132. Compare Giambattista Vico, *The New Science*, trans. Jason Taylor and Robert Miner (New Haven, CT: Yale University Press, 2020), especially books 4 and 5.

13. See Friedrich Nietzsche, "The Seven Seals (or: The Yes- and Amen-Song)," in *Thus Spoke Zarathustra*, trans. Clancy Martin (New York: Barnes and Noble, 2005), 196–99.

14. Löwith, *Meaning in History*, 165.

15. Löwith, *Meaning in History*, 192.

16. Löwith, *Meaning in History*, 204.

17. Patočka, *Heretical Essays*, 54.

18. Patočka, *Heretical Essays*, 55–56.

19. Patočka, *Heretical Essays*, 57.

20. Patočka, *Heretical Essays*, 63.

21. Jan Patočka, "Negative Platonism: Reflections concerning the Rise, the Scope, and the Demise of Metaphysics—and Whether Philosophy Can Survive It," in *Jan Patočka: Philosophy and Selected Writings*, ed. and trans. Erazim Kohák (Chicago: University of Chicago Press, 1989), 175.

22. Patočka, "Negative Platonism," 178.

23. See in particular Eugen Fink, *Zur ontologischen Frühgeschichte von Raum—Zeit—Bewegung* (The Hague: Martinus Nijhoff, 1957). Thanks to the efforts of Hans-Rainer Sepp, the late Ronald Bruzina, and many others, Fink's philosophy has recently been attracting the attention it deserves, including the publication of an impressive collection of his writings in German. See *Eugen Fink Gesamtausgabe*, 20 vols., ed. Stephan Grätzel, Cathrin Nielsen, and Hans-Rainer Sepp (Freiburg: Alber, 2006–); and also Ronald Bruzina, *Edmund Husserl and Eugen Fink: Beginnings and Ends in Phenomenology* (New Haven, CT: Yale University Press, 2004). On Patočka and Fink, see Eugen Fink and Jan Patočka, *Briefe und Dokumente 1933–1977*, ed. Michael Heitz and Bernhard Nessler (Freiburg: Alber, 1999).

24. And earlier, beginning in earnest with Patočka's postwar lectures on Socrates. See Jan Patočka, *Socrate: Cours du semestre d'été 1946*, trans. Erika Abrams (Fribourg: Academic Press Fribourg, 2017).

25. See Martin Heidegger, "Metaphysics as History of Being," in *The End of Philosophy*, trans. Joan Stambaugh (Chicago: University of Chicago Press, 2003), 1–54.

NOTES TO PAGES 138-149

26. Patočka, *Plato and Europe*, 75.
27. Patočka, "Negative Platonism," 180.
28. Patočka, "Negative Platonism," 180.
29. Patočka, "Negative Platonism," 180.
30. Patočka, "Negative Platonism," 181.
31. Patočka, "Negative Platonism," 181.
32. Patočka, *Plato and Europe*, 85.
33. Patočka, *Plato and Europe*, 84.
34. See Plato, *The Republic of Plato*, trans. Allan Bloom (New York: Basic Books, 1968), 328c–331d.
35. Patočka, "Negative Platonism," 188.
36. Patočka, "Negative Platonism," 193.
37. Patočka, "Negative Platonism," 196.
38. Patočka, "Negative Platonism," 182.
39. Patočka, "Negative Platonism," 182.
40. Patočka, "Negative Platonism," 182.
41. Patočka, "Negative Platonism," 182. See Plato, "Letters VII," trans. L. A. Post, in *The Collected Dialogues of Plato*, ed. Edith Hamilton and Huntington Cairns (Princeton, NJ: Princeton University Press, 1961), 341c; Plato, *Republic*, 509b; Plato, *Timaeus*, trans. Benjamin Jowett, in Hamilton, *Collected Dialogues*, 50b–51b. See also Aristotle, *Nicomachean Ethics*, 1142a25ff. and 1143a36ff., a comparison noted in Arendt, *The Human Condition*, 291.
42. Patočka, "Negative Platonism," 198.
43. Patočka, "Negative Platonism," 199.
44. Plato, *Republic*, 507c–509c.
45. Heidegger, "Metaphysics as History of Being," 10–19.
46. Patočka, "Negative Platonism," 199.
47. Patočka, "Negative Platonism," 199.
48. Patočka, "Negative Platonism," 204.
49. Patočka, *Plato and Europe*, 109.
50. Plato, *Phaedrus*, trans. R. Hackforth (Cambridge: Cambridge University Press, 2018), 246a–248e.
51. Patočka, *Plato and Europe*, 120–21.
52. See, for example, the description of the pleasure-addled tyrant at *Republic* 585d as "wandering through life" (*planōntai dia biou*). "As over and against this wandering," James Ambury points out, "the soul that cares for itself achieves a healthy condition synonymous with organization and order (*Gorgias* 504b4ff, *Phaedrus* 247a8-b3, 256a7-b7, *Republic* IV.443c9–444a2, *Laws* X.898a8-c8)." James Ambury, "Dialectical Epimeleia: Platonic Care of the Soul and Philosophical Cognition," *Plato: The Internet Journal of the International Plato Society* 17 (2018): 88.
53. Patočka, *Plato and Europe*, 77.
54. Patočka, *Plato and Europe*, 106.
55. Plato, *Republic*, 571d–572b.
56. Patočka, *Plato and Europe*, 77. On Democritus, see McKirahan, *Philosophy before Socrates*, 303ff.; G. S. Kirk and J. E. Raven, *The Presocratic Philosophers* (Cambridge: Cambridge University Press, 1971), 440–41; and *Democritos: Science, the*

Arts, and the Care of the Soul, ed. Aldo Brancacci and Pierre-Marie Morel (Leiden: Brill, 2006).

57. Patočka, *Plato and Europe*, 77; see also Patočka, "*Europa und Nach-Europa*," 207–12.
58. Patočka, *Heretical Essays*, 65.
59. Patočka, *Plato and Europe*, 81; see also 91, 128.
60. So Democritus, known in antiquity as the "laughing philosopher," an attitude expressed in this fragment from Diogenes Laertius: "The goal of life is cheerfulness, which is not the same as pleasure . . . but the state in which the soul continues calmly and stably, disturbed by no fear or superstition or any other emotion." McKirahan, *Philosophy before Socrates*, 337.
61. Patočka, *Plato and Europe*, 180; see also 97–98, 109–10.
62. Patočka, *Plato and Europe*, 180.
63. Plato, *Republic*, 368c–369b.
64. Patočka, *Plato and Europe*, 180; see also 86, 97.
65. Patočka, *Plato and Europe*, 125.
66. Patočka, *Plato and Europe*, 125.
67. Plato, *Republic*, 501c.
68. Patočka, *Heretical Essays*, 64.
69. Patočka, *Heretical Essays*, 64.
70. Patočka, *Plato and Europe*, 122–27.
71. Patočka, *Plato and Europe*, 192.
72. Patočka, *Plato and Europe*, 192–94.
73. Plato, *Timaeus*, 36e–37v.
74. Aristotle, *De anima*, trans. C. D. C. Reeve (Indianapolis, IN: Hackett, 2017), 431b21, 432a2.
75. Patočka, *Plato and Europe*, 205–6.
76. Aristotle, *Nicomachean Ethics*, 1097a15–1098b9, 1103a15–1104b4, 1178a9–1181b25.
77. Patočka, *Plato and Europe*, 205–6.
78. Patočka, *Plato and Europe*, 208–9.
79. Heidegger, *Being and Time*, §§16, 40.
80. Patočka, *Heretical Essays*, 58–59.
81. Patočka, *Heretical Essays*, 58–59. See Wilhelm Weischedel, *Denken und Glauben: Ein Streitgespräch zusammen mit Helmut Gollwitzer* (Stuttgart, 1965), 268–74.
82. Patočka, *Heretical Essays*, 58.
83. Patočka, *Heretical Essays*, 59.
84. See, for example, Friedrich Nietzsche, "The Problem of Socrates," in *Twilight of the Idols*, in *Twilight of the Idols/The Anti-Christ*, trans. R. J. Hollingdale (New York: Penguin, 1988), 29–34.
85. Patočka, *Heretical Essays*, 59.
86. Patočka, *Heretical Essays*, 61.
87. Patočka, *Heretical Essays*, 63.
88. Patočka, *Heretical Essays*, 63.
89. Patočka, *Heretical Essays*, 64.

90. See Patočka, *Heretical Essays*, 79–94; Jan Patočka, "Was sind die Tschechen?" in *Schriften zur tschechischen Kultur und Geschichte*, ed. Klaus Nellen, Petr Pithart, and Miloš Pojar, *Jan Patočka: Ausgewählte Schriften* (Stuttgart: Klett-Cotta, 1992), 29–106; and Patočka, "Europa und Nach-Europa," 207–87.
91. Patočka, *Plato and Europe*, 89.
92. Patočka, *Plato and Europe*, 97.
93. Patočka, *Heretical Essays*, 66.
94. Patočka, *Heretical Essays*, 66.
95. Patočka, *Heretical Essays*, 66.
96. Patočka, *Heretical Essays*, 67.
97. Patočka, *Heretical Essays*, 69.
98. Patočka, *Heretical Essays*, 69–70.
99. Patočka, *Heretical Essays*, 71.
100. Patočka, *Heretical Essays*, 83.
101. Patočka, *Heretical Essays*, 84.
102. Jan Patočka, "Two Senses of Reason and Nature in the German Enlightenment: A Herderian Study (1942)," in *Jan Patočka: Philosophy and Selected Writings*, ed. and trans. Erazim Kohák (Chicago: University of Chicago Press, 1989), 157–76.

Chapter 5

1. On the history of the months following the invasion of August 1968, see Jonathan Bolton, *Worlds of Dissent: Charter 77, The Plastic People of the Universe, and Czech Culture under Communism* (Cambridge, MA: Harvard University Press, 2012), 47–71; and Harold Gordon Skilling, *Czechoslovakia's Interrupted Revolution* (Princeton, NJ: Princeton University Press, 1976), 813–23.
2. There are several excellent studies of the theme of sacrifice that demonstrate how interwoven it is in the whole of Patočka's philosophical oeuvre, including Marcia Schuback, "Sacrifice and Salvation: Jan Patočka's Reading of Heidegger on the Question of Technology," in *Jan Patočka and the Heritage of Phenomenology*, ed. Erika Abrams and Ivan Chvatík (Dordrecht: Springer, 2011), 23–38; L'ubica Učník, "Patočka on Techno-Power and the Sacrificial Victim (*obět'*)," in Abrams and Chvatík, *Jan Patočka and the Heritage of Phenomenology*, 187–201; Claire Perryman-Holt, "Jan Patočka and the Sacrificial Experience," in *Religion, War, and the Crisis of Modernity: A Special Issue Dedicated to the Philosophy of Jan Patočka*, ed. Ludger Hagedorn and James Dodd, *The New Yearbook for Phenomenology and Phenomenological Philosophy*, vol. 14 (London: Routledge, 2015), 23–30; Wolfgang Palaver, "War and Sacrifice: Comparing Jan Patočka and René Girard, *Metodo* 6, no. 2 (2018): 42–69; and Francesco Tava, "Sacrifice as a Political Problem: Jan Patočka and Sacred Sociology," *Metodo* 6, no. 2 (2018): 71–96.
3. For a reflection on these themes, see Eva Kantůrková, "On the Ethics of Palach's Deed," trans. Milan Pomichalek and Anna Mozga, in *Good-bye, Samizdat:*

Twenty Years of Czechoslovak Underground Writing, ed. Marketa Goetz-Stankiewicz (Evanston, IL: Northwestern University Press, 1992), 175–80.

4. See the suggestive discussion of this theme in Jason Alvis, "'Scum of the Earth': Patočka, Atonement, and Waste," *Labyrinth* 19, no. 1 (Autumn 2017): 71–88.

5. Jan Patočka, "The Dangers of Technization in Science according to E. Husserl and the Essence of Technology as Danger according to M. Heidegger (Varna Lecture, 1973)," in *Jan Patočka: Philosophy and Selected Writings*, ed. and trans. Erazim Kohák (Chicago: University of Chicago Press, 1989), 327–39; Jan Patočka, "Séminaire sur l'ère technique," in *Liberté et sacrifice: Écrits politiques*, ed. and trans. Erika Abrams (Grenoble: Millon, 1990), 277–324.

6. See Martin Heidegger, "The Question Concerning Technology," in *The Question Concerning Technology and Other Essays*, ed. and trans. William Lovitt (New York: Harper and Row, 1977), 3–35; and Husserl, *Crisis of European Sciences*, §§1–7.

7. Husserl, *Crisis of European Sciences*, §9h.

8. See Edmund Husserl, *Krisis der europäischen Wissenschaften und die transzendentale Phänomenologie*, ed. Walter Biemel, *Husserliana: Edmund Husserl Gesammelte Werke*, vol. 6 (The Hague: Martinus Nijhoff, 1954), Beilage XXIV (supplement to §73).

9. Patočka, "Dangers of Technization," 330; see also Heidegger, "Question Concerning Technology," 19.

10. Patočka, "Dangers of Technization," 331.

11. Heidegger, "Question Concerning Technology," 28. The phrase is from the first strophe of the poem: "Wo aber Gefahr ist, wächst / das Rettende auch." Friedrich Hölderlin, "Patmos," in *Gedichte: Eine Auswahl*, ed. Gerhard Kurz (Stuttgart: Reclam, 2015), 88. Also compare the discussion of the same lines in Martin Heidegger, "The Turning," in *The Question Concerning Technology*, 42ff.

12. Patočka, "Dangers of Technization," 331–32.

13. Patočka, "Dangers of Technization," 332.

14. Heidegger, "Question Concerning Technology," 35.

15. Heidegger, "Question Concerning Technology," 35.

16. Patočka, "Séminaire," 282–85.

17. Heidegger, "The Turning," 44.

18. Martin Heidegger, "The End of Philosophy and the Task of Thinking," in *On Time and Being*, trans. Joan Stambaugh (Chicago: University of Chicago Press, 2002), 55–73.

19. Heidegger, "End of Philosophy," 56.

20. Patočka, *Plato and Europe*, 177.

21. See Martin Heidegger, *Introduction to Metaphysics*, trans. Gregory Fried and Richard Polt (New Haven, CT: Yale University Press, 2000), 155–63.

22. Patočka, "Séminaire," 285.

23. Patočka, "Dangers of Technization," 332.

24. Patočka, "Dangers of Technization," 336.

25. Patočka, "Dangers of Technization," 332.

26. Patočka, "Dangers of Technization," 332.

27. Patočka, "Dangers of Technization," 332.

28. Patočka, "Dangers of Technization," 333.
29. Patočka, "Dangers of Technization," 336.
30. Patočka, "Dangers of Technization," 336.
31. Patočka, *Heretical Essays*, 129.
32. Patočka, *Heretical Essays*, 129.
33. Patočka, *Heretical Essays*, 129-130.
34. Patočka, *Heretical Essays*, 130.
35. Patočka, *Heretical Essays*, 130.
36. Patočka, *Heretical Essays*, 131.
37. Patočka, *Heretical Essays*, 126–28; see Henri Barbusse, *Under Fire: The Story of a Squad*, trans. Fitzwater Wray (London: J.M. Dent, 1917).
38. Patočka, "Dangers of Technization," 336.
39. Patočka, "Dangers of Technization," 336.
40. Patočka, "Dangers of Technization," 336.
41. Patočka, "Séminaire," 298.
42. Wilfred Owen, *The Complete Poems and Fragments of Wilfred Owen*, vol. 1, ed. J. Stallworthy (London: Chatto and Windus, 1983), 174.
43. Patočka, "Dangers of Technization," 337.
44. As illustrative, see Pierre Teilhard de Chardin, "The Nostalgia of the Front," trans. Nicolas de Warren, in *Phenomenologies of Violence*, ed. Michael Staudigl (Leiden: Brill, 2014), 245–56; and Ernst Jünger, *Storm of Steel*, trans. Michael Hofmann (New York: Penguin 2004).
45. Patočka, *Heretical Essays*, 134.
46. Patočka, *Heretical Essays*, 131.
47. Patočka, *Heretical Essays*, 132.
48. Patočka, "Dangers of Technization," 337–38.
49. Patočka, "Dangers of Technization," 338.
50. Patočka, "Dangers of Technization," 338.
51. Patočka, "Dangers of Technization," 339.
52. Whereas most commentators in the literature, such as Ludger Hagedorn and Eddo Evink, approach the problem from a specifically philosophical perspective, a few have taken up the question from a more theological angle, such as Martin Koci and, very briefly, Jean-Luc Marion. See Ludger Hagedorn, "Beyond Myth and Enlightenment. On Religion in Patočka's Thought," in Abrams and Chvatík, *Jan Patočka and the Heritage of Phenomenology*, 245–61; Ludger Hagedorn, "'Christianity Unthought'—A Reconsideration of Myth, Faith, and Historicity," in Hagedorn and Dodd, *Religion, War, and the Crisis of Modernity*, 31–46; Eddo Evink, "The Gift of Life: Jan Patočka and the Christian Heritage," in Hagedorn and Dodd, *Religion, War, and the Crisis of Modernity*, 3147–63; Martin Koci, "Sacrifice for Nothing: The Movement of Kenosis in Jan Patočka's Thought," *Modern Theology* 33, no. 4 (2017): 594–617; and Jean-Luc Marion, *The Reason of the Gift*, trans. Stephen Lewis (Charlottesville: University of Virginia Press, 2011), 90.
53. Patočka, "Dangers of Technization," 339.
54. Patočka, "Dangers of Technization," 339.
55. See René Girard, *Violence and the Sacred*, trans. P. Gregory (Baltimore, MD: Johns Hopkins University Press, 1977); see also Girard's *Things Hidden since*

the Foundation of the World, trans. S. Bann and M. Metteer (Stanford, CA: Stanford University Press, 1987). For a (critical) comparison of Girard and Patočka on the problem of sacrifice, see Palaver, "War and Sacrifice."

56. Patočka, "Séminaire," 286, 309–10.

57. See Jacques Derrida, "Secrets of European Responsibility," in *The Gift of Death*, trans. David Wills (Chicago: University of Chicago Press, 1992), 1–34.

58. See the seminal study by Jay Winter, *Sites of Memory, Sites of Mourning: The Great War in European Cultural History* (Cambridge: Cambridge University Press, 2014).

59. Elzbieta Matynia, ed. and trans., *An Uncanny Era: Conversations between Václav Havel & Adam Michnik* (New Haven, CT: Yale University Press, 2014), 150.

60. For a different perspective, see Nicolas de Warren, "Homecoming: Jan Patočka's Reflections on the First World War," in *Phenomenologies of Violence*, ed. Michael Staudigl (New York: Routledge, 2013), 207–46.

61. David Jones, *In Parenthesis* (New York: New York Review Books, 2003), xv.

Chapter 6

1. Paul Ricoeur, "Preface," in Jan Patočka, *Éssais hérétiques sur la philosophie de l'histoire*, trans. Erika Abrams (Lagrasse: Éditions Verdier, 1981); "Preface to the French Edition by Paul Ricoeur," trans. James Dodd, in Jan Patočka, *Heretical Essays in the Philosophy of History*, ed. James Dodd, trans. Erazim Kohák (Chicago: Open Court, 1996), viii.

2. Jan Patočka, "On Masaryk's Philosophy of Religion (1977)," trans. Jiří Rothbauer, in *Religion, War, and the Crisis of Modernity: A Special Issue Dedicated to the Philosophy of Jan Patočka*, ed. Ludger Hagedorn and James Dodd, *The New Yearbook for Phenomenology and Phenomenological Philosophy*, vol. 14 (London: Routledge, 2015), 95–135. For an English translation of the first of the two studies on Masaryk, see Jan Patočka, "An Attempt at a Czech National Philosophy and Its Failure," trans. Mark Suino, in *T.G. Masaryk in Perspective: Comments and Criticism*, ed. Milič Čapek and Karel Hrubý (SVU, 1981), 1–24.

3. For an informative presentation of Patočka's engagements with Masaryk both as philosopher and politician, see Ivan Chvatík, "Jan Patočka's Studies on Masaryk," in Hagedorn and Dodd, *Religion, War, and the Crisis of Modernity*, 136–60.

4. Jan Patočka, "Titanism (1936)," in *Jan Patočka: Philosophy and Selected Writings*, ed. and trans. Erazim Kohák (Chicago: University of Chicago Press, 1989), 139–44; and Jan Patočka, "Masaryk's and Husserl's Conception of the Spiritual Crisis of European Humanity (1936)," in Kohák, ed., *Jan Patočka*, 145–56. See also Václav Černý, *Essai sur le titanisme dans la poésie romantique occidentale entre 1815 et 1850* (Prague: Éditions Orbis, 1935); and Tomáš Garrigue Masaryk, *Modern Man and Religion*, trans. Ann Bibza and Václav Beneš (London: Allen and Unwin, 1938), 215–315.

5. Masaryk, *Suicide and the Meaning of Civilization*; T. G. Masaryk, *The Mak-*

ing of a State: Memories and Observations 1914–1918, trans. Henry Wickham Steed (New York: Ishi, 2009).

6. For a detailed—if also on some points admittedly controversial—account of the rise and fall of the Czechoslovak state that gives a revealing account of the complexity of the political situation in which Masaryk rose to prominence, see Mary Heimann, *Czechoslovakia: The State That Failed* (New Haven, CT: Yale University Press, 2009), esp. chapters 1–3.

7. See Masaryk, *Making of a State*, 345–56.
8. Patočka, "Titanism (1936)," 139.
9. Patočka, "Titanism (1936)," 140.
10. Patočka, "Masaryk's and Husserl's Conception," 153.
11. Karel Čapek, *Hovory s T.G. Masarykem* (Prague: Čin, 1936), 98, cited in Patočka, "Titanism (1936)," 150. Compare in English translation: *Conversations with Masaryk: Masaryk on Thought and Life*, trans. M. Weatherall and R. Weatherall (London: Allen and Unwin, 1935).
12. Patočka, "Masaryk's and Husserl's Conception," 155.
13. Patočka, "Titanism (1936)," 141.
14. Patočka, "Titanism (1936)," 143.
15. Patočka, "Titanism (1936)," 142.
16. Patočka, "Titanism (1936)," 142–43.
17. Patočka, "Titanism (1936)," 143.
18. See Immanuel Kant, "On the Miscarriage of All Philosophical Trials in Theodicy (1791)," trans. George di Giovanni, in *Religion and Rational Theology*, ed. Allen Wood and George di Giovanni (Cambridge: Cambridge University Press, 1996), 19–38.
19. Masaryk, *Modern Man and Religion*, 99; see also 200–212.
20. Patočka, "Titanism (1936)," 142.
21. Kant, *Critique of Pure Reason*, Bxxx.
22. Patočka, "Masaryk's Philosophy of Religion," 96.
23. See in particular Kant, *Critique of Pure Reason*, A462/B490ff. ("The Antinomy of Pure Reason. Third Section. On the interest of reason in these conflicts").
24. Kant, *Critique of Pure Reason*, A542/B570.
25. See Immanuel Kant, *Critique of Practical Reason*, in *Practical Philosophy*, ed. and trans. Mary Gregor (Cambridge: Cambridge University Press, 1999), 5:122ff.
26. See Kant, *Critique of Practical Reason*, 5:73ff. ("On the incentives of pure practical reason").
27. See Kant, *Critique of Pure Reason*, A810/B838ff.; *Critique of Practical Reason*, book 2, chapter 2.
28. Immanuel Kant, *Critique of Judgment*, trans. Werner Pluhar (Indianapolis, IN: Hackett, 1987), 336, cited in Patočka, "Masaryk's Philosophy of Religion," 97–98.
29. Kant, *Critique of Practical Reason*, 5:109.
30. Yirmiyahu Yovel argues that this special imperative articulated by the postulates should be understood as *historical* in both form and intention: "To

make coherent sense, this rational ideal should be construed as the regulative ideal of history; and correspondingly, Kant's special imperative ('Act to promote the highest good in the world') can properly be called the *historical* imperative." Yirmiyahu Yovel, *Kant and the Philosophy of History* (Princeton, NJ: Princeton University Press, 1980), 7.

31. Patočka, "Masaryk's Philosophy of Religion," 112. See Iakov Golosovker, *Dostoevsky i Kant* (Moscow: Izdatel'stvo Akademii nauk SSR, 1963).

32. Fyodor Dostoevsky, *The Brothers Karamazov*, trans. Richard Pevear and Larissa Volokhonsky (New York: Farrar, Straus and Giroux), 235.

33. Patočka, "Masaryk's Philosophy of Religion," 100.

34. Dostoevsky, *Brothers Karamazov*, 235–36.

35. Dostoevsky, *Brothers Karamazov*, 244.

36. Dostoevsky, *Brothers Karamazov*, 244.

37. Dostoevsky, *Brothers Karamazov*, 245.

38. Dostoevsky, *Brothers Karamazov*, 245.

39. Dostoevsky, *Brothers Karamazov*, 237–38.

40. The *locus classicus* for Dostoevsky's exploration of the psychology of the underground man is, of course, his *Notes from Underground*, trans. Richard Pevear and Larissa Volokhonsky (New York: Vintage, 1994). Patočka will also cite the short stories "The Sentence" and "The Dream of a Ridiculous Man: A Fantastic Story," the latter of which, as will be seen shortly, takes on particular importance. Both stories can be found in Fyodor Dostoevsky, *A Writer's Diary*, trans. Kenneth Lantz (Evanston, IL: Northwestern University Press, 2009), 228–34 and 379–86, respectively.

41. See Richard Pevear's foreword to Dostoevsky, *Notes from Underground*, xiii–xvii; also see Nikolai Chernyshevsky, *What Is to Be Done?*, trans. Michael Katz (Ithaca, NY: Cornell University Press, 1989).

42. For an excellent interpretation of the scene of Ivan with the devil (in book 11, chapter 9 of Dostoevsky, *Brothers Karamazov*) in light of Patočka's essay, see Ludger Hagedorn, "The Fatigue of Reason: Patočka's Reading of *The Brothers Karamazov*," in Hagedorn and Dodd, *Religion, War, and the Crisis of Modernity*, 181–98. Ivan's scene at the trial occurs in book 12, chapter 5 of Dostoevsky, *Brothers Karamazov*.

43. Patočka, "Masaryk's Philosophy of Religion," 103; also see Dostoevsky, *Notes from Underground*, 9ff.

44. Dostoevsky, *Notes from Underground*, 7.

45. Dostoevsky, *Notes from Underground*, 16.

46. Dostoevsky, "The Sentence," 231.

47. Dostoevsky, *Notes from Underground*, 130.

48. Patočka, "Masaryk's Philosophy of Religion," 104.

49. Dostoevsky, "Dream of a Ridiculous Man," 381.

50. Patočka, "Masaryk's Philosophy of Religion," 105.

51. Patočka, "Masaryk's Philosophy of Religion," 105. Dostoevsky's narrator does not use the explicit term "boredom" to name his condition, but it is clearly apt to his description of how his growing sense of ridiculousness has led to a condition of detachment. See Dostoevsky, "Dream of a Ridiculous Man," 379–80.

NOTES TO PAGES 222-226

52. Dostoevsky, "Dream of a Ridiculous Man," 380.
53. Dostoevsky, "Dream of a Ridiculous Man," 380.
54. Quoted in Patočka, "Masaryk's Philosophy of Religion," 105. The passage is from Martin Heidegger, "What Is Metaphysics?," trans. David Farrell Krell, in *Pathmarks*, ed. William McNeill (Cambridge: Cambridge University Press), 87. Also see Martin Heidegger, *The Fundamental Concepts of Metaphysics: World, Finitude, Solitude*, trans. William McNeill and Nicholas Walker (Bloomington: Indiana University Press, 1995), esp. §§29–38.
55. Heidegger, "What Is Metaphysics?," 87.
56. See Heidegger, *Fundamental Concepts of Metaphysics*, §19.
57. Quoted in Patočka, "Masaryk's Philosophy of Religion," 105; also see Dostoevsky, "Dream of a Ridiculous Man," 380.
58. Dostoevsky, "Dream of a Ridiculous Man," 381.
59. Hans Holbein the Younger's *Dead Christ* (1521–22). Dostoevsky had been shaken by this painting during a visit to Geneva in 1867, an experience that finds its way into *The Idiot*, in the scene of Prince Myshkin's own unsettling encounter with a copy of Holbein's painting. See Fyodor Dostoevsky, *The Idiot*, trans. Alan Myers (Oxford: Oxford University Press, 2008), 229.
60. Patočka, "Masaryk's Philosophy of Religion," 107; also see Dostoyevsky, "Dream of a Ridiculous Man," 387ff.
61. Patočka, "Masaryk's Philosophy of Religion," 108. In this context, Patočka again quotes Heidegger: "The anxiety of those who are daring cannot be opposed to joy or even to the comfortable enjoyment of tranquilized bustle. It stands—outside all such opposition—in secret alliance with the cheerfulness and gentleness of creative longing." Heidegger, "What Is Metaphysics?," 93. Nevertheless, a certain parting of ways with Heidegger is being prepared here, one that not only takes us to Dostoevsky, but to the question of love at the heart of Christianity. See Nicolas de Warren, "The Gift of Eternity," in Hagedorn and Dodd, *Religion, War, and the Crisis of Modernity*, 161–80, especially 165–68.
62. Dostoevsky, *Brothers Karamazov*, 295–301, 768–76; also see Patočka, "Masaryk's Philosophy of Religion," 113.
63. De Warren, following this distinction, ties love in this sense to *agape*: "The revelation of truth, as documented in the *Dream of a Ridiculous Man*, is not the gift of death, but the gift of *agape* that is timeless and eternal" (de Warren, "Gift of Eternity," 178). This characterization of Patočka's reading, however, is only valid—as de Warren certainly knows—if *agape* is shorn of any specifically ontic associations, as for example those that are still operative in Alyosha's response to Ivan's rebellion: "You asked just now if there is in the whole world a being who could and would have the right to forgive. But there is such a being, and he can forgive everything, forgive all *and for all*, because he himself gave his innocent blood and for all and for everything" (Dostoevsky, *Brothers Karamazov*, 246). Compare Patočka, "Masaryk's Philosophy of Religion," 113.
64. Dostoevsky, "Dream of a Ridiculous Man," 389.
65. Dostoevsky, "Dream of a Ridiculous Man," 393.
66. Patočka, "Masaryk's Philosophy of Religion," 110. Compare Heidegger, *Being and Time*, §§55–59, esp. p. 334.

67. Patočka, "Masaryk's Philosophy of Religion," 113. The biblical passage cited is John 12:24.
68. Dostoevsky, "Dream of a Ridiculous Man," 397.
69. Patočka, "Masaryk's Philosophy of Religion," 108.

Chapter 7

1. Matynia, *An Uncanny Era*, 75.
2. Adam Michnik, "When Socrates Became Pericles (2011)," in Matynia, *An Uncanny Era*, 170. Michnik is here citing Václav Havel, *Disturbing the Peace: A Conversation with Karel Hvížd'ala*, trans. Paul Wilson (New York: Knopf, 1990), 54.
3. See Bolton, *Worlds of Dissent*, 31.
4. Quoted in Bolton, *Worlds of Dissent*, 83.
5. Quoted in Bolton, *Worlds of Dissent*, 80. See Milan Šimečka, *The Restoration of Order: The Normalization of Czechoslovakia 1969–1976*, trans. A. G. Brain (London: Verso, 1984), 78–79.
6. Bolton, *Worlds of Dissent*, 88.
7. Jan Patočka, "The Intellectuals and Opposition," trans. Francesco Tava and Daniel Leufer, in *Thinking after Europe: Jan Patočka and Politics*, ed. Francesco Tava and Darian Meacham (London: Rowman and Littlefield, 2016), 7–26.
8. Patočka, "Intellectuals and Opposition," 20.
9. See the translator's notes to Patočka, "Intellectuals and Opposition," 5.
10. See Bolton, *Worlds of Dissent*, chapter 4: "Legends of the Underground," for a detailed account of the trial and its broader context. See also H. Gordon Skilling, *Charta 77 and Human Rights in Czechoslovakia* (London: Allen and Unwin, 1981), 7–16.
11. See Skilling, *Charta 77*, 199–200.
12. See Bolton, *Worlds of Dissent*, 134ff.
13. Jan Patočka, "On the Matters of The Plastic People of the Universe and DG 307," in Skilling, *Charta 77*, 205–7.
14. Matynia, *An Uncanny Era*, 118.
15. Václav Havel, "The Power of the Powerless," trans. Paul Wilson, in *The Power of the Powerless: Citizens Against the State in Central-Eastern Europe*, ed. and trans. Paul Wilson (Armonk, NY: M.E. Sharpe), 23–96. This text appeared in 1978, and was dedicated by Havel to the memory of Patočka.
16. Havel, "Power of the Powerless," 28.
17. Havel, "Power of the Powerless," 28.
18. Havel, "Power of the Powerless," 33.
19. Havel, "Power of the Powerless," 33.
20. Havel, "Power of the Powerless," 37.
21. Havel, "Power of the Powerless," 41; also see §VII.
22. For an excellent point of departure for further reflection on its meaning for both what came in 1989 and beyond, see Jeffrey Goldfarb, *Beyond Glasnost: The Post-Totalitarian Mind* (Chicago: University of Chicago Press, 1992).

NOTES TO PAGES 236-245

23. Havel, "Power of the Powerless," 93. See §§XX–XXII.
24. Havel, "Power of the Powerless," 96.
25. For an English translation of the text of Charter 77, see Skilling, *Charta 77*, 209–12.
26. For the history of Charter 77, see Skilling, *Charta 77*; and Bolton, *Worlds of Dissent*, chapter 5: "Everything Changed with the Charter."
27. See the account in Bolton, *Worlds of Dissent*, 143ff. Also see Havel, *Disturbing the Peace*, 134–36; and Skilling, *Charta 77*, 19–40.
28. Jan Patočka, "The Obligation to Resist Injustice" and "What We Can and Cannot Expect from Charta 77," both in *Jan Patočka: Philosophy and Selected Writings*, ed. and trans. Erazim Kohák (Chicago: University of Chicago Press, 1989), 340–47. On the circumstances surrounding the composition of these texts, as well as an account of Patočka's final days, see Bolton, *Worlds of Dissent*, 155–60.
29. Patočka, "Obligation to Resist Injustice," 341.
30. For two texts that offer a nuanced approach to these issues, see Jakub Čapek, "Le devoir de l'homme envers lui-même: Patočka, Kant et la Charte 77," *Tumultes* 32–33 (2009): 351–70; and Daniel Leufer, "The Wound Which Will Not Close: Jan Patočka's Philosophy and the Conditions of Politization," *Studies in East European Thought* 69, no. 1 (2017): 29–44.
31. For example, see Kohák, ed., *Jan Patočka*, 130–31, 347.
32. Patočka, "Obligation to Resist Injustice," 342: "The participants in Charta 77 do not seek any political role or privilege for themselves, and least of all do they wish to be any moral authority or social conscience."
33. See Patočka, *Heretical Essays*, 13; see also Patočka, *Plato and Europe*, 43–44.
34. Patočka, *Heretical Essays*, 38.
35. Patočka, *Heretical Essays*, 38 (translation modified).
36. Patočka, *Heretical Essays*, 38–39.
37. See Arendt, *The Human Condition*, 177–78.
38. This is meant to echo, without necessarily endorsing, something of a quasi-consensus in the literature on Patočka to the effect that his adherence to the thought of Heidegger prevented him from fully embracing the humanism and liberalism, not to mention the optimism, of T. G. Masaryk, that other great figure of Czech philosophy and democratic politics in the twentieth century. If Patočka in the end supports democratization, then in this view it is at most in accordance with an agonistic conception of democracy, comparable perhaps to what one can find in the writings of an Ernesto Laclau or a Chantel Mouffe. See two studies that are more or less compatible with this line of interpretation: Aviezer Tucker, *The Philosophy and Politics of Czech Dissidence from Patočka to Havel* (Pittsburgh, PA: University of Pittsburgh Press, 2000); and Edward Findlay, *Caring for the Soul in the Postmodern Age: Politics and Phenomenology in the Thought of Jan Patočka* (New York: SUNY Press, 2002). For more nuanced readings, see Michael Gubser, *The Far Reaches: Phenomenology, Ethics, and Social Renewal in Central Europe* (Stanford, CA: Stanford University Press, 2014), esp. 151–73; Alexandra Laignel-Lavatine, *Jan Patočka: L'esprit de la dissidence* (Paris: Michalon, 1998); James Mensch, *Patočka's Asubjective Phenomenology: Toward a New Concept of Human*

Rights (Würzburg: Königshausen & Neumann, 2006): and Aspen Brinton, *Confronting Totalitarian Minds: Jan Patočka on Politics and Dissidence* (Chicago: University of Chicago Press, 2021).

39. See Heraclitus, *Fragments: A Text and Translation with a Commentary*, ed. and trans. T. M. Robinson (Toronto: University of Toronto Press, 1987), fragments 53 and 80.

40. Patočka, *Heretical Essays*, 42. Patočka is here citing fragment 113 (Heraclitus, *Fragments*, 66–67), which echoes the phrase *polemon eonta xunon* in fragment 80 (*Fragments*, 48–49).

41. Heidegger, *Introduction to Metaphysics*, 94–133. On Heidegger, Heraclitus, and *polemos*, see Gregory Fried, *Heidegger's Polemos* (New Haven, CT: Yale University Press, 2000), esp. 21–86; Nicolas de Warren, "Homecoming: Jan Patočka's Reflections on the First World War," in *Phenomenologies of Violence*, ed. Michael Staudigl (Leiden: Brill, 2014), 219–23; and Sandra Lehmann, *Der Horizont der Freiheit: Zum Existenzdenken Jan Patočka's* (Würzburg: Könighausen & Neumann, 2004), 84–95.

42. "*Logos* is constant gathering, the gatheredness of beings that stands in itself, that is, Being. So *kata ton logon* in fragment 1 means the same as *kata phusin* [according to *phusis*]. *Phusis* and *logos* are the same." Heidegger, *Introduction to Metaphysics*, 138.

43. Heidegger, *Introduction to Metaphysics*, 106.
44. Heidegger, *Introduction to Metaphysics*, 139.
45. Patočka, *Heretical Essays*, 42–43.
46. Patočka, *Heretical Essays*, 39.
47. Patočka, *Heretical Essays*, 41.
48. Patočka, *Heretical Essays*, 43.
49. Patočka, *Heretical Essays*, 44 (translation modified).
50. Patočka, *Heretical Essays*, 83–86.
51. Patočka, *Heretical Essays*, 136–37.
52. Patočka, "What We Can and Cannot Expect," 346.

Conclusion

1. Havel, "The Power of the Powerless," 48. The line is from Jan Patočka, "What We Can and Cannot Expect from Charta 77," 346.

2. See the account in Bolton, *Worlds of Dissent*, 158.

3. Jan Patočka, "Erinnerungen an Husserl," in *Texte, Dokumente, Bibliographie*, ed. Ludger Hagedorn and Hans Rainer Sepp (Freiburg: Alber, 1999), 282.

4. Edmund Husserl, "Philosophy as Rigorous Science," in *Phenomenology and the Crisis of Philosophy*, trans. Quentin Lauer (New York: Harper, 1965), 71–47.

5. Erazim Kohák, *Hearth and Horizon. Cultural Identity and Global Humanity in Czech Philosophy* (Prague: Filosofia, 2019), 165.

6. Patočka, "Masaryk's Philosophy of Religion," 130.

7. Václav Havel, "Last Conversation," trans. Milan Pomichalek and Anna Mozga, in *Good-Bye, Samizdat: Twenty Years of Czechoslovak Underground Writing*, ed. Marketa Goetz-Stankiewicz (Evanston, IL: Northwestern University Press, 1992), 211.

8. Havel, "Last Conversation," 212.

9. Havel, "Last Conversation," 213.

Epilogue

1. Peter Demetz, *Prague in Black and Gold: The History of a City* (London: Penguin, 1997), xi.

2. Jan Patočka and Krzysztof Michalski, "Letters between Krzysztof Michalski and Jan Patočka (1973–1976)," in *Religion, War, and the Crisis of Modernity: A Special Issue Dedicated to the Philosophy of Jan Patočka*, ed. Ludger Hagedorn and James Dodd, *The New Yearbook for Phenomenology and Phenomenological Philosophy*, vol. 14 (London: Routledge, 2015), 241.

3. Patočka and Michalski, "Letters," 247.

4. Václav Havel, "Anatomy of a Reticence," trans. Erazim Kohák, in *Open Letters: Selected Writings 1965–1990*, ed. Paul Wilson (New York: Vintage, 1992), 308.

5. I owe this comparison to an anonymous reader.

6. I owe the formulation of this question to the film *The Socrates of Prague: Jan Patočka and Charta 77*, directed by Sam Willems and produced by Francesco Tava and Nicolas de Warren.

Index

Abrams, Erika, 268n37
absurd, the, 229
action: Arendt on, 114–16; political, 245
adikia (injustice), 109–11
affectivity: and body, 107; vs. instinct, 77–78; and others, 110–12
Alexander the Great, 167
alienation: Dostoevsky on, 218–19, 221; Masaryk on, 6; modern order of, 4; and others, 113; Patočka on, 117, 123, 223–24; of technological civilization, 177; in twentieth century, 201
Anaximander: on *adikia* (injustice), 109–11; and Socrates, 139; and soul, 152
anchoring: earth and, 107–8; as first movement, 106–12
animality, human, 78, 80–82
appresentation: and reflection, 51–54
Arendt, Hannah: on action, 114, 125–26; on appearance, 124; on *homo faber*, 121; on labor, 99, 114, 125–26; on natality, 105, 106; on the new, 244; Patočka on, 86; on the political, 89; on violence, 117–18; on work, 87, 114, 125–26
Aristotle: on body, 68; on excellence, 125; and mathematical thinking, 22; and metaphysics, 153–54, 167; on movement, 62–65, 73–74; Patočka on, 3, 19, 163; on *phusis* (nature) as manifestation, 24, 25; and Plato, 153–56
art, and technology, 179–81
asceticism, 113, 212
Athenaeum (journal), 205
Atrahasis myth, 97–99
attitude: natural, 13, 28, 32, 34, 66, 269n13; personalistic, 66; theoretical, 13–14, 28, 31
Augustine, 128, 130

Austro-Hungarian Empire, 4, 204, 205
Avenarius, Richard, 28, 32

Bacon, Francis, 168
Barbusse, Henri, 187–88
being: of beings, 190; Heidegger on, 45, 55; in-between, 147; meaning of, 48–49, 156–61; objective, 57; as *phusis*, 81–82; subjective, 53–54; and technology, 176
Being and Time (Heidegger), 55–56, 65, 81
blindness: and death, 102, 121; and natural attitude, 30; of Oedipus, 97, 101–4, 121, 148; willful, 175
bliss: and need, 107, 110; of rest, 116
body, the: and affectivity, 107; and freedom, 69–72, 74; and movement, 64–75, 81–82; and others, 75–77; and perception, 67–68; phenomenology of, 107–8; as subject and thing, 66–69, 74–75; and world, 72–77, 82
Body, Community, Language, World (Patočka), 3, 105
Böll, Heinrich, 232
Bolton, John, 230
Bondy, Egon, 232
boredom, 221–24
Brentano, Franz, 209, 255
"Brentanoism," 43–44, 52
Březina, Otokar, 103–4
Brothers Karamazov, The (Dostoevsky), 214–28
Burckhardt, Jakob, 130

Čapek, Karel, 206
care: body's need of, 73; vs. care for power, 166; ethic of, 148; Heidegger on, 66, 105; for self, 170. *See also* care for the soul

295

care for the soul: and Aristotle, 153–56; and catastrophe, 163; and Christianity, 165–66; and Europe, 18–19, 161–70, 254; and freedom, 156; and history, 156–57; Kant and, 168–69; and meaning, 159; origins and history of concept, 161, 166, 168–69; in Patočka's thought, 106, 146–53; in philosophy of history, 128; and Plato, 146, 151; self-discipline as, 148, 151; in Western metaphysics, 26, 146–47
Cartesianism, 39, 43, 55, 257
Cartesian Meditations (Husserl), 32
catastrophe: and care for the soul, 163; and Europe, 161–70
Černý, Václav, 204, 207, 208–9, 238
Charles University, 3, 171, 205, 259
Charter 77 essays: history in, 251–52; *polemos* in, 250–55
Charter 77 manifesto: democratic liberalism and, 239–40; Havel role in, 237; Patočka's writings on, 237–41; phenomenology in, 241–50
Charter 77 movement: Havel in, 233–37; and Helsinki Accords, 252–53; and moral ideal, 254; Patočka as spokesperson for, 19, 231–32, 264; phenomenology and, 241; police methods in response to, 230; and techno-civilization, 239
Chernyshevsky, N. G., 218
chōrismos, as sense of separation, 145, 154, 165
Christ, 197–98
Christianity: and care for the soul, 165–66; eschatology of, 127–30, 161; Greek absorption of, 162–63; rise of, 5; sacrifice in, 196–98
City of God (Augustine), 165
clarification: Husserl on, 30; in phenomenology, 35, 54–55; reflection as, 44, 54–57;
clarity: and history, 247; ideal of, 121; meaning and, 123, 124; and necessity, 23; of non-indifference, 82; of objective being, 57; philosopher and, 254; of praxis; and reflection, 50–56
Club of Rome, 5–6
Cold War, 169, 192
Comenius (Jan Amos Komenský), 19, 162

commonality, 248
Communism, 231, 236
Communist Party, 3, 235, 238
community, 75–76
comportment, human: and body, 80; and cooperation, 133; and openness, 85, 120; and playing role, 113; and "soul," 64; and time, 244; and world, 72–73
consciousness: absolute of, 46; Greek, 12; European, 127–36; historically oriented, 85–86; of historicity, 10; as "mirror of nature," 59; and others, 107; reflection and, 51–52, 54, 61; self-distancing of, 61–62; as suffering, 219–21; and technology, 176
Constantine, 165, 167
consumerism, 240
Conversations with Masaryk (Čapek), 206
"Crisis of European Humanity and Philosophy, The" (Husserl), 7
Crisis of European Sciences, The (Husserl): lifeworld in, 28, 30, 33–35, 39; Patočka and, 6–7, 14–15, 18; two paths in, 33
Critique of Pure Reason (Kant), 210–14
Czechoslovak democratic state, 4–5, 204, 205, 256, 287n6
Czechoslovakia: Charter 77 movement, 233–37, 252–53, 254; dissidence in, 229–54, 264–65; as former state, 261, 263; normalization in, 3, 171–73, 200, 229–30, 233, 234; Prague Spring, 3–5, 173, 230–31, 264; Russian invasion in 1968 and aftermath, 4, 5, 171, 229–30, 238, 264; resistance in, 171–74
Czech Realist Party, 205

"Dangers of Technization in Science according to E. Husserl and the Essence of Technology as Danger according to M. Heidegger, The" (Varna lecture) (Patočka), 174, 176, 178–79, 181, 188, 194, 196
Dasein: and affectivity, 78; as being-at-a-distance, 63–64; as being-in-the-world, 45; and conscience, 226; and history, 156–57; and openness, 84–85; Patočka on, 65; and reflection, 58–59; and sacrifice, 183; and self-understanding, 55–56, 81; spatiality of, 65
Dead Christ (Holbein), 223, 289n59

INDEX

death: and blindness, 102, 121; of Europe, 15, 19, 258; freedom for, 199; and history, 160; individuation of, 152; mystery of, 259; in myth, 94–95, 97–98, 100, 103, 121; of Palach, 171–73; of polis, 164; and the political, 246; as sacrifice, 185, 187, 191, 194, 197–98; of selfishness, 227; of Socrates, 261
Demetz, Peter, 263, 264–65
Democritus: and philosophy of object, 143–44; and Plato, 146–54, 282n60
de Musset, Alfred, 208
Descartes, René, 167, 168
DG 307 (music group), 232
Dilthey, Wilhelm, 29
dissidence: Charter 77 as, 229–54, 264–65; of Patočka, 264; as *polemos*, 251–54; as principal form of resistance, 170, 173; and strife, 245–50
divine, the: Christ and, 197–98; and philosophy, 156
Doctor Faustus (Mann), 49
"Does History Have a Meaning?" (Patočka), 131–32
Dostoevsky, Fyodor: on alienation, 218–19, 221; on love, 225, 289n61, 289n63; and Masaryk, 204; and moral theology, 214–28; Patočka on, 48, 214–15, 218, 221, 227–28, 232; and philosophy of love, 228; and "underground" condition, 218–22, 288n40, 288n51
"Dream of a Ridiculous Man, The" (Dostoevsky), 221–27, 232, 288n40, 288n51
Dubček, Alexander, 3, 171, 230

earth: as anchoring, 107–8; and sky, 72–75
empathy, 62
"End of Philosophy and the Task of Thinking, The" (Heidegger), 180
Enlightenment, the, 168–69, 255–57
epochē, the: and active reflection, 32–33; in Husserl, 45–46; as transcendental experience, 33–35; unrestricted, 46–47
"*Epochē* and Reduction" (Patočka), 43, 45–47
eschatology, 127–30, 161
Essai sur le titanisme (Černý), 204
eternity, problem of, 152–53
"Europa und Nach-Europa" (Patočka), 128, 146, 162

Europe: and care for the soul, 18–19, 161–70, 254; and catastrophe, 161–70; as dead, 14–15, 164–65, 258–59; Greek philosophy and beginning of, 9, 10–11; Guénoun on, 12; history of, 162–63; Husserl on, 7–20; as idea, 7; identity and, x, 12; legacy of, 15–16, 18; in 1930s, 7, 12; and "other," 12–13; Patočka on, 7–20, 161–70; religion in, 204–9; and sacrifice, 198–99; spiritual crisis in, 169–70, 204
evil, 207–8, 209–10, 215–17
existence: "natural," 13–14; philosophical problem of, 49
experience: of absolute, 186; of freedom, 36–37, 143–44, 146–47; horizon of, 81; intentionality of, 40–41; of self, 51; of time, 79–80, 90–91; transcendental, 45–46; of wonder, 26

faith: in God, 219; and moral theology, 210–28; and philosophy, 104, 256, 258; rupture of, 91–92; and titanism, 203–9
Faulkner, William, 48
Fichte, Johann, 169
field: bodily, 75; phenomenal. 44–45
Filosofický časopis (journal), 3
Fink, Eugen: current attention to, 280n23; and Greek thought, 136–37; and manifestation, 81; and phenomenology, 257
First World War, 162, 172, 185, 192, 193, 200, 204–5
Force and Freedom (Burckhardt), 130
form: as attribute of movement, 104; objective, 41
Formation of the Historical World in the Human Sciences, The (Dilthey), 29
Franco-Prussian War, 163
freedom: and body, 69–72, 74; and care for the soul, 156; for death, 199; experience of, 36–37, 143–44, 146–47; Greeks and, 89, 139–41; Havel on, 235; of "I can," 69; internal, 22–23; Masaryk on, 255–56; and nothingness, 247–48; and openness, 84–85; and phenomenology, 27; problematization of, 139–41, 146–47; and sacrifice, 185–86, 195; situated, 117; and titanism, 208; wandering as, 227–28; and work, 98, 113–14

INDEX

Frege, Gottlob, 131–32
French and American revolutions, 163, 169

German Idealism, 27
Gilgamesh myth, 88, 97, 98, 99–103, 125
glasnost, 171
God: and evil, 207–8, 215–16; existence of, 210, 214–15; faith in, 219; and meaning, 132–33; and morality, 212; rebellion against, 215, 217; will of, 129
Goethe, Johann Wolfgang von, 208
Golosovker, Iakov, 214
good: faith and, 253; highest, 196, 212–13; saving and, 197
Good, the: Plato on, 144; and soul, 155–56
Gorbachev, Mikhail, 171
Grandma (Babička), Němcová, 95
Greek philosophy: and beginning of Europe, 9, 10–12; and care for the soul, 164–67; and Heidegger, 180; metaphysical tradition of, 27; and myth, 88–90; as origin of philosophy, 10–11; and phenomenology, 136–46; and philosophy of history, 128; on whole, 24–25
Guénoun, Denis, on Europe, 12

Hájek, Jiří, 238
happiness: and highest good, 196, 212–13; and pleasure, 112; Solon on, 277n51; and suffering, 216, 220
Havel, Václav: on the absurd, 229; in Charter 77 movement, 19, 233–37; and Patočka, 255, 259–62; on post-totalitarian state, 237, 264–65; on sacrifice, 200–201; and underground scene, 231–33
Hebrew tradition: eschatology in, 127; future in, 129
Hegel, G. W. F.: on absolute, 130; on alienation, 116–17; on subject, 167
Heidegger, Martin: on affectivity, 78; on being-in-remove, 38; on body, 65–66, 75; on boredom, 221–22; on conscience, 226; on earth and sky, 72–73; and Heraclitus, 248; on history, 156–57; on Husserl, 58, 257; on manifestation, 17–18; on material intelligibility, 132–34; and metaphysics, 27, 43; on movement, 62; on openness, 84–85; Patočka on, 3, 45, 55–56, 58–59, 65, 176, 178–81, 199, 289n61, 291n38; and philosophical anthropology, 80–81; on *phusis*, 247–48, on Plato, 145–46; and reflection, 58; on Socratic thinking, 137, 139; on technology, 172, 174–79. See also *Being and Time*; "The End of Philosophy and the Task of Thinking"; *Introduction to Metaphysics*; "What Is Metaphysics?"
Hellenistic empire, 162
Helmholtz, Wilhelm von, 30, 33
Helsinki Accords, 237, 245, 246, 252–53
Heraclitus: on *polemos*, 247–49; and Socrates, 139; and soul, 152; on wonder, 89
Herder, Johann, 169
Heretical Essays (Patočka): absolute meaning in, 158–59, 213; care for the soul in, 162; as crowning achievement, 203; dissidence in, 230–31; historical reflection in, 15, 250–52; injustice in, 109; Michalski and, 264; prehistory in, 83, 85–86, 121; philosophy of history in, 90–92, 127–28; *polemos* in, 250–54; and Prague Spring, 231; religion in, 227–28; Ricoeur on, 227; sacrifice in, 172, 191–93; technology in, 174; war in, 185, 201–2, 203
Herodotus, 128, 277n51
Hippasus, 22
history: and being, 156–58; composed by power, 191; Czech, 162; end of, 134; and Europe, 7–8; and the ideal, 11–12; meaning of, 123, 127–36, 160–61; as movement, 120–26; and openness, 83–92; vs. parable, 15–16; of philosophy, 3–4, 19, 23–24, 27, 242–43; philosophy of, 18–19; and *polemos* (conflict), 124–26, 133–34; and the political, 241–45; of Prague, 263–64; and prehistory, 86–87, 121; relief from, ix; and seeing, 247–48; and the spiritual, 10; stages of, 122–26; and truth, 178–81. See also prehistory
Hobbit, The (Tolkien), 95
Holbein, Hans, 223, 289n59
Holy Roman Empire, 162–63, 263
Homer, 88, 95–96

INDEX

hope: and meaninglessness, 207, 216, 217, 219, 221–24; as principal form of resistance, 170
horizon: and asubjective approach, 50; of bodily field, 75; of experience, 81; living in, 76–77; of others, 110–11; political act in, 245; world and, 40–43, 69
human being: and ethical bonds, 261; and movement, 63–65, 68–71; and nothingness, 178; as openness, 17–18, 56–60; and sacrifice, 183; in twentieth century, 202
Human Condition, The (Arendt), 86, 114, 116
human existence: and absolute meaning, 158–59, 199; basic structures of, 104–6; as being in-between, 147; corporeity of, 64–65; and destruction, 251–52; and faith, 207; historicity of, 156–57; individuation of, 98–99; as movement, 60, 74; openness of, 100–101; and the political, 243–44; self-givenness of, 57–58; as value, 251; as wandering, 228
humanity: and identity, 14; universal, 8–9, 12, 14–15
human rights, 239
Hus, Jan, 171
Husák, Gustáv, 171
Husserl, Edmund: on affectivity and instinct, 77–78; and Avenarius, 28, 32; on body, 66–68, 71; Cartesian approach of, 32–33, 39, 257; on crisis, 6; on earth and sky, 72–73; on *epochē*, 45–46; on Europe, 7–20; and Fink, 136–37; on history, 15–16; as Jewish, 8; on Kant, 29, 32–33; on lifeworld, 29–31; on manifestation, 17–18; on natural attitude, 28, 269n13; Patočka on, 3, 6, 27, 29–30; Patočka relationship, 6–7, 204, 255; phenomenology of, 27–35, 42, 49–60; on positivism, 28; on "principle of all principles," 57–60; and philosophical anthropology, 80–81; on reflection, 51–52, 58, 61, 272n86; on science, 31; on spiritual unity, 10–11; subjectivism of, 50–51, 53–54; on technology, 174–76; transcendentalism of, 43–44; on whole, 27. See also *Cartesian Meditations; Ideas I; Ideas II; Logical Investigations*

"I," the: asubjective approach to, 50–51, 56–57; and body, 67, 69–70, 74–75; and ownness, 56; and reflection, 58–59
Idea, the: in Platonism, 144–46; unchanging reality of, 26
ideal: as attribute of movement, 104; of clarity, 121; history and, 11–12; reason as, 8; science as, 256–58
idealism: German, 27; Patočka rejection of, 257–58; transcendental, 35
Ideas I (Husserl), 28, 32, 39, 45–46, 51–52, 54, 57, 61
Ideas II (Husserl), 66, 274n15
identity: and Europe, x, 12; national and folk, 12–13; and philosophy, 11; vs. universal humanity, 14–15
ideology, 171–72, 206, 233–37, 260
Iliad, the (Homer), 95–96
imagination, 49, 62, 63, 93, 102
individuation: and *adikia*, 110, 111; and body, 81–82; and conflict, 247; of death, 153; of freedom, 113; and guilt, 225–26; and inwardness, 69; in myth, 99, 102; and natural life, 38; Silenus on, 277n51; and worldhood, 82
"Intellectuals and Opposition, The" (Patočka), 230
intentionality: horizon and, 40–41; of object experience, 41–42; and transcendence, 46–47; unfulfillable, 35–49
Introduction to Metaphysics (Heidegger), 181, 247–48
Ionesco, Eugène, 5–6
Islam, 162

Jaspers, Karl, 105
Jirous, Ivan, 229, 231–32
Jones, David, 202
Jünger, Ernst, 191–92
justification: in clarity, 254; and faith, 153; life as, 251; and the political, 239; rational, 165, 207, 215; self-, 9; in Socratic thought, 138–39, 142; of values, 132

Kafka, Franz, 263, 264–65
Kant, Immanuel: and care for the soul, 168–69; Husserl on, 29, 32–33; and Masaryk, 204, 209–10; moral theology of, 209–18; on objectivity, 26

Kohák, Erazim, ix, 256
Kolář, Jiří, 259
Kritik der reinen Erfahrung (Avenarius), 28

labor: and alienation, 117; Arendt on, 99, 114–16; and slavery, 115, 116; self-projection of, 119–20; and work, 99–100, 115–18
legacy, 15–16, 18, 71
life: affective, 111; bondage to itself, 120; conversion to, 220–27; of Europeans, 9; individuated, 82; as modification, 53; in movement, 84; mythical, 90, 93; partiality of, 59–60; philosophical, 151; pre-subjective, 80; rational, 13–14; and risk, 89–90, 125, 244–45; in truth, 235–36; as upswing, 124; world of, 28–35
lifeworld: obviousness of, 28–32; as subject-relative, 39
Linear B tablets, Knossos, 88
Logical Investigations (Husserl), 54
love: and conversion to life, 224–26; philosophy of, 228
Löwith, Karl: on European consciousness, 127–28; on meaning, 131–32, 134; Patočka on, 127–28, 136, 160, 166, 279n3; on philosophy of history, 130–36

Macedonian empire, 166–67
manifestation: and openness, 83; and reflection, 44–45, 59; and situation, 17–18; space of, 243–44; and technology, 178; and world, 40, 81, 82
Mann, Thomas, 48–49
Marx, Karl: on alienation, 116–17
Masaryk, Tomáš Garrigue: on alienation, 6; and Czechoslovak state, 4–5, 256, 287n6; on freedom, 256–57; and Husserl, 255; in intellectual history, 19; and moral theology, 209–14; Patočka on, 203–9, 256–58, 291n38; on religion, 204–9
"Masaryk's and Husserl's Conception of the Spiritual Crisis of European Humanity" (Patočka), 204
"Masaryk's Philosophy of Religion" (Patočka), 204, 221, 223, 253
material intelligibility, 132–34
mathematical thinking, 22, 150, 153

meaning: absolute, 158–59; of being, 48–49, 156–61; Christian conception of, 166; and faith, 213; of history, 123, 127–36, 160–61; horizontal character of, 39–40; human as arbiter of, 92; and interpersonal comprehension, 34; Löwith on, 131–32; and myth, 94; and nothing, 199; philosophy as affirming, 259; and position, 175–76; problem of, 43–49; and risk, 134; of sacrifice, 197; shaking of, 161; and technology, 175–81; types of, 105; world as horizon of, 27
meaningfulness, 66, 100, 102, 126, 132–33, 158–59, 200, 208, 213, 223, 228, 243, 249
Meaning in History (Löwith), 127
meaninglessness: and care for the soul, 129, 133, 157–59, 161; and hope, 207, 216, 217, 219, 221–24; and natural world, 257; and sacrifice, 176–77, 193–94, 200
memory: and the "I," 62; and writing, 88
menschliche Weltbegriff, Der (Avenarius), 28
Merleau-Ponty, Maurice, 67, 174–76
Mesopotamia, civilizations of, 16, 96–97, 99
metaphysics: and Aristotle, 153–56; and experience of freedom, 143–44; "from above," 150; Heidegger and, 27, 43, 181; Kant and, 210; Patočka on, 135–36, 138–39, 150, 154; Plato and, 141, 146, 154; and the political, 25–27; and positivism, 167; and revealed truth, 165; of sacrifice, 181–82; Socrates and, 137–38, 140–46; and technology, 184, 188–89; and titanism, 205–6
Michalski, Krzysztof: and Patočka, 263–65; on philosophy as living tradition, ix
Michnik, Adam, 200–201, 229
modernity: and Christianity, 166; and technology, 5
Modern Man and Religion (Masaryk), 204, 209
moral, the: as ideal, 254; Kant on, 168, 210–16; Plato on, 153; and the political, 240, 241–42
moral theology: and Dostoevsky, 214–28; and Kant, 209–18
movement: anchoring as, 106–12; Aristotle on, 62–65; and body, 64–75, 81–

INDEX

82; disruption of, 119–21; earth and sky as poles of, 72–75; existence as, 60; form as, 104; history as, 120–26; ideal as, 104; life in, 84; of natality, 106–7, 111; as ontological category, 61–62; and openness, 77–82; outward, 76–77; and *polemos*, 248; and the political, 242–43; self-projection as, 112–20; as situated, 64–65; soul as, 154–55; three types of, 83, 104–6, 126, 257; and time, 79–80
myth: Babylonian, 88, 96, 97, 98, 99–103, 125; and death, 121; and eternity, 153; and faith, 91–92; and Greek philosophy, 88–90, 92–96, 103–4, 277n47; and meaning of history, 160–61; and oral vs. written tradition, 87–89, 123; Patočka focus on, 48–49; and philosophy, 126; and the political, 242, 244–45; as representation, 99; and sacrifice, 188; and self-consciousness, 102–3; temporality as, 104; two-sidedness in, 95–98, 100, 108

Napoleon, 163, 168, 169
natality, 105, 106–7, 111
" 'Natural' World and Phenomenology, The" (Patočka), 38, 72–73
Natural World as Philosophical Problem, The (Patočka): Europe and, 35–36; Havel and, 259–60; Husserl in, 37; 1970 edition, 37; world in, 28
need: biological, 115, 118–19; and bliss, 107, 110; radical, 112
"Negative Platonism" (Patočka), 135, 136, 139, 144–45
Němcová, Božena, 95
neutrality, as false, 59–60
Nicomachean Ethics (Aristotle), 155, 277n51
Nietzsche, Friedrich: on absolute meaning, 159; Patočka on, 204; on recurrence, 130
nihilism: vs. care for the soul, 166–70; and Europe, 36; of Nietzsche, 159; of power, 161; questioning as response to, 228
non-indifference, 58–59, 82, 180–81, 188–94, 197
normalization, 3, 171–73, 200, 229–30, 233, 234

Notes from Underground (Dostoevsky), 218–21, 288n40
nothingness: as central for Patočka, 178, 246–47; and conversion to life, 223–27; of death, 148; and meaning, 199; positivity of, 223, 253; and sacrifice, 187; of underground man, 219
nullity, 101, 178, 187, 188, 196, 199, 219, 221, 224, 226–28, 254

object(s): body as, 67, 70–72; Husserl, on, 50–51, 54; individuals as, 29; and meaning, 49, 213; in metaphysics, 143; oneself as, 43; philosophy of, 143–44; in use, 115, 118; world as aggregate of, 251
objectification, 54–55, 57, 67, 144, 272n86
objectivity: absolute, 145–46; and faith, 207–8; logic of, 26; rationally ordered, 41–44, 205; and science, 31–32, 36; and subjectivity, 39, 40–41, 47, 60, 212; and value, 132
"Obligation to Resist Injustice, The" (Patočka), 239, 241, 245–50
Oedipus at Colonus (Sophocles), 101
Oedipus myth, 97, 98, 101–2, 148, 228
Oedipus Rex (Sophocles), 101
"On the Matters of the Plastic People of the Universe and DG 307" (Patočka), 232
ontology: of lifeworld, 32–35; movement as category of, 61–62; phenomenological, 18–19, 257; and self-distancing, 62
openness: and body, 82; and comportment, 85, 120; and freedom, 84–85; and history, 83–92; human being as, 17–18; of human existence, 100–101; and love, 225–26; and material intelligibility, 133; and movement, 77–82; and *phusis*, 124; and *polemos*, 248–49; whole as, 135
Opletal, Jan, 171
other: and affective bonding, 110–12; and alienation, 113; and body, 75–77; and comportment, 107; self-projection and, 112–20; spatiality of, 75–76, 80; and three movements, 83; and time, 90–92
Owen, Wilfred, 190–91, 200

Palach, Jan, public suicide of, 171–74, 193–94, 198–99
"Parable of the Old Man and the Young, The" (Owen), 190–91
past: as ever-closing, 78–79, 80; legacy of, 71; -ness, 87–88; passivity of, 106
Pasternak, Boris, 260
Patočka, Jan, life of: in Charter 77 movement, 19; and crisis, 6; death of, 233, 239, 253, 255, 259; and Europe, x; Husserl relationship, 6–7, 255; Michalski visit, 263–66; personal history, 3–6; Prague Spring, 3–5, 173, 230–31, 264; private seminars of, 5, 260–62; sacrifice in, 173; as teacher, 3–5, 173, 259–62; and underground scene, 232–33
Patočka, Jan, work of: on alienation, 117, 123, 223–24; on Arendt, 86; on Aristotle, 19; on the body, 61–82, 104–8; on care for the soul, 146–53; on crisis, 6; democratic liberalism and, 239–40; devotion to philosophy, 265–66; on Dostoevsky, 48, 214–15, 218, 221, 227–28, 289n63; on Europe, 7–20, 161–70; experience of reading, 20; on Greeks, 124–25, 136–46; on habit, 71–72; on Heidegger, 3, 45, 55–56, 58–59, 65, 176, 178–81, 199, 289n61, 291n38; as heretical, 80–81; as historian of philosophy, 19, 23–24; Husserl, departure from, 35, 37–43, 46–49, 50–51, 257–58; Husserl, influence of, 3, 6, 27, 29–30, 33; on Kant, 26, 209–10, 213; as legacy, 255–62; on love, 224–26; on Löwith, 127–28, 136, 160, 166; on Masaryk, 203–9, 256–58, 291n38; on meaning, 39–40; on melody, 63; on metaphysics, 135–36, 138–39, 150; and Michalski, 263–65; on movement, 62–65, 68–82, 104–26; on myth, 92–104; on natality, 106–7; as non-Cartesian, 39, 42; nothingness as central to, 178, 246–47; on openness, 84–85; phenomenology in, 3, 15, 19–20, 27, 39–60, 240–50, 255–56, 260, 264; philosophical anthropology in, 80–81, 83; philosophy of history in, 15–16, 19, 90–92, 127–36; on Plato, 3, 144–47, 149–50; on *polemos*, 195, 247–49, 250–54; on the political, 25–27, 89–90, 240–50; on possibility, 77; problematicity in, 195, 250; on religion, 196–98; on resistance, 170, on sacrifice, 172–74; on self-distancing, 62; significance of, 240–41; translation of, 268n37; on value, 132–33; on war, 185–88, 201–2; world in, 21–22. See also *Body, Community, Language, World;* "The Dangers of Technization in Science according to E. Husserl and the Essence of Technology as Danger according to M. Heidegger" (Varna lecture); "Does History Have a Meaning?"; *"Epochē* and Reduction"; "Europa und Nach-Europa"; *Heretical Essays;* "The Intellectuals and Opposition"; "Masaryk's and Husserl's Conception of the Spiritual Crisis of European Humanity"; "Masaryk's Philosophy of Religion"; "The 'Natural' World and Phenomenology"; *The Natural World as Philosophical Problem;* "Negative Platonism"; "The Obligation to Resist Injustice"; "On the Matters of the Plastic People of the Universe and DG 307"; *Plato and Europe;* "Séminaire sur l'ère technique"; "Time, Myth, Faith"; "Titanism"; "Was sind die Tschechen?"; "What We Can and Cannot Expect from Charta 77"
Paul, Saint, 128
Peloponnesian War, 15, 141
Phaedrus (Plato), 147, 151, 154
phenomenality, 57, 60
phenomenology: asubjective, 21–60, 80–81; of body, 107–8; Cartesianism in, 55; and Charter 77, 241–50; and clarification, 35, 54–55; classical, 57; as eidetics of lived experience, 42; and Greek philosophy, 136–46; Husserl and, 27–35, 42, 77–78; logic of experience in, 27; vs. Marxist ideology, 260; Patočka on, 3, 15, 19–20, 27, 39–60, 240–50, 255–56, 260, 264; and philosophical anthropology, 80–81; as philosophy of manifestation, 15–18; as political, 240–50; Socrates and, 137, 139; transcendental, 35–37

philosophical anthropology, 80–81, 83
philosophy: of body, 104; care of the soul in, 26, 106, 128, 156, 254; and Christianity, 165; and the divine, 156; and Europe, 7–11; and faith, 104, 256, 258; Greek origin of, 10–11, 15, 124; history of, 3–4, 19, 27; of history, 18–19, 124, 127–36, 242–43; of love, 228; modern, 206; and myth, 103–4, 126; and neutrality, 59–60; vs. nihilism, 170; Patočka devotion to, 265–66; place of phenomenology in, 15–18; and *polemos*, 249–50; and the political, 243–44; and prehistory, 86–88; proto-, 139, 140; reflection in, 37–43, 61; of religion, 204; and renewal, 175; on risk, 238–39; and "space between," 202; spiritual vs. natural teleology and, 9–10; and tradition, 3–4, 11–12, 15–16, 258–59; and transcendence, 21–22; transcendental, 33–37; in troubled times, 5–6; as wandering, 259; and wonder, 25–26
phusis (nature): of being, 81–82; and cooperative action, 113; and eternity, 152–53; as manifestation, 24; and movement, 62; and openness, 124–25; and *polemos*, 247–48; as term, 248
Physics (Aristotle), 62
Plastic People of the Universe, 232
Plato: and Aristotle, 153–56; and care of the soul, 146–47; and Democritus, 146–53; Heidegger on, 145–46; on Homer, 88; Idea and, 144–46; on joints forming the whole, 49; and mathematical thinking, 22; and metaphysics, 141, 146, 154, 167; Patočka on, 3, 144–47, 149–50; on *polemos*, 249; on power, 166–67; and Socrates, 137–46, 148–49, 152, 198; on state, 164–65; on wonder, 89
Plato and Europe (Patočka): care of the soul in, 128, 146–47; crisis in, 5; death of Europe in, 164–65; democratic liberalism in, 240; Heidegger in, 180; historical reflection in, 15; myth in, 94–96, 101; and Prague Spring, 231; and Socratic thinking, 138
Platonic philosophy, 15, 26

polemos (conflict): and Charter 77, 250–54; as confrontation, 180–81; Heraclitus on, 247–49; and history, 124–26, 133–34; as meaningfulness, 126; and problematicity, 195; and risk, 246; as strife, 245–50
polis, the: collapse of, 15, 162, 163, 164–65; life of, 124–25; and meaning, 159–60; and *oikos*, as public vs. private, 86–87; and philosopher, 166; and power, 243–44
political, the: Arendt on, 89, 117–18; and death, 246; and history, 124; and metaphysics, 25–27; phenomenology on, 240–50; and prehistory, 86; and the pre-political, 118–19; as problematicity, 245; and strife, 245–50
positivism, 28
"post-Communism," 234–37
potentiality, 63, 64
power: absurd, 229–37; vs. care for the soul, 166; contested, 243–44; history composed by, 191; knowledge as, 251–52; mass mobilization of, 5; nihilism of, 161; peace as serving, 187; resistance to, 193; and war, 184–88
"Power of the Powerless, The" (Havel), 233–37, 255
Prague Cercle philosophique, 6–7, 204
Prague Spring, 3–5, 173, 230–31, 264
prehistory: and history, 87, 90; and humanity, 122–23; and openness, 83; and philosophy, 86–88; and the political, 244–45; and third movement, 121
problematicity: Aristotle and, 155–56, 159; Democritus and, 150; embrace of, 138–39; of freedom, 134, 140, 155–56; and meaning, 57; Plato and, 150, 155–56, 159; and the political, 245, 246; and sacrifice, 189, 195; of sense, 49, Socrates and, 141, 159; of transcendence
propaganda, 233–34
Putík, Jaroslav, 229
Pythagoreans, 22

reason: and faith, 209–14; as historical, 8–9; universal, 10–12
Reed, Lou, 232

INDEX

reflection: active, 32–33; as clarification, 44, 54–57; critical, 89; *epochē*-reduction axis of, 46–47; historical, 8–11, 15, 123; on human condition, 18–19; Husserl on, 46–47, 50–52, 58, 61, 272n86; and manifestation, 44–45, 59; as non-indifferent, 58–59; phenomenological, 30, 37, 56; and problem of meaning, 48–49; self-, 51, 175; and selfhood, 50–54, 57–58; and subjectivity, 37–38; and time, 53
religion: in *Heretical Essays*, 227–28; Michalski and, 265; and moral theology, 209–14; Patočka on, 196–98, 227–28; philosophy as, 153; and reason, 209, 210
Renaissance, the: mathematization in, 174–76
Republic (Plato), Cephalus in, 141–42; Homer in, 88; Patočka on, 145–46, 149, 151; *polemos* in, 249; state in, 164–65; wandering in, 277n47, 281n52
resistance: dissidence as, 170, 173; meaning of, 176; principal forms of, 170; vs. protest, 193–96; public suicide as, 171–74; and risk, 253–54; sacrifice as, 170, 171, 183, 194–95; to techno-civilization, 189–90
responsibility: and morality, 217–18; Patočka on, 238–39
Ricoeur, Paul, 227
risk: of conflict, 126; and historicity, 172; and life, 89, 125, 244–45; and meaning, 134; Patočka on, 238–39; and *polemos*, 250–51, 253–54; and strife, 246
role: and comportment, 113; and work, 116
Roman Empire, 7, 15, 162, 165, 198
Russian invasion of Czechoslovakia in 1968, 4, 5, 171, 229–30

sacrifice: absolute, 186, 191; ambiguities of, 181–84, 185; Christian conception of, 196–98; and conversion to life, 226–27; and historicity, 172; and non-indifference, 180–81, 188–93; and nullity, 178; Patočka on, 172–202; as resistance, 170, 171, 183, 194–95; self-, 193–95, 198–99; war as, 184–88; as waste, 173–74

samizdat, 3
Scheler, Max, 6, 14
Schelling, F. W. J., 169
science: a priori, 34–35; Husserl on, 31; ideals of, 256–58; as knowledge, 251; vs. natural understanding, 29; and progress, 8; rise of, 15, 167, 168; and technology, 175
secularism, 205–7
self-discipline, 148, 151
self-distancing, 61–62
self-givenness, 57, 273n108
selfhood, 50–54
self-loving, 219, 220
self-projection: of *Dasein*, 45, Husserl on, 8; as movement, 104, 112–20, 122
self-understanding, 36, 55–56, 85, 218–19, 257–58
"Séminaire sur l'ère technique" (Patočka), 174, 181, 190
sense-formation, 37–38
"Sentence, The" (Dostoevsky), 220, 221
shaken, the: non-indifference of, 188–93; solidarity of, 186–88, 192–93, 203
Siduri, 102
Silenus, 102, 277n51
Šimečka, Milan, 230
situation: concrete, 16–17; freedom and, 117; and manifestation, 17–18; movement and, 64–65
Sleep of Reason Produces Monsters, The (Goya), 149
Socrates: and Christ, 198; death of, 261; dialectic of, 142; and metaphysics, 140–46; Patočka on, 3, 137–43, 280n24; and phenomenology, 137–46; and Plato, 137–46, 148–49, 152; and problem of freedom, 139–41; as transitional figure, 139
Sophocles, 101, 277n47
soul: and city, 151–52; and comportment, 64; and good, 155–56; and happiness, 213; as movement, 154–55; Platonic conception of, 147–48. *See also* care for the soul
Soviet Union: end of, 201; invasion by, *see* Russian invasion of Czechoslovakia in 1968
Stalinism, 230

INDEX

state, the: Plato on, 164–65; post-totalitarian, 237, 264–65; theories of, 239
subject: affirmation of, 137; in asubjective phenomenology, 47–48, 58; body as, 66–71; Descartes on, 167, 168; free, 69; Hegel on, 167; Kantian, 211, 215, 216; and reflection, 50–51; transcendental, 42–43; and truth, 179; understanding, 79; and world, 26–27
subject-body, 68, 71
"subjectivism," 205, 207–9
subjectivity: autonomous, 80–81; and immanence, 38–39; Patočka revision of Husserl on, 47–49, 50–51, 53–54; and reflection, 37–38; and self-understanding, 36; and space, 75; and time, 34–35; and titanism, 205; transcendental, 30, 33
suffering: consciousness as, 219–21; and happiness, 216, 220; and morality, 217–18; work as, 116
suicide: and alienation, 224; Dostoevsky on, 220, 223; Masaryk on, 204; public, 171–74; and "underground" condition, 223

techno-civilization: being and, 177; and Charter 77, 239; and historicity, 172; metaphysics of, 188–89; nihilism of, 170; resistance to, 189–90; and truth, 196; and war, 184–85
technology: dangers of, 174–78; Heidegger on, 172, 178–79; as knowledge, 251; and metaphysics, 184; and modernity, 5; and sacrifice, 196–98; "saving" in, 178; truth under, 177–81
Teilhard de Chardin, Pierre, 191–92
teleology: inborn, 16; spiritual vs. natural, 9–10
temporality: as attribute of movement, 104–6; and lifeworld, 35; of present, 106; and reflection, 60; and subjective being, 71
Theater on the Balustrade, 260
theodicy, 207–8, 216
thing(s): body as, 66–71, 74–75; contingency of, 17; kinds of, 190; mastery of, 137; meaningfulness of, 132; nature as

an order of, 42; relation to whole, 24, 25; separation between, 145
thinking: agency of, 137; Socratic, 137–39
Thirty Years War, 162–63, 169
Thitch Quang Duc, 171
Thucydides, 128
Timaeus (Plato), 151
time: and body, 71–72; consciousness of, 46; cyclical vs. linear, 128–30; and ever-closing past, 78–79, 80; experience of, 79–80, 90–91; and praxis, 65; and reflection, 53; self-distancing modifications of, 61–62; and subjectivity, 34–35; and understanding, 78–81
"Time, Myth, Faith" (Patočka), 90–92, 93–94
titanism: and faith, 203–9; and morality, 209; as term, 91
"Titanism" (Patočka), 204
Tolkien, J. R. R., 95
tradition: historical, 125; oral vs. written, 87–89; philosophy and, 3–4, 11–12, 15–16
tragedy, Greek, 88–89
transcendence: and body, 70, 75; and intentionality, 46; and inwardness, 38–39; and movement, 63–64; and mythical world, 94–95; philosophy and, 21–22; and sacrifice, 184, 186; and sky, 73; and subject, 26–27; and whole, 23, 24–25, 27
transcendental, the: and lifeworld, 33–34; and subjectivity, 30, 42–43
truth: living, 235–36; questioning after, 228; and sacrifice, 184, 195; under technology, 177–81; and untruth, 18
twentieth century, the, 200–202

"underground" condition, 218–22, 228
underground scene, 231–33
understanding: problematic, 48–49; and reflection, 44; and time, 78–81
universality: of humanity, 8–9, 12, 14–15; and tradition, 11–12
Unknown Soldier, 200

validity: and the obvious, 29; structures governing, 31–32

value: body and, 66; and experience, 140; of life, 186, 189–90; meaning as, 132–33; moral, 212–15
van der Stoel, Max, 255
Velvet Revolution, 4, 172
Velvet Underground, the, 232
Vico, Giambattista, 130
violence: Arendt on, 118–19; and necessity, 119–20; salvation in, 197–98
Voltaire: on future, 129; on philosophy of history, 127
vulnerability, 75–76

wandering: blind, 103, 121, 123, 124, 126, 148; and care for the soul, 254, 281n52; as common reality, 262; as discursive, 20; as freedom, 227–28; groundless life as, 247; of Oedipus, 97, 101–2; philosophy as, 259
war: and modern condition, 191–92; as nuclear holocaust, 252; as pursuit of the possible, 249–50; as sacrifice, 184–88, 198; twentieth century as, 200–202
Warsaw Pact, 3, 171
"Was sind die Tschechen?" (Patočka), 161
Weil, Simone, 96
Weischedel, Wilhelm, 158–59
"What Is Existence?" (Patočka), 48–49
"What Is Metaphysics?" (Heidegger), 222–23

"What We Can and Cannot Expect from Charta 77" (Patočka), 239, 250–54, 255
"When Socrates Became Pericles" (Michnik), 229
whole: in Greek philosophy, 24–25; as openness, 135; world as, 23–24, 27, 37–38
wonder: experience of, 26; of manifestation, 138; and meaning, 159; Patočka as inspiring, 266; and philosophy, 24–25, 104; Plato and Aristotle on, 89
work: Arendt on, 87, 114–16; and building of world, 98–99; labor and, 99–100, 114–16; movement of self-projection as, 112–20; as suffering, 116
world: and body, 72–77, 82; as both concrete and abstract, 21–22; as context for moral life, 213; horizontal character of, 39–43; and internal freedom, 22–23; of life, 28–35; and manifestation, 40, 81, 82; meaning of, 48–49; "natural," 26–27, 28, 93, 108; obviousness of, 29; as phenomenon, 32–33; as real, 77; redemption of, 216; as term, 21; unity of, 31; as whole, 23–24, 37–38; work and building of, 98–99; worldhood of, 157
writing: vs. oral tradition, 97–98, 121–23; as work, 99

Zeit, Die (newspaper), 255
Zprávy (newspaper), 17